Roman Architecture and Society

Ancient Society and History

Roman

JAMES C. ANDERSON, jr.

Architecture and Society

The Johns Hopkins University Press
Baltimore and London

© 1997 The Johns Hopkins University Press
All rights reserved. Published 1997
Printed in the United States on recycled acid-free paper
06 05 04 03 02 01 00 99 98 97 5 4 3 2 1

The Johns Hopkins University Press
2715 North Charles Street
Baltimore, Maryland 21218-4319
The Johns Hopkins Press Ltd., London

Library of Congress Cataloging-in-Publication Data will be found at the
end of this book.
A catalog record for this book is available from the British Library.
ISBN 0-8018-5546-2

Uxori Carissimae
Filio Carissimo
Filiae Carissimaeque

Contents

Contents

Illustrations

The original published source of each figure is given in brackets at the end of each entry. For full bibliographical information on the sources, see the Bibliography.

Acknowledgments

I am deeply and sincerely indebted to any number of friends, colleagues, and institutions, both for having had the opportunity to investigate and to write this book and for the fact that it was at last completed. The idea was broached to me, and an advance contract issued, by the Johns Hopkins University Press in January of 1990, and all staff of the Press have been consistently helpful and supportive in every imaginable way. The research itself was supported most generously by a Senior Faculty Research Grant in the Humanities from the Office of the Vice-President for Research of the University of Georgia during 1992–93, and—most essentially—by a Fellowship for College Teachers granted by the National Endowment for the Humanities for 1994–95. Various computer equipment grants between 1993 and 1995 from the University of Georgia's Research Office permitted the manuscript to be prepared in an acceptable and attractive form. Released time from teaching duties in 1992–93 permitted me to undertake the initial research; during 1993–94, when I had the privilege of serving as A. W. Mellon Professor-in-Charge of the Intercollegiate Center for Classical Studies in Rome, and during the summers of 1992, 1993, and 1994, while serving as director of the Classical Summer School of the American Academy in Rome, I was able to visit all the monuments essential to this study and continue my reading and reflecting; the grant of the NEH Fellowship for 1994–95 permitted me to conclude the research and prepare the actual manuscript for submission, both of which were accomplished while I was a visiting scholar at the American Academy in Rome, making use of its superb library and facilities.

Over the years of its gestation I have received support, encouragement, advice, and helpful criticism from many, and to attempt to name them all would be overlong and likely to give offense by unintentional omissions. Assistance far above and beyond the call of duty, however, must be acknowledged. I am grateful to Eric Halpern (former editor-in-chief) and his successor, Douglas Armato (associate director) at Johns Hopkins University Press, as well as to the anonymous outside reader who offered sound advice and constructive criticism on the first full draft of the book; to my manuscript editor, Jean Eckenfels, for her skill and good judgment; to Richard A. LaFleur (head, Department of Classics, University of Georgia), Joe L. Key (vice-president for research, University of Georgia), Caroline Bruzelius (director, American Academy in Rome), Malcolm Bell (Mellon Professor, American Academy in Rome), Christina Huemer and Antonella Bucci (director and associate director of the library at the academy), and to many others at the locations—both in Rome and in the United States—where I labored. Other very special and deeply appreciated contributions of scholarly advice, discussion, and many and varied kinds of support from Lawrence Richardson, jr., William V. Harris, Gerhard M. Koeppel, Katherine E. Welch, Susann S. Lusnia, James E. Packer, Nicholas Horsfall, Rogers Scudder, and Eileen Torrence must be acknowledged individually, as well as stimulation, consideration, and assistance from a host of others too numerous to mention here. Thanks are owed also to my students in the Classical Summer School of the Academy in Rome for 1992, 1993, and 1994, and at the Intercollegiate Center for Classical Studies in Rome during 1993–94, who read or listened to much of this material in one form or another and provided valuable feedback to it. I am deeply grateful to them all, as I am to supportive friends—especially Abigail Gillespie in Rome—and to my family.

The idea for this book was conceived in January 1990, just as my daughter, Helena, was born. Throughout the project, the love, support, and patience of my wife, Dana, and son, Owen, as well as the joy of a new daughter, have not only made the work possible but delightful, since we all were able to share in it during nearly two years' residence in Rome. Perhaps without the addition of Helena to our family, the work would have been completed more rapidly, but nothing could be more touching than hearing my learned five-year-old daughter correctly identify colored marbles in the floor of the Pantheon by their Italian names! Hence, it is to Dana, to Owen, and to Helena that I dedicate this book, together with its many wonderful memories.

Introduction

The architectural achievements of ancient Rome have long excited admiration and praise. The influence of Roman architecture upon building after its own heyday had passed has been incalculable, and the influence of Roman construction techniques and discoveries has been equally important throughout the post-classical Western world. The history of Roman architecture has been investigated since the dawning of the Italian Renaissance, and its aesthetic principles and presumptions—communicated to posterity in part through the remains themselves but at least equally through the importance attached to the treatise *De Architectura,* written during the last quarter of the first century B.C. by Vitruvius and brought back to world attention by the humanists of the Renaissance—long shaped the architectural vision of the West. In our own century the practical application of the methods, decoration, and style of ancient Roman architecture has lessened a great deal, but the fascination of it as a subject for scholarly study has increased, resulting in the availability of a wealth of information about the history and development of architecture, which was, arguably, the area of their greatest achievement among the plastic arts practiced by the ancient Romans. With the historical development and spread of Roman architecture much more thoroughly understood, a second trend in scholarly study in the twentieth century A.D. has been the attempt to comprehend the technical side of Roman building—the nature of construction as practiced by the Romans—and this has generated a substantial technical literature of tremendous importance.

One area of interest in the study of ancient Roman architecture has recently come to be of increasing concern to scholars: the interaction between architecture and the society that produced it. Studying architecture in its societal context has been pioneered in other areas of architectural history, but only within the last twenty years or so have such concerns become a focus of study for scholars and students of the architecture of ancient Rome. At the same time, the increase in our knowledge of construction and the continuing increase in documentary evidence published—notably epigraphical evidence—have provided the possibility of attempting an assessment of Roman architecture's position within its own society. This book is offered primarily as a synthesis of the current state of knowledge in this area. The inquiry is divided into six major topics: (1) Roman architects and what we know of them and of architecture as a profession in the ancient Roman world; (2) the legal, economic, and entrepreneurial organization of the "business" of building in ancient Rome and the people involved in that business; (3) the supply of manpower and materials for Roman architecture and how these requirements developed into and became organized as industries in their own right; (4) how Romans planned and organized their urban and suburban spaces into cities and towns that they found compatible with the lives they lived; (5) how public forms of architecture functioned in the daily and in the long-term physical world of ancient Romans; and (6) the nature of the everyday, or "quotidian," architecture—domestic, funerary, and commercial— by and into which Romans organized the spaces in which they had to live and work. None of these is a topic about which everything is known and merely awaiting synthesis and analysis. Rather, all are areas for continuing research and interest for many outstanding scholars, much of whose work will be cited and discussed throughout this book. The analysis of Roman architecture as a part of

Roman society is an ongoing and tremendously important part of classical archaeology, of Roman historical scholarship, and of the history of ancient art and architecture, and the many important discoveries already made will continue to be advanced, refined, perhaps overturned, and certainly revised by the process of ongoing scholarly questioning and evaluating of the growing body of evidence available.

One of the most exciting elements in this study is the conviction that Roman builders—architects, contractors, supervisors, patrons, construction specialists, even laborers, and slaves—are beginning to emerge as identifiable human beings from the mass of evidence, as are their professions and businesses, and that at the same time we can gather some understanding and appreciation of the architecturally defined spaces that were the borders and parameters of their physical world and their quotidian existence. It is the nature of the majority of this evidence to be fragmentary, however, and fragmentary evidence often and inevitably engenders the frustration of "running head-on into a brick wall," that is, discovering that the line of evidence you have been following suddenly and completely runs out, leaving only rational speculation as a method for continuing the investigation.

The evidence is, of course, largely archaeological in nature, not just those few remaining Roman buildings—always significantly altered from their original state and often sadly battered by time—but in addition the very bricks and cement, paving stones and slabs of marble, that often carry much information about the people who worked them and the society that wanted them, if we can manage to read it. Beyond individual buildings and their materials, the street patterns of ancient cities and towns, the distribution of public and private architecture, and the interrelationship between the various elements of architecture within their actual settings can now, largely thanks to archaeological and topographical research in many parts of the Roman world, permit us to analyze and evaluate to some degree the topography of the physical settings in which Romans existed. The Roman habit of inscribing stone, brick, tile, and almost every other possible surface that could be written upon offers a wealth of information on our subject, and the contribution of epigraphy and epigraphers to our knowledge has been essential and extensive.

Finally, the literature preserved so precariously to us from the ancient Roman world also provides remarkable amounts of evidence for analyzing the architecture of the times, not just specifically architectural or constructional texts such as Vitruvius's ten books on architecture or Frontinus's description of the aqueduct system of Rome, but documents such as the correspondence of Cicero or, much later, the gossipy imperial biographies of Suetonius and the *Historia Augusta* provide vivid insights into how buildings were built, for what purposes, and by whom. The sheer variety of the sources of evidence may occasionally prove bewildering, but it is hoped that a fairly consistent picture will emerge, always bearing in mind the fragmentary and sometimes random nature of the evidence that has been preserved to us over more than two millennia. Much has been learned and there remains much more to be discovered.

With these limitations in mind, then, *Roman Architecture and Society* is offered as a useful synthesis of that evidence for the *realia*—the people and organizations, planning and topography— of building in the world of ancient Rome. The idea for this book grew from a need I felt as a graduate student to have the *realia* of Roman architecture brought together in one relatively easy to find and affordable sourcebook since the information and evidence for these topics was spread over a vast range of scholarly publications and appeared in many languages. Hence, this is not a book intended, first or foremost, for scholars of Roman architecture or archaeology or for specialists in Roman social history. Rather, it is designed and written for anyone who would like to know more about how architecture was done, who did it, who paid for it, and how it affected the daily lives of those who lived and worked within it. Perforce, the majority of this material concerns the city of Rome itself since so much of our evidence comes from the capital of Rome's farflung empire, but corroborating or contradicting evidence from all over the Roman world, especially from Italy, is of tremendous importance and will be cited regularly. No history of Roman architecture, and no analysis of its monuments as artistic creations or for their aesthetics, is attempted. Excellent histories and equally excellent analyses of Roman architecture as an art are readily available in all modern languages. The focus of this book is instead specifically on the subject of its title and the areas of investigation listed above. The evaluation of the beauty, the grandeur, and the aesthetics of Roman architecture I leave to others better equipped for that task. This book only asks the questions "Who?" and "How?" of ancient Roman architecture and attempts to supply some answers and point the way toward gaining more knowledge of a fascinating subject's practitioners and practices.

I have intentionally restricted—severely—the number of illustrations published with this book and have limited those included to previously published drawings and plans, rather than photographs. However, sources of other plans and of high quality photographs of archaeological remains are given in the notes for every building or location discussed. These should be sought out by the reader who wishes to explore in more depth. In the same way, many of the brief discussions and evaluations of buildings included here can be expanded by consulting the extensive scholarly literature cited in the notes and bibliography. Two items, Donderer (1996) and Packer (1996), listed in the bibliography were not yet available when this book went to press; I list them because they are essential to their particular topics. As always, any and all errors of fact, citation, or interpretation herein are my sole and entire responsibility.

This book is an introduction, no more, to a vast and fascinating subject. If it leads the reader to search for more information, while providing a reliable initial summary of the evidence, then it has, in one way at least, done its job.

PART I

HOW THE ROMANS
ORGANIZED BUILDING

One

The Roman Architects

The Latin word *architectus* is surprisingly ambiguous. In the modern world we have established a common (if not always consistent) distinction between the "architect," who designs a building and is trained primarily as an artist and draftsman, and the "engineer," who manages and supervises the actual act of construction and takes complete responsiblity for creating the nonglamorous functional elements essential to cities and buildings. While such a distinction is not nearly as clearcut even in our own times as is sometimes implied, it is only in part applicable to the ancient world. Many projects that we would label "civil engineering" today were undertaken by men called "architects" by the ancient Greeks and Romans. While a Roman *architectus* was first and foremost the designer of a building, he could be and often was called upon to serve in addition as contractor or advisor in the formation of a building contract, as construction supervisor, and as building inspector.

There was a theoretical distinction between architect, contractor, and skilled builder in the Roman world, but it was by no means

3

rigid or even consistent.[1] For instance, in Roman literature we find that the word *architectus* means a house designer or a ship designer in the plays of Plautus; Vitruvius applies the label equally to both designers of temples and builders of siege engines; and the elder Pliny calls the builder of a lighthouse as well as the creator of a temple *architectus*.[2] Some builders whom both we and the Romans would call "engineers" in certain of their capacities functioned at other times as true designing "architects" in any sense of the word. Apollodorus of Damascus, the architect of Trajan's Forum in Rome—one of the supreme masterpieces of ancient architectural design—was also the engineer renowned for spanning the Danube River with a bridge during Trajan's Dacian campaigns; Vitruvius was certainly serving as an "engineer" when he worked on armaments assignments for Augustus or recalibrated the dimensions of pipes for Agrippa's aqueduct project, yet he designed and built an elegant basilica for the town of Fanum Fortunae, too.[3]

Thus, for the Romans, the scope and functions of an architect in the public sphere were conceived of much more broadly than they often are today. The distinction seems to be more applicable to private building, in which the "architects" seem to have been primarily responsible for design and to a lesser extent for contracting and supervisng building projects for private patrons. Vitruvius (1.1.10) implies that the *architectus* was responsible even in a private project for guiding the owner through the entire process of construction—from plans to contract to overseeing actual construction—but the majority of the evidence of private building activities, notably that provided by Cicero in his letters, indicates that design was considered the first and foremost of these duties, with the others required only in particular cases.[4] But while the scope of the *architectus* on any particular private commission may have been limited to certain areas, it is equally clear that in public building projects as well as in private contracts from time to time, the architect had to employ the full range of skills suggested by Vitruvius.

In order to study the nature of the architectural profession in ancient Rome, we must begin with Vitruvius's *De Architectura*, the only original manual of Roman architecture that survives to us.[5]

Vitruvius opens the first book of his work with a theoretical description of what the Roman architect ought to be. Given that he wrote at the end of the first century B.C., during the period of transition between the Roman Republic and the Roman Empire, Vitruvius, to some extent, represents typical Roman thinking (or at least a particular Roman practitioner's thinking) on this profession. Hence, any study of Roman architecture and society, which must take into consideration the people who actually practiced this profession, may start with the *architectus* in theory, in the ideal, as he was conceived in the ten books Vitruvius wrote on architecture.[6]

In the third paragraph of the introduction to his first book, Vitruvius writes:

> Both in general and especially in architecture are these two things found; that which signifies and that which is signified. That which is signified is the thing proposed about which we speak; that which signifies is the demonstration unfolded in systems of precepts. Wherefore a man who is to follow the architectural profession manifestly needs to have experience of both kinds. He must have a natural gift and also readiness to learn. (For neither talent without instruction nor instruction without talent can produce the perfect craftsman.) He should be a man of letters, a skilful draughtsman, a mathematician, familiar with scientific inquiries, a diligent student of philosophy, acquainted with music; not ignorant of medicine, learned in the responses of jurisconsults, familiar with astronomy and astronomical calculations.

What he is describing seems, at first glance, to be the well-educated minor aristocrat or citizen aiming to rise in his society, in part through a typical gentleman's rhetorical education. The term *architectus* is employed as an honorific title for practitioners trained in a broad but specific curriculum urged, perhaps invented, by Vitruvius. His theoretical basis for this curriculum is a simple dichotomy: while the knowledge needed by an architect is enhanced by learning techniques from various other crafts and skills, the actual practice of architecture requires a balance between skill or craftsmanship (*fabrica*) and theory (*ratiocinatio*).[7] This dichotomy between skill and theory corresponds to Vitruvius's distinction between "that which signifies and that which is signified." The essential balance

between these two elements is a constant theme throughout Vitruvius's book. He goes even further when he asserts that anyone
wanting to become an architect must possess both innate talent (the
"natural gift" of the passage quoted above) and a "readiness to learn"
the skills and the theory that Vitruvius will prescribe and must be
able to keep these two sides of his discipline in correct balance.

Vitruvius lays out nine areas of learning that he thinks essential
for the architect: literature (*litteratus*), draftsmanship (*peritus graph-
idos*), geometry (*eruditus geometria*), history (*historias complures*),
philosophy (*philosophos*), medicine (*medicinae*), law (*responsa iuris-
consultorum*), and astronomy (*astrologiam*).[8] His selection is interesting, particularly since Vitruvius states that he himself had received the normal liberal arts education of the Roman gentleman,
that is, training first in grammar, dialectic, and rhetoric, and only
then in the more advanced subjects of geometry, arithmetic, astronomy, and musical theory.[9] It would appear that his own education
was not entirely what he recommended for the "ideal" architect.
Grammar, dialectic, and rhetoric—the entire primary group of
studies—are not mentioned; arithmetic appears only as a subfield
of geometry; drafting, history, philosophy, medicine, and law go
beyond the standard curriculum. Only in geometry, astronomy, and
musical theory does there appear to be congruence. Even more
surprising is his insistence on technical education (*fabrica*), which
further distances his curriculum from that of the rhetorical and
grammatical education of a Roman aristocrat, although to some
degree he may be following the well-known "nine disciplines" pro-
moted by the scholar Varro during the first century B.C. as the
proper areas of study for an educated person.[10]

Vitruvius offers brief but interesting justifications for his selection of these areas of study (1.1.4).[11] He asserts that architects need
to know literature in order to be able to write clear and reliable
commentaries on, or descriptions of, what they have built. In the
preface to his seventh book (sec. 18), Vitruvius developed this point
when he lamented that many Roman architects had failed to publish commentaries describing their accomplishments, although the
Romans were no less talented than many Greek architects, who
were well known for their writings as well as their buildings. But

this aspect of an architect's education, while important to Vitruvius, was not given much attention in Rome in the later first century B.C., or his lamentation would have been unnecessary. His reason for emphasizing training in draftsmanship is also practical: "By his skill in drawing he [the architect] will find it easy by coloured drawings to represent the effect desired." Skilled drafting, then, will allow the architect both to prepare clear plans—blueprints, sections, elevations, sketches of details and structure—for the design and construction of a building in the practical sense and at the same time permit him to provide drawings that will clarify and decorate his publication of the building itself. Vitruvius, in his list of important publications in architecture prior to his own time (7. Pref. 12), cites ten such monographs on individual buildings, written by their architects, all Greeks, and presumably illustrated. *Geometria,* for Vitruvius's architect, consists of geometry proper, which teaches how to use rule and compass, lay out buildings on sites, and solve problems of symmetry; of optics, which provides for the lighting of buildings; and of arithmetic, by which the cost of building is determined and measurements are correctly taken. Here again, the study is grounded in a thoroughly practical concept of what the architect will actually make use of from the various subfields of the discipline of mathematics.

This practical but limited view of the architect's educational needs and requirements runs throughout Vitruvius's treatment of the remaining subjects also. The architect's need for a grounding in history seems almost entirely rhetorical, "because in their works they often design many ornaments about which they ought to render an account to inquirers" (1.1.5). He follows this somewhat vague remark with anecdotes drawn from Greek architecture concerning the origins of Caryatids and of the Persian colonnade, which seem more colorful than significant, but here again his emphasis on the publication of commentaries and descriptions of architects' achievements seems to be the reason behind his emphasis on history as an essential study for the prospective architect.

His reason for insisting on philosophy as an important grounding for the architect is twofold (1.1.7): "Philosophy . . . makes the architect high-minded, so that he should not be arrogant but rather urbane, fair-minded, loyal, and what is most important, without avarice."[12] The other area of philosophy that Vitruvius espouses for study is that of natural science, since "philosophy, moreover, explains the 'nature of things.'" Much later in his manual, Vitruvius himself tells us that he drew directly from Lucretius's famous epicurean poem "On the Nature of Things" (9. Pref. 17–18). The only example he adduces is a practical one again: the need for an architect to understand the fundamental principles of the natural world in order to create proper and safe water channels.[13] He concludes with a warning that the architect not instructed in philosophy may not be able to understand the works of engineers such as Ctesibius and Archimedes, which he thought essential to good architectural practice.

Knowledge of music is also justified by a practical twist. According to Vitruvius, an architect needs to know music in order to be aware of acoustic ratios and the mathematical relationships of sound in order to make the correct adjustments in machines of war such as the catapult, the scorpion, and the *balista*. He proceeds to explain these points with examples, first, of how the ropes of catapults are adjusted by "half-tones" (1.1.8) and, then, of how the acoustics of theaters may be improved (1.1.9). Vitruvius dispenses with his last three "required" subjects in one brief paragraph (1.1.10) again focused on practical applications. Studying medicine will instruct the architect in choosing healthy sites upon which to build; studying law will make him aware of the boundary rights of any building and how to avoid their violation as well as of how (and how not) to prepare contracts and meet contractual obligations; and studying astronomy will instruct him in the form of the physical world beyond the building itself and with the measurement of time.

From this quite specific curriculum for the education of the architect, Vitruvius proceeds to a more general discussion of the nature of the architect and what sort of person should be encouraged to pursue this profession. While innate talent and enthusiasm for mastering the prescribed course of study are essential, Vitruvius asserts later in his work (6. Pref. 6) that those trained as architects must be of respectable birth and honorable upbringing, with a true sense of moral responsibility and possessed of such qualities that money could be entrusted to them without hesitation. All this relates to Vitruvius's original justification for prescribing a required course of study for the architect: so that the architect will be equally skilled in practice (*fabrica*) and in theory (*ratiocinatio*), and from this joining of practical and theoretical skills, he will come to possess the authority (*auctoritas*) that he needs to be a successful artist and craftsman (1.1.2): "So architects who without culture [learning] aim at manual skill cannot gain a prestige correponding to their labours, while those who trust to theory and literature obviously follow a shadow and not reality. But those who have mastered both, like men equipped in full armour, soon acquire influence and attain their purpose." For Vitruvius, then, it would appear that the proper end of training is that the architect will not only be able to direct all elemenьs of his profession but will be a cultivated person with a well-rounded education. However, having said all this, Vitruvius feels he must make sure his audience thinks the goal attainable (1.1.12–18). He does not think it necessary that the architect possess total and complete mastery of every discipline listed; a moderate level of knowledge in each seems sufficient (1.1.18).[14]

Fascinating and valuable as Vitruvius's prescription for the education of the architect is, there are many questions that the author leaves unanswered. Nowhere does Vitruvius say where his curriculum is to be acquired, whether in the classroom, in apprenticeship to a master architect, or through training in an architectural workshop. No real idea of the amount of time involved in the acquisition of the necessary education and skills is provided, and Vitruvius says little if anything about the social status or the earning power of the architects of his own time. These subjects will bear some investigation, but the evidence is woefully inadequate. It is a pity that Vitruvius did not concern himself with these very practical types of information, for otherwise his treatise is by far the finest example preserved to us from antiquity of a craftsman's view of his own profession. It is clearly the work of someone who has worked as an architect,[15] but it does not provide the comprehensive social and sociological information that we would have liked about the Roman architect. For that, insofar as it is available at all, and to test to what extent Vitruvius's theoretical construct of the architectural profession corresponds to the facts preserved, we will have to turn to what we know of actual architects attested in the Roman world and their careers, including Vitruvius himself.

Before considering these people, however, we should return to Vitruvius's book briefly to outline his view of the duties and responsibilities of the Roman architect, since these things are clearly inherent in the nature of the education and training he prescribes. On the question of how the aspiring architect was trained we are almost without evidence earlier than the third century A.D., and such meager evidence as there is points up only extraordinary cases, not the usual practice. During the reign of Alexander Severus (A.D. 222–235), it appears that the emperor set up at public expense professors of a number of the liberal arts including architecture, to whose classes even poor parents could send their children. However, this was clearly an unusual public benefaction, and there is no evidence to demonstrate that it continued after A.D. 235.[16] Prior to the third century A.D. our sources are not very helpful. It has been generally assumed that before the reform instituted by Alexander Severus the training required for an architect was probably obtained by some type of apprenticeship to a master architect or in an architectural workshop, which seems to have been the usual method in Greece.[17] That workshops existed seems well attested from the monuments and the technical similarities that can sometimes be identified among different building commissions from the same general period, as well as from epigraphical evidence.[18] But some of the studies prescribed by Vitruvius (music theory, for instance) would have been at best infrequent occurrences in a normal workshop and probably would have been much more effectively inculcated in a classroom or school. What is clear is that the constant focus on the practical application of theoretical knowledge, as Vitruvius's justifications for his various areas of study clearly show, made the Roman architect as much a practitioner of construction as a designer of buildings in theory and on paper: the study of optics, perspective, theoretical mathematics—which were expected of architects in the Greek world—did exist but appear to have been less prevalent in the Roman system, and the balance between theory and practice more closely observed. But beyond such a generality, there is little evidence upon which to compare the training or the practices of Greek architects with those Vitruvius maintains for Romans.[19]

The evidence of actual architects, Vitruvius included, leads us to distinguish three possible career paths for the aspiring architect, each with its own inherent method of training: private study in the liberal arts and then with a master architect aiming toward a private career; training and career service in the Roman military, especially in roles involving construction and maintenance; or, primarily during Imperial times, training and a career in the Imperial building and maintenance services. It is important to note that there is no reason to think these three professional options were mutually exclusive; indeed Vitruvius himself seems to have moved in and out of all three, as we shall see.[20]

The duties and responsibilities of the Roman architect are, however, more easily determined; to a great extent they are clearly implied in Vitruvius's description of the ideal architectural education. The *architectus* was responsible for the design and planning of buildings without doubt; this was provided for by his education in draftsmanship and in geometry; between the two of these he learned both the principles and the concepts of building design. Certainly, one of a Roman architect's most important functions seems to have been the drawing up of plans for projects, and this was probably one of his distinguishing characteristics. There is a variety of ancient testimony to show that such plans actually existed: Cicero found it difficult to conceptualize what his brother Quintus's house would look like from the architect's plans, Aulus Gellius mentions plans for bath complexes being exhibited in public, and Plutarch says that builders competing for a city contract provided plans for the magistrates.[21] Vitruvius apparently incorporated or appended sketch plans to the original publication of his *De Architectura*; he enumerates three different types of plans for which an architect might be held responsible: ground plans (*ichnographia*), elevations (*orthographia*), and perspective drawings (*scaenographia*).[22] Thus draftsmanship and geometry seem to be assigned a central place in Vitruvius's scheme of architectural education although not at the beginning of his list of subjects. The architect is furthermore charged with knowing optics so he can undertake lighting design and acoustics when that is a consideration in the plan of a building (Vitruvius cites the apposite example of designing a theater).[23]

As a direct corollary to the architect's responsibility for the physical design of the building to be created, Vitruvius also charges the Roman architect with responsibility for choosing and laying out the site, assuring its salubriousness and suitability for what is to be put on it, and for being able to lay out not just a building but the street pattern and city blocks of an entire town if called upon.[24] In his prescribed education, the study of medicine, geometry and drafting, natural philosophy, and astronomy would all contribute to the architect's acquiring skills now thought of as belonging to a city planner, a sanitary engineer, and a landscape architect rather than the designing architect per se, and exercising his authority over all these elements should they enter into his building project.

While Vitruvius nowhere states that the Roman architect was ever responsible for the financing of his projects—indeed, it is very clear that, in Vitruvius's opinion and to some degree in fact, a Roman architect designed and built only after receiving and accepting a commission, not prior to financing[25]—nonetheless the architect was responsible for balancing the books and keeping, or attempting to keep, the cost of the project within reasonable limits. To possess such ability in accounting and cost maintenance, it is necessary that the architect be trained in arithmetic and also that he be morally high-minded through training in philosophical ethics and morals; indeed Vitruvius is vitriolic in his denunciation of fraudulent and unprofessional financial activities by some builders, and strongly advocates stringent controls on the finances of construction.[26]

The last duty specifically laid out by Vitruvius in his prescribed education for the architect is that of publishing treatises ("commentaries") about his creations, and for this purpose there is included in the curriculum training in literature and history. This was apparently something of a hobby horse of Vitruvius's since he regularly laments the lack of such treatises being written by Roman architects, compared with their abundance among the Greeks (7. Pref. 14). He is firm on the point that it should be the duty of every architect to publish treatises that describe what he has built, as well as more theoretical and practical works, and clearly he views his own manual of architecture as doing his duty in this sphere of activity, especially when he describes the basilica he designed and built at Fanum Fortunae (5.1.6–10).[27]

Beyond design and planning, cost estimation and control, and publication, it seems implied at various points in Vitruvius's text, that the Roman architect, like Vitruvius himself in his project at Fanum, was or could be expected to serve as general supervisor and organizer of the entire process of building. Hence the architect had to concern himself directly with such duties as providing building materials and supplies, hiring labor (both skilled and unskilled) and arranging for contracts to be let: the actual day-to-day operation of the building site, and the construction team; making revisions and adaptations to plans as construction progressed or problems arose; and with the legal requirements of contracting that were part and parcel of building, especially in cities. Furthermore, it is clear that, while the initial decision about what sorts of materials were to be used in a building was not necessarily the architect's, his knowledge of and experience with many of them made his advice on their applicability, and his intervention in their procurement, very important.[28] All these are mentioned at various points in the text of Vitruvius but not specifically provided for in the theoretical education, except possibly contracting since the ideal architect is to have a practical training in the law, though the author leaves the exact nature of that legal training rather ill-defined. But it seems quite clear that these were further expectations that might be, though were not necessarily in every commission, placed upon the architect when he was at work. Private building projects seem to have divided these responsibilities more specifically than did public building. Evidence from legal texts as well as that of Cicero shows that in private projects primary responsibility for design was placed on the architect, but contracting and supply were left largely to a contractor (*redemptor* or *conductor*), and the practical side of the project to the actual builders, while in a number of instances the

owner of the property being built upon served as his own inspector.
There are instances of the architect serving in various of these roles
for a private patron, but assignment of such duties to the architect in
private construction seems to have been entirely ad hoc.[29]

The last area of interest upon which Vitruvius sheds some light,
and we can gain much more insight, is the question of the social
position or status accorded architects in the Roman world. It is
reasonable to note that while Vitruvius seems to be prescribing a
gentleman's education for the architect at first glance, in fact his is a
much more practical scheme than the rhetoric surrounding it may
imply. Vitruvius does say that "the ancients," by which he presumably means the pre-Hellenistic Greeks, preferred architects of good
family (6. Pref. 6) and that it had been normal for son to follow
father in the profession (10.2.12).[30] We know that Cicero deemed
architecture an honorable profession, but the orator added that it
was honorable specifically for members of the lower classes.[31] Perhaps the contradiction that some have seen here is not real, however, but reflects a different societal reality. It is now well established, as we shall see when we turn to named Roman architects,
that architects were drawn from every class of society, ranging all
the way from the emperor Hadrian himself to slaves and freedmen.
An important factor in this entire consideration, which has been
studied in detail by Gros, is that architects were as (or more) often
imported into the western Roman Empire, most particularly from
Greece, as produced on Italian or western European soil. The status
of talented "foreigners" in the Roman West was always ambiguous,
and that ambiguity helps to explain the ambiguous (and sometimes
contradictory) impression we receive from ancient literature and
inscriptions about the social status of architects in the Roman
world. Before drawing many conclusions on this subject it will be
best to turn to the evidence available to us for the names and careers
of architects who practiced in the Roman world between the second
century B.C. (when our evidence begins) and later antiquity.[32] By
investigating what we know of attested architects who practiced in
the Roman world—who they were, where they came from, for
whom they worked, what they built, what became of them—we
can attempt to exercise a certain type of "reality check" upon the

theoretical and, perhaps, ideal *architectus* known to us from Vitruvius's pages. However, it must be noted immediately that our evidence will be, for the most part, fragmentary and random, and much may have to be deduced from meager evidence.

Roman Architects and Architects in the Roman World, in the Second and First Centuries B.C.

To begin the search for Roman architects,[33] we must turn first to Greece. The names of more than one hundred Greek architects are known to us from ca. 650–50 B.C.[34] In the great majority of these cases we know little about these builders beyond their names and, sometimes, certain of their buildings, and even less about their education, career path, and social status.[35] Their artistic influence upon the development of Roman architecture and its practitioners is made clear not only by Vitruvius but by the history of those architects who worked in Rome and in the increasingly Roman-dominated Mediterranean world of the second and first centuries B.C. Vitruvius's manual is drawn overwhelmingly from treatises written by Greek architects of the centuries prior to his own, as well as from technical literature of the Greek world, and the author mentions a large number of Greek sources in the course of his work, including such well-known figures as Archimedes, Aristotle, Plato, and Pythagoras.[36] While he may have consulted many, even most, of these technical and philosophical works only through compilations and abridgements,[37] nonetheless the overwhelming influence exercised upon Vitruvius by these Greek sources is abundantly clear.

Vitruvius lists fourteen specific architects whose handbooks on architectural orders or monographs on individual buildings he singles out for special praise (7. Pref. 12). These include, in the order Vitruvius mentions them, Silenus on the Doric order; Rhoecus and Theodorus on the Ionic temple of Juno (Hera) at Samos; Chersiphron and Metagenes on the Ionic temple of Diana (Artemis) at Ephesus; Pytheos on the Ionic temple of Minerva (Athena) at Priene; Ictinos and Carpion on the temple of Minerva (Athena) on the Athenian acropolis (i.e., the Parthenon); Theodorus Phocaeus on the tholos at Delphi; Philo on the symmetries of temples and on his arsenal at the port of Piraeus; Hermogenes on the Ionic temple of Liber Pater (Dionysus) at Teos; Arcesius on symmetries in the Corinthian order and on the Ionic temple to Aesculapius (Asclepius) at Tralles; and Satyrus and Pytheos on the Mausoleum at Halicarnassus.[38] Of these individuals, Hermogenes appears to have exercised the greatest influence upon Vitruvius—indeed the majority of our remaining information about this important architect is transmitted to us by Vitruvius—and upon Roman conceptions of architecture and architects. He requires closer scrutiny.

HERMOGENES

Hermogenes was a practicing architect in Hellenistic Asia Minor between 250 and 150 B.C. Vitruvius mentions him by name five times, and it seems fairly apparent that much of Book 3 of *De Architectura* employs Hermogenes' writings as its major source.[39] Vitruvius turns to Hermogenes' temple of Artemis Leucophryne at Magnesia (3.2.6) when he wants to cite an example of a pseudodipteral temple, for none was available to him in Rome. Hermogenes' temple to Dionysus at Teos (3.3.8) is the example of the eustyle column arrangement, an invention Vitruvius attributes to the Greek architect. Shortly thereafter (3.3.9), Hermogenes is somewhat grandiloquently praised for this invention, and, by implication, for the general characteristics of his architectural designs. Vitruvius cites Hermogenes' agreement with Arcesius and Pytheos (4.3.1) that the Doric order was unsuitable for temples and other religious architecture, shown by his change of mind in converting the plan for a temple of Dionysus from Doric to Ionic though he managed to build it with the materials already laid in.[40] Finally, Vitruvius specifically names Hermogenes as the author of treatises on the Artemis temple at Magnesia and the Dionysus temple at Teos (7. Pref. 12), which seems to imply that these were his most famous and most innovative works.[41]

The two passages in praise of Hermogenes (3.3.9 and 7. Pref. 12) imply that certain characteristics that Vitruvius admired and wanted other Roman architects to admire were exemplified by the Hellenistic architect. These included inventiveness combined with cost efficiency, the creation of dignified spaces (such as a walkway that did not detract from the overall appearance of the building), and Hermogenes' authority over both the architectural design and the execution of it. Whether this represents the actual nature of Hermogenes or perhaps what Vitruvius wanted Hermogenes to have been in order to furnish a good example is impossible to tell, since Vitruvius is to such a degree our main source of information. What does emerge clearly is the inventiveness of the Greek architect, and the importance of his written treatises both to Vitruvius and to Roman architects in general. It seems fair to assert that Vitruvius probably derived a good deal of his own theoretical education from Hermogenes' writings.[42] Hermogenes is portrayed by Vitruvius as a proper model to be emulated by Romans wanting to become architects and seems to have provided such a model at the very least for Vitruvius himself. The importance of Hermogenes and the other renowned Greek architects cited by Vitruvius to Roman architecture during the second and first centuries B.C. must have been primarily educational, through the surviving examples of their architectural masterworks and the treatises they left behind. Although they never actually practiced in Rome or Italy or on commission to Roman patrons, their writings served as the textbooks from which a Roman could learn the art and craft, or the theory (*ratiocinatio*) and practice (*fabrica*) of architecture.

HERMODORUS

The other Hellenistic Greek architect who influenced Vitruvius directly, and who certainly had a tremendous impact on the development of Roman architecture out of the tradition imported from Hellenistic Greece, was Hermodorus of Salamis, renowned as the first Hellenistic Greek actually to have built a public monument in the city of Rome. Our sources for Hermodorus are more diverse than those for Hermogenes. Vitruvius mentions him only once (3.2.5) as the designer of the peripteral temple of Jupiter Stator in the Porticus Metelli. He is not mentioned in Vitruvius's list of his written sources (7. Pref. 12), presumably because Hermodorus failed to publish a treatise on his work, although this assumption is at best disputable, and it certainly does not prove him illiterate.[43]

The career and creations of Hermodorus have come under a good deal of scrutiny in the last twenty-five years, and much can now be discerned, but there is still a good deal of hypothesis involved. We know from Vitruvius that Hermodorus built the temple of Jupiter Stator in the porticus set up by Q. Metellus Macedonicus, and the connection between the two men can be reasonably dated to around 143 B.C., although the exact extent of Hermodorus's responsibility—whether for entirely original construction or just for completion, whether for the temple alone or also for the porticus—is unclear. Certainly Metellus Macedonicus was one of the leading importers of Greek art and architecture into Rome during the second century B.C. and his temple to Jupiter Stator was the primary basis for his reputation, since it was the first marble temple to be built in the city.[44] The ancient sources emphasize the significance of this introduction of marble into temple architecture and strongly imply that marble was an important part of the appeal that Greek Hellenistic architecture held for Romans of the second century B.C. An increase in the use of marbles from Greece, notably Pentelic, was a natural result of the conquest of the Greek mainland through the destruction of Corinth in 146 B.C. The great *triumphatores* such as, in addition to Metellus Macedonicus himself, Scipio Aemilianus, Lucius Mummius, and Decimus Junius Brutus Callaicus were constantly in contest with one another to embellish Rome with magnificent contemporary monuments, and they made use of the materials newly available to them through conquest in the East that would most accurately reflect the new Roman ideology of imperialism and triumph. But Italian architects of the time had little if any knowledge of marble and probably only the meagerest experience in using it in building. Therefore it became necessary to call upon Greek master architects like Hermodorus of Salamis, not to mention the skilled marble workers already engaged by those architects' workshops.[45]

That Hermodorus came to Rome and, apparently, stayed is attested by his likely execution of a commission for Decimus Junius Brutus Callaicus—the building of a temple to Mars possibly ca. 132 B.C.—and by Cicero, who says that he (or at least an architect named Hermodorus, presumably the same man) was responsible for building the *navalia* for Marcus Antonius in the city between 100 and 99 B.C.[46] While neither of these later projects can be attributed with certainty to Hermodorus, the likelihood remains fairly strong that, in Hermodorus of Salamis, we see the next step in the importation of Hellenistic architectural practices, styles, and aesthetic into Rome and Roman Italy: a renowned Hellenistic Greek architect who brought his training, his sensibilities, and probably his pretrained craftsmen and stonecutters to Italy with him and stayed to take a leading role in the hellenization—or more correctly the hellenisticization—of Rome and thereby of Roman architecture. The apparent freedom Hermodorus enjoyed to move from project to project surely attests that he was in great demand, or else a master at soliciting commissions. If the latter, then Vitruvius may mention him only once because he did not fulfill the writer's idealistic image of the architect always waiting to be asked to accept building commissions (5. Pref. 6). On the other hand, it may be that Hermodorus was one of the first professional builders to turn architecture in Rome into a full-time occupation. While Vitruvius would not have approved, particularly if Hermodorus had been too busy during his career to publish a proper treatise on the temple of Jupiter Stator, nonetheless Hermodorus appears to provide an important example of the arrival of the architect as professional in the Roman world.

COSSUTIUS

If we turn from Greek to Roman architects attested by Vitruvius, we find only three whose actual buildings are mentioned or described: Quossutius [*sic*] (7. Pref. 15, 17), Mucius (3.2.5 and 7. Pref. 17), and Vitruvius himself.[47] All three are described as master craftsmen and have known and datable buildings attributed to them. Cossutius, a Roman citizen, was chosen by the Romanophile Seleucid king of Syria, Antiochus IV Epiphanes, as architect for his undertaking to complete the long-unfinished temple to Olympian Zeus at Athens.[48] The story is well told by Vitruvius (7. Pref. 15):

> For at Athens the architects Antistates and Callaeschrus and Antimachides and Porinus laid the foundations for Pisistratus when he was

building a temple to Olympian Jupiter. After his death they abandoned his undertaking because of the interruption caused by the Republic. About two hundred years after [i.e., after the accession of Alexander the Great in 336 B.C.], King Antiochus undertook the cost of the building. A Roman citizen Quossutius [*sic*], an architect of great skill and scientific attainments, finely designed the great sanctuary with a double colonnade all round and with the architrave symmetrically disposed. And this building is famous owing to its magnificence not only with the crowd but with the experts.

It is important to note here that Vitruvius uses a rare Latin deponent verb—*architector* [*Quossutius nobiliter est architectatus*]—which in this context strongly implies that Cossutius was responsible for designing or planning every aspect of the project.[49] Vitruvius does criticize Cossutius for not having left any written treatise or description of the building behind (7. Pref. 17). Our information is confirmed, and perhaps slightly refined, by Velleius Paterculus (1.10.1), who states that Antiochus began the Olympieion at Athens, but both Vitruvius's testimony and the archaeological evidence at the site show clearly that Antiochus was reworking and completing a building begun in the late sixth century B.C., so Velleius must have meant the Hellenistic restoration project. Cossutius is also attested by the inscription on an honorific statue base found on the site of the Olympieion, which calls him "Decimus Cossutius Roman citizen,"[50] and this can leave little doubt of the veracity of Vitruvius's story. But if so, there is an interesting puzzle here. How did a Roman citizen gain such prestige as an architect in the second quarter of the second century B.C. to be selected for what must have been a major and singularly prestigious commission from a powerful Seleucid monarch, and one to be carried out in the symbolic center of Greek culture and architecture, Athens itself? Was this a fluke? Why was such a commission not entrusted to a Hermogenes or a Hermodorus? And can we connect D. Cossutius to any other architectural projects, major or minor, in the Hellenistic or Roman world of the second century B.C.?

First, the fact of Cossutius's Roman citizenship is emphasized not only by Vitruvius but also by the honorary inscription from the temple site. From this it is fair to deduce that such recognition for a

Roman citizen was indeed extraordinary. Vitruvius nowhere else mentions the citizenship of any non-Greek architect in his manual, so here he is probably simply translating the wording of the Athenian inscription to Cossutius since this was a noteworthy achievement for a Roman citizen as well as a noteworthy piece of architecture. D. Cossutius himself is not attested anywhere in Rome or Italy but, as Rawson has shown, other Cossutii are attested at Puteoli and Pompeii in Campania as early as the second century B.C. and in various Roman trading posts in the eastern Mediterranean, notably in Delos, by the mid-second century B.C. as contractors dealing with marble quarries and in various official capacities.[51] From these family connections it can be hypothesized that D. Cossutius received his training and pursued his early career either in Greece or, more likely, in Campania (where it is often asserted that architecture was developing more rapidly than at Rome itself during the second century B.C.).

Rawson adds weight to the evidence for a Campanian architectural training for D. Cossutius by citing the other evidence for the architect, often regarded as hopelessly confusing. His name appears scratched, in Latin letters, into the interior of an aqueduct above Epiphaneia, a suburb of Antioch in which Antiochus built a *bouleuterion* and several temples. If this is the same Cossutius, and both the date of the aqueduct and the connection with Antiochus must lend credence to the attribution, then this ought to be the architect of the Olympieion at Athens, engaged upon further commissioned work for Antiochus. Rawson suggests that these two inscriptions may be the signature of a freedman of D. Cossutius who had adopted the cognomen and continued to work for his master after manumission; whether or not that is correct, the two Latin inscriptions surely imply that Cossutius had at least one, and perhaps a number of, Latin-speaking workmen with him in Syria, and in turn that he had been initially based in Italy, not in Athens, which would explain the presence of Latin speakers among his personal assistants and skilled workmen.[52] Polybius (26. 1) tells us that Antiochus Epiphanes liked to converse with craftsmen, and Livy (41.20.11–13) says that Antiochus sponsored gladiatorial games "in the Roman manner" and in time trained young Greeks to fight in them so that he could forego hiring costly gladiators from Rome. The fact that Antiochus spent a number of years as an official hostage (*obses*) in Rome helps to explain his Romanophile instincts and makes his association with and eventual patronage of a Campanian architect who was also a Roman citizen more likely.

It is noteworthy that there is nothing specifically Italic, or Italian-influenced, in the remains of the temple of Olympian Zeus at Athens, but this should not occasion surprise, since the work was a continuation and updating of the original Pisistratid project, including changing the temple's order from Doric to Corinthian and introducing Pentelic marble, but incorporating the original foundations as well as the overall design of the sixth-century plan.[53] It would have been inappropriate for Cossutius to have introduced any Italic elements into this project, even had he wished to. Various other projects known to have been built by Antiochus have been attributed to D. Cossutius—notably the temple of Jupiter Capitolinus at Antioch, which may have stood in Epiphaneia[54]—but there is no real proof. Nonetheless, it is reasonable to assume that an important part, if not the whole, of Decimus Cossutius's career as architect was spent in the service and under the patronage of Antiochus IV Epiphanes. Whether Cossutius was Campanian- or Greek-trained, it is fairly clear that he worked strictly in the Greek Hellenistic architectural tradition, but kept up his Roman contacts and was identified by his contemporaries very specifically as a *civis Romanus*.

Given the connections of various Cossutii to Delos and other Roman trading centers in Greece and to Campania with its strong Hellenic cultural traditions, Decimus Cossutius's career may well represent a new phenomenon, one that would become increasingly important in the history of architecture in the Mediterranean basin: a freeborn Roman citizen trained in the Greek Hellenistic architectural tradition who employed Italian as well as Greek craftsmen in his entourage and undertook major projects at the commission of a wealthy aristocratic patron who exhibited no prejudice against the insurgence of Rome and Romans into every sphere of influence in the ancient world. From the time of Decimus Cossutius onward,

Roman architects become ever more common in and ever more important to the history of Western architecture: a fairly direct lineage can be traced from Cossutius to the great architects of the high Roman Empire, Rabirius and Apollodorus.

The family of the Cossutii continues to appear on inscriptions that connect them to the architectural and, increasingly, the sculptural trade of the Roman world throughout the first century B.C. and on into the Empire. Most of the inscriptions are those of freedmen laborers who adopted the Cossutius family name after their manumission, which indicates both the economic and social status of the Cossutii. These mention both Greek and Italian workers, often marble-cutters or workers in sculptural workshops, and indeed a few inscriptions attest Cossutii still involved in these trades as late as the second century A.D. It appears that a fairly widespread "family" business, already reaching from Rome and Campania to Greece and the Aegean islands in the second century B.C., remained a going concern at least to the latter part of the first century B.C., and individuals bearing the name remained involved well beyond that, although the evidence is insufficient during the Empire to assume a family "firm" under specific control of any Cossutius or Cossutii.[55] These inscriptions clearly attest to the renown, the status, and the wealth acquired by the family probably in the generation in which Decimus Cossutius served as architect to Antiochus IV Epiphanes of Syria. This is the first such "family" firm connected to architecture and sculpture that we find securely documented in the Roman world. With the growth of architectural activity on a grand scale in Rome after 146 B.C., other such family enterprises appear to have arisen, and increasongly we see the architects who followed Cossutius working in their native land and capital city, rather than for foreign kings. Whether the Roman citizen Decimus Cossutius might have been engaged, if he were still alive in the 140s B.C. (for which there is no evidence one way or the other), rather than the Greek foreigner Hermodorus of Salamis, to construct the first marble temple in Rome must remain moot and idle speculation; nonetheless, the career of Decimus Cossutius marks the true starting point of Roman success in the profession of architect.

MUCIUS

In the same paragraph (3.2.5) in which he mentions Hermodorus's temple to Jupiter Stator, Vitruvius singles out as the second perfect example of a peripteral temple "the temple of Honos and Virtus built without a *posticum* by Mucius near the *Mariana* (Monument of Marius)."[56] At a later point (7. Pref. 17) Vitruvius remarks that "Gaius" Mucius's temple to Honos and Virtus would have been one of the finest in the world, if only it had been built of marble. It would seem likely that the avoidance of marble was part of the original commission to Mucius, which came from Marius himself after the victory over the Cimbri and Teutones in 102 B.C., the spoils of which were to pay for the temple's construction.[57] Marius was renowned as an "anti-Hellene" and might well have wanted his "victory temple" built of native Italian materials, thus distancing both temple and himself from the Hellenizing tendencies of previous *triumphatores*.[58] If so, Vitruvius fails to mention, or perhaps to appreciate, the significance of the building materials used; but given Vitruvius's deep-seated admiration of Hellenistic architectural traditions, especially as embodied in the principles and practices of Hermogenes, this is not very surprising.

Vitruvius mentions Mucius—first by *nomen* only, with *praenomen* G(aius) only at 7. Pref. 17—as if his name would be familiar to his readers;[59] nowhere does Vitruvius specifically apply the title *architectus* to him, but instead uses the past participle *facta* to describe Mucius's responsibility for this temple, a linguistic construction more commonly used (especially in inscriptions) to refer to the responsibilities of magistrates who commissioned or presided over building projects than to architects. It is even more unusual that, in the second passage devoted to Mucius, Vitruvius uses a phrase (*qui magna scientia confisus*) that means Mucius built the temple "by trusting in his own great learning." Such vocabulary is elsewhere employed by Vitruvius (e.g., 6. Pref. 6–7) to praise private persons who could supervise their own building projects and improvements because they were confident in their own literary training. Could this imply that Mucius was the magistrate responsible for the temple of Honos et Virtus and that he exercised important influence on the actual appearance of the building, perhaps even to the point of claiming to have designed it, though an amateur? The evidence is meager, but worth investigating. A Gaius Mucius was said by Livy (*Peri.* 70) to have served as proconsul of Asia in 97 B.C., but the *praenomen* Gaius seems to be an error in the text, since it is now fairly firmly established that the proconsul of Asia in that year was Quintus Mucius Scaevola, who had held the office of curule aedile under Marius in 100 B.C. Perhaps the "architect" Mucius, mentioned in specific connection with Gaius Marius by Vitruvius but never called *architectus*, should be identified with Quintus Mucius Scaevola,[60] and Vitruvius's "G(aius)" attributed to a similar error. While attractive, this identification cannot be proven. Vitruvius's Mucius might be identified instead as a freedman or client of Scaevola who had sufficient training to serve as architect for the temple and who had adopted his former master and patron's *nomen*. Another possibility is that Mucius was a free agent, probably of servile origin, whose family had for at least a couple of generations been connected to that of Q. Mucius Scaevola, possibly through the manumission of an ancestor a generation or two earlier who took his family's *nomen* from the Mucii.[61]

If Vitruvius's Mucius is identified with Q. Mucius Scaevola, it points up another aspect of the "profession" of architecture in Rome: the fact that Roman architects were not in general men of humble origin (as seems clear from Vitruvius's description of the architect's education) but were often either professionals drawn from the middle (even the upper middle) classes who worked on commission for distinguished patrons, or were sometimes themselves rich and powerful men of the highest social status, well-trained amateurs indulging in architecture as an avocation. There would have been nothing demeaning to a man of the stature of Q. Mucius Scaevola in designing a temple on commission of the *triumphator* and consul G. Marius, given that Marius apparently did not wish to design it himself. It is certainly fair to conclude that, as Richardson[62] asserts, the Mucius who designed the temple of Honos et Virtus was "a person of consequence," whether he was Q. Mucius Scaevola himself or an *ingenuus* architect connected to the family. In the Roman world of the second and first centuries B.C.

25

there seems to have been nothing inconsistent or incongruous about a patrician and senator practicing the art of architecture or serving as an *architectus,* as long as he was not called one. Some slight support for assuming that Vitruvius did mean Scaevola himself and merely mistook Mucius Scaevola's *praenomen,* is provided by the fact that he scrupulously avoided referring to the ex-consul as a practitioner of a profession (i.e., not calling him an *architectus*), thereby respecting the traditional prohibition against senators indulging in, or at least appearing to indulge in, money-making enterprises. An architect not called "architect" was merely a gentleman amateur indulging in his favorite skill for honor and prestige, without the taint of profit even implied, and this was thoroughly suitable behavior.[63] But the professional *architectus,* too, while also generally expected to be a man of good family and social standing, worked on commission from others, and for such men the title does not seem to have been an honorary but a professional designation. We see similar situations of a nobleman fulfilling many of the functions of an *architectus* for himself at various points throughout the first century B.C.: Quintus Cicero apparently served as his own architect to some extent,[64] and it would appear that L. Aemilius Paullus may have taken a good deal of personal responsibility for his two successive reconstructions of the Basilica Aemilia—which thereafter was always called Basilica Paulli—first restoring it in or prior to 54 B.C. as cheaply as possible due to financial exigencies, but then doing the job right after 54 with Julius Caesar's financial support. Paullus here was clearly not providing the funds but was directly involved in planning the project, as Cicero's remark about Paullus's reuse of the columns from an earlier phase of the building in his earlier reconstruction seems to indicate.[65] But L. Aemilius Paullus is nowhere labeled the "architect" of the Basilica Paulli; such a label could not have been applied with propriety to an aristocratic amateur.

L. CORNELIUS

With the coming of the first century B.C. and the rise of a quasi-professional military in place of the traditional citizen volunteer army that had previously been the Roman tradition, another path for receiving the training needed for the practice of architecture, and for gaining the experience expected of an *architectus* while still avoiding the possible stigma of seeming to work for money, was opened up. Its influence is apparent in the careers of the two best-documented architects of the first century B.C., L. Cornelius and Vitruvius himself. At the same time, we have an unexpectedly rich source of information about a wide variety of architects and builders otherwise unknown to us through the correspondence of Cicero, in which we can see extremely wealthy Romans getting their projects built and the people they employed to do the jobs.

The first architect to appear in our sources practicing in Rome during the first century B.C. is attested only by a single inscription which can be dated to between 65 and 35 (fig. 1.1).[66] It commemorates one Lucius Cornelius, son of Lucius, a member of the Voturia voting tribe, then lists the two most significant posts of his career: *praefectus fabrum* (literally "prefect of builders") of the consul Quintus Catulus and *architectus* of the censor, presumably again—since no other censor's name is given and the inscription is obviously complete—Quintus Catulus. There is nothing ambiguous in the text. It should occasion no surprise that the gentile *nomen* of the consul and censor is omitted, since that is not at all uncommon in inscriptions of the first century B.C.[67] Furthermore, the Quintus Catulus listed here is almost without doubt one of the two men of this name who rose to the consulate in the first century B.C.: the father and son Quintus Lutatius Catulus. The father held the consulate in 102 B.C., but insofar as we know never served as censor; the son, a close associate of L. Cornelius Sulla, the dictator, was consul in 78 B.C. and was appointed censor in 65. Unless further evidence appears to suggest a censorship for the father, it seems reasonable to assume that the Quintus Catulus of this inscription is Quintus Lutatius Catulus consul of 78 B.C.[68]

Quintus Lutatius Catulus is associated with two extremely important building projects carried out in Rome in the first half of the first century B.C.: the building of the city record office, the Tabularium, sometime around 78 B.C. and the reconstruction of the temple of Jupiter Optimus Maximus on the Capitoline Hill, which was completed in 62 B.C. and upon the epistyle of which Catulus's

Figure 1.1 The L. Cornelius Architectus inscription from the via Praenestine, located on Tiber Island, Rome. [Courtesy of the Soprintendenza Archeologica di Roma and the Ospedale Fatebenefratelli, Rome]

name was inscribed.[69] The Tabularium has been identified for over a century with the substantial remains still to be seen beneath the Palazzo Senatore on the Capitoline Hill. Two inscriptions, said to have been found in the building, attribute the construction to Catulus during his consulate. Strangely enough, so important a building as the central record office for Rome from the time of Sulla onward is never mentioned anywhere in the surviving literary sources, but in addition to the two construction inscriptions, we are told by further epigraphical evidence that it was restored by the emperor Claudius in A.D. 46 (so was obviously still in use at that time) and that military diplomata were hung there.[70] It would appear, then, that L. Cornelius was serving on Catulus's staff as *praefectus fabrum* at the time of the construction of the Tabularium and so would in all probability have been some sort of building supervisor, if not more, on that project.

The magnificent reconstruction of the temple of Jupiter Capitolinus was necessitated by the temple's destruction by fire on 6 July 83 B.C. Its rebuilding was entrusted to the dictator Sulla, who is reported to have brought marble columns (or possibly column capitals) from Cossutius's rebuilding of the temple to Olympian Zeus in Athens to Rome for the project.[71] It was Catulus, long a supporter and right-hand man to Sulla, to whom the Senate assigned the actual reconstruction of the temple, and it was Catulus who finally dedicated the completed rebuilding in 62 B.C.[72] By the 60s B.C., perhaps because of the success of the Tabularium project, L. Cornelius had risen to the position of *architectus* on Catulus's staff, and it seems safe to list him as the architect of this major rebuilding project on the Capitoline Hill. Here we seem to have a well-documented and successful career for an architect serving, presumably on commission, an important Roman nobleman and political figure. Two questions must be addressed, however, before any further conclusions can be posited from the evidence: What was the social status of L. Cornelius and what does his name tell us? And what was a *praefectus fabrum?*

The architect's name, Lucius Cornelius, seems to imply a direct connection with L. Cornelius Sulla Felix, the dictator, possibly as a freedman or the son of a freed slave. The association with Catulus clearly reinforces the assumption of a connection to the family of Sulla. But the lack of a *cognomen* for Cornelius in the inscription—which had become the normal practice in inscriptions of freedmen from 85 B.C. onward, as Molisani points out—as well as the presence of his father's *praenomen* ("son of Lucius") and of a voting tribe are much more characteristic of inscriptions for the sons of freeborn fathers. Such a person, at least two generations free, was an *ingenuus,* and this was considered the rank of a gentleman.[73] The voting tribe Voturia, one of the most ancient in Rome, was in particular the tribe to which citizens of Ostia belonged (together with the Palatina) and is otherwise attested only in Italy outside Rome. Therefore, it is quite possible, though by no means proven, that L. Cornelius was the son of a freeman, an *ingenuus* of good rank and family, and came from Rome's port city at Ostia.[74] Such an origin and social status would accord well with the background we have so far seen in architects like Cossutius, or among the Hellenistic Greek professionals (e.g. Hermodorus) though he would not be a patrician aristocrat of the stripe of Q. Mucius Scaevola (if that identification of the architect is correct).

The office called *praefectus fabrum,* which Cornelius held during 78 B.C., had, until this inscription was published, not been thought to be specifically associated with the profession of architect or with building in general, despite the vocabulary. Certainly by the middle of the first century B.C., specifically during the hegemony of Julius Caesar, the *praefectus fabrum* was not a builder's post at all, but a generalized and convenient label given to subordinate positions, both military and civilian, filled by men who accompanied Roman magistrates to their assignments in the provinces and who were responsible for the widest variety of duties. While the office may originally have been linked with the so-called college of builders (*fabri*) as the title for a supervisor of public works undertaken by the college, it is also clear that at some point there developed a clear distinction between civil and military *praefecti fabrum* since military prefects of building appear from the epigraphical record to have been supervisors responsible for construction work undertaken by any legion of the Roman army.[75] The specific connection of this post to an architect's career is unknown prior to the time of L. Cornelius; most of the evidence even for the Republican period comes from later in the first century B.C. and demonstrates that by the time of Caesar and on into the early principate the office is most commonly attested in military careers and can be defined overall only in general terms as a post likely to be reached at the culmination of his career by a *primipilus* of equestrian rank, a career army man who did not necessarily have much to do with construction, except in the vaguest sort of supervisory capacity.[76] But the evidence of the L. Cornelius inscription shows clearly that the post could imply direct technical responsibility for construction projects in the civil sphere as well as in the military, since it was held by Cornelius during the Tabularium building project and apparently served for him as a penultimate job title before he achieved the distinction of being labeled *architectus* for the reconstruction of the Capitoline temple.[77]

In L. Cornelius, then, we may be able to see a successful career architect rising to great prestige and renown in the era of Sulla and afterward. Given the importance of the military to both Sulla's and the younger Q. Lutatius Catulus's careers and the frequent use of the title *praefectus fabrum* among career officers in the Roman army, it is tempting to assume that Cornelius may first have distinguished himself as a military *praefectus fabrum*,[78] then continued his winning ways by serving as construction supervisor to Catulus's project to build the Tabularium while holding the same title in a civilian capacity, and that the success of his work on that project led in turn to his obtaining the title *architectus* and the overall responsiblity for reconstruction of the temple of Jupiter Optimus Maximus. While the first part of this career can only be hypothesized, the latter seems reasonably secure from the text of the inscription. Since it would appear that Cornelius was himself of good birth and estimable rank as an *ingenuus*, we can assume further that his lengthy connection to the younger Quintus Lutatius Catulus—one of the most successful patrician politicians of the first half of the first century B.C.—worked to their mutual advantage. Cornelius may be seen as the next stage in the development of the professional architect in the Roman world after Decimus Cossutius: a Roman citizen of middle rank and station who chose to be an architect because it interested him and he was good at it and rose to the top of his profession in Rome initially through ability and merit, first demonstrated perhaps in the military and subsequently through ability combined with the right connections.

Middle class Cornelii appear at various points in Roman architecture and may constitute a family firm of architects, similar to (though probably not as extensive as) that of the Cossutii. The evidence is slight, but intriguing. Two inscriptions found in Rome mention three Cornelii who were architects, or who at the very least had taken on the word *architectus* or a variant, *architectianus*, as surnames. The texts mention, specifically, a Publius Cornelius Thallus, son of Publius Cornelius Architectus, and a Publius Cornelius Architectianus, the grandson.[79] Both later Cornelii rose to important posts: Thallus is attested as *magister quinquennalis* of the professional builders' association—the *collegium fabrum tignariorum*—in Rome, while Architectianus was a member of the *ordo decurionum* perhaps at Ostia. Unfortunately, there is no further evidence beyond the inscriptions, and these do not specifically mention any commissions or achievements that would clearly label these men as practicing architects, although the use of such invented *cognomina* as Architectus and Architectianus (which seem to recall the L. Cor-

31

nelius inscription) as well as Thallus's membership in the *collegium* seem quite clear. Whether there was any family connection with L. Cornelius remains speculative but certainly accords well with the evidence of extended families involved in architecture over several generations revealed by the Cossutii and subsequently, perhaps, by the various Vitruvii.[80]

CYRUS AND OTHER ARCHITECTS MENTIONED BY CICERO

Cyrus

Other than Cornelius, we are rich in the names of architects and builders during the first century B.C., but almost solely in the private sphere with the exception of Vitruvius himself.[81] We hear of Mamurra serving as *praefectus fabrum* to Caesar in Gaul in the 50s B.C., but no specific architectural responsibilities are ever mentioned for him. By far our richest source for individuals involved in architecture and construction during this period is Cicero, whose many references to projects, mostly private, appear in his letters. But when we turn to this evidence briefly, it is important to admit immediately that for no single individual attested by Cicero can we construct a full or even a moderately complete career and that the evidence provided by Cicero for the social status and life history of any of these men is at best minimal.

The most important architect attested by Cicero is Vettius Cyrus, whose name provided the orator with the opportunity to make a poor pun on the title of Xenophon's *Cyropaedeia* when he wanted to reply to his friend Atticus's criticism of the windows in a villa owned by the orator. Cyrus's *praenomen* may well have been Vettius, but we cannot be certain. Cicero tells us quite a lot about Cyrus when he says that Atticus's criticism must also be taken as a slur on Cyrus's education as an architect; Cyrus had chosen to introduce large windows to take advantage of the view over a garden and may very well have provided Cicero with the rather elaborate optical argument that was sent on to Atticus in the letter.[82] Clearly Cyrus could defend his architectural decisions with the rational arguments of an educated man. His name certainly suggests Greek origin, and he is shown by Cicero at various points as wealthy, able to speak Greek, and free to work for whomever he chose, much in the manner of Hermodorus. Cyrus's social status is uncertain: at the very least he must have been a freedman (*libertus*), but his wealth and mobility might suggest rather a free foreigner under Roman rule who lacked citizenship (*peregrinus*).[83] We find him engaged on architectural projects for both the orator Marcus Cicero and his brother Quintus at least through 56 B.C. and possibly until the architect's death in 52 B.C.; in a letter to Marcus, Quintus seems to imply that Cyrus might not be available because he had other commissions, and so Cyrus was apparently not a slave or a bonded or indentured worker.[84]

That Cyrus was a highly successful architect is demonstrated by the story of his will.[85] It is a bizarre tale. According to Cicero, in the revised version of his speech in defense of Milo on the charge of having murdered the infamous gangster and politician P. Clodius, Clodius's supporters said that it was news of Cyrus's death that prompted Clodius to leave his estate in Alba and set out for Rome. On the way he encountered Milo with an armed band. Clodius's own retinue got into a pitched battle with Milo's, and in the scuffle Clodius was struck down. But although he knew Cyrus was dying when he set out from Rome for Aricia on business of at best minor importance, Clodius had set out anyway, so why would he then chuck the business at Aricia and return to Rome immediately on hearing the already anticipated news of Cyrus's decease? Cicero goes on to point out that he himself had been with Cyrus at the same time as Clodius, that they had both witnessed Cyrus's will, and that the two of them were named his heirs. Cicero further asserts that this odd will—which named two determined enemies as the architect's heirs—had been made openly and without coercion by Cyrus. Cicero's point as far as his defense of Milo was concerned was to cast doubt on the reason for which Clodius left Alba at the fateful hour when Milo was on the road. But the implication of the tale for the career of Cyrus is more interesting for us. It can reasonably be assumed, from Cicero's remark, that Cyrus had undertaken important architectural commissions for P. Clodius as well as for the Ciceros. We know that Clodius was infamous for the extravagance of his own home, which the elder Pliny compared to the insanity of kings. It is not unreasonable to assume that Cyrus

33

may have been the architect, or one of the architects, in charge of the creation of this grandiose home, for which Clodius had paid (again according to Pliny) the unbelievable sum of 148,000,000 sesterces.[86]

Chrysippus

Cyrus had in his establishment at least one freedman who followed him into the profession of architecture, Vettius Chrysippus. Cicero mentions him in 53 B.C., when Chrysippus brought a letter to the orator from Trebatius, who was in Gaul with Caesar,[87] and he seems to have been rather more fully under Cicero's control than Cyrus had been. We do hear of him as an independent functionary "on loan" to Cicero's favorite correspondent, Atticus, in the spring of 45 B.C., when he analyzed the condition of Atticus's gardens as well as offering suggestions for alterations that might solve some problems in one of Cicero's many house properties.[88] The passage shows that Chrysippus could be expected to plan gardens, design construction projects, and estimate their costs; furthermore Cicero is quite open about the fact that his knowledge of the situation is not firsthand but comes largely from Vettius Chrysippus, from whom the construction proposals must, then, have originated. This indicates a high level of trust placed in the architect by his patron.

Chrysippus may well have continued some sort of association with Caesar, too, during the 40s B.C. and could have been commissioned by the dictator to design some of his planned public works in Rome, although this is entirely hypothetical.[89] The next year, in April 44, Cicero somewhat peremptorily recalled Chrysippus from Athens to oversee the rebuilding of two tenements Cicero owned that were on the verge of collapse.[90] Although Chrysippus had been a *libertus* at least since 53–52 B.C.—the period when Cicero specifically refers to him as "freedman of the architect Cyrus"[91]—Cicero seems to have been able to expect instant obedience to his wishes and whims from the builder, even to requiring him to abandon other projects to engage in what must have been fairly routine rebuilding work on the orator's behalf. Although Chrysippus seems to have fulfilled all the functions of an architect just as his master Cyrus had before him, he is never referred to by Cicero as *architec-*

tus. Whether or not this has any significance is doubtful; certainly Chrysippus functioned in all the various capacities expected of the architect engaged in a private practice and accepting commissions from patrons. Perhaps he was simply willing to protect his profitable connection with Cicero and his circle by a certain amount of abject grovelling or perhaps he was honestly grateful to Cicero for having essentially permitted him to fill Cyrus's place upon the latter's death.

Corumbus, Rufio, Numisius, Cluatius, and Diphilus

In a number of Cicero's letters it is clear that aristocrats regularly and reciprocally shared the skills of architects of servile or freedman status. The orator himself borrowed Corumbus, whom he says had the reputation of being a fine architect, from L. Cornelius Balbus, although whether Corumbus was slave or freedman is not indicated.[92] Clearly Corumbus, whether slave or free, had done sufficient architectural work to have gained a good reputation among the aristocrats. The letter also makes fairly clear that a major duty awaiting Corumbus on his arrival was the supervision of Cicero's (hungry!) construction workers (*structores*) who were already in place. This short passage provides fascinating insights on the methods of private architecture among the rich and powerful in Rome in the middle of the first century B.C., as well as emphasizing the relatively privileged treatment accorded to reputable architects whatever their actual social position in the Roman world might be. A similar situation, though in reverse, is recounted when Cicero has to forego the services of a builder named Rufio when Rufio is transferred back to a project sponsored by his patron, Trebatius.[93] Cicero says: "your Rufio is missed as much as if he were one of us. But I do not blame you for transferring him to your own building project." The status of Rufio seems to be ambiguous just like the status of Vettius Chrysippus and of Corumbus. Other builders mentioned in the letters include Numisius, who had devised a house plan for Quintus Cicero; Cluatius, who was commissioned to design a shrine after the death of Cicero's daughter, Tullia, and whose plans were so much admired by Cicero that the orator asked to engage him to supervise the actual building site as well; Diphilus, whose dilatoriness Cicero criticized when he inspected a project the architect was undertaking for Quintus and which had to be turned over to Caesius, who may also have been an architect or a building contractor who stepped in to help.[94] The *vilicus* of Quintus Cicero's estate at Laterium, Nicephorus, is also credited with building skills and even accepted a contract for such work with Quintus, but whether he would have been classified as an architect or not is impossible to say.[95]

The last architect of the first century B.C., for whom Cicero's letters constitute our only source, is something of a conundrum. Writing to Atticus in 45 B.C., Cicero speaks of a nameless architect whom Julius Caesar was planning to put in charge—presumably as architect—of his ambitious building program in the city of Rome, although the man had only lived in Rome for two years. Since this important figure is not named by Cicero, we are left with little further information; no such architect is mentioned in our other sources for Caesar's building program.[96] It has been suggested that this person was Vettius Chrysippus, who had been in Gaul with Trebatius and thus in contact with Caesar and who may have continued as both architect and go-between for Caesar and Cicero, but it is equally possible that this unnamed architect was not a professional builder at all, but a friend or acquaintance of Caesar's whom the dictator could trust to carry out his wishes; Cicero's information is too ambiguous to permit further extrapolation.

These skilled men were highly valued not only by Cicero but by their patrons and were permitted to accept work on a variety of commissions, but whether because they were slaves or because they were essentially clients bound to a particular master when he called for them, they apparently had little choice in where or for whom they worked, but went to jobs outside their own master's possessions essentially on temporary loan which could be instantly revoked. It is most likely this class of architects and building supervisors whom Cicero had in mind when he made his remark that while architecture was an honest profession, it was nevertheless one suitable for the lower classes.[97]

Of those architects mentioned by Cicero, Cyrus appears to be the exception. He seems to have functioned on an altogether higher and more independent plane, but even he tended to work regularly for the same wealthy patrons. This pattern of sticking fairly regularly to a particular patron who likes and appreciates the architect's work is a consistent feature in the careers of ancient architects, including, so far as our evidence goes, Cossutius and Cornelius, although prestigious men such as Hermodorus and Cyrus could accept a variety of commissions.

In contrast to the likes of Cossutius, Mucius, and Cornelius, the majority of the builders mentioned in Cicero, like the majority mentioned in inscriptions of all periods of the Roman world, were foreigners, freedmen, or slaves.[98] Their social status seems to have been quite variable, and many appear to have been upwardly mobile within the constraints of the Roman social caste system (e.g., Cyrus, Chrysippus). They appear to have occupied a somewhat ambiguous social position. That is hardly surprising in the case of foreigners such as Hermodorus or Cyrus, since Greeks, though much praised and valued for their skills and expertise, were always regarded with suspicion. But something of the same ambiguity seems to surround thoroughly Roman architects; even Cossutius was regarded as praiseworthy though somewhat "Greekified" for working under the aegis of Antiochus IV Epiphanes.

Free architects seem to have had a certain amount of mobility and choice in accepting commissions during the Republic, but that should not be overestimated. Many seem to have been tied quite closely to the fortunes and careers of a single patron, whether their own social status was that of *ingenuus* or *libertus* or *servus*; we have no indication whether this was by choice or due to custom or necessity. A foreigner who was an architect, however successful, wealthy, and highly sought after, remained suspect as a foreigner; a Roman who was an architect—unless he was a patrician amateur never disgraced by a professional label—remained suspect because he was practicing a profession more properly left to foreigners or to slaves or to freedmen attached to patrician households.[99]

In any case, credit for buildings was regularly given first to the official who had paid for it or, less often, to the *redemptor* who contracted for it or the *officinator* who supervised the construction.

The *architectus,* in surviving dedicatory inscriptions, is often relegated to fourth place or even lower, if he is mentioned at all. Exactly the same phenomenon is apparent on the gravestones and funerary reliefs of builders. The ambiguity in our sources, then, probably reflects a real ambiguity in Romans' own perceptions of the *architectus:* architects themselves were either too far down the ladder of distinction to gain much notice or mention, or—as foreigners or Romans behaving like foreigners—could not and should not really expect much more recognition.[100] Both Cicero and Vitruvius seem well aware of this discrepancy in perception of social status, which architects seem to have shared with other skilled professions such as teaching. Such was the fate, but such also the opportunities, open to the *architectus* in the Roman Republic.

One reason for this ambiguity in the social status of *architecti* was probably directly due to the aristocratic enjoyment of practicing architecture that is evidenced again and again in our sources. If the identification is correct that the Mucius who designed Marius's temple of Honos et Virtus was the consular Q. Mucius Scaevola, then we can certainly see in this man's indulgence in architecture, as we see in the evidence surrounding Quintus Cicero and L. Aemilius Paullus, the place that aristocratic amateurs made for themselves, whereby they to some degree established architecture as a uniquely suitable area for a nobleman to indulge in as an avocation. Roman aristocrats ever since King Tarquinius Superbus seem to have taken quite an active role in their own building projects. With the arrival of Hellenistic styles of architectural planning and the valuable and beautiful building materials characteristic of such construction in Rome during the second century B.C., the desire to impress the populace could be combined with that aristocratic avocation. On into the first century B.C. a strong tendency for nobles to be active in architecture continues. To a great degree, from the second century B.C. onward, building design seems to have mandated enlisting the services of a trained professional architect, except perhaps in rare cases, but wealthy amateurs turn up in a variety of architect's roles, such as selecting sites and inspecting projects.[101]

A professional builder, whether architect or contractor, seems often to have been kept available and called in when deemed necessary by the noble amateur or when there were obvious problems. Cicero did precisely this when, after inspecting a new villa being built for his brother Quintus (apparently to plans in which Quintus had a hand), he sharply criticized much of what had been done by the builder in charge and engaged a different builder to repair the damage.[102] To the patrician nobleman, then, an *architectus* may have been a necessary service person, though one who often was not of servile or freed status and so had to be acquired through long-time family loyalties or through friends and personal connections. The nobleman might enjoy the idea and the periodic practice of architecture, but professional assistance of the very highest skill had to be available from the beginning when the project designs were drawn up, which must often have mandated a professional's training, through the contracting and organization of the project, and indeed throughout in case of problem or crisis. Hence while primarily the designer of the project, the *architectus* could be and was expected to supervise the work of other specialists concerned (*redemptores, fabri,* etc.) and sometimes to fulfill their roles himself. This aristocratic fascination with and participation in architecture could have greatly increased the demand for trained professional architects in the Roman world, but at the same time abetted the ambiguous, though respectable and admired, social status to which architects appear to have been relegated. In turn, the association of architects with the pet projects of distinguished patricians may well have contributed to their own proud perception of their standing and acquired them a reputation for snobbery.[103]

Vitruvius and the Architects of the Age of Augustus

As in so many other areas of Roman history, we are particularly rich in sources of evidence for the profession of architect during the principate of Augustus. While the best-documented career in the period is that of Vitruvius himself—since the author tells us a good deal about his own life in his book—we have the names and in some cases the projects undertaken by a variety of other architects as well and can determine a good deal about their careers and social status. We should begin with Vitruvius himself.

VITRUVIUS

There has been a good deal of controversy over the date and career of Vitruvius and even over his identity. The last question arises because the surviving manuscripts of *De Architectura* provide neither a certain *praenomen* nor *cognomen* for him, and he is seldom mentioned by other ancient writers. The name "Vitruvius" does occur in a variety of inscriptions, notably examples from Verona in Italy and from Thilbilis in North Africa;[104] Thielscher has suggested that the Vitruvius named on the Thilbilis inscription—Marcus Vitruvius Mamurra—was in fact the author and architect and should be identified with the notorious Mamurra pilloried by the poet Catullus in poems 29, 41, and 57. Mamurra may have served as Caesar's *praefectus fabrum* in Gaul after 58 B.C. and in Britain in 55 and 54 (although this is not specifically attested but must be inferred from the text of Catullus 29). He became a metaphor, courtesy of the poet, for financial and sexual debauchery, and his immense wealth a subject of popular legend. Mamurra is last attested in a datable context in the year 45 B.C., but his reputation for profligacy lived after him at least to the end of the first century A.D.[105]

Thielscher's equation of Mamurra with Vitruvius is attractive primarily because of the chronological coherence of the two men, and the well-attested connection of both to Julius Caesar; it appears even more attractive when the evidence of the L. Cornelius inscription is recalled, since that attests clearly to the architectural experience and skill of someone who had held the post of *praefectus fabrum,* and thus might suggest how Mamurra the *praefectus* became in later life Vitruvius the *architectus.*[106]

The equation has, nonetheless, won few adherents and can be criticized on a number of important points. First, Cicero seems to imply that Mamurra was dead by December 45 B.C., well before Vitruvius wrote;[107] second, there is no absolute or even probable reason to connect the Thilbilis inscription with either the author Vitruvius or the profligate Mamurra since the inscription lacks any internal or external dating evidence;[108] third, any of the other inscriptions that mention the name "Vitruvius" and cannot be dated might just as easily be connected with the author, since his *praenò-*

men and *cognomen* are not certainly attested in manuscripts or other ancient sources;[109] and fourth, while the most important point about Mamurra in our ancient sources was his extraordinary wealth, Vitruvius tells us quite specifically that he himself was not well off and that but for a stipend provided him by Augustus he would have ended his life a pauper.[110] The last objection should, in and of itself, militate strongly against identifying the struggling architect Vitruvius with the spendthrift parvenu Mamurra. For all these reasons, it seems best to dispense with the Mamurra-Vitruvius equation altogether, although it remains a perversely intriguing suggestion.[111]

The ancient evidence for Vitruvius outside his own text offers a little help. The elder Pliny mentions his name three times as a source of information on trees and timber, painting and color, and building stone, while Frontinus mentions him twice in connection with the water system of Rome.[112] Sometime around the beginning of the third century A.D., Cetius Faventinus adapted and abridged Vitruvius's manual and published it as his *De Diversis Fabricis Architectonicae;*[113] Servius mentions a "Vitruvius"—possibly not our author, since the passage quoted there does not appear in *De Architectura*—in his commentary on Vergil's *Aeneid*; and at the end of the fifth century A.D. Sidonius Apollinaris praises him in two separate epistles.[114] All these authors refer to him by *nomen* only except Faventinus (1.1), who seems to supply the *cognomen* Pollio (actually Polio in the manuscripts) but whose text can just as well be read to mention two different architectural writers, Vitruvius and Pol(l)io. Some manuscripts from the fifteenth century include the *cognomen* Cerdo, adopted from the inscription at Verona. The manuscripts of Vitruvius supply a bewildering variety of *nomina:* M(arcus), L(ucius), C(aius), and A(ulus) are all to be found here or there; no one can be better justified than the others.[115] Of the numerous inscriptions from around the Roman world on which the name "Vitruvius" appears, none can be securely associated with the author.[116] Nothing more can be ascertained about his name.

Vitruvius does tell us a good deal about his own career as an architect, and that information is supplemented by Frontinus and by scholarly conjecture. What Vitruvius tells us is straightforward and makes good sense. His parents were able to provide him with a gentleman's education of which, like the poet Horace, he took full advantage (6. Pref. 4). Nonetheless, his architectural career was a minor and obscure one (6. Pref. 5). He began that career in the military, attached to Julius Caesar's army, perhaps as early as the unsuccessful siege of Massilia (Marseilles) in 49 B.C., which he describes in a manner that some assert implies he was an eye-witness (10.16.11–12).[117] He is the only ancient source for an-other battle of Caesar's—the siege of Larignum in the Alps (2.9.15–16), which he describes so vividly that most commenta-tors assume he was present—but the date of the battle can be put either at the beginning of the Gallic campaigns or later, at the beginning of the Civil Wars and so offers no chronological help in understanding his career.[118] He was certainly with Caesar during the campaigns in Numidia in 46 B.C. (8.3.24–25), though in what capacity he does not state specifically; he seems to have spent most of his career in the direct employ of Caesar and his heir, Octavian (1. Pref. 2).[119]

At some date after Caesar's assassination in 44 B.C. Vitruvius, who had quickly allied himself with Octavian, was granted an army surveyorship over the construction and repair of military engines of war (1. Pref. 2)—together with three other men, M. Aurelius, P. Munidius, and Cn. Cornelius—and subsequently he was contin-ued in this post upon the recommendation of Octavian's sister, Octavia, who may have been Vitruvius's direct patron. This sur-veyorship has often been assumed to be a *praefectura fabrum*[120] although it would be extremely unusual to have four *praefecti* serv-ing together with responsibility for the same thing. If this post was not *praefectus fabrum,* it could have been something like a *decurialis scriba armamentarius,* a scribe responsible for keeping track of weapons—the sort of post that seems often to have been offered to educated Italians deemed worthy of patronage. If Vitruvius did hold such a scribal position, it would further indicate that he was regarded by Octavian and his sister as an *apparitor.*[121] Whatever the exact designation of the surveyorship, the nature of the position helps clarify Vitruvius's social status: he was most likely a freeborn and educated Italian, as he himself implies (6. Pref. 4), of sufficient culture and standing to enter the growing ranks of Italians who received patronage from the *princeps*.

Vitruvius seems to have left the army, possibly as a veteran after twenty years' service, and entered the civilian side of his profession. He continued essentially dependent upon Imperial favor, however, and was employed, directly or indirectly, through the influence of Augustus and his family. Vitruvius writes from direct experience about aqueducts and the water system (8.6.2), for Frontinus confirms that Vitruvius had worked on the water system during the aedileship of M. Agrippa (33 B.C.) and had even invented a new measurement for lead piping.[122]

At some point he accepted a commission and served as *architectus* of a public basilica for the Caesarian or Augustan colony town of Fanum Fortunae (5.1.6–10), but at what precise date we do not know.[123] The commission for the basilica also seems to have come to him through direct connections to the house of Augustus, as did the grant that supported him in his last years. By the time of writing the preface to Book I of his manual, Vitruvius tells us he was a stipendiary of Octavian (1. Pref. 2–3) and, apparently, no longer actively involved in architecture.

Thus Vitruvius would seem to provide a clear example of the sort of career path that is implied for other Roman architects (e.g., L. Cornelius). The requirements would appear to have been the social status of an *ingenuus* or (preferably) higher, an education of some quality, and military experience that provided practical training. The fact that Vitruvius was never much of a success in his chosen profession was in no way the fault of his apparent qualifications for it.

Finally, we can look for clues to Vitruvius's life and career in considering the date of composition and publication of his book. There has been some debate—not especially productive—over this, but the general conclusion still seems the correct one, that is, that the first book, and probably the first four books at least, were composed before 27 B.C. and presented to Octavian (i.e., published) in that year, since the *princeps* is referred to as Octavian in the dedication rather than Augustus, a title granted him in 27. There is one use, and only one, of the title *Augustus* in the entire work, when Vitruvius mentions a temple of Augustus at Fanum Fortunae (5.1.6), but this does suggest at least that Book 5 was emended—and possibly published—after 27.

Vitruvius also uses vocabulary (8.3.24) that seems to derive from Horace (*Odes* 1.22.15–16) to describe buildings constructed by King Juba at Zama, which would imply that Vitruvius had read the Horatian poem (published in 23 B.C.) and so was at work on the eighth book after publication of the ode. It would seem certain that the last books were published later than the first: in addition to the evidence above, it should be noted that Vitruvius's prediction of immortality for the writings of Lucretius, Cicero, and Varro (9. Pref. 17) implies fairly clearly that all three were dead when the passage was written, and we know that the last of them to survive, Varro, died in 27 B.C.

The latest more-or-less secure datable reference within Vitruvius's text appears to be his statement that praetors, as well as aediles, were the Roman officials in charge of games and spectacles (10. Pref. 4), a responsibility that Cassius Dio (54.2.4) tells us was first extended to the praetors by Augustus for games held in 22 B.C. Thus the most likely chronology that can be assigned to *De Architectura* is that it was written over a period of a decade more or less, that the first books appeared in or just prior to 27 B.C., and that the rest became available presumably by the end of that decade.[124] After its publication there is no further evidence of its author, no indication of the date of his death.

L. COCCEIUS AUCTUS AND C. POSTUMIUS POLLIO

It is one of the anomalies of the random preservation of information from antiquity that while we know a tremendous amount, courtesy of Vitruvius, about the practice of architecture and the profession of architect in general from the age of Augustus, we do not know the name of a single architect who participated in the design or construction of the great monuments of the time: Augustus's Forum and temple to Mars Ultor, his Mausoleum, the Ara Pacis, or any other surviving Augustan monument. Perhaps this reflects a certain level of envy or resentment for his own lack of success in the profession on Vitruvius's part. Indeed beyond Vitruvius himself—

whose posterity is due to his writing, not his building—we have nothing more than names, relatively randomly attested and difficult to connect to any specific architectural projects, from all over the Roman world during Augustus's reign. Only one other figure emerges with anything like clarity or precision: Lucius Cocceius Auctus, whose sphere of activity, insofar as we know it, seems to have been exclusively in Campania.

Cocceius is known to us from two inscriptions: a signature scratched on a wall of the temple of Augustus at Puteoli and an otherwise unlocalized architrave fragment from ancient Cumae.[125] Each inscription provides a piece of interesting information. The signature from Puteoli gives us Cocceius's social standing—he is called *C. Postumi libertus,* a freedman of Gaius Postumius—while the Cumaean inscription lists Cocceius as a *redemptor,* a contractor in his own right. We know who Cocceius's former owner was: C. Postumius Pollio dedicated the temple of Augustus at Terracina, and his name also occurs on the lintel of an unidentified public building at Formiae.[126]

This testimony is puzzling in light of the *nomen* the architect assumed: "Cocceius" as adopted *nomen* would normally imply that he had been owned, and presumably manumitted, by a member of the *gens Cocceia;* his adoption of the *praenomen* Lucius has led most scholars to conclude that his manumittor was probably L. Cocceius Nerva, one of the more important figures who attempted to intercede between Octavian and Antony during the early years of the second triumvirate (notably as suffect consul in 39 B.C.) and finally allied himself with Octavian, and that C. Postumius (with whom he appears later to have joined in an architectural concern in Campania) had been a previous owner, mistakenly identified as Cocceius's manumittor in the inscription. L. Cocceius Nerva had property and important attachments in Campania to the extent that Gros would suggest that it was he who started L. Cocceius Auctus on the road to his successful career in Campania.[127] The *cognomen* Auctus suggests that the architect was of Greek origin, but clearly he arrived in Italy as slave rather than distinguished free architect in the tradition of Hermodorus.

None of this would be particularly remarkable, however, were it not for the fact that Strabo attributes the massive tunnel cut between the Mediterranean coast at Cumae and Lake Avernus and an even more impressive tunnel that connected Puteoli to Neapolis, to an architect called Cocceius.[128] Although Strabo does not specifically say so, it seems extremely likely that this Cocceius is L. Cocceius Auctus, and that the tunnels formed part of the immense project of military architecture undertaken on the Cumaean Peninsula, at Lakes Avernus and Lucrinus, at Misenum, and around the Bay of Puteoli between 38 and 36 B.C.[129]

If this identification, now generally accepted, of the L. Cocceius Auctus of the Campanian inscriptions with the Cocceius mentioned by Strabo, is correct, then it is clear that the freedman architect and engineer achieved a career of remarkable importance during the reign of Augustus, while working (apparently exclusively) in Campania. It would seem a tribute to his skills that, despite coming from a social status not generally productive of men who rose to the level of designing and supervising *architecti,* Cocceius Auctus was engaged in the design and construction of a major dynastic sanctuary for Augustus at the most important seaport in Italy of the time and in the largest single piece of military engineering undertaken during that reign. His connections to the distinguished L. Cocceius Nerva would have been instrumental in his success, of course; nonetheless it is a surprise to find a freedman architect so successful at that time in Italy. His Greek derivation was, presumably, not quite such an impediment in Campania as it would have been in Rome or Latium, and his skill (if the remains of the project at Cumae and Lake Avernus are any indication) must have been extraordinary.

Nonetheless, presumably upon the death of L. Cocceius Nerva, Auctus had to attach himself to another patron of free birth, and in this case joined another architect, C. Postumius Pollio, who as a freeborn Roman citizen could serve in that capacity for him (and may have been his former owner). Gros would go so far as to propose, logically enough, that Auctus and Pollio must have formed a sort of architectural firm that offered freedom of choice to Auctus, who now functioned in the official role of *redemptor* (contractor) under the legal and technical aegis of Pollio. Certainly

Auctus would appear to have had financial and technical control of various projects, far beyond that normally apportioned to a contractor. He was in fact functioning as a true *architectus/redemptor.*[130]

Although it is not an issue specifically connected to architects of the age of Augustus, the *libertus* status of L. Cocceius Auctus allows the introduction of the next important element that must be considered in relation to the social status of architects in the Roman world. As we have seen above, those Roman architects whose names come down to us from Vitruvius and from other textual sources tend to be of relatively high social status, mostly freeborn *ingenui* if not more. Since it is for these men that we have fairly secure dates and careers, on the whole, it is inevitable that they should receive a preponderance of the consideration given by most historians of architecture. But our other great source of attestations for Roman architects— inscriptions—offers a very different picture. However, the overwhelming majority of inscriptions that mention architects cannot be dated with any kind of precision if at all. Hence while they can provide a general picture of another segment, as it were, of the Roman building profession, they do not provide any specific evidence for the situation of architects and their profession as it developed through the centuries. Nonetheless, it is worth considering their information briefly because they are in many instances the sole evidence we have that a large number of men who were sufficiently skilled to be honored by the title *architectus* in their epitaphs were of servile origin, either slaves or freedmen. Taking the most comprehensive list of *architectus* inscriptions that has so far been drawn up, that of Pearse,[131] we find that of a total of 15 persons specifically labeled *architectus* on funerary inscriptions from the city of Rome, five are definitely listed as freedmen (*liberti*), one is a slave (*servus*), and the other nine appear to be freemen, mainly of *ingenuus* status. If we look at Pearse's list for the rest of ancient Italy, we find a total of seventeen attested *architecti;* five are definitely freedmen, one is certainly labeled a slave, the social status of four more is missing from the surviving texts of the inscriptions, and the remaining seven are *ingenui* or higher in social status. A few of these inscriptions can be dated and provide us with further names of practicing *architecti* in the Roman world. Amianthus Nicanorianus was a slave architect during the reign of Augustus, and Tychichus Crispinillianus was a *servus* architect of Domitian.[132] Four more are Imperial freedmen who can be assigned likely dates.[133]

This epigraphical evidence is indicative of the overall situation in the Roman world: architects tended to be, if freeborn, either foreigners, probably classified as *peregrini*, or native Italian *ingenui* (and occasionally of higher status) or, if of servile origin, those graced with the name *architectus* were generally skilled *liberti* very often still closely attached to the individual who had freed them or to his family, or sometimes remained *servi*. The evidence, then, is generally consistent with the picture we might draw from the evidence provided by Cicero's letters and other first century B.C. sources, but it reveals a wider stratum of freedmen and slaves who were practicing architects than the somewhat wishful evidence drawn from Vitruvius alone might lead us to suppose.[134] Freedmen architects rose to wealth and important success in the Roman world, as is witnessed by L. Cocceius Auctus, and architecture may well have been a promising path to freedom for talented slaves. Without more specifically datable evidence, however, there is not a great deal more that the epigraphical record can provide us except general corroboration of, and specific correction to, the textual evidence.

OTHER NAMED ARCHITECTS OF THE AGE OF AUGUSTUS

The names of four other architects of the age of Augustus or thereabout are preserved to us, three in inscriptions and one by the elder Pliny; Pliny also provides us with two dubious names of contemporary architects. The most securely dated of these figures is Titus Vettius, son of Quintus, who is called *architectus* in charge of building porticoes that were to be paid for by public funds in an inscription from Grumentum that gives the names of the consuls Aulus Hirtius and Gaius Vibius of the year in which it was inscribed, 43 B.C.[135] The inscription is also interesting for the language employed, which in turn parallels almost exactly the wording used by Vitruvius (5.1.6) when he describes his own functions as architect of the public basilica at Fanum Fortunae, and this would certainly seem to indicate that Titus Vettius was expected to function not only as designer and planner of the building but also had to assume certain contracting responsibilities for the construction project, just as Vitruvius indicates was his situation at Fanum.[136]

The three Augustan architects attested by the elder Pliny are a very mixed bag indeed. Valerius of Ostia was praised in these words: "[Should I not mention] the roof of the ballot office made by Agrippa? Although before that Valerius of Ostia, the architect, roofed a theater at Rome for the games of Libo."[137] He seems on the whole a perfectly likely figure. While the passage reveals little enough, it does assume that Valerius was a contemporary of M. Agrippa and hence provides a fairly convincing dating for his project in the latter part of the first century B.C. However, he is nowhere mentioned again. Pliny is also the source for a pair of Augustan architects who seem likely to be apocryphal: the Lacedaemonian(!) architects associated with Octavia's reconstruction of the Porticus Metelli and the two temples it surrounded, dedicated to Jupiter Stator and Juno Regina. Pliny's story is almost ludicrous:[138]

> Nor should we forget Saura and Batrachus, who built the temples that are enclosed by the Porticus of Octavia. They were natives of Sparta. And yet, some people actually suppose that they were very rich and erected the temples at their own expense because they hoped to be honoured by an inscription; and the story is that, although this was refused, they attained their object in another way. At any rate, on the moulded bases of the columns there are still in existence carvings of a lizard [*saura*] and a frog [*batrachus*] in token of their names.

It seems best to assume that Saura and Batrachus are imaginary figures from a traditional pun, although we are otherwise well informed about the Porticus Octaviae; they are never mentioned elsewhere.[139]

Also Augustan are two architects from the cities subsequently destroyed by Vesuvius. Marcus Artorius Primus, freedman of Marcus, is called *architectus* in an inscription, probably Augustan, from the Large Theater, at Pompeii, which was constructed in 28 B.C. by the aediles Rufus and Celer;[140] Publius Numisius, son of Publius and also called *architectus,* is named as the architect of the theater at

Herculaneum during the same period.[141] Beyond these names and attestations of known projects, we have very little in the way of further information about the architects of the time of Augustus. A late writer, Macrobius, tells us that Augustus used to joke about how the procrastination of the *architectus* in charge of building the Augustan Forum had slowed down completion of the whole project but, to our frustration, Macrobius does not give this architect's name.[142]

As we turn to the architects of the Imperial period it will be clear that the first century B.C. had established the role of the architect and his profession in a very real way, and the text of Vitruvius— despite its sometimes wishful nature—is on the whole a valid reflection not only of the thinking of educated architects of the time but also of the entire profession of architecture as the Republic passed into the Empire and of the nature of those who practiced it.

Architecti *during the Empire*

In the first and second centuries A.D. our evidence for *architecti* comes more and more to center upon the massive building projects and programs undertaken periodically in and near the city of Rome by various emperors, generally following the example set by Augustus. Any list of the "great builders" of Imperial Rome usually includes the emperors Nero (reigned A.D. 54–68), Domitian (A.D. 81–96), Trajan (A.D. 98–117), and Hadrian (A.D. 117–138), and it is no surprise that for the reigns of these four figures we have attested the names of, and some projects attributable to, specific architects. Beyond these extremely important figures, however, our information tends to be random and obscure. There were individual building projects in Rome and in various parts of Roman Italy of tremendous scope during the reigns of Tiberius (A.D. 14–37), Claudius (A.D. 41–54), Vespasian (A.D. 70–79), Marcus Aurelius (A.D. 161–180), Septimius Severus (A.D. 193–211), Caracalla (A.D. 211–217), Aurelian (A.D. 270–275), Diocletian (A.D. 285–305), Maxentius (A.D. 305–312), and Constantine (A.D. 312–337) as well, but we do not have the names of any architects clearly involved in them, and very few names of architects at all from these centuries.

Part of the explanation for this must lie in the centralization of responsibility (and of credit) for major public buildings in the hands of the Imperial administration, which paid for them, taking over that responsibility from wealthy private aristocrats who had traditionally undertaken public construction in the cities of the Roman world, and especially in Rome herself, as a type of familial obligation and glory. Since the name of the person paying for and dedicating a building seems always to have been thought more important than the name of its architect, once public building becomes effectively a monopoly of the emperor, the names of associated people like the architect are preserved less and less often.

Certain facts are clear about the position of architects under the Empire. Frontinus tells us, on the one hand, that *architecti* held permanent official positions in the administration of the water board of the city,[143] and it is quite possible, though nowhere specifically confirmed in our sources, that there were other such permanent posts for specialized *architecti* within the Imperial bureaucracy, for instance, attached to such offices as the *curator viarum* in charge of roads and the other maintenance boards. On the other hand, there does not appear to have been any kind of permanent or quasi-permanent official in charge of new Imperial works at Rome at any time during the Empire. Architects, at the highest level at least, were presumably engaged ad hoc for specific projects,[144] although there were almost certainly various architects and other building specialists attached to the office of the *opera Caesaris*, once it was established, which was not before Domitian's principate. Such top-level appointments as those of Severus and Celer by Nero, Rabirius by Domitian, and Apollodorus by Trajan seem to have been examples of personal preferment by the emperor, not appointment to any kind of long-standing official post. The epigraphical record attests that emperors did maintain *architecti*, often slaves or freedmen, within their own personal staff (*familia*) and could send these architects to building projects outside Rome at need,[145] but the same source records the names of architects brought into Rome from elsewhere by the Imperial bureaucracy.[146] Presumably these outsiders reflect Imperial appointment through recommendation or on the basis of personal knowledge in the manner approved by Vitruvius (3. Pref. 2); there is no direct evidence that there was any kind of system of competition for appointment to and service on Imperial projects.[147] With this general background on the nature of our evidence in place, we can turn to the attested *architecti* who served the emperors of the first and second centuries A.D., then to the evidence for the later centuries of the Roman Empire.

SEVERUS AND CELER, *ARCHITECTUS ET MACHINATOR NERONIS*

Tacitus provides us with the names of the two men who were responsible for the design and execution of Nero's second, and most incredible, royal palace in Rome, the so-called Domus Aurea ("Golden House"): Severus and Celer. This immense example of bringing the countryside into the city (*rus in urbe*)—literally—was made possible by the extensive damage done to the city center, especially to the Palatine Hill and the slopes of the Esquiline and Caelian, by the great fire of A.D. 64:[148]

> Nero turned to account the ruins of his fatherland by building a palace, the marvels of which were to consist not so much in gems and gold, materials long familiar and vulgarized by luxury, as in fields and lakes and the air of solitude given by wooded ground alternating with clear tracts and open landscapes. The architect and engineer were Severus and Celer, who had the ingenuity and courage to try the force of art even against the veto of nature and to fritter away the resources of a Caesar. They had undertaken to sink a navigable canal running from Lake Avernus to the mouths of the Tiber along a desolate shore or through intervening hills; for the one district along the route moist enough to yield a supply of water is the Pomptine Marsh; the rest being cliff and sand, which could be cut through, if at all, only by intolerable exertions for which no sufficient motive existed. Nonetheless Nero, with his passion for the incredible, made an effort to tunnel the heights nearest Avernus, and some evidences of that futile ambition survive.

There is a good deal of useful information and implication here. First of all, it is notable that Tacitus refers to Severus and Celer, respectively, as master (*magister*) and engineer (*machinator*), implying that Severus was the master architect who designed their projects and Celer the engineer who carried them out, when possible.

Nothing much need be made of the omission of the word *architectus* in the passage; Tacitus probably felt no need to use the obvious label for either man, since they would have been quite well-known anyway, and it seems safe to accept that Severus was regarded by Tacitus and probably by most other educated Romans as the leading architect of his time.[149] The syntax of the Latin indicates clearly that Severus is to be regarded as the master architect and Celer as engineer, not both men as serving both functions. As MacDonald has pointed out, too, Severus must have been not only an architect in modern terms but a landscape architect as well to have designed the elaborate gardens attested for the Domus Aurea, and Celer must have been a master of hydraulic as well as mechanical engineering. Both men must have had substantial administrative responsibilities not only in the almost inconceivably complicated Domus Aurea project but in the abortive attempt at an Avernus-Tiber canal as well. They may well have worked on a number of elaborate projects for Nero prior to the Domus Aurea, but Tacitus chooses only the most infamous; and the typically Tacitean barbs about wastefulness and unbearable labor should be regarded as aimed at Nero, not at Severus and Celer.[150] The renown of the Domus Aurea for its size, gardens, remarkable mechanical inventions, and hydraulics is attested elsewhere in Latin literature, but the names of architect and engineer are, surprisingly, not mentioned in any of those passages.[151]

For our purposes, perhaps the most important suggestion we might draw from Tacitus comes from the position and subject matter of the passage that follows immediately upon the one describing the Domus Aurea and the Avernus canal.[152] In that passage, immediately after detailing the accomplishments of Severus and Celer, Tacitus proceeds to describe—and even to give praise, albeit with notably modified enthusiasm, to—Nero's and his administration's efforts to rebuild the city after the fire and introduce building codes and reforms long overdue.

> In the capital, however, the districts spared by the palace (i.e., Domus Aurea) were rebuilt not, as after the Gallic fire, indiscriminately and piecemeal, but in measured lines of streets, with broad thoroughfares,

buildings of restricted height, and open spaces, while porticoes were added as a protection to the front of the insulae. These porticoes Nero offered to erect at his own expense, and also to hand over the building sites, clear of rubbish, to the owners. . . . The buildings themselves, to an extent unspecified, were to be solid, untimbered structures of Gabine or Alban stone, that particular stone being proof against fire. Again, there was to be a guard to insure that the water supply . . . should be available for public purposes in greater quantities and at more points; appliances for checking fire were to be kept by everyone in the open; there were to be no joint partitions between buildings, but each was to be independent, with its own walls. These reforms, welcomed for their utility, were also beneficial to the appearance of the new capital.

Tacitus's placement of this elaborate description of Nero's attempt to impose a building code upon the city of Rome can be read to imply that Severus, *magister* of the Domus Aurea and Avernus-Ostia canal projects, also served as director of this entire rebuilding project and hence was a sort of supervising or directing architect charged with the entire project of creating the *urbs nova* that seems to have been Nero's intent. While this grandiose assignment of such responsibility to Severus goes well beyond the actual evidence, the implications of Tacitus's and, to a lesser extent, Suetonius's passages are important. Severus would appear to represent the sort of architect described by Vitruvius in his model of a proper professional education and training that would result in a professional who could rise to the very top level of accomplishment in the Roman world. Certainly, the kind of training that Vitruvius prescribed would have been essential to the designer of the Domus Aurea; if Severus did also assume responsibility for Nero's rebuilding of the entire city, then that broad education would surely have proved even more necessary. Perhaps, in Severus, we see the evidence for what could be accomplished by a talented man of sufficient social status who received the proper education and training. Sadly, we do not have any direct evidence for his birth, education, or early experiences,[153] and so the rather grandiose descriptions of his career sometimes advanced in the scholarly literature must be accepted only with care.[154] But the importance of the designing architect of the Domus Aurea, and the fact that he also had experience on at least one major (if unsuccessful) engineering project, remains manifest. Severus is the first of the great figures, however shadowy the details may be, of Roman Imperial architecture.

Of Severus's companion, the *machinator* Celer, we know even less. Tacitus connects him to the same two projects as Severus but provides us with no other information. Since he is clearly distinguished from Severus by being called an engineer, it seems reasonable to assume that he may have been the most important employee—possibly the "right-hand man,"—of Severus's architectural practice, but little more can be deduced. He may be mentioned on a problematical inscription that would call him a freedman (*libertus*), but the inscription itself is thought by many epigraphers to be a fake.[155] Freed status in and of itself would be no surprise even for an engineer who rose to the fame that Celer apparently did, but the lack of a *cognomen* is surprising (unless this is simply a stylistic device preferred by Tacitus, which seems reasonably likely in the passage). But beyond attaching him to the architectural practice of Severus and noting that he must have been an unusually gifted engineer both in hydraulic and in mechanical devisings, there is little to be added. That an engineer received such recognition in the literary record of ancient Rome at all is unparalleled and attests to the extraordinary reputation Celer must have earned.

RABIRIUS

Just as with Nero's architect and engineer, we have only one literary source for the name of the architectural genius who appears to have been responsible for the building program undertaken in Rome during the reign of Domitian (A.D. 81–96) and left unfinished at the emperor's death. The poet Martial speaks of Rabirius in two different poems; in the first he attributes to him the design of the remarkable Imperial palace created on the top of the Palatine Hill:[156] "Heaven with its stars you, Rabirius, have conceived in your pious soul, who by wondrous art built the mansion of the Palatine. If Pisa shall be set to give Phidian Jove a temple worthy of him, she will beg of our Thunderer these hands of yours." In another poem, Martial is even more hyperbolic when he says, of seeing the great palace: "you could believe that the seven hills were rising up together."[157] Rabirius is again mentioned by Martial, but in a nonarchitectural context, in a poem offering the poet's condolences on the death of the architect's parents. The very fact that Rabirius was a central enough figure in Domitianic times to be addressed by a court poet in a personal, rather than a professional, situation in and of itself attests his importance in the Imperial hierarchy:[158]

> Whoe'er thou art who for thy parents prayest for a happy and a late death, regard with love this marble's brief inscription. In this earth Rabirius has hidden dearly-loved shades: with fairer lot none of the old lie in death. Twice six lustres of wedded life one night, kindly and their latest, closed; on one pyre two bodies burned. Yet he looks for them as if they had been snatched away from him in early years: naught more unwarranted can be than such a lament.

We gain little personal information from these poems. Rabirius has often been called a freedman (*libertus*) on no evidence whatsoever; Martial's use of the *nomen* alone would make *ingenuus* status (if not higher) seem more likely, as would the very fact of addressing a poem to a distinguished Imperial functionary on the death of his parents who, one would assume, were probably also of good family.[159] Rabirius is never mentioned in the inscriptional record, but we would not expect his name to appear on building inscriptions, which would of course have mentioned only Domitian himself.

The essential information in Martial's poems is the direct attribution to Rabirius of the centerpiece of Domitian's building program, the Palatine palace. The remains and the architecture of this immense complex are well known, although much is required of the autoptic imagination of the visitor to gain any real impression of its ancient grandeur.[160] Oddly enough, in antiquity there seems to have been an ongoing controversy, if the epigraphical record is correct, over whether the building's name was to be spelled Domus Augustiana or Augustana.[161] Far more important, however, is the fact that the architectural interests, styles, and techniques exhibited in the remains of the Palatine palace can offer the possibility of assigning responsibility for the design of other buildings of the Domitianic program specifically to Rabirius. There has been a tendency sometimes to be immoderate in this and to assign to Rabirius practically every major building known from at least the time of Titus until well into the reign of Trajan. While many of these attributions are possible, and some fairly likely, the grounds upon which they are made must be investigated first, then the likelihood of them established.[162]

That Domitian had in mind a building program that, if completed, would have revised the whole physical appearance of the city center of Rome in the first century A.D. is becoming ever clearer. In a number of important remains associated with Domitian, there appear certain architectural details characteristic of Domitianic architectural decoration that can be seen in the Palatine palace, including the insertion of two small rings between the dentils in entablature blocks, extremely deep carving out behind the eggs in the same entablatures, and, more generally, elaborate foliate carving that tends to cover every available surface of the entablature not otherwise decorated.[163] These techniques of decoration are often assumed to be "signature" characteristics of Rabirius and have led to the attribution of buildings in which they are found, and for which there is independent attestation of Domitianic construction, to Rabirius as designing architect. In a number of cases, the attribution seems both reasonable and convincing, if we accept the idea that Rabirius was serving as master architect of Domitian's building program in the same way that it has been supposed Severus served for Nero's. The most likely assignments to Rabirius include: the Forum Transitorium and its temple to Minerva, the renovation of the temple of Jupiter Optimus Maximus on the Capitoline, the rebuilding of the temple of Venus Genetrix and at least in part the Forum of Julius Caesar in which it stood, and the magnificent villa on the shore of Lake Albanus (now in part enclosed in the papal gardens at Castel Gandolfo) which Domitian called his Albanum.[164] None of these attributions to Rabirius need be doubted, and in their grandeur and variety they demonstrate the remarkable range of this architect.

The list can be, and has been, extended by more controversial assignments to the master architect. This may reflect not so much our knowledge of Rabirius's specific architectural traits as the strong tradition in later antiquity of Domitian's responsibility for at least beginning a great number of buildings that were only completed in the succeeding reigns of Nerva and Trajan.[165] It seems reasonable that Rabirius might have been involved at least as supervisor in such massive Domitianic undertakings as the restoration of much of the public and sacred architecture of the Campus Martius, which had been severely damaged during the fire of A.D. 80. This work included such projects as building or restoring the Stadium (now the Piazza Navona) and Odeum, the Porticus Divorum and Minucia Vetus, temples to Fortuna Redux, Minerva Chalcidica, Isis and Serapis, the Pantheon, and the Saepta Julia. He may also have served as supervisor for the completion of the huge public entertainment center southeast of the Forum Romanum in what had been the grounds of Nero's Domus Aurea, which included not only finishing the Flavian Amphitheater begun by Vespasian but also building the gladiatorial schools, two important bath complexes (the baths of Titus and Trajan), and the Meta Sudans fountain. Direct responsibility has been argued for Rabirius for the designs of such remarkable buildings as Trajan's Baths (assigned to Domitian by both St. Jerome in his translation of Eusebius's *Chronicle* and by the independent list of the Chronographer of A.D. 354) and for early elements of the area that became the Forum and "Markets" of Trajan on the south slope of the Quirinal, but the evidence is indirect and open to interpretation.[166]

Whatever specific buildings may be assigned to Rabirius, what seems abundantly clear is that he served for Domitian in the capacity of presiding genius over one of the most extensive building programs the Imperial city ever knew. He clearly rose to the very top of the Imperial administration, as Martial's praise certainly seems to indicate, and may still have been functioning (given the date at which Martial could still write sympathetically of him in *Epigrams* 10.71) after Domitian's assassination in A.D. 96. Hence it is reasonable to assume that he may have completed the Forum Transitorium and temple of Minerva, which Nerva dedicated in 97, but he had certainly been replaced as master architect for the Imperial administration by fairly early in the reign of Trajan, making way for Apollodorus. We hear no more about him after Martial's later epigram, and his reputation must inevitably have suffered from the *damnatio memoriae* visited on his emperor, but the greatness of Domitian's architectural contribution to Rome remained a byword at least into the fourth century A.D., and Rabirius's name survived with it.

APOLLODORUS OF DAMASCUS

The fame of Trajan's master architect, Apollodorus of Damascus, was widespread during his own time and remained strong into very late antiquity. At least three important passages mention the man and his works and provide us with a picture and a story that have provoked much discussion.[167] His reputation seems to have been established while serving with Trajan during the Dacian campaigns, when he was able to span the Danube River with a bridge. Procopius tells us that Trajan "was eager to span it with a bridge so that he might be able to cross it and that there might be no obstacle to his going against the barbarians beyond it. How he built this bridge I shall not be at pains to relate, but shall let Apollodorus of Damascus, who was the master builder of the whole work, describe the operation."[168] Clearly Apollodorus had, in the best Vitruvian tradition, published a monograph about his accomplishment that was still available to Procopius during the reign of Justinian. Upon Trajan's return to Rome after the successful completion of his conquest of Dacia, Apollodorus, who may well have been *praefectus fabrum* for the Dacian army on Trajan's own staff, seems to have taken over the sort of responsibilities that had been previously entrusted to Rabirius in the city of Rome.[169]

After Domitian's death, both Nerva and Trajan avoided indulging in any sort of extensive building in the city or in Latium, probably to avoid public opprobrium should they seem to be continuing the sort of expenditure Domitian had been involved in. This hiatus certainly lasted until ca. A.D. 104, and possibly longer.[170] But with Trajan's return to Rome, a conscious decision seems to have been made to redesign and complete many—indeed most—of the projects left unfinished in A.D. 96. Apollodorus's name appears to be connected with the variety of buildings completed in the reign of Hadrian in exactly the same way that Rabirius's was with Domitian's accomplishments. He must have continued to serve as a civilian master architect, master of public works for Trajan, and had at least supervisory and perhaps a good deal more direct influence on and control over what was being built. He is generally credited with the architectural plans of the Forum and Markets and the Baths of Trajan although all three of these projects seem to have been begun, perhaps in only the most preliminary manner, before Trajan's accession. He has sometimes also been seen as the master sculptor responsible for the frieze of Trajan's column and the "Great" Trajanic frieze now attached to the Arch of Constantine, a speculative attribution that would render Apollodorus the Roman equivalent of Phidias, mastermind of the Periclean building and sculptural program on the Athenian acropolis, and subsequently at the sanctuary of Olympia, during the fifth century B.C.[171] While it is extremely difficult to determine what projects traditionally credited to Trajan and Apollodorus may have had their beginnings under Domitian and Rabirius, there can be no real doubt that the ultimate form and appearance of much of Trajan's Forum, Markets, and Baths was due to Apollodorus.

Apollodorus seems to have continued to function as master architect in Rome during the first years of the reign of Trajan's successor, Hadrian (A.D. 117–138). The *Historia Augusta* biography of Hadrian says that he was involved in the planning of a statue to the Moon (*Luna*) with Hadrian, a statue intended to match the great Colossus of Nero, which Hadrian had transformed into a representation of the Sun (*Sol*).[172] More important and more informative, however, is the gossipy tale about the rivalry between Apollodorus, the established architect, and Hadrian, amateur building designer, both before and after Hadrian's accession to the purple. The story is preserved for us only in Xiphilinus's abridged version of Cassius Dio, but it is worth quoting for its information about both Apollodorus and Hadrian in the architectural world of their time.[173]

[Hadrian] first banished and later put to death Apollodorus, the architect who had built the various creations of Trajan in Rome—the Forum, the odeum,[174] and the baths. The reason assigned was that he had been guilty of some misdemeanor; but the true reason was that once when Trajan was consulting him on some point about the buildings he had said to Hadrian, who had interrupted with some remark: "Be off, and draw your pumpkins. You don't understand any of these matters"—it chanced that Hadrian at the time was pluming himself upon some such drawing. When he became emperor, therefore, he remembered this slight and would not endure the man's freedom of speech. He sent him the design of the temple of Venus and Rome by way of showing him that a great work could be accomplished without his aid, and asked Apollodorus whether the proposed structure was satisfactory. The architect in his reply stated first, in regard to the temple, that it ought to have been built on high ground and that the earth should have been excavated beside it, so that it might have stood out more conspicuously on the Sacred Way from a higher position, and might also have accommodated the machines in its basement, so that they could be put together unobserved and brought into the theater[175] without anyone being aware of them beforehand. Secondly, in regard to the statues, he said that they had been made too tall for the height of the cella. "For now," he said, "if the goddesses wish to get up and go out, they will be unable to do so." When he wrote this so bluntly to Hadrian, the emperor was both vexed and exceedingly grieved because he had fallen into a mistake that could not be righted, and he restrained neither his anger nor his grief, but slew the man.

Clearly Apollodorus was no courtier, at least not to Hadrian! The story and its various bits of information have been much discussed, and certain things seem quite clear, including its essential lack of verifiable historicity. Apollodorus was obviously in a dominant position in architectural endeavors in Trajanic Rome, to such a degree that he felt secure in condescending to Hadrian while Trajan was alive and still felt sufficiently sure of his position to continue to criticize Hadrian's architectural endeavors after Hadrian's accession, unwisely as it turned out. The conversation among the three men—Trajan, Apollodorus, and Hadrian—can be dated either to A.D. 104–5, before the Dacian campaign, or just after it, about 107–8. The "pumpkins" Apollodorus seems to have sneered at perhaps refer to the sort of segmental domes Hadrian experimented with in his villa at Tivoli, in the domed rooms at either end of the so-called Piazza D'Oro and in the Terme Piccole.[176]

Apollodorus's extraordinary standing in matters architectural is certainly attested in the later section of this passage by Hadrian's sending the blueprints for his temple to Venus and Rome to the older man and inviting his criticism of them; the same sentence implies that Hadrian himself was the architect who had drawn them. Here the story as it is given us becomes rather more puzzling. Apollodorus's criticism is aimed at two points: (1) the temple should have been raised on a high platform, and (2) the cella roof should have been higher. Sound as these critiques may appear in Dio's story, they do not make sense in the context of what we know of the actual temple of Venus and Rome. The temple's platform still stands to the northwest of the Flavian amphitheater, raised on substantial—though not towering—vaulted substructures that feature large tunnels opening inward from the amphitheater side. Investigation of the substructures has demonstrated convincingly, primarily on the evidence of brick stamps, that they are Hadrianic, but the tunnelled passageways turn out to be medieval reworkings to them. The fragmentary remains of the superstructure are almost entirely from a reconstruction by Maxentius in the early fourth century A.D., which was in turn converted in part into the church of S. Francesco Romano, but certainly the reconstructed temple did not lack for height as the remaining evidence of its double-apsed cella shows. It is difficult to imagine that this does not to some degree at least reflect the height of Hadrian's original.

From the architectural remains, then, we must conclude either that Hadrian followed Apollodorus's criticisms and redesigned the temple plans before they were executed (which is contradicted by the passage, since Hadrian is said to have "fallen into a mistake that could not be righted"), or that Apollodorus's criticisms were in fact unjust and Hadrian had a certain right to feel slighted by the older man. Neither conclusion is acceptable and it seems all too likely that the entire tale is a slanderous fiction. Given that the other important source for this period and similar events—the *Vita Hadriani* of the *Historia Augusta*—makes no mention whatsoever of what would surely have been a scandalous cause célèbre had it actually occurred, there seems little reason to concede it any basis whatsoever.[177]

Although as history, Dio's (or Xiphilinus's) story is best regarded as apocryphal, if not outright falsehood intended to blacken Hadrian's reputation, it does have some relevance to this investigation in that it points up the extraordinary status in the architectural profession and in the Imperial bureaucracy to which Apollodorus rose in the first decades of the second century A.D. It also ties him firmly to the building of Trajan's Forum and his Baths, though also, and unfortunately, to an otherwise unknown odeum. If we accept the comparison between the status achieved by Rabirius under Domitian and that of Apollodorus under Trajan, a case can be made for attributing to him supervisory and (possibly) design responsibility for Trajan's Markets, the new harbor at Portus and extensive development at Ostia herself, the port at Centumcellae (modern Civitavecchia), the cutting for the via Appia at Terracina, a circus-naumachia, the arches at Benevento and Ancona, and any and every other Trajanic monument in the entire Roman world, as well as for regarding him as the master sculptor of Trajan's Column and the so-called Great Trajanic frieze.[178] He has even been credited with having designed and built the Pantheon as we know it, or at least having participated in it while still in favor early in Hadrian's reign.[179]

Although it seems best to avoid the hyperbole inherent in many of these attributions of direct responsibility to Apollodorus, it is significant to remember that he was, both on the basis of his name and his origin in Damascus, a product of the Greco-Roman, rather than the Italo-Roman, world and hence is to some extent the inheritor of the mantle of Hermogenes and Hermodorus during the Imperial period. Nowhere in our sources is he criticized for being "Greek" or stigmatized as a foreigner and therefore somehow suspect.[180] After him, also, master architects seem to become all but entirely anonymous, though it is difficult to know whether this is due to the increasing domination of public architecture by the emperors or to the random preservation of names and information in our historical sources. Nonetheless, the central importance of Apollodorus of Damascus to Roman Imperial architecture must be acknowledged, as that of Severus and of Rabirius must.

The name of an architect contemporary with Apollodorus may be preserved to us. The younger Pliny wrote a letter to a man named Mustius concerning the restoration of a temple that had fallen into disrepair on one of Pliny's estates.[181] While Mustius is not specifically referred to as an *architectus* in the text of the letter, it is probably significant that according to Pliny he had supplied the plan for the whole restoration project, which sounds very much like the primary duty of an architect on a private commission. Certainly Mustius must have had a fair level of expertise in building and perhaps was an architect who also served as a contractor, since Pliny in addition charges him with obtaining four marble columns as well as other marble and leaves the choice of them up to him. Mustius would seem then to offer evidence that the *architectus/redemptor* figure attested in the first century B.C. was apparently still to be found in private building in the early second century A.D. No other mention of Mustius has survived.

HADRIAN AND AFTER

The tale told by Cassius Dio allows us not only to draw conclusions about the career and importance of Apollodorus, but also to begin an assessment of the contribution of the most renowned aristocratic amateur architect of all, the emperor Hadrian, to the profession during the Roman Empire. Hadrian as architect is a much-debated and tortured subject. The direct evidence is slight but implies a great deal. In Dio's passage we have the clear implication that he liked to experiment with architectural forms at least in drawings and that he was capable of creating the blueprint for an entire building of massive size. The remains of his renowned villa near Tivoli, with their elaborate series of experiments in stone that seem to play with every element of ancient architectural form and vocabulary, would seem to bear out the testimony of Hadrian's direct personal interest and skill in architectural design. At Rome our sources credit him with the Pantheon, the temple of Venus and Rome, the temple of the Deified Trajan, and the Mausoleum (now Castel S. Angelo) and Pons Aelius, as well as a wide variety of rebuildings and repairs.[182] Of these, direct responsibility for the architectural design is assigned to Hadrian only for the temple of Venus and Rome, but his participation in all the other items seems likely.

Hadrian was apparently interested in most areas of accomplishment both public and private, according to Cassius Dio,[183] and demonstrated talent in most of them, architecture being near the top of both his interests and his talents.[184] It seems safe to say that Hadrian, as architect, liked to experiment within the boundaries of Greco-Roman architecture, even to the extent of introducing elements from other architectural traditions into his work (e.g., the so-called Canopus at the villa at Tivoli supposedly reproduced the original Egyptian Canopus; but if the area identified as the Canopus at Tivol. today is correctly labeled, it was a very Hellenized view of Egyptian architecture that Hadrian espoused). No master architect is mentioned during Hadrian's reign, or indeed ever again after Apollodorus; perhaps Hadrian had no use for another such *architectus* after his disputes with Apollodorus.

During Hadrian's reign one other architect is named and attached to a particular project. According to the *Historia Augusta,* "With the aid of the architect Decrianus he [Hadrian] raised the Colossus and, keeping it in an upright position, moved it away from the place in which the temple [of Venus and Rome] is now, though its weight was so vast that he had to furnish as many as twenty-four elephants for the work. The statue he then consecrated to the Sun, after removing the features of Nero, to whom it had previously been dedicated."[185] This is our only mention of Decrianus, and although he is specifically labeled *architectus* in the passage, the deed described seems more a feat of engineering and clearly represents a project carried out at Hadrian's behest and to his specifications.

After the reign of Hadrian the names of few architects before the reign of Justinian survive, and we are equally wanting in further evidence about the status of the profession and its practitioners. An Imperial freedman named Cleander is said to have constructed baths at Rome for the emperor Commodus (A.D. 180–192) but is not specifically called *architectus* and may just as likely have been financier or supervisor of their construction as the designing architect.[186] A fragmentary Oxyrynchus papyrus names one Sextus Julius Africanus as architect of a library at Rome on behalf of the emperor Severus Alexander that was located near or opening onto the precinct of the Pantheon, part (presumably) of Alexander's massive reworking of the Baths of Agrippa and of Nero (immediately south and west, respectively, of the Hadrianic temple) as the *thermae Alexandrinae* prior to A.D. 235.[187] A Greek inscription, from the early fourth century A.D., from Mylasa near Miletus in ancient Asia Minor, has been interpreted as providing us with the name of the architect responsible for Maxentius's redesigning and restoration of Hadrian's temple of Venus and Rome, one Pericles of Mylasa, who is otherwise unknown to us.[188]

There is another collection of names of architects who practiced in Ravenna, Constantinople, and elsewhere during the sixth century A.D., thanks almost entirely to the testimony of Procopius,[189] that includes Aloysius, Julianus, Cyriades, Entinopus of Candia, Dalmatius of Rhodes, Anthemius of Tralles, and Isidorus of Miletus. Of these, Anthemius and Isidorus, who built the church of Sta. Sophia in Constantinople, are the best known to us. A passage of Procopius both documents their achievements and shows that they were still working very much within the tradition inherited from their pagan Roman forebears:[190]

> The Emperor [Justinian], disregarding all questions of expense, eagerly pressed on to the work of construction, and began to gather all the artisans from the whole world. And Anthemius of Tralles, the most learned man in the skilled craft which is known as the art of building, not only of all his contemporaries, but also when compared with those who had lived long before him, ministered to the Emperor's enthusiasm, duly regulating the tasks of the various artisans, and preparing in advance designs of the future construction. Associated with him was another master-builder, Isidorus by name, born in Miletus, a man who was intelligent and worthy to assist the Emperor Justinian. Indeed this was also an indication of the honor in which God held the Emperor, that He had already provided the men who would be most serviceable to him in the tasks which were waiting to be carried out.

The pagan Roman origins of Procopius's description seem clear: the association of Anthemius with Isidorus is remarkably congruent to that of Severus and Celer, and the relationship of both men, and of the great building they designed and executed, to Nero and his Domus Aurea is also transparent, though in a Christian world the connection is now with God and the building a great church.[191]

Anthemius became known throughout the early Christian world as much as a geometrician as an architect, and Isidorus seems to have founded or been part of a familial workshop of architects, since it was his son Isidorus the Younger who reconstructed the central dome of Hagia Sophia after Anthemius's original design proved too attenuated and collapsed in A.D. 558. The Justinianic architects are the inheritors of the tradition of Roman *architecti* from Hermogenes to Hadrian, but at such a chronological remove that we can learn little else that is useful to us from the little we know of them. About all we can say is that the profession of *architectus* does not seem to have altered much from the time of Vitruvius to the time of Anthemius. In short, our evidence for the Roman *architectus* as individual and for architecture as a profession in the pagan Roman world peters out after Hadrian's reign. There seems no obvious explanation other than the increasing dominance of the Imperial system in many areas for the anonymity that afflicted architecture from the mid second century A.D. onward, and perhaps it is just the happenstance of what information is lost and what is preserved that accounts for the phenomenon, particularly given the visibility of architects of the sixth century A.D. who were working very much in the same tradition. Nonetheless, it brings us to the end of our search for the Roman architects.

Two

The Organization of Building in Ancient Rome

Building Contracts

Any sort of building or construction requires that the labor essential to it, skilled and unskilled, and the materials necessary for it be organized before the actual work begins. This coordination of organization and supply was regularly handled in the ancient Roman world by forming a legally binding contract between the landowner who wanted something built on property he owned and a builder who had or could provide the needed expertise.[1] Since a contract is concluded between the proprietor and the builder, it can be set up in such a way that, for each specific job, all the various essential elements can be provided for, and the employer can choose how much or how little specific control he wants to exercise over the project, frequently allowing the employer to transfer all real control (and responsibility) onto the builder who has agreed to organize the job and who must then assume the burden of accountability, while the landowner takes no, or very little, part in the project.

In the Roman world, at least well into the second century A.D. and probably much later, private contractors continued to furnish the majority of the labor and supplies necessary for public and private building, although from the late first century A.D. onward the increasing size of the Imperial bureaucracy—especially the creation of the office called *opera Caesaris*, probably during the reign of Domitian—meant that public building came more and more under governmental administrative control. But the importance of the contract system continued; prior to that time it constituted the only means by which architectural projects were realized.[2]

Because of the paucity of examples preserved, it is impossible to provide more than a general description of how a Roman building contract was formed. It must be noted, first, that contracts for construction are not discussed in our surviving Roman legal texts under their own heading, but are included only as occasional examples of two important types of contracts: *stipulatio,* which meant a legal form by which a promise made by one party to another was enforceable, and *locatio conductio,* which was the general term for any kind of contract involving hire and lease. Such details as we know of each type of contract will be discussed below. But it is important to realize that the evidence is meager; for instance, aside from the periodic building contracts cited as examples here and there in the *Digest* of Roman law compiled in the time of Justinian,[3] we have only two important building contracts attested epigraphically: the remarkable inscription that records the contract terms for building a wall around the sanctuary of Serapis at Puteoli in 105 B.C. (often called the *Lex Puteolana*),[4] and the fragmentary inscriptions that record contracts for the repair of sections of the via Caecilia probably during the early first century B.C.[5] Literary sources that actually provide any specific terms of building contracts—as opposed to brief notices that some sort of building was constructed and presumably contracted for, which are fairly common in annalistic historical sources such as Livy and Polybius—are equally sparse: a fragment of Cato describing how to contract for new construction on a farm[6] and Cicero's highly rhetorical description of a maintenance contract for the temple of Castor in the Roman Forum, which must be used as evidence only with care.[7] The evidence we do have concerns Roman Italy only, nowhere else in the

Roman world. Nonetheless, it is possible to form a general description of each type of Roman contract for construction, and that in turn can lead us to consider the history and organization of construction in ancient Rome.

Stipulatio appears to have been the less common, but probably the older, type of contract used in construction (as well as in many other types of formal agreements).[8] A valid contract through *stipulatio* required a formalized verbal exchange, in the form of a question and answer, between the prospective employer, often called the stipulator (*reus stipulandi*) and the employee or promissor (*reus promittendi*). An apposite example of this sort of verbal contract through formulaic question and response is given in the Justinianic *Digest* 45.1.124;[9] the stipulator asks the promissor, "do you promise to build an apartment building in that location within two years?" and the promissor must respond, "I promise."[10] Just as in much of Roman religious ritual, so too in early Roman law, the validity of the contract required that the verbal exchange be performed exactly right; even the slightest flaw in the oral presentation of question and answer could invalidate the whole contract. Nothing was written down in this form of agreement, and it is notable that, since a *stipulatio* was considered unilateral, the sort of contract recorded here may not have been sufficient to bind the employer to pay the builder! Probably either a second *stipulatio* for payment had to be undertaken at the same time between the two parties or a provision for payment could be included within the basic *stipulatio*, perhaps together with any other essential reciprocal obligations.[11] What little further evidence we have for contracts arranged by *stipulatio* indicates that the contract was valid only if the specific location of the building site was included and usually a date for completion of the project indicated.[12]

Seemingly in more common usage for construction contracts was *locatio conductio*. A valid contract of this type required that the parties come to a specific agreement on all the terms of the activities covered by the contract and that they agree on a fixed price. Because of this, contracts in *locatio conductio* were developed for specific types of hire and lease agreements, such as leasing places to live or for storage or for hiring workers, skilled or unskilled, for a day or other specific period of time.[13] Such contracts for construction were certainly in use by the time of Cato, since he provides an example of one in his advice for contracting to build on a farm and many of the building activities described in Cicero's letters appear to have been conducted under this type of agreement. In its simplest form, a contract in *locatio conductio* required that one party, called a *locator*, place his thing, job, labor, and the like at the disposal of the second party, called the *conductor*, and that they agree upon a fixed price (*merces*). In a contract to build, the *locator* had to agree with the *conductor* on exactly what type of work was to be done—a wall or an entire building constructed, a pipeline laid, a road paved, and so on—and had to furnish the land that would receive the building. The *conductor* was then legally bound by the contract to build the edifice agreed upon, and the *locator* was bound to pay the previously agreed price for his work to the *conductor*. These were the essential terms. While *conductor* is the label generally applied to the builder in private building contracts of this type, in contracts for public construction it is always replaced by *redemptor*, and *redemptor* also appears periodically in private contracts, while *conductor* is not known in contracts for public building. Hence *redemptor* is actually the more common of the two terms in our sources, but they indicate the same party to the contract in legal terms.[14]

There were a number of other elements in a contract in *locatio conductio*. The contract contained a "good faith" clause (*ex bona fide*), which meant that, if a suit was filed over the contract, the judge had to decide whether the defendant had completed his obligation under the terms of the contract according to the standard of "good faith."[15] It seems fairly certain that provisions were made within such building contracts for supply of materials—whether they were to be supplied by the landowner or by the builder—and that the agreed price for building was calculated accordingly. There appears to have been some discussion among Roman jurists about whether a situation in which the builder supplied the building materials for the project would affect ownership of the finished building, but the legal conclusion was that, given the nature of the contract, materials supplied by the builder within the terms of the contract became the property of the landowner once they were used in the agreed construction.[16] Essentially, the builder was hired as a skilled craftsman (*artifex*) and his degree of control over the project, as well as his responsibility for meeting the terms of the contract, was great.[17] The juristic sources emphasize that the *conductor* or *redemptor* had such extensive control precisely because of his expertise: he had to supervise the work and take responsibility for the quality of the finished product. At the end of the project, the builder and his building had to pass an inspection (*probatio*) for approval, which seems to have consisted of an examination of how well the building conformed to the original specifications in the contract and of the quality of the work.[18] Since the initial form of the agreement in *locatio conductio* was more detailed than the question and answer used in *stipulatio*, the former seems to have become the preferred form for construction contracts. Such contracts, springing from the presumption that the *conductor* or *redemptor* is a skilled professional, placed the majority of liability upon him, not just for actual construction but also for coordination of the project as a whole. He was put entirely in charge, was assumed to act in "good faith," and was obliged to submit his work for approval before the contract could be terminated. Hence, the *redemptor* or *conductor* became an extremely important figure in the entire system by which construction was organized in Roman society.

The clearest way in which to understand the form and content of building contracts in *locatio conductio* is provided by the example given by Cato in his manual *On Agriculture*. Cato describes in some detail how a contract for the construction of a new farm—clearly of the type called *villa rustica*—should be let, and the extraordinary precision included is instructive:[19]

> If you are contracting for the building of a new steading from the ground up, the contractor should be responsible for the following: all walls as specified, of quarry-stone set in mortar, pillars of solid masonry, all necessary beams, sills, uprights, lintel, door-framing, supports, winter stables and summer feed racks for cattle, a horse stall, quarters for servants, 3 meat racks, a round table, 2 copper boilers, 10 coops, a fireplace, 1 main entrance, and another at the option of the owner, windows, 10 two-foot lattices for the larger windows, 6 window-shutters, 3 benches, 5 stools, 2 looms, 1 small mortar for crushing

wheat, 1 fuller's mortar, trimmings, and 2 presses. The owner will furnish the timber and necessary material for this and deliver it on the ground, and also 1 saw and 1 plumb-line (but the contractor will fell, hew, square and finish the timber), stone, lime, sand, water, straw, and earth for making mortar. . . . The price of this work from an honest owner, who furnishes duly all necessary materials and pays conscientiously: one sesterce per tile. The roof will be reckoned as follows: on the basis of a whole tile, one which is one-fourth broken is counted two for one; all gutter tiles are counted each as two; and all joint-tiles each as four.

In a steading of stone and mortar groundwork, carry the foundation one foot above ground, the rest of the walls of brick; add the necessary lintel and trimmings. The rest of the specifications as for the house of rough stone set in mortar. The cost per tile will be one sesterce. The above prices are for a good owner, in a healthful situation. The cost of workmanship will depend upon the count. In an unwholesome situation, where summer work is impossible, the generous owner will add a fourth to the price.

There are a number of interesting features to this model building contract. Its most obvious characteristic is its explicitness. The details of responsibility of the builder and of the owner are laid out in great detail with exact numbers of items provided, as well as clear division of responsibility. In this particular example it should be noted that the owner is agreeing to provide all materials and that the cost of the project is carefully calculated with the owner's contribution included (presumably if the builder were contracted to supply the materials, the price "per tile" would be higher in order to recompense the extra outlay involved). The "good faith" implicit in contracts in *locatio conductio* is made fairly explicit by the references to the "honest" or "generous" owner (in each case the Latin is *dominus bonus*). In the final paragraph Cato demonstrates the different ways in which the price of the project might be calculated based upon the particular situation prevailing at the building site. Cato simply assumes that the building site has been agreed upon and stated explicitly; otherwise it would be impossible to calculate, and for the parties to the contract to agree upon, the pricing formula for the job. While Cato's "contract" is really intended as a didactic example, it is a very good one, since in it Cato specifies absolutely everything needed to complete the construction. What Cato is describing is a purely private construction contract between two individuals. But the form and clauses of contracts for public building work seem to have been very much the same.

The two actual building contracts whose terms have come down to us—the via Caecilia repair inscriptions and the so-called *Lex Puteolana*—are examples of contracts in *locatio conductio* and represent contracts formed with private builders to undertake public construction projects. The contracts to repair sections of the via Caecilia are preserved only in fragments, but their form and intent are clear.[20] All four individual contracts represented were let by the Roman censor T. Vibius Temundinus, acting as caretaker of public roads (*curator viarum*), and each was concluded with a different contractor (the contractors are referred to in these inscriptions as *mancupes*).[21] The contracts seem to have been valuable ones: one appears to have involved 600,000 sesterces if not more, another perhaps 150,000. The responsibilities are laid out quite thoroughly, defining exactly what is to be done in each stretch of the road; for example, where there is a fallen arch (*arcus dela[psus]*) it must be repaired. The requirements upon the contractors were clear and explicit, and the price for the work set out in advance, as essential to a valid contract in *locatio conductio.*

The construction contract from Puteoli survives intact. It was let in 105 B.C. and has long been a subject of study.[22] Again, as it should be in a contract in *locatio conductio,* the terms, obligations, and liabilities under this contract—which runs to three lengthy texts carved on individual slabs of Luna marble—are quite explicit, even though the actual work involved, and the price agreed upon for its completion, are quite small if compared to the via Caecilia contracts. The contractor, C. Blossius, son of Quintus, is contracted by the *duoviri* of Puteoli for the year 105 B.C., N. Fufidius and M. Pullius, to build a wall with a gateway in front of the sanctuary of Serapis in the town, for which he is to receive a *merces* of 1,500 sesterces. All details of the wall are described in numbing detail; little if anything is left to the discretion of the builder. Blossius is referred to in the contract by the term *praes,* which seems to mean that he acted as his own guarantor or surety, although this has been disputed; the other three men named in the contract may have been additional guarantors.[23] The fullness of the terms in this contract demonstrates clearly why contracts in *locatio conductio* came to be preferred for building contracts: their very completeness must have served as a "sword of Damocles" suspended over the neck of the contractor who had to fulfill their terms to the satisfaction of those who had let the contract and had to undergo a *probatio* to insure it. The builder, however, was given the protection of the "good faith" presumption in such a contract. He was not liable if he could demonstrate to the satisfaction of a judge, should any dispute or disagreement about the work arise, that he had acted *ex bona fide*.

The Administration of Public and Private Building

During the centuries of the Roman Republic, this system of contracting for construction projects was the dominant, indeed for all practical purposes the only, method of realizing building projects. The basic form of building contracts—either *stipulatio* or *locatio conductio*—was employed for both private and public building, that is, the government of Rome let contracts with private builders just as private Roman citizens did in order to build. Since the documentation for public building is sufficient to allow us to devise something of a history of it, we will concentrate on that, looking first and only briefly at the specific evidence of private building.

PRIVATE BUILDING DURING THE REPUBLIC AND EMPIRE

No elaborate chronology of private construction during the Republic can be devised. Our two main sources are Cato's example of a building contract, discussed above, and numerous remarks and stories in Cicero's letters. Cicero describes a number of undertakings that would seem to constitute private projects; one of the best-known is that of the *fanum* in memory of his daughter Tullia, the construction of which he let out on contract with a man named Cluatius in 45 B.C.. It is clear that Cluatius was responsible for the entire project, serving as *architectus, conductor,* and probably supervising stone mason.[24] Two months later, another letter tells us that

75

the site for the *fanum* still had not been settled, and Cicero asks Atticus to encourage Cluatius and perhaps goad him a bit toward completing the project, which, in fact, was never done since Cicero could never acquire the gardens he wanted for its location.[25] Given the nature of a building contract in *locatio conductio*, the delay can hardly be designated Cluatius's fault, since the site would have had to be agreed upon before the contract could be considered valid. In general, however, the sort of fairly informal, though contractual, arrangement described by Cicero seems to be typical of the sort of project that characterized private construction. Cluatius probably worked at Rome, since Cicero was writing to Atticus from Astura, but we do not know his social status nor exactly how Cicero had found and engaged him. In other situations, too, it is difficult to tell whether the builders Cicero refers to, whether labeled *architectus* or not, are really architects or contractors. Many, like Cluatius, probably served as both.[26]

Cicero provides an excellent example of the type of wealthy landowner from the Roman upper classes who was most likely to let contracts for private construction. His projects concentrated on housing, tombs, commercial property, and maintenance or repair work. We have direct attestation in his letters of building in all four categories.[27] Certain points can be noted. While Cicero purchased and sold a number of houses and villas during his lifetime, he was apparently quite scrupulous about maintaining and repairing them; he did similar service for his brother Quintus's personal property while Quintus was with Caesar in Gaul.[28] The story was quite different with rental and commercial properties, such as *tabernae* and *insulae*, that Cicero owned. He was interested solely in the profits to be earned from those and farmed out all maintenance and repair on rental property to be taken care of by others. We know that he owned, or in one case co-owned, apartment buildings (*insulae*) in Rome on the Argiletum and on the Aventine hill, that he rented out shops (*tabernae*) in Puteoli, and that both were excellent, if not trouble-free, sources of income for him.[29]

What is abundantly clear is that the brothers Cicero, while they probably maintained a small number of semi- or minimally skilled workers able to undertake maintenance and repair jobs on their permanent staffs, turned to *redemptores* and *architecti* whenever they indulged in larger projects or those that required any kind of specialized skill. Labor costs money, of course, and skilled labor of the kind needed to build a new house or totally refurbish a villa or build a top-quality funeral monument required contracting with private builders; it could not have been cost efficient, or even conceivable, for the Ciceros to have supported such skilled builders permanently (i.e., as slaves), since they did not engage in sufficiently extensive building projects to justify the expense.[30]

We hear of two other landowners in Republican times who engaged in more radical forms of speculative property development. C. Sergius Orata, early in the first century B.C., together with a physician named Asclepiades of Prusa, made a lot of money out of buying up aging and run-down country houses, fixing them up with heated baths (*balneae pensiles*) and reselling them. Since this seems to have been a business proposition engaged in a number of times, it is possible that Orata maintained his own crew of builders skilled in exactly the jobs he needed done, contracting out only if and when he would have needed some specialized construction skill. Orata also had a sideline: he exploited the renowned oyster beds at Baiae and did well out of that, too.[31]

Much more famous is the speculation—an early form of damage insurance scam—by which M. Licinius Crassus, colleague of Pompey and Caesar in the first triumvirate and renowned as the richest man in Rome of the mid-first century B.C., is said to have made a good deal of his fortune. Plutarch[32] tells us that:

> observing how natural and familiar at Rome were such fatalities as the conflagration and collapse of buildings, owing to their being too massive and close together, he proceeded to buy slaves who were architects and builders. Then, when he had over five hundred of these, he would buy houses that were afire, and houses which adjoined those that were afire, and these their owners would let go at a trifling price owing to their fear and uncertainty. In this way the largest part of Rome came into his possession.

The tale is odd at best. Clearly it was unusual that Crassus kept a force of builders on hand; the cost must have been astronomical, and either fires must have been a more regular occurrence than seems likely, or we have to postulate the intentional setting, at Crassus's command, of more fires than would have occurred naturally in order for the scam to have justified his expenses, much less turned a profit. Perhaps the figure of five hundred slaves is exaggerated; while the story seems to give us firm evidence for large-scale use of slave gangs in building, at least by one exceedingly wealthy aristocrat, the utterly anomalous nature of this testimony should urge caution in reading too much into it. It is more an exaggerated *exemplum* of Crassus's renowned avarice, and a chance to portray him as a promoter of arson, than sober fact.[33] In contrast however, to such aristocratic landholders as the Cicero brothers, who clearly let contracts with *redemptores* or *conductores* and *architecti* for their building schemes, the tales of Orata and Crassus do offer evidence that teams of skilled, or semi-skilled, builders—probably mostly or entirely slaves—could be possessed and used in extraordinary and large-scale construction businesses.

Evidence for private building becomes even scarcer during the Empire. From the time of Augustus we do possess a certain quantity of information about the building concerns and activities of the family of the Statilii Tauri, whose grave monument on the via Appia contained over four hundred inscriptions that included those of three (or possibly four) slave and one (or possibly two) freed builders, called *fabri*. The inscriptions attest that these builders functioned within the *familia,* which was conceived in the broadest terms to include all servants of the Statilii Tauri as well as actual relations. The freed builders all appear to have been manumitted by the *familia* and continued to work for the family business.[34] Clearly the family's construction business justified the expense of keeping slave builders. We know that T. Statilius Taurus was one of the wealthy Romans whom Augustus urged to put up buildings in Rome that would contribute to the architectural glorification of the city. We also know that their property in Rome included gardens on the Esquiline and the first stone amphitheater ever erected in the city; it was maintained by the family slaves until its destruction in the fire of A.D. 64.[35] The Statilii Tauri may have had financial interests in the building trade beyond property development, for

they also appear to have invested in importing timber from Dyr-
rachium, a connection that must have increased their interest in the
construction business and might help to explain how it was economically feasible for them to maintain skilled builders in their
familia. The Statilii Tauri were not the only wealthy family known to
engage in the trade of supplying building materials, as we shall
see.[36]

After the reign of Augustus, the evidence for private building in
the Roman world becomes even more random. Pliny the Younger is
often cited since we know that he bought houses and country villas
and rebuilt them to his own tastes, but he never seems to have
owned any commercial property in Rome and so does not seem to
have engaged in building for profit.[37] There is good epigraphical
evidence from Ostia of the building of houses and commercial
properties, especially during the second century A.D., and it seems
to show that the standard methods of contracting for construction
were still in place and largely unchanged well into that century.[38]
Very little seems to have changed in the private building industry—
once the procedures, methods, and legal forms of contract had been
established—well into late antiquity. The major changes in the
administration of building, just like the major advances in Roman
architecture, were concentrated in public building, just as they had
been from the second century B.C. onward.

PUBLIC BUILDING DURING THE REPUBLIC

We are told by Polybius that, by the second century B.C., expenditure for public construction, including new projects and the
maintenance of existing structures, was the biggest single drain on
the Roman treasury.[39] But public building by contract is attested
at least two centuries earlier and probably can be seen as far back
as 435 B.C., when the censors gave their approval of the newly
built *villa publica*, which certainly implies approval of its construction by the magistrates (*probatio operis*) and, in turn, strongly suggests that they had let a contract for its construction, which they
were seeing completed in the required manner.[40] Indeed, there is
reason to suppose that public contracting, for all sorts of necessities in addition to construction, may have been in existence as far

back as the fifth century or even the regal period of Roman history.[41]

The first absolutely attested contract for a public building project was let in 378 B.C., when the censors Sp. Servilius Priscus and Q. Cloelius Siculus let a contract for the construction of a stone wall for the city.[42] Public construction seems to have been the responsibility primarily of the censors, but the record of their activity in this field is neither consistent nor particularly reliable for the fourth and third centuries B.C.[43] A few of these early censorial construction programs are well known, including the project undertaken by Gaius Maenius in 318 B.C. to add balconies to the façades of the *tabernae* in the Forum (as well as other hypothetical alterations there)[44] and, most notably, the extensive program that was forced through over strong senatorial opposition by a combination of bullying and chicanery by Appius Claudius Caecus in 312 B.C., the project that built both the Aqua Appia and the via Appia. As told by Frontinus, the story is colorful and provides a glimpse of the sway available to the censors in matters of public building:[45]

> In the consulship of Marcus Valerius Maximus and Publius Decius Mus, thirty years after the beginning of the Samnite War, the Aqua Appia was brought into the city by the censor Appius Claudius Crassus, later called Caecus, who also had charge of the construction of the via Appia from Porta Capena to Capua. His fellow censor was Gaius Plautius, called Venox for discovering the veins of this supply [of water]; but this man resigned after eighteen months, deceived by Appius pretending he would do the same: so the honour of giving his name to the aqueduct fell to Appius alone, who is said to have extended his censorship by many subterfuges, until he had completed both road and aqueduct.

That this sort of important public construction was the responsibility of the censors is clear from this tale, and that building was a sufficiently prestigious part of the office to reward the kind of behavior indulged in by Appius is also significant. Otherwise, we are told that the censors elected for a relatively brief period in 272 B.C. were given the spoils from the Pyrrhic War to finance construction of the Anio Vetus aqueduct and that, at the expiration of their censorship, they were appointed to an extraordinary magistracy—

as *duumviri aquae perducendae*—so that they could complete the project.[46] The plebeian censor of 220 B.C., Gaius Flaminius, gained tremendous popularity on account of using his office to build the via Flaminia and the Circus Flaminius, although exactly what the latter entailed is unclear.[47]

Public building projects in the earlier Republic were by no means a monopoly of the censors, although this is sometimes implied in the scholarly bibliography. The same sort of vocabulary derived from contracts is used by Livy for the building of temples at Rome by various magistrates from the fourth to the second century B.C.[48] Early examples of such projects include the dictator M. Furius Camillus's letting of a contract in 396 B.C. to build a temple to Juno on the Aventine Hill, and the consul Sp. Carvilius Maximus contracting for the construction of a temple to Fors Fortuna in 293 B.C.[49] During the early centuries of the Republic, special pairs of magistrates—called *duumviri aedi locandae* or *duumviri aedi dedicandae*, essentially special commissioners, the former for letting building contracts and the latter for approving and dedicating the finished buildings—were sometimes appointed to deal with construction and completion of temples. The earliest of these *duumviri* are attested in 344 B.C. charged with building the temple to Juno Moneta on the Arx; they were appointed precisely because it was decided that some kind of extraordinary appointment was required for so important a project, and they were charged with devoting their full attention to it. The temple was completed in the following year, an unusually rapid fulfillment of the contract.[50] We again hear of a major project, the restoration of temples throughout the city, being given to *duumviri* in 217 B.C., but the Second Punic War prevented completion of this project.[51] Various men holding the office of aedile, whether curule or plebeian, are recorded by Livy as having undertaken public building during the fourth and third centuries B.C.,[52] and this evidence confirms the magistrates' broad use of contracting during those centuries. Since books eleven through twenty of Livy are missing, our record of such public building breaks off until the beginning of the Second Punic War, thus leaving us with little information for much of the third century B.C. But the generalization that Roman magistrates by the early third

century were well accustomed to letting contracts for public building projects remains acceptable.

The near cataclysm and associated expenses of the Second Punic
War caused an understandable hiatus in magisterial building projects at Rome, and the period of recovery after the defeat of Hannibal in 202–201 B.C. seems to have continued into the following
decade. But in 196 B.C., Livy provides his first specific reference to a
building contract let in that year by the aediles for the construction
of a temple.[53] In 193 the curule aediles built two *porticus* (sing. and
pl.), both called Aemilia, for utilitarian purposes as well as a huge
wholesale market, called *Emporium,* next to the Tiber.[54] The next
year, the curule aediles built another porticus, which was paid for
with revenue from fines they had levied.[55]

By the 180s B.C. the economic recovery was complete and the
censors returned to public building in an extremely important way
beginning in 184 B.C. when M. Porcius Cato and L. Valerius Flaccus
held the magistracy and spent large amounts of money on new and
repair work to drains, the water supply, and the roads, as well as the
construction of the first basilica, the Basilica Porcia, in Rome. While
the evidence indicates that there was some senatorial opposition to
these schemes, it was much less than that exerted in the fourth
century B.C. against Appius Claudius Caecus's program of construction and probably reflects a generally more positive attitude toward
censorial proposals aimed at coping with the problems brought on
by the city's growth.[56] There were problems, however. We are told
that Cato and Valerius let their contracts in 184 at very low figures
in an attempt to cut down on the extraordinary profits being realized by contractors from public contracts. The Senate, under lobby-
ing pressure from the *equites,* cancelled those contracts, but Cato
and Flaccus managed to outmaneuver senators and knights by
forbidding any builders who had bid for the contracts in the first
auction to participate in the second. They ended up letting their
contracts for only slightly more than they had in the first round of
bidding.[57]

In 179 B.C., the censors M. Fulvius Nobilior and M. Aemilius
Lepidus enjoyed the allocation of an entire year's *vectigal,* or tax
revenue, for public building projects, which included the usual

provisions for maintenance and repair of the aqueducts, the road system, harbors, drains, and sanitation but also allowed the construction of the Basilica Aemilia in the Forum and was supposed to permit the construction of a new aqueduct. The last item was blocked by M. Licinius Crassus, who would not give right of way for it to cross land that he owned.[58] While we do not know the overall value of these contracts, Dionysius of Halicarnassus tells us that Fulvius and Aemilius spent some six million denarii on the sewers alone, and there seems no real reason to doubt his testimony.[59]

Sometimes it seems to have been necessary to manage different parts of a building project when holding different magistracies. Q. Fulvius Flaccus had vowed a temple when a *propraetor* in 181 B.C., arranged the appointment of *duumviri aedi locandae* during his consulate to oversee its construction, and finally dedicated the completed building while censor in 173.[60] In 169 B.C. the censors C. Claudius Pulcher and Ti. Sempronius Gracchus received an allocation of half a year's *vectigal* for public building projects, and they jointly let a whole series of contracts for projects that included the construction of the Basilica Sempronia. For a reason or reasons that remain unclear, Claudius and Sempronius chose to make it a condition of letting their contracts for that year that no contractors who had bid under the previous censors, in 174, could participate again. The contractors affected induced a tribune to intercede for them, but the censors managed to win a crucial vote in the Senate by the narrowest of margins and their contracts were enforced.[61]

The events of 169 B.C. offer a unique opportunity to study the censorial, and from their example the general magisterial, system of contracting for construction as it had evolved by the second century B.C. It has never been clear why the censors, in particular, came to be associated with public construction projects. Upon first glance at the general duties of magistrates under the Republican *cursus honorum*, it makes far more sense that this would be the more-or-less exclusive duty of the aediles. But responsibility for public building had been taken over in large part by the censors by the time of Appius Claudius Caecus, if not before, and they remained much more important in building than the aediles until the time of Augustus. Strong has given a convincing summary of the censors' finances:[62] the funds to be used for building during any five-year censorship were voted by the Senate and included any balance left to the credit of the new censors by the previous pair. Extraordinary additional grants could be made to the censors—as was done in 179 and 169 B.C.—from tax revenues. The decision on what to build with the money seems to have been left, usually, to the censors. There is only one instance in our sources when the Senate actually intervened and prevented the censors from building what they wanted: in 155 B.C. two censors who were widely distrusted wanted to build a permanent theater on the slope of the Palatine Hill. What had been constructed was destroyed on the ground that it was not a building that would be useful to the people in general.[63] Once in office and with funds appropriated, it appears that the censors' first duty was to let out maintenance contracts for public works by public auction held in the Forum. These auctions could be held only if the work of the last five years' contractors for maintenance had been approved by the previous censors. For new building, it seems that the censors usually divided responsibility for the component parts, one letting the contracts for one element, the other for another. It was considered very unusual when, in 169 B.C., the censors let all their contracts together.[64]

As Strong quite rightly points out, the censorial system of contracting for public building had serious disadvantages. Nonetheless it worked quite well, at least through the second century B.C. The problems included the fact that the censorship was a unique magistracy within the governmental system of Republican Rome, which was otherwise primarily made up of annually elected offices. But the censors were elected for a term of eighteen months only once every five years. Eighteen months was hardly sufficient time for the holders of the office to plan, contract for, and see to completion any kind of major building project, and, as we have noted, special exceptions and arrangements had to be made repeatedly in order for an important building to be completed according to the contract. Even more problematical, however, must have been the utter lack of any kind of professional staff to advise on, supervise, or carry out public works. This left the censors, generally aristocratic amateurs, at the mercy of contractors who seem quite often to have been untrustworthy. This was a problem that continued into the first century B.C. and was solved only under the early Empire.

It must be assumed that some sort of system of tendering competitive bids for these censorial contracts existed, but we do not know what it was. The building contract that survives from Puteoli may provide evidence for one element in the system. In that contract, payment was to be rendered to the builder in two parts, with the first half paid as an advance when the contract was signed but the remainder not payable until the work was completed and had successfully passed *probatio*.[65] Difficulties seem to have been fairly common with the censorial system of letting these contracts, as the disputes of 179 and 169 B.C. reveal. Nonetheless, the censorial system was surprisingly effective at least through the second century B.C., even when two unlikely figures served simultaneously as censors. Especially in the second century, it was to a large degree censorial contracting that resulted in the design and execution of new and very advanced works of architecture, new and exciting developments in construction technique (most important, of course, the discovery of the bonding properties of *pulvis puteolanum*, or pozzolana sand, which led to the development of *opus caementicium*), and the greatly extended and improved amenities necessary to a rapidly expanding city.

At the end of the second century B.C., however, the hegemonies of the Gracchi made it abundantly clear that, whatever the successes of the haphazard censorial system of public works, a professional public works administration for the city was badly needed. The Gracchi demonstrated for all to see that utilitarian projects, so essential to the comforts and indeed to the survival of Rome's inhabitants, could be accomplished most efficiently by one determined politician backed up by a great deal of money and some competent technical advisors. The roads Gaius Gracchus built and the speed with which they were completed underlined all too clearly the inherent weakness of the traditional system,[66] but until the dictatorship of Sulla nothing much was changed.

As in so many other areas of Roman life, the first century B.C. proved a crucial but crisis-oriented period of substantial change in the system of public building. While the censorial system remained intact, the rise to power of the great Roman *condottieri*—Marius, Sulla, Pompey, and Caesar—combined with the tremendous new technical possibilities that had been opened up to Roman architects and builders by the advances in techniques and design made during the second half of the second century B.C. led to a major change in the methods and control of public building. It was Sulla who combined, during his dictatorship in Rome, the necessary power, resources, and ambition and took advantage of the opportunity to undertake the first massive public building program in the capital. He indulged in all manner of grandiose projects including the rebuilding of the temple of Jupiter Capitolinus, the repaving of the Forum and (perhaps) rebuilding of the Curia and the Rostra, and the creation of the Tabularium.

The presiding genius, and completer, of most of these projects was Q. Lutatius Catulus, but Catulus seems, as was Sulla, to have had no interest in and wasted no time on, utilitarian projects, much less maintenance. The program of Sulla and Catulus was truly an attempt not just to maintain the city and provide an occasional new building, but to change the face of it for propagandistic ends.[67] This use of public works for proganda purposes and political prestige presaged what would happen soon thereafter; public building would become a kind of power play between the participants in the struggle for supremacy of the last decades of the Republic.

Not only did Sulla not overhaul the general system and functioning of public works administration, he rendered it even less efficient since no censors were appointed for a decade after his death and their absence rendered the old system utterly unusable. Other annual magistrates, with other duties to handle in addition, found themselves swamped under more maintenance contracts than they could possibly manage, and so extortion and fraud ran riot.[68] To keep the system from collapsing completely the whole spirit of the Republican system had to be abrogated and curators appointed to handle public works for long periods of time. Even so, public works were badly managed throughout the first two-thirds of the first century B.C., and by the time of Octavian's rise to power, their condition was desperate.

Pompey and Caesar, especially Caesar, continued the sort of building program that Sulla had initiated and at the same time added to the problems afflicting the traditional administration of public works. Pompey built a massive theater and porticus in the southern Campus Martius, along with a temple of Venus Victrix and a private mansion, projects that substantially altered the topography of that part of the city.[69] Meanwhile, Caesar bought up land for a new extension of the Forum and a huge new assembly and voting precinct in the Campus Martius. The new extension to the Forum removed senatorial business from the old city center, and the assembly and voting precinct nullified the need for the ancient Comitium in the Forum and replaced the ancient villa publica.[70] Needless to say, Caesar's new projects were just as much propaganda as Pompey's had been, but there does seem to have been a perception in them that the entire administration of public building had fallen into disarray and needed revamping. Even his most grandiose projects could be justified, for political purposes, as falling within the realm of necessary public works—such as finding larger and more efficient meeting places for Senate and Assembly—but nonetheless they also constituted blatant personal propaganda. By the last years of his dictatorship, there is some evidence that Caesar had come to realize the grave needs of the city and, following the example that had been apparent since the time of Gaius Gracchus, turned the absolute authority of his dictatorship, as well as the limitless resources of his *manubiae,* toward maintaining and repairing the city's fabric, as well as glorifying it with masterpieces of architecture. For instance, a comprehensive city plan seems to have been in preparation in 45 B.C., and we know that the Senate passed a bill for enlargement of the city which included a project that would have completely reshaped the Campus Martius even canalizing the Tiber River into a new course, as Cicero somewhat grumpily told Atticus in a letter of (probably) early July, 45 B.C.:[71]

> Capito happened to be talking of the enlargement of the city, saying that the Tiber is being diverted at the Mulvian bridge to run alongside of the Vatican hills, that the Campus Martius is being built over and the other Campus, the Vaticanus, is becoming a new Campus Martius.

"What's that?" said I, "I was going to the auction to buy the Scapula estate if I could get it at a reasonable figure." "Better not," said he. "This law will go through. Caesar wants it."

Even to Cicero, Caesar's plan seemed extraordinarily far-reaching. Equally, if not more, important for the administration of public building in the city, it seems clear that Caesar was reorganizing the whole procedure, supplying himself with a staff of trained architects and engineers (at least as consultants for his projects), and aiming at achieving absolute control over all aspects of building for public purposes.[72] This comprehensive reorganization was interrupted by his assassination in 44 B.C., but much of it, as we shall see, was finally completed by Augustus, though probably in somewhat different form and a good deal more slowly than Caesar had intended. It was reform nearly a century overdue.

PUBLIC BUILDING DURING THE EMPIRE

Octavian continued and completed many parts of Caesar's building program, but the comprehensive reorganization of the city plan itself was mostly abandoned. Octavian encouraged all sorts of wealthy aristocrats to contribute to the architectural glorification of the city, and managed to persuade distinguished men such as Asinius Pollio, Munatius Plancus, Domitius Ahenobarbus, Statilius Taurus, Marcius Philippus, Lucius Cornificius, and Domitius Calvinus to contribute major new buildings.[73] Of course, he also did extensive building himself, including the temple to Apollo on the Palatine, the Porticus Octaviae and its libraries, the theater dedicated in memory of Marcellus, the Mausoleum, and his own Forum with its temple to Mars Ultor. Propaganda played a part in most of these items, to be sure, as did remembrance of his murdered adoptive father, but they also contributed to his ultimate aim of turning Rome into a city visually and architecturally worthy to be considered the center of the universe.[74] But Octavian realized that he needed to go far beyond glorious architectural creations: the functioning fabric of the city was deteriorating alarmingly, and the system for maintaining and repairing it was in hopeless disarray. His efforts to convince some of the wealthier senators to put some of their own money, or spoils of war (*manubiae*), into the repair of roads, for instance, met with little success.[75]

As early as 33 B.C., it had become apparent to Octavian that he would have to reorganize the public works administration, and in that year he began by persuading Marcus Agrippa to assume the office of aedile, in which he was to take on a vast responsibility for every facet of public works and public building in the city. The aedileship, like the censorship, had fallen largely out of use in the decades preceding 33 B.C., and very little of the office's traditional *cura urbis* had been exercised,[76] much to the city's detriment. Agrippa's program as aedile would have been unthinkably broad at any previous point in Roman history. Agrippa undertook repairs and long-deferred maintenance of the roads, buildings of every sort, and the water system, while at the same time reorganizing the services that were responsible for them. He repaired the three republican aqueducts—the Appia, Anio Vetus, and Marcia—and began the new Aqua Julia. He also made detailed arrangements for the maintenance of the aqueducts in the future and continued to take direct responsibility for them after 33 B.C. To carry out this last task, Agrippa had to reorganize the whole water operation, and he did so by setting up a permanent staff of stonemasons and other skilled or semiskilled workmen, who provided the core of an efficient department responsible for this essential public work.[77] For these and other building projects, Agrippa maintained a large, professional, highly organized staff of advisers, supervisors, architects, and agents, which at his death in 12 B.C. may have numbered as many as 240 workers involved with the aqueducts alone. This staff must have provided the model not only for the Imperial water board but also for what was to become in later reigns the permanent construction board called the *opera Caesaris*.[78]

While Agrippa may well have provided the model for the later Imperial public works administration, it is quite clear that Augustus (as Octavian became in 27 B.C.) did not attempt to set up any kind of single central authority to handle these tasks. That was a reform for a later reign. What he did do was twofold: he removed his program of new building projects completely from contact with those officials responsible for maintenance and repair of public works (for which he devised a permanent bureaucracy) and initiated a policy of setting up permanent boards supervised by *curatores* which would have the responsibility in perpetuity for maintaining and repairing essential public works. Augustus did this only after the failure of his effort to revive the office of censor in 22 B.C., but that debacle was followed in 20 by creation of a permanent maintenance board for roads under a *curator viarum*, and in 11 by a board to maintain and repair the water system supervised by a *curator aquarum*. Late in his reign, though the date is uncertain, a third board was created that had responsibility for public buildings and shrines (the *curatores operum publicorum*), and at the very end of his reign, in ca. A.D. 14, he created a fourth board to oversee the condition of the banks and riverbed of the Tiber.[79] Of these boards, we know by far the most about the water board, but before investigating it as an example of the administration of public building under the high Empire, we must survey briefly how public building was administered from the death of Augustus in A.D. 14 until the establishment of the *opera Caesaris*, possibly by Domitian, near the end of that century.

Augustus's reformed system of administration remained essentially unchanged well into the last years of the first century A.D. Control of public works passed slowly but seemingly inexorably out of private control into the Imperial administration. The process is well described by Strong.[80] We know that, beginning with the reign of Claudius (A.D. 41–54), all the various boards for public works administration were operating officially *ex auctoritate Caesaris*, no longer even attempting to preserve the myth of functioning *ex auctoritate senatus*, as Augustus had maintained.[81] Their finances were provided not from the nominally senate-controlled *aerarium* but directly from the Imperial *fiscus*. More and more, every form of public works, whether new or not, came under the control of Claudius's staff, probably in part because of the increase in private and quasi-private building undertaken by the Julio-Claudians. As more and more buildings were put up by the emperors and their relations, they seem to have needed and maintained an ever growing staff of architects and other skilled builders who were kept completely distinct from builders working on public construction projects for the official boards. Their main charge was to maintain and repair the Imperial family's own possessions. After the fire of A.D. 64, Nero assumed responsibility for rebuilding the city, apparently making use of his own architects and planners. While his plan for altering the whole face of the city seems never to have been completed,[82] it did add to the power and influence of the emperor's building staff and put them in positions of supervisory authority over much of the city's architecture.

The accession of the Flavians seems to have led to ever greater concentration of public works administration in Imperial hands. This development led eventually to the establishment of a massive public works department called the *opera Caesaris,* which became the dominating official presence in Roman public architecture from that time forward.[83] By Trajan's reign it had become customary for all public building projects to be scrutinized by the emperor's staff, which now controlled almost every aspect of architecture and city planning and was even exercising supervisory rights over maintenance and repair. The emperors wanted such control over building, in part, for propaganda purposes, given how effectively architecture and public building had served to promote the policies of Augustus and Domitian. While our information is too dispersed and fragmentary to undertake anything like a full study of the *opera Caesaris* in all its vast size and myriad duties, we can look more closely at the water board, as it was set up and functioning at the end of the first century A.D., contemporary with the creation of the *opera Caesaris,* as a microcosm of the whole Imperial system of public works administration.

It is important to remember that, despite the growth of the Imperial construction bureaucracy just described, private builders and building contracts, including contracts for builders who provided services to the state, did not disappear with Augustus. On the contrary, the evidence is quite extensive that they continued to function in much the same way, using the same sorts of contracts, as they long had. Certainly, there is plenty of evidence to show that, until the foundation of the *opera Caesaris,* which cannot be before A.D. 81 and may well have been later, and possibly afterward, the contract system for building continued to function throughout Roman Italy.[84] While the Roman state was beginning to organize the resources needed to carry out building projects on its own under Augustus, contracts continued to be let regularly for private supply of public building projects until the reign of Domitian. What we see developing throughout the first century A.D. is a branch of the civil service controlled by the emperor rather than the senate, with responsibility for public works administration and at the same time a general Imperial organizing of the industries that supplied building materials and, to a lesser extent, manpower under the management of an Imperial board. The water board continued at least through the curatorship of Frontinus to let contracts with private builders for certain specific things that needed to be done and for which the contractors could provide the skilled workers and specific supplies required.

Our detailed knowledge of the water system of Rome is due primarily to the survival of Frontinus's treatise *De Aquae Ductu.* Sextus Julius Frontinus was an important public official throughout the Flavian period and into the reign of Trajan. He served as *curator aquarum* for only a year, A.D. 97, and published his description of the water system in ca. A.D.100. Thus he is describing the water system as it existed at the very end of the first century A.D. He seems to have been born in Gallia Narbonensis, and he began his career in the military. He first held important office in A.D. 70, when he was *praetor urbanus;* he was consul in either 72 or 73; in 73 or 74 he replaced Petilius Cerealis as governor of the province of Britannia, a command he only relinquished in 77 or 78 to Gnaeus Julius Agricola. He was probably involved in military campaigns during the reign of Domitian, perhaps the first war against the Chatti, and was also honored by that emperor with the post of proconsul of Asia in A.D. 85–86. He then disappears from our record for a decade but returns with the accession of Nerva to the purple, in the autumn of A.D. 96, first elected to a commission charged with reducing public expenditure, then appointed *curator aquarum* in 97. He was consul for a second time in 98 and for a third time in 100. He died ca. A.D. 103–104.[85]

The water board as set up under Agrippa had used a gang of some 240 slaves. Upon Agrippa's death, Augustus made these slaves *servi publici* who would work for the *curator aquarum,* and they were called the *familia publica.* With the construction of two new aqueducts under Claudius—the Claudia and the Anio Novus—the workforce attached to the *familia* of the *curator aquarum* was increased by 460 men, called *familia Caesaris,* to a total of 700, and these men were distributed throughout the city.[86] Frontinus states that within this *familia aquarum* there were men with various quasi-specialized skills, including *vilici* (overseers), *castellarii* (reservoir-keepers), *cicitores* (inspectors), *silicarii* (pavers), *tectores* (plasterers) and, more vaguely, *alii opifices* (other workers).[87] Of altogether higher status and free, or at least freed, within the *cura aquarum* were the members of the so-called office staff, which included *architecti* (architects),[88] *scribae* (secretaries), *librarii* (clerks), *accensi* (assistants), and *praecones* (heralds). These various persons are labeled *apparitores* (attendants) slightly later in the same passage, which would seem pretty well to describe their social rank as well as their function.[89] Two other specialists mentioned elsewhere in Frontinus's treatise probably shared the rank of the "office staff," but there seems no way to tell whether these were regular positions in the *familia* or terms for specialists brought in for consultation as needed: the *libratores* (levellers) and the *plumbarii* (plumbers). Their titles clearly refer to hydraulic engineers, whom one would suppose must be part of the regular staff of the water board, but the context in which Frontinus mentions them makes them sound like part of a different division of the *cura,* so perhaps they had their own engineering department.[90]

While such an extensive bureaucracy clearly demonstrates that a great deal of the constant maintenance and repair required by the aqueducts was performed by the water board's *familia* and *cura,* Frontinus himself clearly indicates that in his administration the water board still contracted with independent specialists for their services when needed, including *architecti* outside the *cura,*[91] presumably for second opinions when there were major problems or disagreements. It is also interesting to note that, before 11 B.C., *curatores aquarum* had always contracted with private *redemptores* for the labor and skills needed to keep the water system working well and that those *redemptores* who wanted to bid for the contracts

were legally required to maintain fixed numbers of slaves sufficient
to accomplish the work inside and outside the city.[92] Certainly the
noticeable expansion of the aqueduct system in the early Empire
required a much larger workforce to keep them clean and functioning, and perhaps it was thought cheaper or more efficient (or both)
if they were under the direct control of government officials. But the
use of contractors was by no means eliminated. Frontinus states
specifically that the *curator aquarum* is responsible for deciding
"what is to carried out by public contractors and what by his own
regular workmen," and later he mentions hiring "contractors for
repairing the conduits."[93] Beyond maintenance and repair, it would
seem that specific initiatives begun by the *curator aquarum* would
also have been contracted out. Frontinus mentions that he arranged
to have maps of all the aqueduct lines extant in his administration
drawn and mentions that the details on these maps included valleys
crossed by the aqueducts, rivers, and hillside sections. It seems
extremely likely that this work would have been done by professional mapmakers, probably chosen from the ranks of the *agrimensores* (land measurers), a professional body of surveyors in Imperial
times, since Frontinus clearly implies that such a mapping of the
aqueducts was so rare as to be unprecedented and therefore not a
part of the regular duties of the *familia aquarum*.[94] Clearly a dual
system of government workers and contracted labor—brought in
either from private sources or, as is probable in the case of the
mapmakers, from other agencies of the Imperial bureaucracy—
existed through the end of the first century A.D., and there is no
particular reason to assume it disappeared later.

The contracts let may well have been, at times, quite substantial.[95] Sadly we have no real way of calculating the scale in supplies
and manpower, and very little way of calculating the price, of any
major building projects; recent attempts at statistical analysis have
proven woefully inadequate.[96] But that long-term requirements
such as the water system or the roads, as well as sudden huge spurts
of building activity, might require the services of building and materials contractors over and beyond what could be supplied by the
Imperial administration should not, perhaps, surprise us. And of
course, private building seems to have continued under the Empire

and it was not managed, staffed, or supplied by the Imperial bureaucracy.

The Organization of Public and Private Building

During the Republic, practically all construction work, public or private, in the Roman world was accomplished by building contracts formed between two parties, one the landowner and the other the builder.[97] We have seen that from at least the fourth century B.C. the Roman censors let contacts for major public works to *redemptores,* and the other magistrates, including the aediles and praetors as well as specially appointed *curatores,* proceeded in the same manner. Private construction throughout Roman history remained a matter of contract between the landowner and builder. In order to understand how building was accomplished, then, we need to turn to the people who accepted these contracts and explore the ancient evidence concerning them. We need to know who bid for and accepted building contracts and what kinds of people they in turn employed.

THE CONTRACTORS: *REDEMPTORES* AND *PUBLICANI*

For the earliest centuries of Roman history we have little if any evidence for who accepted building contracts. In the very earliest times, there may have been relatively little contracting; we know that in the sixth century B.C. Roman citizens were required by Tarquinius Priscus to donate their labor (*plebis manibus*) for the construction of essential drains,[98] much to their disgruntlement. Until the middle of the Roman Republic we cannot tell whether contracts were let with individual builders and artisans or, as subsequently became the practice, with entrepreneurs—the *redemptores* and *conductores* of Roman contract law—who could provide some of the required elements and knew where to subcontract the rest. The first really useful evidence we find comes from Livy and dates to 215 B.C. Livy tells of men who were engaged in contracting (though not necessarily building) and that nineteen of them were grouped into three associations (*societates*) which were offering to provide on contract (*conducendum*) clothes and food for the military.[99] The senate apparently went along with the suggestion since the members were not willing to offend the *ordo publicanorum,* to which these associations belonged. Indeed, Livy specifically describes one of the nineteen men in one of the associations as a *publicanus.*[100] Livy paints a picture that suggests that, as early as the late third century B.C., there were certain types of men who regularly attended censorial auctions of public contracts and knew the procedures and requirements involved. These men he terms *publicani.*

Roman *publicani* tend to receive a very bad press in historical and popular writing because in the New Testament they are tax collectors in Judaea, regarded as officials of the very lowest type and morally as sinners not worthy of association. Jesus' solicitude for them was considered at best unwise, rather like his consideration for lepers.[101] In fact, *publicani* were private citizens who, for a price and for concessions, contracted with various branches of the Roman government to provide various services the government found too inconvenient or too costly to undertake itself. One of these, and obviously the most infamous, was collecting taxes in the provinces. This is what the *publicani* of the New Testament were up to; actually they were not *publicani* at all but the local agents of *publicani* who were themselves working on contract or long-standing agreement for the actual publicans in Rome. The local agents were loathed as tax collectors on behalf of a foreign power are usually loathed, and they were labeled by the Latin word which properly described their employers.

But tax collecting was not the only form of contract that *publicani* could and did accept in the Roman world. Those who undertook government contracts for public building were also classified as *publicani.*[102] Livy records a number of examples of building work contracted out by various magistrates, not only the censors, after 215 B.C., and he regularly calls those who accepted such contracts *redemptores,* but until 184 B.C. and the censorship of L. Valerius Flaccus and M. Porcius Cato, he does not once identify these men or provide any other essential information about them.[103] As mentioned previously, when these censors tried to let the building contracts for that year at extremely low prices in order to save money for the state treasury, the senate was so dismayed by the uproar of the *publicani* who intended to bid that the contracts were disbarred and the censors ordered to try again. Flaccus and Cato did so, but (in a puzzling move, presumably to punish them) eliminated all *redemptores* who had refused the earlier contracts from bidding for the new ones, and some money was ultimately saved when the contracts were let at prices a little lower than the previous ones.[104] An interesting implication of this odd story is noted by Badian: Plutarch seems to indicate that the low prices of the first round of contracts would have permitted the *publicani* to make no profit at all on them. Even in the second round these same bidders may have been forced to bid for all sorts of contracts, specifically revenue contracts and contracts for *ultro tributa* (among which building contracts were included), in order just to break even. If Badian's interpretation is correct, it would seem to show that as of 184 B.C. the *publicani* were not rigidly specialized but capable of accepting contracts for the collection of revenues and for furnishing supplies at the same time if necessary, although they presumably were not happy about it.[105] If this is true there can be little doubt that the contractors, who were being squeezed by the censors, would simply have in their turn forced their collection agents and employees to accept smaller profits, and those agents would then have extorted profit in other ways from their collecting or out of what they supplied. Earlier in this episode, Livy implies that the *publicani*, to whose troubles he is just turning, were severely treated during this censorship as were the *equites* in general.[106] This would appear to set building contractors, along with all those accepting public contracts, firmly into the Roman equitorial class.

Dealing with the censorship of a decade later, 169 B.C., Livy directly links the *publicani* with the *equites*. He states that the censors in that year, C. Claudius Pulcher and Ti. Sempronius Gracchus, found much to criticize in the class of the *equites* and removed a number of them from that rank, also attempting to bar, as we have seen, any *publicani* who had held public contracts under the previous censorship (i.e., contracts issued in 174 B.C.) from bidding for new contracts. The *publicani* invoked tribunician intervention and later nearly defeated the censors in a trial over their actions.[107] The whole episode brings a number of important pieces of evidence to us in our search for Roman *redemptores*. Here for the first time Livy states clearly that contractors for public duties were drawn from the *equites*. Thus they were generally from the upper middle class of Roman society and quite respectable, men who were the leaders of the emerging middle class that controlled so much of commerce, trade, and industry in the Roman world. Their influence was obviously considerable if they could come so close to nullifying and overturning a decree of the censors, since the censorship was one of the oldest and most respected of the traditional Roman magistracies. In the last phrase of the edict issued by the censors to prevent the previous contractors from participating in the auction, Livy uses these words: *sociusve aut adfinis eius conditionis esset* ("nor should he be a partner nor a sharer in the contract").[108] This is wording typical of contracts. It shows for the first time that an individual might be regarded as a partner (*socius*) or a sharer or participant (*adfinis*) in a censorial contract, and the vocabulary recalls directly the description of the supply contractors of 215 B.C. who were divided into three *societates*. Livy himself clearly sees these contractors as men of substantial wealth and social position, as *equites,* by the middle Republic, even to the suggestion that they were attempting to gain some form of political influence when he calls them the *ordo publicanorum*. There can be little doubt that the *publicani* had increased their power to an extraordinary degree during this period, but evidence for any attempt to abrogate political power as an ordo is slight.[109]

By the second quarter of the second century B.C., as we have seen, there had begun a notable increase in the number and probably in the value of public building contracts to be let, which implies that more and more regular work was available to the *redemptores* and their crews. This is substantiated when we recall that some of the building work recorded by Livy for the early second century B.C. was construction aimed at delivery, storage, and distribution of building materials and supplies (as well as other materials), when projects such as the Emporium on the banks of the Tiber and the portico for timber dealers set up outside the Emporium were built.[110] Growth in the building industry and the increased complexity of what was contracted for from the censors are surely also implied in situations such as that in 169 B.C. when the projects let on contract were so extensive that the censors were unable to perform the required *probationes* within their statutory eighteenmonth terms of office and applied unsuccessfully for a prolongation of their term.[111] Such demands on the building industry presumably led to higher levels of organization—probably reflected in the *societates* mentioned by Livy—and also to some form of specialization among the various builders.

The *societates* are much better attested among the tax-farming *publicani* than among those involved in building, but their function was likely the same: they were groups of able and usually wealthy businessmen who contributed capital to the schemes and initiatives of their *societas* and probably also constituted its top levels of management. They would be Livy's "partners and sharers" in contracts, and in building contracts they would presumably have been responsible for providing surety money and covering expenses not handled by the state.[112] In turn, the actual building work would be in part subcontracted to specialists—for decorative stone carving, supplying and cutting timber, decorative stucco work, and the like—and it is relatively unlikely that the building contractors or the *societates* would have maintained huge labor forces or staffs of specialists, since they would have had little if any certainty of obtaining sufficient contracts for specific types of building to make the expense of such a force worthwhile. As so often happens in building in any age, it would seem probable that particular contractors had firm, if unwritten, agreements with various subcontractors to whom they regularly let parts of the work for which they held contracts, but these would have been independent subcontractors, not part of a permanent staff for the *publicanus*. It is equally likely that the very *societates* themselves were not permanent, but were fluid associations of men who could raise money for particular contracts. In sum, as Pearse wisely puts it, their "importance and function can perhaps be better comprehended if we term them not contractors but entrepreneurs."[113]

There is some apposite confirmation for this analysis in Polybius,[114] who says he is describing the building contractors and their industry as it existed at the start of the Second Punic War.

> Throughout the whole of Italy a vast number of contracts, which it
> would not be easy to enumerate, are given out by the censors for the
> construction and repair of public buildings, and besides this there are
> many things which are farmed (out), such as navigable rivers, habours,
> gardens, mines, lands, in fact everything that forms part of the Roman
> dominion. Now all these matters are undertaken by the people, and one
> may almost say that everyone is interested in these contracts and the
> work they involve. For certain people are the actual purchasers of the
> contracts, others are the partners of these first, others stand surety for
> them, others pledge their own fortunes to the state for this purpose.

Polybius may exaggerate the extent of censorial contracting when
he extends it to all of Italy, at least for building, since there is no
evidence at all to back up the statement, and we know that by the
first century B.C., after the Social War, building contracts outside
Rome were let by local magistrates and that this had begun at least
as early as the *Lex Puteolana* of 105 B.C., which was let locally.[115] It is
interesting that Polybius does not specifically mention the *equites,*
but rather says that everyone takes part. But on the specific groups
involved in the contracts he is remarkably specific. He lists those
who purchased the contracts from the censors, Livy's *publicani* or
redemptores (ἀργράζουσι τὰς ἐκδόσεις); partners of these, the
socii (κοιωοῦσι); those who stand surety, the *adfines* (ἐγγυῶνται);
and those who pledge their fortunes on behalf of the contractors,
whom he terms τὰς οὐσίας διδόασι. The parallel between this
terminology and Livy's Latin vocabulary is apparent, and it further
confirms Livy's testimony in that Polybius, too, clearly thinks of
these builders and their associates as men of wealth. Thus the legal
structure of censorial contracting, and its primary practitioners,
seem clearly described by Livy and Polybius.

If any confirmation of the terminology and the existence of
contracting is needed beyond this testimony, both Appian and Plutarch, describing Rome a century later than Polybius purports to,
state that because there was a great deal of building instituted by
Gaius Gracchus, many contractors (ἐργολαβόι) and craftsmen
(χειροτέχναι, τεχνῖται) obtained employment at that time.[116] So
the contracting system, the contractors themselves, their business
associates, and presumably all the skilled subcontractors, artisans,

stonemasons, woodworkers and so on with whom they had to work were a well-organized sector in Roman working society by the middle to later second century B.C. C. Blossius, son of Quintus and the contractor of the *Lex Puteolana* in 105 B.C., is the first *redemptor* named in the history of Roman architecture. Blossius seems to have acted as his own surety; four other names are added to the contract after his, and their function has been variously described. Following the terminology laid out by Polybius, these men ought to be examples of those who pledged their own fortunes (or property) on behalf of Blossius.[117]

The evidence for *redemptores* becomes much fuller and more revealing in the first century B.C., particularly in the information provided by Cicero. For public building there are a number of informative testimonia. In his Second Verrine oration, while discussing how Verres had handled building maintenance as praetor, Cicero offers testimony from two men who had given money to Verres so that he would, we presume, allot contracts to them. Cn. Fannius is directly described as an *eques Romanus,* and Q. Tadius was a relative of Verres' mother and so most likely also an *eques.*[118] This passage immediately precedes the notorious tale of Verres' fiddling the contract for maintenance of the temple of Castor in the Roman Forum, in which two more building contractors are named. The first is P. Iunius, who had accepted the original contract from the consuls in 80 B.C. and who had equestrian relatives although Cicero describes him as a plebeian;[119] the second is named Habonius (or Rabonius), the man whom Verres tricked into taking the much more costly new maintenance contract, whose status is not mentioned, but whom Cicero explicitly labels *redemptor,* and who was apparently not under Verres' influence and so had to be deceived.[120] This becomes doubly interesting if Iunius and Habonius, as Cicero states in the first case and implies in the second, were plebeians rather than knights; if so they provide direct evidence that not just equestrian *publicani* but men of lower rank could also take part in, and perhaps even bid at, the auctions for public building contracts.[121] By the 80s and 70s B.C. it is clear that *redemptores* were a regular feature—indeed together with architects one of the two most essential features—of the Roman building industry. They continue to be the producers of almost all public building well into the age of Augustus, and it is significant that they appear in the *Lex Iulia Municipalis,* where they are an accepted and normal part of the system.[122]

In a brief passage that is describing the procedures of maintaining the aqueducts during the Republic, Frontinus says:[123]

> The care of the several aqueducts I find was regularly let out to contractors (*redemptoribus*) and the obligation was imposed on these of having a fixed number of slave workmen (*servorum opificum*) on the aqueducts outside the City, and another fixed number within the City; and of entering in the public records the names also of those whom they intended to employ in the service for each region of the city.

It is no real surprise that the maintenance of individual aqueducts was let out on contract; that was standard practice, as we have seen, for other public buildings, too. What is significant here is that these contracts were such a regular and expected thing that *redemptores* who wished to bid for them were required to keep gangs of slaves for the work and that the names of those slaves had to be entered in the public records for every area of the city. There is no doubt at all that the aqueducts were leaky and in constant need of attention and that at the same time they were of primary importance to the city's sanitation and well being.[124] But the terms laid out by Frontinus as those required of *redemptores* hoping to win maintenance contracts for an aqueduct or a section of an aqueduct surely indicate that these were fairly specialized arrangements. It is difficult to conceive of there being several different contractors with the required labor force all properly registered risking so substantial an investment on a truly competitive contract. Surely we should assume that these contracts tended to be allotted to the same *redemptores* every time. But the aqueducts are a special case. This testimony does not imply that regular building contractors kept their own personal labor forces. General public building contracts must have been far more competitive and could be fulfilled mostly or entirely through subcontracting and ad hoc hiring for all needed skills, materials, and unskilled labor.

Cicero's letters give us the names, and glimpses, of several private building contractors during the first century B.C. Despite the political and military unrest of much of that century in Italy, it would appear that there was a substantial boom in private building throughout the period, and it is quite likely, since the public contract system was already in place as was the industry to support it, that this new demand for private work was handled, to a large degree at least, by many of the same people who accepted public construction contracts.[125] In chapter 1 we investigated the named, and probable, *architecti* who worked for Marcus and Quintus Cicero—including Cyrus, Chrysippus, Corumbus, Numisius, Caesius, and Rufio—and we have also already considered Cluatius (who was commissioned to create Tullia's *fanum*). Here I want to turn to the remaining builders attested in the letters who are either described directly as *redemptores* or whose duties are described in such a way that it seems a better case can be made for them as building contractors than as architects. Inevitably some of these designations are matters of individual interpretation; where others who have studied this material do not agree with my view, I shall cite the various alternatives proposed.

Longilius

Twice Marcus wrote to Quintus in Sardinia in the spring of 56 B.C., after he had visited the site, concerning repairs that were being carried out to Quintus's house on the Palatine Hill. He reports in the first letter that he has made payment of half the agreed price to the *redemptor.* Apparently Marcus had the *redemptor* working together with various *fabri*, and a significant revamping of the Ciceros' properties on the Palatine was underway; Marcus's house next door was also being repaired while he was at the same time involved in remodeling others of his houses and building new structures on three more sites, all of which has stretched Marcus's finances.[126] In a follow-up letter written in April, Marcus is far more informative. He reports to his brother that everything is moving along well, there are lots of builders (*structores*) at work on the house, the *redemptor,* whose name is Longilius, has promised to give satisfaction, and Marcus thinks he will do so.[127] Longilius is referred to only by his *nomen*, which probably indicates *ingenuus* status, certainly that of a *libertus* at least. He has obviously accepted a building contract from Quintus Cicero, and there seems no reason to doubt he is the *redemptor* to whom Marcus paid the *dimidium* the month before. We know that Longilius and his *structores* were building to a plan (*forma*), but there is no mention at all that Longilius had drawn it up. Indeed it would seem a good deal more likely that it might be from the hand of one of the Ciceros' usual architects, Cyrus or Numisius, if not by Quintus himself.[128]

There are a number of things we do not know: how many builders were working with Longilius (*multi* can mean almost anything here)? Were they slaves or free workers on contract to Longilius? Was Longilius also in charge of the repairs to Marcus's adjacent dwelling? Was he connected to any of the other projects Marcus mentions in the same letter? It does appear, from the tone of Cicero's remarks (in which Longilius appears to be very much the man in charge), that Longilius is the contractor for the entire project let out by Quintus. Marcus's tone of approval of Longilius's work, and the close eye he is clearly keeping on the progress, might imply that he was also contractor for repairs to Marcus's own house, but that is nowhere stated. It would appear that work to Quintus's house was still going on two years later, when Marcus comments that there are *redemptores* there doing plastering and finishing (*expolitiones*), but we are not told whether Longilius is still involved or not. Indeed Longilius is never mentioned again.[129] He seems a fairly straightforward example of a building contractor working in the private sphere. He took on a contract for apparently fairly extensive rebuilding of Quintus's pre-existing house on the Palatine, was paid half the agreed price in advance, had brought in *structores* to handle the actual work and was working along with them, had the good business sense to be extremely polite to Quintus's brother when he came nosing around the site, and in general seems to have behaved as a professional builder should. If the *multi structores* were only a handful—between five and ten, for example— it is possible to hypothesize, with Pearse,[130] that he may have kept a small permanent labor force as part of his business, but there is absolutely no need to do so. He could just as well have hired workers as he needed them.

Mescidius, Philoxenus, and Cillo

The Cicero brothers were still deeply involved with construction in 54 B.C., when Marcus described to Quintus the complications he encountered in getting some sort of irrigation canal dug on the Arcanum, a property near Arpinum. Two men, named Mescidius and Philoxenus, had already dug one watercourse and had agreed with Quintus to do another one on his nearby estate at Bovillae for a price of three sesterces per foot. Apparently the contract is already settled, when Marcus summons Cillo, also a builder of some kind, but finds out that four of Cillo's workers have recently been hurt or killed in the collapse of a tunnel.[131] The passage is at best ambiguous. We are told that Mescidius was not a member of Quintus's *familia,* so was working as an independent contractor; Philoxenus could be his partner, his slave, or one of Quintus's slaves on the estate who had been told to help Mescidius. The summons of Cillo carries the implication that he, or at least his *conservi et discipuli,* were intended to provide the extra labor needed for this second watercourse. What is clear is that it was Mescidius, and possibly Philoxenus as partner, who had concluded the contract with Quintus; Cillo and his gang were mere afterthoughts of Marcus's, and they were not available anyway because of their mishap. While it is reasonable to assume that Mescidius, or Mescidius and Philoxenus, were functioning as independent irrigation contractors, there is no reason at all to assume that Cillo was involved except as a possible source of extra labor.

The social status of these three named builders is difficult to assess. It seems most likely, on account of his rare *nomen,* that Mescidius was an *ingenuus,* and we know he was not a permanent employee of the Arcanum estate. Philoxenus could be either slave or freedman but probably not higher in rank (although that does not in any way preclude his having functioned as a contractor) and his association with Mescidius could be of long standing or merely situational if he were attached to the estate. Of Cillo we can really say very little. He was not the contractor for this job. The manner in which Marcus thinks he can presume on Cillo and his workers would not imply much independence, and it is perfectly possible that Cillo was a local Arpinate contractor whom Marcus thought would be easily available to lend muscle or a slave of Quintus's who specialized in building projects and led a group of men or (in some ways most likely of all) a *libertus* who had continued to work with his former, and still servile, companions. It is an error to label him a building contractor on the evidence of this letter, since it says nothing of the sort nor implies it.[132] What is more interesting in this situation is the clear implication that Mescidius, the contractor, was not required to provide the labor himself. This is in keeping with the model contract for country building preserved to us from Cato, as we have seen, but is fairly unusual.

Nicephorus

In the same letter, Marcus tells Quintus that he has paid a visit to Laterium, where Quintus hopes to build an *aedificatiuncula* (a very small building). His *vilicus,* Nicephorus, had contracted to complete the job for 16,000 sesterces but subsequently withdrew from the contract since Quintus had added requirements to the job but not increased the price to be paid for it. It seems most probable that Nicephorus, since he was a *vilicus* (overseer), was also a slave. The reason for the contract would be, presumably, that this was a very special and expensive job that could have—and probably should have—been let to an independent builder, and Quintus agreed to let it to Nicephorus precisely so that the slave would be bound by its legal terms and obligations. Quintus then appears to have presumed on Nicephorus's servile status to behave illegally himself and try to get more for his money than the contract stated. Clearly, Nicephorus had the legal option of withdrawing from the contract and did so; what the long-term consequences were to a slave who reneged on his master, even when the master behaved improperly, we are not told.[133]

Diphilus

Lastly, returning for a moment to the episode at Quintus's Manilian property near Arpinum, the description that Cicero gives of that project—either new construction or extensive remodeling and upgrading—gives the distinct impression that the builder, Diphilus, whom Cicero upbraids for his dilatoriness, is serving in the role of *redemptor.* Cicero's inspection tour has all the marks of a *locator's* interim *probatio operis,* and it is clear that Marcus was fulfilling the role of *locator* on his brother's behalf throughout his brother's absence. The reassurance Marcus sent to Quintus, that Caesius is now in place and overseeing the job carefully (*curat*), suggests that Caesius is an *architectus* who, at Cicero's behest, is keeping a sharp eye on the contractor Diphilus in response to an unsatisfactory interim *probatio.* Of course, neither Diphilus's nor Caesius's exact role is given by title in the letter, but this reading of the evidence seems both appropriate and likely given the circumstances described.[134]

Several conclusions may be drawn from this evidence before we turn to *redemptores* of the Imperial period. It is interesting that Cicero does not tell us if any of these contractors had any specific area(s) of expertise in building. It would seem reasonable to assume that Mescidius (and Philoxenus if he is a partner rather than a workman) specialized in exterior hydraulic projects, like irrigation canals, but there is no specific mention of this. Longilius seems to be overseeing a major project of domestic architectural restoration and expansion and one can hypothesize a specialization in it, but since he is nowhere mentioned again, it must remain a supposition. Nicephorus, as a *vilicus,* was really an estate supervisor who had unwisely taken on an architectural contract; Diphilus like Longilius seems to be in charge of a major suburban villa construction, but there is no reason to think he was any kind of specialist. In short, we cannot draw from this information the conclusion that *redemptores* specialized in specific types of buildings, although it would appear to offer possible corroboration to such a conclusion. Only for the aqueducts can we safely draw the conclusion that *redemptores* who worked on them specialized in it and could rely on being awarded such contracts regularly. We should note that the development of *opus caementicium* by the second century B.C. must have greatly speeded up the process of building and also reduced the number of workers needed for any one project; construction from cut stone would require a much larger number of workers.[135] Since jobs such as finishing, plastering, and painting are indicated as part of the contracted job, it seems reasonable to assume that the contractor had to sublet those parts of the job to specialists and that the contracts would have contained specifications for them.

From the time of Augustus onward, it becomes increasingly difficult to distinguish contractors engaged on public projects from those involved in private construction. Their names, together with the label *redemptor,* appear on inscriptions from various parts of the Roman Empire. Some can be dated with fair precision, others not. They appear hardly at all in our literary sources for the Empire. The only possible exception may be the Imperial freedman Narcissus, whom Claudius put in charge of the gigantic project to drain the Fucine Lake, but he is at least as likely to have been a unique supervisory appointee trusted by the emperor to oversee a pet project as to have been functioning as a contractor.[136] Aside from so unusual a case as Narcissus's, the *redemptor* was a well-recognized type of businessman in Augustan Rome, one sufficiently common on the city streets that Horace could poke gentle fun at him as a character type:[137]

Overheated the contractor hurries with his mules and porters;
His huge machine hoists now a block of stone, now a wooden beam.

Twenty-one inscriptions,[138] ranging in date from the 30s B.C. to the third century A.D. and many of them not susceptible to fixed dating at all though clearly Imperial, preserve the word *redemptor* applied to individuals who were clearly part of the building industry. Of these, six are from Rome, four more from Latium, three from Campania, two more from other areas of Italy, and two from Roman Africa. In the majority of these cases the inscription gives us fairly good information about what kind of contracts these men took, and a number are quite specific about the contractor's role in construction. Nine of them, all from the Augustan to the Trajanic period, provide specific and extremely useful information that fills in the picture of Imperial *redemptores;* the remainder corroborate this picture without expanding it.[139]

L. Cocceius Auctus

We have already discussed L. Cocceius Auctus, mentioned on a fragmentary epistyle from Cumae and labeled *redemptor*. He can very likely be identified with the L. Cocceius Auctus called *architectus* on an inscription from Puteoli and also with the Cocceius whom Strabo identifies as a military architect and engineer of the early 30s B.C. If all three testimonia do record the same man—as seems likely since the inscriptions will easily bear an Augustan dating—then we have direct evidence of an architect who also served as a contractor, though not on the same project. He was a *libertus*, connected with the aristocrats L. Cocceius Nerva and C. Postumius Pollio.[140]

Q. Olius Princeps

Princeps is labeled *redemptor oper(um) publicorum Lanivinorum* [*sic*] on a dedicatory inscription to Juno from Lanuvium that Pearse dates to the early first century A.D. Since the label puts the *opera publica* in the plural, it seems reasonable to assume that he was a regular contractor for public construction there, possibly for maintenance of the numerous temples in the town.[141]

Redemptores from Africa

Four *redemptores* from Thuburbo Maius in Tunisia are recorded on a bilingual inscription that can be reasonably dated to the first century A.D. but no more closely. The inscription itself marked the building of a *cella proma* near the city. The inscription does not tell us what specific duty each *redemptor* had, but it does indicate that the four worked under the general supervision of an *exactor* (overseer) who is also unnamed. The Latin of the text employs vocabulary usual in public contracts known at Rome, thus attesting to the universality of the system for letting public contracts throughout the Roman world.[142]

L. Mucius Felix

Felix shows that a *redemptor* often specialized in one seemingly minor area of materials supply. He is described on the inscription as *redemptor* involved with a *navis harenaria*, or ship that brought sand up the Tiber. He has often been thought to have supplied sand for building projects under the supervision of (as the inscription puts it: *sub*) L. Arruntius Stella; a man of that name was in charge of the games given by Nero in A.D. 55. Pearse has suggested that the two Stellas are the same and that what Felix supplied sand for was the arena in which the games were held. It is a reasonable suggestion but not susceptible to absolute proof; certainly if Felix did not supply sand to builders, some other *redemptores* must have, as it was a necessary commodity.[143]

C. Avillius December

December is called *redemptor marmorarius* on an inscription from Puteoli that can be dated precisely to A.D. 62. He was a specialist contractor for supplying marble to building projects, and the title is attested twice more in our inscriptions (*Artema* and *Clemens*). December was presumably a *libertus*; his wife Vellia Cinnamis is described on the inscription as *cont(ubernalis)* which would only be applied to the spouse of a freedman.[144]

L. Paquedius Festus

Festus appears on a dedication dated specifically to July 3, A.D. 88, found in the countryside around Rome, probably near Monte San Angelo. The dedication is to the *Bona Dea,* a deity for whom he had rebuilt a temple as recompense for her aid in helping him repair a section of the *aqua Claudia Augusta.* He calls himself *redemptor operum Caesar. et puplicorum* [sic]. His work as contractor in repairs to the Claudian aqueduct nicely corroborates Frontinus's indication that, even as late as the end of the first century A.D., the *curator aquarum* regularly made use of private contractors.[145]

Ti. Claudius Cela[dus]

Celadus is described as a *redemptor intestinarius,* which usually indicates a contractor who arranged for the carpentry needed for the completion, the finishing touches, of a building. His status is not given on the inscription, which was found near Velitrae, but he and his wife have Greek *cognomina* which would suggest that he was a freedman of the emperor Claudius and so datable to the late first century A.D. The huge size of his family's funeral monument suggests that he prospered as a contractor.[146]

[Ti. Clau]dius Aug. l. Onesimus

Onesimus was also a freedman of Claudius and states as much on his tombstone, which itself can be dated to the late first or early second century A.D. He also calls himself [rede]mptor operum Caesar(is), and apparently did very well accepting public building contracts, since he rose to a level of such respectability as to become a magistrate of the collegium fabrum tignariorum at Rome.[147]

Q. Haterius Tychichus

This Haterius, who calls himself redemptor, tells us that he erected at his own expense a marble shrine and a signum of Hercules at Rome. He is usually identified as one member of the family of builders whose tomb carries reliefs (now in the Lateran collection of the Vatican Museums) of a number of important public monuments of Flavian times, as well as a scene that shows a group of builders clambering around on a huge crane set up next to the Haterii's tomb itself, as if it had just been used to complete construction of the monumentum. The public monuments shown on the tomb reliefs certainly include the arcus ad Isis [sic]—possibly that known to have stood on the via Labicana—and the Arch of Titus (called arcus in Summa Sacra Via), which are labeled, the Flavian Amphitheater, a temple to Jupiter (possibly that of Jupiter Stator near the Roman Forum), an unknown Quadrifrons arch (perhaps that of the Forum Transitorium), and a small arch turned in three-quarter perspective that is nestled up against the amphitheater and might conceivably represent a Domitianic predecessor of the Arch of Constantine. There is no acceptable evidence for any elaborate topographical or thematic link amongst the monuments shown. A Flavian, or at best early Trajanic, date for these reliefs is supported not only by the monuments portrayed, all of which are Flavian, but by the hairstyle worn by Quintus's wife in her portrait, which is an excellent example of the relatively simple hairstyle regularly worn by free women, parted in the middle and brushed out in deep waves, of the time of Domitian. If Haterius was involved in the contracting of such major public monuments as those shown on the reliefs, then he must have accepted contracts from the Imperial bureaucracy throughout the Flavian period. He was clearly tremendously successful, as the size and elegance of the family *monumentum* attests.

Haterius has been identified as descended from a *libertus* of Q. Haterius Antoninus, *consul ordinarius* of A.D. 53, and if this is so, as seems likely, it may have been Antoninus who sponsored their business and used his influence to help the Haterii obtain public building contracts.[148]

With this evidence collected, several observations about the Imperial *redemptores* can be made. The majority are freedmen or the descendants of freedmen, obviously upwardly mobile entrepreneurs rising from their own or their family's servile origins. It would seem likely that the original slave forebears had been trained in architecture as part of a servile *familia,* then entered the building industry on their own when manumitted.[149] The ones whose names are preserved to us are undoubtedly the successful ones, in general men who enjoyed sufficient success to erect (often elaborate) funeral monuments for themselves and their families. A number of them seem to be part of family businesses (e.g. the Haterii, the Turpilii, possibly the Cocceii) that might continue for several generations. It is interesting that the inscriptions tend to be rather specific. We have three marble contractors, a theater stage contractor, a number of contractors who specialized in accepting public building contracts, a contractor for a villa, and so on. This suggests a growing specialization among *redemptores* during the Empire, a suggestion that I think is corroborated by the evidence of an Imperial contractor still specializing in maintenance and repair of aqueducts. It seems likely that a number of these contractors would have maintained some kind of permanent labor force.

A further interesting point is that these men, as they became specialists in certain areas of building (which most were), became less and less comparable to the *publicani* of the Republican era, who were true entrepreneurs mainly providing financial backing for contract projects that were then let out on subcontract. The men we see in these inscriptions are, for the most part, skilled technicians who can do a particular sort (or sorts) of building extremely well and make their and their workmen's living by specializing.[150] Despite the huge growth of the Imperial building monopoly from the time of Augustus onward, private contractors remained important and able to make a living out of building at least into the third century A.D. (as these inscriptions attest) and probably throughout Roman times. But things were unquestionably different during the Empire. The emergence of the massive, centrally organized Imperial maintenance boards was presumably to some degree responsible for the clear growth in specialization of *redemptores*. Their services were not needed for general purposes so much as for specific ones, and the intelligent contractors realized this and adapted.

THE SKILLED WORKERS: *MENSORES, TECTORES, STRUCTORES, FABRI,* AND *FABRI TIGNARII*

All sorts of words for different sorts of building workers survive in Roman texts and, especially, inscriptions. We have already looked at the arguably most important of these positions, that of *architectus*. But what of the skilled and semiskilled builders and craftsmen? How much information survives about them? The answer is: not very much, except in rare cases. These workers were humble men, for the most part, and did not erect elaborate family *monumenta* or put up self-aggrandizing inscriptions to their family pride. What little we can say about them concentrates entirely on their functions within the building industry. Their specialties tend for the most part to be made clear by their occupation's names.

Mensores were "measurers" or surveyors who would periodically have been employed on building work much as surveyors are today. *Mensores* are mentioned in connection with the *familia aquarum*— and it makes sense that they would have been needed in aqueduct building and repair[151]—and there is also evidence for them in the Imperial civil service connected with building, where they are usually labeled *mensores aedificiorum*. These surveyors were involved in maintenance work, where they were supervised by the *curatores operum publicorum,* and on new construction, where they came under the supervision of the ad hoc commissioners assigned to each project. Pearse has noted thirteen instances of the term *mensor* on inscriptions, and their duties seem overall to involve the surveying and the measuring of completed buildings or completed parts of buildings, prior to the contract price being paid.[152] Of the eleven *mensores aedificiorum* attested in the thirteen inscriptions, none was a slave and the majority appear to have been *ingenui*, thus sharing the social status of the majority of *architecti* attested in our sources. There are *mensores* (not modified by *aedificiorum*) who are Imperial slaves and freedmen, but the duties of such surveyors were probably varied and sundry, while those of the *mensores aedificiorum* seem to be fairly circumscribed.[153]

Two other terms that come down to us connected with building workers are even less well-attested, although that may well be due solely to random preservation of the information. *Tectores* were as a rule plasterers. *Structores* are sometimes builders, but the term is also applied to meat carvers and arrangers of food(!).[154] Undoubtedly the term used more generally to describe skilled building workers, in which *tectores* and *structores* were included, was *fabri*. *Fabri* were skilled builders, but beyond that generalized description there is little distinction drawn. Our sources indicate that all *fabri* underwent a training period—perhaps in workshops or, if they were slaves, in the *familia*—and then worked for contractors on whatever projects they were assigned.[155] Not surprisingly, their level of skill and accuracy seems to have been variable.[156] There is evidence that they could be employed in a variety of different manners: they could take contracts on *locatio conductio* themselves, be hired by the day as skilled labor by a *redemptor*, or work in direct league with an architect, possibly forming small offices to provide architectural plans and designs and actual building advice and expertise, presumably primarily for private commissions. A passage from Aulus Gellius that describes the beginning of a building project implies this sort of business arrangement between architect and *faber*:[157]

> By Fronto's side stood several builders (*fabri*) who had been summoned to construct some new baths and were exhibiting different plans (*pictas*) for baths, drawn on little pieces of parchment. When he had selected one plan and specimen of their work (*formam speciemque operis*), he inquired what the expense would be of completing that entire

project. And when the architect (*architectus*) had said that it would probably require about three hundred thousand sesterces, one of Fronto's friends said, "And another fifty thousand, more or less."

The passage clearly connects the *fabri*, who could give direct building advice, with the *architectus*, who had presumably drawn the plans with their advice to hand and was able to provide an estimate of the cost of construction. That the plans were standard ones which the men had at their disposal (presumably kept at the headquarters or office), that they also had models of them available to show the prospective customer,[158] and that the architect could make a fair estimate of what it would cost to build them, all this implies that these men had some degree of specialization in building baths and that they had a fair amount of experience with just such a commission. Quite clearly they worked together, as associates in a group business.

We find evidence of the training of *fabri* on the monument of the Statilii Tauri with its numerous builder inscriptions. Those inscriptions list three *fabri* and two *fabri tignarii* who were slaves, one *faber tignarius* whose status is uncertain, and one freed *faber structor parietarius*, this last a specialist in putting up walls.[159] We find *liberti* of the Statilii Tauri in important roles with the *collegium fabrum tignariorum*, notably several in the *collegium* at Rome during the first century A.D., and slaves of the family must have been bought already trained as builders or else trained within the *familia*. The inscriptions make it clear that the Statilii Tauri regularly freed slave builders who then continued to work in the family business; whether or not they could in addition have pursued independent careers, at least moonlighting, in building is not revealed. The association of the *liberti* with the *collegium* is a reasonable indicator that they were successful and prosperous.[160]

The *collegium fabrum tignariorum* was a social organization composed mainly, but not exclusively, of men involved in the building trade. There seems to have been no connection, however, between membership in the college and the actual organization of the building industry. The college was a social grouping; membership was restricted on the basis of prosperity since members had to be able to pay required contributions. The college did not furnish builders or crews for projects, and there could be members who were not builders. Nonetheless, the very name of the organization implies a connection to the building trade: *faber tignarius* means a carpenter or a builder working with wood. Certainly it is fair to assume that, as has been pointed out before, since the membership was drawn overwhelmingly from freedmen and the freeborn of low-to-middle status, membership must have provided a social setting and constituted a type of recognition among fellow builders and craftsmen. Thus it is an important element, though not a professional association per se, among the builders of Rome from the first century A.D. onward. Of builders we have mentioned previously, we should recall that Ti. Claudius Onesimus, the *redemptor,* was a *magister* of the college in the eighteenth *lustrum,* and the architect/builder P. Cornelius Thallus, sprung from a family that could boast at least three generations in the industry, is listed as *magister quinquennalis* in the twenty-seventh *lustrum.* A funerary inscription mentions Q. Haterius Euagogus, who may well have been connected to the family whose monument survives from Flavian times, as a college member and a *decurio* in the first or second century A.D.[161] There was a flourishing *collegium fabrum tignariorum* at Ostia, too, which is well documented by inscriptions. We are told, for instance, that it was founded between A.D. 58 and 63 and that by the late second century it had 350 members. The membership is much like that at Rome, made up largely of *liberti,* and these freedmen were wealthy (and becoming wealthier) and upwardly mobile in society's ranks.[162] The evidence confirms and strengthens what seems to be the situation at Rome: the *fabri* were rising professional builders of various skills who were gaining wealth and wanted to gain social position and recognition, with the *collegia* as one means of achieving that end.

From skilled builders it might seem appropriate at this point to turn to consideration of the supplying of unskilled labor, the sheer muscle and sweat needed for major building projects. However, unskilled labor was a matter of supply and demand, not of training or professionalism, and so I shall leave it to be considered in the next chapter, as one of the supply industries.

The conclusions we can draw from our study of the contract system and the builders other than architects who made up the construction industry in Rome are now fairly clear. During the Republic, the industry was entirely a matter of contracting. The *redemptores* seem mostly to have functioned as, and been, *publicani*. They had *socii* and *adfines* whose responsibilities were almost entirely financial and managerial. When contracts were won, these financiers then subcontracted them out to the appropriate builders, who may sometimes have had small staffs of trained specialists but most often must have sublet the work further, since there was no guarantee of obtaining the same sort of contracts sufficiently often to justify the expense of keeping a labor force on permanent retainer or as slaves who had to be kept alive whether they were working or not. With the coming of Augustus and empire, public building began to come increasingly under the control of the Imperial bureaucracy, culminating in the institution of the office of *opera Caesaris*, perhaps under Domitian. Government agencies, like the *curatores viarum* and *aquarum,* which had contracted for skilled building, repair, and maintenance just like the censors and aediles had for major and minor construction work previously, now received Imperially funded corps of slave workmen and office staffs of skilled freedmen and freemen specialists. But these provisions did not eliminate the need to contract out specialized work or work that was over and above what the *familia* of the *curator* could manage. The *opera Caesaris* came to function in a similar way for all major new Imperial building projects. Private construction appears to have continued as a system of individual contract relationships between landowner and builder, functioning pretty much as it had during the Republic. The epigraphical record attests to the continued existence of *redemptores* and of the contract system in general throughout the Empire, although the contractors were no longer financier *publicani* but much more specialized builders probably with skilled labor forces in their keeping or readily hired. *Architecti* seem to have been able to create small businesses for specific kinds of building with skilled *fabri,* and builders of all kinds who were of the freed and free but lowly ranks joined together in *collegia.* Thus the building industry itself became to some degree a route to social advancement, as well as to prosperity, during the first and second centuries A.D. It remained a highly organized contract-based system, collaborating easily, so it would seem, with the increasingly totalitarian tendencies of the Imperial bureaucracy.

Three

Supplying the Roman
Building Industry:
Manpower and Materials

I n any type of building, whether public or private, there are two
essential requirements that must be obtainable by the landowner
or magistrate or contractor before any project can get underway:
the manpower that provides the largely unskilled labor—the
muscle—demanded by all construction large or small, and the
materials to be used in the building. Given the tremendous range of
building in Rome, in Italy, and throughout the Roman world between the second century B.C. and the third century A.D., it should
occasion no surprise that these requirements of supply—especially
in building materials—themselves developed into business concerns all their own. But the quantity and quality of the evidence
available to us for these supply industries varies widely. For unskilled manpower we find relatively little solid evidence, for reasons
to be discussed below; for the supply of materials we are in far better
shape for evidence primarily because of the epigraphical record.

Supply of Manpower to the Building Trade

What evidence we have for how manpower was supplied to the
building industry in the Roman world is concentrated almost exclusively on the city of Rome itself. While this might give cause for

suspicion—that the situation in what was by far the largest city of antiquity might be unique rather than exemplary—recent investigations of what little evidence there is outside Rome have, instead, tended to corroborate the evidence from the city on how unskilled labor was supplied, not only to the building trade but in general. Thus it seems reasonable to analyze the situation in the city and allow it to serve as a general model for the Roman world.[1]

To understand the nature of the supply of manpower to the building trade in Rome, it is necessary first to review quickly what we know of the makeup of the city's population. There are notoriously few reliable pieces of evidence with which to determine the actual numbers of people in the ancient city at any point during its existence: such evidence simply has not been preserved, and what little there is is open to dispute and interpretation. For Italy as a whole, information is even more sketchy, and for the Empire the evidence is effectively nonexistent. It is now widely assumed that a figure between 750,000 and 1,000,000 is not too far wrong for the city in the age of Augustus, based on the known numbers of male citizens who are attested as recipients of the grain dole for the years 46, 45, 44, 29, 24, 23, 12, 5, and 2 B.C., and for A.D. 14 and 37.[2] Whether the Imperial city grew beyond such a figure is at best a tortured subject, and one not really susceptible of proof.[3] For our purposes, however, the simple realization that by the latter half of the first century Rome was far and away the largest urban concentration of people in the ancient Mediterranean world and that she must have remained so well into the Empire will at least permit us to analyze the nature of the unskilled labor supply that was available there.

We are told over and over again in literary sources for the late Republic and early Empire that the countryfolk of Italy tended to drift to the city in large numbers and that this constituted a significant societal problem in the ancient city. Sallust, describing the complaints that led the urban poor to rally to Catiline's cause in 63 B.C., says:[4]

But the city populace acted with desperation for many reasons. To begin with, all who were especially conspicuous for their shamelessness and impudence, those too who had squandered their patrimony in riotous living, finally all whom disgrace or crime had forced to leave home, had all flc ﬡed into Rome as into a cesspool. . . . Besides this, the young men who had maintained a wretched existence by manual labour in the country, tempted by public and private doles, had come to prefer idleness in the city to their hateful toils.

The phenomenon of Italian peasant migration into Rome, and the resulting problems of massive urban unemployment and reliance on public dole, continued at least well into the reign of Augustus, if not later, and it is mentioned by a number of authors subsequent to Sallust as well.[5] The question then becomes: aside from reliance on the grain dole, which was hardly sufficient to support one man and utterly insufficient for a family, how did this burgeoning mass of largely unskilled immigrant labor survive? Rome's great size and power resulted, after all, from military and subsequent political conquest. The city never possessed any sort of industry that, in a modern sense, could provide widespread employment, with the single exception of the very trade and transport that supplied it with food and raw materials. Thus, as Brunt has pointed out,[6] the very necessity of supplying Rome's artificially swollen population must to a large degree have created a demand for cheap and unskilled labor to service that supplying. Clearly there would have been a demand for muscle at docks, on transport from the docks to the city (both up the river from Ostia and, before the mid first century A.D. if not later, on coastal routes to Ostia from Puteoli and other ports on the western coast of Italy), at the unloading sites such as the Emporium in the city, and to the *macella* and other wholesale and retail markets throughout the city. Thus the supply of transport could have made use of a certain proportion of the unskilled labor available in Rome, and it is easy then to hypothesize other areas of demand for muscle and sweat that would have stemmed from that industry. By the same token, it seems reasonable to assume that substantial numbers of unskilled laborers might have come to be employed in the building trade, from its initial expansion in the second century on well into the second century A.D. at least. We have seen from our survey of the history of building in Rome that not only did public construction increase dramatically from ca. 181 B.C. onward, but that private construction in and around the city also was on the rise throughout the central centuries of Roman history. Wealthy citizens, like Marcus and Quintus Cicero, constantly seem to have been engaged in building projects, both new and reconstruction, both in the city and in the nearby countryside. At the same time, it is reasonable to assume that the continuing increase of the city's population from the Italian peasantry provided an ever increasing demand in and around the city for humble dwellings, tenements, and *tabernae* and that the private building trade supplied these, at least in part, by providing employment for unskilled laborers. Thus demand mandated supply, and supply struggled to keep up with demand.

It cannot be denied that Rome's was an economy supported and propelled to a great degree by slave labor. We know that slaves were employed in every capacity in Rome and throughout the Roman world, in skilled work as well as in the most gruelling of manual tasks. But the evidence for the supplying of unskilled labor in the building industry through gangs of slave workmen is practically nonexistent. Such an arrangement is mentioned only in situations in which a *redemptor* could expect regular or constant employment that would justify the maintenance and feeding of such a servile company—attested to us, as we have seen, in the case of contractors who were engaged on the maintenance and repair of the water system during the Republic and who were required by law to maintain the necessary slave labor force in order to be permitted to bid for the aqueduct contracts[7]—and permit the contractor to make a profit even with the relatively heavy expense of maintaining his slaves. In most industries, and particularly in building and construction, the demand must have fluctuated with a number of variables: the season of the year (Frontinus says construction should be undertaken only between April and November and halted when the weather was too hot),[8] the state of the private economy or of the money available for public expenditure on building, and the very nature of a construction industry itself (in which the completion of the building also terminates the demand for the labor that built it). We know that the ancient Roman landowner did not maintain a sufficient slave *familia* on his estate(s) to cope with the seasonal harvests or with major operations beyond normal maintenance of the property[9] but hired a contractor who could provide, as well as skilled workers and (sometimes) materials, the necessary manpower. While we are told that some building contractors did maintain some number of permanent slaves, there can be little question that these regular workers would not have sufficed, and were not intended to, during any period of heavy demand for construction (a "building boom")[10] and may well have been proficient in particular skills that justified their maintenance by the contractor even when there was no immediate demand. There is some apparent confirmation of this in a fragment of the legal writer Venuleius, writing probably toward the end of the second century A.D.:[11]

> The person who has contracted to build an *insula* should not hurry, mustering builders from all quarters and providing a host of day-laborers, nor on the other hand should he be content with one or two, but he ought to avoid extremes in accordance with the rational practice of a careful builder, having regard to time and sites.

It should be noted that the builder advised by Venuleius is quite clearly conceived of as bringing in his unskilled workers (the "host of day-laborers") on hire, and the implication seems also to extend to the more skilled "builders" who are to be brought in from all around the city (perhaps on hire from workshops or other contractors or on individual subcontracting arrangements). The actual contractor appears to have as few as "one or two" workers regularly in his employ, presumably slaves, so for any job beyond the tiniest he has to hire outside labor, skilled and unskilled. Such unskilled manpower, especially in Rome itself, could hardly have been provided by slaves, and certainly not in any sort of affordable or economical manner.

While building certainly requires a pool of skilled workers who can deal with the relatively technical tasks—from the plans and advice of the architect through the specific skills required of the woodworkers, stonemasons, plasterers, painters, and so forth—these seem often to have been either slaves of particular contractors or of a *familia* involved in the building trade, whose special skills

123

were recognized and respected, often leading to their manumission and continuance in the building industry as freed specialists. These were not the men who provided the sheer hard labor of construction. It is important to remember that Rome was an almost completely nonmechanized society where heavy labor required sheer muscle and sweat. Much of what had to be done to erect a building was heavy labor of exactly this back-breaking kind, and little of that labor would be likely to have been supplied by slaves when there was no clearly profitable way in which to maintain a slave force of unskilled workers for a seasonal and occasional industry. Slaves have to be fed, clothed, housed, and kept alive whether they are at work or not, and hence they constitute an expensive commodity unless they can be kept continuously and profitably busy. Construction must always have provided a demand for unskilled manpower during the proper seasons of the year and when other circumstances so dictated. If slaves were not an economical way to meet this occasional demand, then the existence at Rome of a large number of free but poor men who had, to some degree at least, to support themselves (and their families if they had them) must have been exactly what the building contractor most wished for. Such men could be hired solely for the duration of a project or by the day, as needed, and their wages could have been controlled so that their employment was profitable to the contractor yet financially rewarding to them, too.[12] This appears to be the way in which most unskilled labor was provided for building in Rome. The slight evidence that remains indicates that the same pattern of employing nonslave labor for building projects was in use not just in the city, with its readily available mass of urban poor, but throughout Italy and in much of the Empire.[13] It is reasonable, then, to assert that the brute manpower for building tended to be supplied, all over the Roman world, through the hire of free but unskilled laborers for specific projects, rather than by gangs of unskilled slaves maintained by contractor, landowner, or magistrate.

A further point for consideration is implied by this analysis and is put forward by Brunt: since nonslave labor was regularly and widely employed for the construction of public works at Rome—and indeed throughout the Roman world—it can at least be thought probable that the frequent policy of pursuing public build-ing programs and expending a great deal of public funding on public works was, though only secondary or even tertiary to the urbanistic and propagandistic motives behind such policy, in-tended to keep a substantial proportion of the masses of urban poor employed at least part of the year. But while this point seems emi-nently reasonable, it is attested nowhere in our surviving ancient sources. Indeed, the ancient sources for laborers, especially the unskilled, are paltry at best. Even the epigraphical record does not attest to anyone, slave or free, who provided the brute manpower clearly essential to the building industry or to any other labor-intensive enterprise in the Roman world. The poor Roman laborer certainly could not afford to put up an elaborate, or even a simple, epitaph for himself and his family and probably could not have read it even had he possessed the means to commission it. Beyond inscriptions, the evidence is random and open to interpretation. For instance, it is plausible to assume that the urban distress Tiberius Gracchus was seeking to alleviate in the 130s in Rome was in part due to unemployment on account of the completion of the Aqua Marcia, but the sources do no actually state this. Cicero's remark that builders working on his villa at Tusculum returned to Rome to collect the grain dole can be interpreted to indicate that these were free citizens working on hire, but Cicero himself is not anything like so specific and the interpretation can be challenged.[14]

Most famous, and most controversial, of all ancient testimonia about labor supply in Rome is the tale told by Suetonius about the emperor Vespasian's reaction to the proposal that he adopt a labor-saving device on a public building project:[15]

> To a mechanical engineer, who promised to transport some heavy col-umns to the Capitol at small expense, he [Vespasian] gave no mean reward for his invention, but refused to make use of it, saying: "You must let me feed my poor commons."

Suetonius's implication, that the mechanical device if used would have put the laborers hired from the urban poor for the restoration of the Capitoline temple out of work, is clear, but a passage from Xiphilinus's epitome of Cassius Dio indicates that when work was begun on the temple restoration Vespasian actually shovelled out the first clod of earth himself "evidently bidding the other men of most distinction to do likewise, in order that the rest of the populace might have no excuse for shirking the service."[16] This second passage led Casson to assume that Vespasian had attempted to get the earth for the Capitoline temple restoration moved for free and when the citizens proved unwilling to do so he had to send in a gang of slaves. But surely it is more likely that the emperor was reduced to hiring free labor for the project, as seems to have been customary, and the usual interpretation of Suetonius's remark remains the correct one. It bears rare testimony to the assumption that to a minor degree at least, public works were indeed intended to keep the urban poor gainfully employed and out of trouble.

Beyond these fragments the ancient writers are silent, as are Roman inscriptions, which give a notoriously incorrect impression of Roman manual laborers, since only those able to afford them were members of *collegia* or set up epitaphs (two of the three varieties of inscription that mention workers at all), while the manufacturer's marks encountered on bricks, pipes, and pots are largely random and contribute little to evidence outside their own narrow spheres.[17] The lack of testimony concerning labor and laborers extends even to the legal texts, which were concerned, practically enough, with legal precedent and potentiality, that is, cases that had actually been tried in court or seemed likely to be. The truly poor do not turn to the law or the courts, since they can seldom afford lawyers or court costs. Hence the lack of anything resembling a body of labor law in the Roman jurists is only to be expected. We know that labor contracts were drawn up primarily in a particular form of *locatio conductio*—*locatio conductio operarum*—but there is extremely little evidence, and nothing like enough upon which to base conclusions.[18] So, while it seems reasonable and logical to follow the brilliant analysis offered by Brunt, we have to keep in mind that the evidence is minimal. For the building industry it seems, on the whole, most likely that nonslave labor was the major source of manpower for construction projects throughout the Roman world, that slaves attached to the building industry tended to be skilled specialists in a particular phase or element of the building process and were regularly manumitted and continued in the profession as freedmen, and that this system was used precisely because it permitted the maximum profit to be made by the contractor and the maximum use to be made of the biggest source of unskilled labor available. But it is conjecture and hypothesis, not demonstrable fact, however reasonable and appealing a reading of the fragmentary evidence.

Supply of Materials to the Building Industry

The evidence available is much fuller for how the various essential materials for building were obtained. Each major source of material may be considered individually, both in a chronological framework (i.e., how demand for specific building materials and their supply developed through Roman history) and as a business undertaking essential to the building industry (i.e., who were involved in it, where the resources were found, how they were obtained, shipped, delivered, and prepared for use, where these things are known). As with manpower, the bulk of our evidence concerns the city of Rome, but there is substantial information from other parts of the Roman world that can be brought to bear on these supply industries. In the last quarter of the twentieth century, tremendous advances have been made in the study of all these topics, and in a number of cases we can now see much more clearly than ever before the nature of such business endeavors in the ancient world. The specific materials to be studied include timber and wood, tufa and other native building stones, concrete, brick and other tile products, and marble and other decorative stone.

TIMBER AND WOOD

Timber was always essential to construction in the Roman world. Its importance was attested by the elder Pliny, who devoted six books of his *Historia Naturalis* to trees and their uses. More important for discussing wood and timber in Roman architecture and construction, however, are Strabo, who describes the forests of Italy in sufficient detail that from his descriptions a rough distribution map of the species of trees available in the ancient forests could be

127

drawn, and Vitruvius, who considered types of wood appropriate for building and their uses by builders.[19] Italian forests, of course, are mentioned by other authors at various times (e.g., Livy in describing Hannibal's campaign; Dionysius of Halicarnassus periodically in considering earliest Rome). We can most profitably follow Strabo in a quick survey of the forests available to the Romans in Italy; we will consider importation of wood from outside Italy at a later point, since it was apparently a development of the Imperial period only and never reached the same status as an import trade that marble and other decorative stones did.

Strabo begins by asking himself, rhetorically, how such a large city as Rome could possibly continue to stand and to expand despite such constant disasters as fire and building collapse. He responds that it was possible because there were accessible to Rome both sufficient stone quarries and timber and a river system (in the Tiber basin) capable of providing easy transport for them. He then proceeds to description. Latium, Etruria, and Umbria are heavily wooded; Etruria especially provides trees notable for their height and straightness, notably oak trees (*quercus*). Strabo notes that the Sabine country south of Umbria was particularly heavily forested, too. The nearest great forest to Rome was the Ciminian forest north of Sutrium and Nepete in south Etruria, the nature of which in 310 was vividly described by Livy:[20]

> The Ciminian forest in those days was more impenetrable and frightening than until recently were the forests of Germany: up to that time no trader had entered the forest.

After a Roman expedition in that year, the Romans established the via Cassia and extended their control over that part of central Etruria, coincidentally opening up and beginning to exploit the Ciminian forest for timber. While Strabo at first gives the impression that the Romans seldom went beyond the Tiber basin for wood, he later corrects that misleading image when he points out the importance of water transport for bringing in special timbers from farther away, notably from Liguria and from the area around Pisa. Indeed Strabo's description is suggestive:[21]

Pisa is reputed to have been prosperous on a time, and at the present time it is not without repute on account of its fertility, its stone-quarries, and its timber for ship-building; in ancient times, indeed, they utilised this material to meet the perils that faced them on the sea . . . but at the present time most of it is being used up on the buildings at Rome, and also at the villas, now that people are devising palaces of Persian magnificence.

There is no substantial evidence to suggest that, as long as central Italy's forests flourished, the Romans imported woods from elsewhere, with the exception of luxury items such as citrus wood, which was brought from Africa for furniture,[22] although Corsica may have already been providing both fir and pine wood by sea during the later Republic, since specimens of remarkable size had been known there from as far back as the fourth century B.C.[23] As demand continued to grow, the great forests of Liguria to the north and the Sila forest in Calabria to the south may have been opened up to logging and export of timber, but there is little if any direct evidence of such import.[24] That Italy was well forested at the very least through the time of Augustus is attested by Dionysius of Halicarnassus, a contemporary of Augustus, who describes Italy's wealth of timber and its relative accessibility in his own day:[25]

Her woodlands on precipitous slopes, in glens, and on unfarmed hills are most impressive; they provide a plentiful supply of fine ship timber and of timber for other purposes. . . . the abundance of rivers in all parts of the peninsula makes the transport and exchange of the products of the land easy.

Importation of timber for building was considered a highly unusual undertaking. Vitruvius praised the possibilities offered to builders by the larch (*larix*) of the Alpine forests, which was remarkably fire resistant and had impressed Julius Caesar when he attacked an Alpine stronghold built of this wood and found that piling burning brushwood against the larchwood stockade had no appreciable effect on it. The Romans came to call the tree *larix* from the name of the fort, Larignum. It was available commercially in northern Italy by the time Vitruvius built the basilica at Fanum, but he lamented that the cost of transporting it to Rome made its adoption in architecture there impractical.[26] So highly respected had the *larix* become, however, that when Augustus's successor Tiberius had to rebuild the bridge over the Naumachia, which had been burned, he contracted for a shipment of larch wood for the job. The cargo of wood, when it arrived, became famous for the sheer size of the trees, as the elder Pliny attests:[27]

> What is believed to have been the largest tree ever seen at Rome down to the present time was one that Tiberius Caesar caused to be exhibited as a marvel on the bridge of the Naumachia before mentioned; it had been brought to Rome with the rest of the timber used, and it lasted 'til the amphitheater of Nero. It was a log of larchwood, 120 feet long and of a uniform thickness of two feet, from which could be inferred the almost incredible height of the rest of the tree by calculating its length to the top.

The meaning of the last sentence is, at best, unclear, but may imply that the tree when standing measured as much as 150 Roman feet in height.[28] The Neronian amphitheater referred to in the passage was a wooden construction of his second consulship erected in the Campus Martius.[29] But such import was clearly still quite a rarity in the mid-first century A.D. Indeed, there is no indication at all that the supply of tall fir trees from the Apennines was beginning to falter until the early third century A.D., when Dio Cassius indicates that it had proven impossible to replace the wooden roof of the Diribitorium in the Campus Martius, but there is little confirmation for this. While such great late antique buildings as Diocletian's baths and Maxentius's restoration of the temple of Venus and Rome, as well as his basilica near the Forum, employed concrete coffered or cross vaults to span their vast interior spaces, there is no particular reason to think that this was due to a lack of available timber; Diocletian's restoration of the Curia in the Forum had a wooden roof, and not too much later (in the fourth century) the immense Christian basilicas of St. Peter and St. Paul at Rome could be constructed with timber roofs. In fact the timber supply seems to have been sufficient to the demands of construction throughout the Empire, although wood for fuel seems to have been in increasingly short supply in the third and fourth centuries A.D.[30]

The earliest inhabitants of Roman Italy built almost entirely from wood, often covered with mud and roofed in wattle-and-daub. Small wooden huts like those whose postholes can still be seen on the south slope of the Palatine Hill were being built at least by the eighth century B.C. and probably long before, since the entire Italian peninsula was heavily wooded. The hills and valleys that would become the city of Rome were covered with broad-leaved deciduous trees, including (if ancient place names preserve such information from very early times, as they seem to do) oak (*quercus*), osiers (*vimina*), beech (*fagus*), and perhaps cornel trees (*cornus*). Thus there was no shortage of the small but strong timbers needed for such construction immediately at hand.[31] Demand for wood in Roman construction must have grown rapidly with the arrival of the Etruscan kings in Rome and their initiation of temple building in the "Tuscan" style, which required very large amounts of timber and often timber beams of extraordinary size to span their intercolumniations and interior cellae. At the same time, small huts were replaced by the first atrium houses, and the first great wooden bridge across the Tiber, the Pons Sublicius, was built under Ancus Marcius across the river just south of Tiber Island. Early temples are attested to Fortuna and Mater Matuta in the Forum Boarium, to Saturn and to the Dioscuri in the Forum Romanum, and to Jupiter, Juno, and Minerva on the Capitoline. The last of these is the best known archaeologically. Its podium seems to attest a size that is difficult to credit, 56.63 m. long by 49.73 m. wide, with a hexastyle (six-columned) façade made up of columns 18.64 m. tall. The intercolumniations, which would have had to be spanned by wooden beams, were 7.85 m. across the front and 10.46 m. between the columns of the building's flanks, clearly much too large to have been spanned in stone—weight alone would have brought the structure down—and so were probably instead of local hardwood, perhaps oak. The superstructure would also have been almost entirely of wood, faced in terracotta plaques and tiling.[32] The Capitoline temple was dedicated immediately after the expulsion of the kings in 509 B.C., and there is no mention of any timber having to be brought far in order to complete it. Hence we must assume that a substantial supply of large trees suitable for its construction was readily available to Romans of the later sixth century B.C.

Temples and private houses continued to develop throughout the early centuries of the Republic, always requiring a good deal of wood for their upper sections especially. Despite Livy's indication that at the time of the Gallic sack of the city (ca. 390–389 B.C.) the nobility were living in *atria,* which has sometimes been taken to mean atrium-style houses of the type well known to us from early Imperial Pompeii and Herculaneum, there is no solid archaeological evidence for such a house plan before ca. 300 B.C. Livy may have used the term anachronistically, or meant it to be taken only in its simplest and strictest meaning as "halls," which could indicate more or less any large dwelling.[33] Between the early fourth and the end of the third century B.C. we know almost nothing about architectural development in the city, except that the atrium house with its central *impluvium* opening in the roof formed by large wooden beams was developed and must have demanded a ready supply of good building timber of fair size, as must periodic construction of temples and maintenance and repair of those in place.

With the vast expansion in construction attested for the second and first centuries B.C. following on widespread conquest by Rome throughout the Mediterranean and in turn the extensive hellenization of Rome and Italy, demand for timber in the city and throughout the Roman world must have become even heavier. A porticus— *porticus inter lignarios*—was built in the dock area along the Tiber south of the Aventine Hill in 192 B.C. that was specifically for timber merchants to store and sell their commodity. The development of the basilica during the first half of the second century B.C., with its wide intercolumniations and pitched or, eventually, clerestory roofs also signals an increase in demand for very large roof beams that could be trussed with tie beams to cover the immense spaces essential to the central open space.[34]

While basilicas must have signaled a further need for large wooden beams for roofing, at the same time the development of *opus caementicium* much reduced the use of mud brick for wall construction and hence reduced the need for timber framing. Once the techniques of Roman construction were developed, experimentation began and the remarkable properties of concrete construction were slowly realized. The development of concrete vaulting to cover large interior spaces eventually reduced the demand for large timber beams in buildings such as temples and baths, but the basilica remained stubbornly wooden in its superstructures as did the atrium house. The huge building programs of Sulla, Caesar, Augustus, Nero, Domitian, Trajan, and Hadrian must all have required impressive quantities and qualities of wood and timber, and in due course there is evidence that huge timbers to be used in trussed roof beams and intercolumniations were shipped into Rome from elsewhere in Italy and were also shipped around the Mediterranean in a regular timber trade. However, there is no real evidence of any serious shortage of timber in the Roman world at any point at least to the end of the second century A.D. and possibly not ever. The demand for timber in construction remained great, despite the development of *opus caementicium,* but the emphasis must to some degree have shifted more toward what was required for domestic construction—both houses and *insulae*—and away from wood to use in public and religious monuments, on the whole. A good deal of timber would always have been needed for repair and reconstruction, too, even though massive buildings such as the temple of Jupiter Capitolinus when restored were given columns and perhaps entablatures of precious stone instead of the earlier wood faced with terracotta plaques and moldings.[35]

A regular supply industry for the timber and wood necessary to the growth of the city of Rome was well established, it would appear, by 192 B.C. and the creation of the *porticus inter lignarios.* Wood, of course, was every bit as essential for fuel as for building in the Roman world, and so it was a precious and profitable commodity, although one quite readily available. The kinds of wood must have been those found in the great forests that covered most of the Italian peninsula, and the literary record supports this. Vitruvius devotes the most space in his treatment of timber for architecture to fir (*abies*), which he describes as light, hard to bend, and able to support a good deal of weight. Seneca cites fir and pine (*pinus, pinaster*) as the most often used woods for building, and Juvenal mentions wagons of fir and pine rumbling through the city and threatening to fall on its inhabitants.[36] These timbers were readily available in Italy; the fir indeed was the tallest of the Italian hardwoods, able to provide lengths up to ca. 100 Roman feet; mountain pines also would grow up to 60 Roman feet or longer; and both were easy to work and considered very beautiful.[37] The other native woods that are most regularly mentioned in construction are hardwood: oak (*quercus*) used especially for doorposts, lintels, and corbels, and elm (*ulmus*) also for doorposts and lintels as well as for beams. Cypress (*cupressus*), which had been imported into Italy from Greece, is mentioned as a building timber by Vitruvius, but there is little archaeological or textual evidence from Italy to support him, and he may have been thinking of its use in Greek temple architecture.[38]

As we have seen, wood was being shipped into Rome from other forests of Italy, notably those of Etruria and the area around Pisa, later perhaps from Liguria and Calabria, and possibly from Corsica, by the first century B.C., and larch came to be imported in the early Empire from Rhaetia in the Alps. But except for such specialty woods as citrus from Africa, import from much beyond the boundaries of Italy seems always to have remained unusual and noteworthy. It appears that the sea-borne trade in timber to Rome was largely limited to imports around the peninsula itself, such as larch brought from the Adriatic ports and perhaps other timbers shipped from places such as Aquileia at the north end of the Adriatic or Salona in Dalmatia, but there is no positive evidence to establish even that trade securely. Meiggs quite rightly dismisses Horace's remark about Pontic pine as evidence that Rome imported pine from the forests around the Black Sea or boxwood from Mysia.[39] Even in the late Empire, there is no evidence for extensive shipment of building timber to Rome, nor is there much evidence of a major trade industry in building timber anywhere in the Mediterranean; clearly forests were still able to fill the demand from relatively nearby. The crisis in wood for fuel that is attested in the third century A.D. and afterward in Italy was not a crisis in timber for building. While the pine and fir of the Apennines may well have been over-logged by that time,[40] and much of the smaller timber in central Italy may have been seriously depleted, it is important to remember that still in the early sixth century A.D. Theoderic was able to plan to build a fleet of a thousand ships without anticipating any difficulties in the supply of timber, since he had discovered that Italy was exporting timber to the provinces. We know that he sent surveyors to choose and purchase pine and cypress along the Italian coast and fir from the Po Valley, and he subsequently is said to be pleased with the progress being made. This can hardly reflect an Italian peninsula denuded of forests; even as late as the sixth century A.D. the timber of Italy was renowned and reliable.[41]

Although our evidence for the quantity and types of wood supplied by the timber trade in Rome is relatively good, it is a sad but true fact that otherwise this is perhaps the least well documented of the major supply industries for building. Such evidence as there is has been collected by Meiggs, and the details of its application to construction are provided by Adam.[42] We do know that quite early on in their expansion through Italy, the Romans were scrupulous about including large tracts of virgin forest in the packets of land that conquered territories were to turn over to them. These forest acreages became public land and could be used for supply of timber as well as to collect a regular revenue from those who acquired forest products, pitch and charcoal as well as timber, from them.[43] These public forest lands eventually stretched all over Italy, near Rome as well as distant, and they seem to have been considered of prime importance. Cicero was well aware of this and assumed that any attack against the forests would produce public outrage. He twice mentions the Scantian forest, otherwise meagerly attested, in his speech *De Lege Agraria*, more extensively in the first passage:[44]

> What they need now is ready money, money that cannot be questioned, money that can be counted. I wonder what this watchful and shrewd tribune has in mind? "The Scantian forest is to be sold," he says. Did you discover the forest in the list of abandoned leaseholdings, or in the register of pastures controlled by the censors? . . . Would you dare to sell the Scantian forest in my consulship? Would you dare to touch any form of public revenue? Would you rob the Roman people of what gives them strength in war, and in peace an easier life?

135

We do know that contracts were regularly let for the exploitation of public forests in order to supply timber for building and fuel for public baths, not just by Rome herself but by most colonies and municipalities around the Roman world. For instance, in the charter of the colony of Urso in southern Spain a clause specifies that public forests may not be sold or leased for a period longer than five years, implying that logging was controlled just as rigidly by contract as was collecting pitch. What evidence there is implies that the forests were always worked by public contractors rather than by state labor, in exactly the same manner as public building itself was largely let out to *redemptores*. The only difference is, this does not appear to have changed radically, at least insofar as our meager evidence shows, under the Empire.[45]

Exact details of the Roman timber trade are also frustratingly meager. We know very little about the felling of the trees, and, as we have seen, only scattered testimonia bring us information about their transport. A certain amount of evidence from the archaeological record corroborates what little we know of the mechanics of harvesting and shaping timber, most notably the various timber operations that are shown in various panels of Trajan's Column and the tools attested on funerary reliefs of timber merchants and carpenters.[46] We do know that, once wood had been brought from the forest to the timberyard, at least some of it was allowed to season before it was used, or else special measures had to be taken to protect the green wood until it dried out naturally, as when Scipio had to dry dock his fleet for the winter in 205 B.C.[47] While the marketing of timber in the Greek world is relatively well documented, the whole trade is poorly represented in Roman sources. As we have seen, timber was shipped to Rome from ports on the west coast of Italy, primarily Pisa and Genoa. On the east coast both Ravenna and Aquileia are mentioned as involved in the timber trade as ports. At the city of Salona in Dalmatia, on the east coast of the Adriatic, an inscription records a *negotiator materiarius* (timber merchant) operating there.[48] To what extent the older Greek exporting cities for timber such as Ambracia, Methone, Amphipolis on the Strymon or those in Asia Minor like Aspaneus in the Troad, Prusa near Apamea, Cyzicus, and Nicomedia continued to serve this function is not readily ascertained, but it seems reasonable to suppose that the trade continued to supply the timber needs of Roman Greece and Asia Minor. Beyond these areas we know nothing.

Of the timber business itself in Roman times we are only slightly better informed. We do have some of its vocabulary preserved to us in inscriptions and a few literary sources. Roman law distinguished between two types of wood: *materia,* which was wood for building, and *lignum,* which was wood to be burned as fuel.[49] In practice, however, as Meiggs has pointed out, the word *lignum* and its derivatives seem to have been used indiscriminately. For instance, while logs to be burned are always *ligna,* people called *lignarii* may be workers in (or marketers of) building timber just as well as sellers or cutters of fuel wood. At Pompeii there are attested in graffiti both *lignari plostrari,* who seem to be carters of wood, and *lignari universi,* who might have any sort of relationship to woodworking, supply or transport. But there were also *materiarii,* and these too seem to have been sellers of wood who had a street—the vicus Materiarius—named after them in the very same sector of Rome in which the *porticus inter lignarios* was founded.[50] We have already noted the wood seller from Salona—*negotiator materiarius*—and another is know from outside Florence; presumably these men located sources for wood and negotiated leases or contracts for exploiting them with the landowners, as well as supplying retail traders in wood like small timberyards. Another and older term for this sort of timber entrepreneur was *abietarius.*[51]

The status of the few of these timber workers who provide the information seems to have been relatively humble, *ingenui* or freedmen. There is a tale, possibly apocryphal considering its source, of one man who rose from a family involved in the timber trade to the highest possible distinction at Rome: he became emperor! This was the short-term (January–March A.D. 193) *princeps* Pertinax.[52]

> Publius Helvius Pertinax was the son of a freedman, Helvius Successus by name, who confessed that he gave this name to his son because of his own long-standing connection with the timber-trade, for he had conducted that business with pertinacity.

The story may gain a bit more credibility from the fact that, after his deification at the insistence of Septimius Severus, who called himself Pertinax' avenger for propaganda purposes, it was the *collegium fabrorum tignariorum* at Ostia who built a temple to the new god, as if honoring a former colleague.[53] But if this story has any truth to it at all, it was an unparalleled event. Timber cutters, shapers, transporters, and sellers otherwise seem to have come from the middle and lower strata of Roman society, insofar as they are documented at all. Nor do we hear, Pertinax aside, of any fortunes made in the timber business nor of any other members of the profession rising to much in the way of political or social influence. The slight evidence available about both prices and wages in the timber trade are so few and of such a late date that it seems doubtful they can form any sort of basis for generalization or extrapolation.[54] Beyond this we seem to know nothing more.

The picture that emerges is one of a primarily Italian industry, owing little to imports from distant areas of the Empire. It was a supply line industry from the place where the tree was felled to the point where its timber was used in a building or as firewood. There is no evidence at all for the elaborate hierarchy of contractors, specialists, supervisors, skilled workers, and unskilled laborers that we have seen in construction and that existed in the stone and brick industries, at least so far as our fragmentary sources allow us to see. Clearly there would have been some, perhaps vestigial, hierarchy that placed the contractors over those who merely felled the trees, and the skilled carpenters and woodworkers must certainly have had a status all their own, although their skills may have put them within the hierarchy of the building industry rather than that of the wood suppliers. The evidence is too scarce to permit us to perceive much in the way of changes or development in the industry or in its work over time. That it was an efficient delivery and supply business seems tacitly attested by the very expansion of the Roman building industry itself, but it was also one that must have been taken for granted to a great degree, and hence was seldom recorded in the lists, much less in the literary texts, that have survived to us. Perhaps since timber was a resource relatively readily available in Italy—like tufa—it seemed unnecessary to say much about it other than describing and praising the properties of particular types of trees.

TUFA AND OTHER NATIVE BUILDING STONES

To build any kind of monument larger or more permanent than a simple hut-type house, materials other than wood were needed. From the very earliest times the peoples of the various parts of Italy exploited native stone as material for construction. While styles and techniques of both construction and masonry in stone walls changed over the centuries, the materials used were almost always local. Before the development of Roman concrete, *opus caementicium*, and its adoption as the most satisfactory method of building walls with sufficient strength to withstand hard use, enemy attack, and the like, city walls, major public buildings, and roads were all made of cut-stone masonry, with blocks cut to fit as snugly as possible to one another[55] and often held together by clamps and dowels, and the remaining interstices filled by mortar, usually a mixture of sand and lime, that would act as bonding agent between the stones.[56] Two types of cut-stone masonry are distinguished by most archaeologists and given the Latin names *opus siliceum*, which indicates polygonal masonry in which the blocks of stone are worked to fit together snugly but are not squared nor set in rows, and *opus quadratum*, which simply means stones dressed into rectangular or squared shapes and generally positioned as "headers and stretchers" so that the joints between the stones in one row do not fall directly over or under the joints between stones in the rows below or above them (fig. 3.1).[57]

Both forms of cut-stone masonry are attested in Italy from the earliest times. In central Italy, *opus siliceum* appears always to have been a popular method, and it survives there quite late in the history of construction, for instance, in the Latin colony of Alba Fucens, which was founded in 303 B.C., as well as at many other Roman towns.[58] Masonry that is much more regularly squared, if not rigidly ashlar, dominates early stone wall construction in the areas of Italy that had been under the domination of the Etruscans, while true *opus quadratum* (see fig. 3.2 below) seems always to have been used in southern Italy and Sicily, undoubtedly because of the

Figure 3.1 Methods of building walls in *opus quadratum*. [Adam (1984) fig. 246, p. 118; reproduced by permission of the author]

early colonization of these areas by the Greek cities, where it was the normal technique.[59] In every case where the stones used in these types of masonry have been studied, they have proved to be of more-or-less local origin. The lack of textual or epigraphical evidence for such early construction allows us to say little about how they were quarried, delivered, worked, and set up beyond assuming a general correspondence, though of course much less developed and refined, between quarrying and dressing methods in later Roman architecture.[60]

The story of building stone in the earlier centuries of the Roman world has been most carefully studied in Rome and Latium. In the architecture of Rome and her environs seven different types of volcanic tufa and one calcareous sedimental stone that was desposited as a result of the volcanic eruptions that produced those tufas form the core of all stone construction.

Cappellaccio *Tufa*

Cappellaccio was the local tufa employed in construction at Rome from the seventh down to the fifth century B.C. It was extracted from quarries along the south slope of the Quirinal and from the slopes of the Capitoline hills. This local stone was easy to obtain and easy to work, though not particularly strong. Its ready availability must have been the reason for its adoption at Rome before the city's great territorial expansion; indeed it was presumably the only building stone available down to the end of the fifth century B.C. *Cappellaccio* dropped out of use, except for rapid repairs to existing structures, as soon as higher quality building tufa from other sources became available at the end of the fifth and beginning of the fourth century B.C. Examples of the use of *cappellaccio* include the podium blocks of the temple of Jupiter Capitolinus, the foundations of the archaic temples of Fortuna and Mater Matuta in the Forum Boarium (in the area sacra di S. Omobono), and some of the lowest strata of the Regia in the Roman Forum.[61]

Fidenae *and* Grotta Oscura *Tufas*

Other tufas became available to the Romans during the early decades of Rome's expansion in Latium and southern Etruria, specifically with the conquests of Fidenae in 426 B.C. and of Veii ca. 396 B.C., where *Fidenae* and *Grotta Oscura* tufas were quarried, respectively. Both were used extensively in Rome until the end of the second century B.C. but seldom thereafter. The use of both types in the so-called Servian walls of Rome has permitted the date of those walls to be correctly assigned to the Republic of the fourth century. Both are also used in the lower levels of temples A and C in the area sacra di Largo Argentina; *Fidenae* can also be identified in the third phase of the temple(s) of the area sacra di S. Omobono. *Grotta Oscura* apparently became very popular during this period; it has been identified in the lowest levels of the Basilica Aemilia, in the temple of Veiovis on the Capitoline, in the round temple of the Forum Boarium, and in the Aemilian and Mulvian bridges. The *Fidenae* tufa quarries are mentioned specifically by Vitruvius, and it is possible that the *Rubra* quarries mentioned in the same passage are those near Veii (if it can be connected with ancient Saxa Rubra and the west bank of the Tiber) from which *Grotta Oscura* was obtained.[62]

Anio *and* Monteverde *Tufas*

Two harder stones than *Grotta Oscura* and *Fidenae, Anio* and *Monteverdi* tufas came into use around the middle of the second century B.C., and they seem quickly to have been preferred, perhaps as soon as the new quarries were established and transport and delivery of the stone arranged. *Monteverde* was mined on the west side of the Tiber on the slopes of the Janiculum Hill, especially to the south in the area now known as Magliana. *Anio* tufa was extracted from the still-evident quarries at Tor Cervara, near the eighth milestone of the via Tiburtina northeast of the city. The ancient name for *Monteverde* is not preserved; Lugli identifies the quarries at *Palla* mentioned by Vitruvius as the *Anio* quarries near Tor Cervara and therefore calls *Anio* tufa *lapis Pallens* (Vitruvius actually employs the form *lapis Pallenses*), but this identification must remain hypothetical. Both tufas were widely used. *Monteverde* was used in a reworking of the foundations of the temple of Apollo *in Circo* ca. 179 B.C., in the temple of Concord in 121 B.C., in the upper level of the Carcer Mamertinum, and in temple B of the Largo Argentina (as well as the second phase of Temple A), all ca. 100 B.C., while *Anio* can first be found in the Aqua Marcia (144 B.C.), and then, extensively, in the reworked platform of Temple A in the Largo Argentina (ca. 120 B.C.), in the Mulvian bridge (ca. 109 B.C.), in the Tomb of the Scipios (ca. 100 B.C.), and in the Carcer Mamertinum (also ca. 100 B.C.). Both tufas remained in regular use into the Imperial period, appearing in the second half of the first century A.D. in various contexts.[63]

Campidoglio *Tufa*

A light red tufa of the same strength, consistency, and geological origin as *Monteverde* and *Anio, Campidoglio* tufa occurs on the Capitoline Hill near the Tarpeian rock, as well as on the Palatine and on the east edge of the Aventine. The local strata seem only rarely to have been quarried, perhaps because of the increased population and urbanization of Rome in the second and first centuries B.C. Blocks of *Campidoglio* tufa can be seen in the steps of the earliest Rostra in the Roman Forum and possibly in the podium of the temple of Concord, but these deposits were little exploited.[64]

Peperino (lapis Albanus)

Alban tufa is named by Vitruvius. It was quarried from the Alban hills near Marino and named for ancient Alba Longa (modern Castel Gandolfo). Its modern name alludes to its dark gray color. It, too, came into use in the middle of the second century B.C. and is probably best known as the pepper-colored stone from which the sarcophagus of Scipio, son of Barbatus, now in the Vatican Museums, was made; this is its earliest certainly datable occurrence. It was also employed for voussoirs in the Aqua Marcia (144 B.C.) and for both columns and entablature of the temple of the Magna Mater on the Palatine (either 191 or 110 B.C.). It was widely used in the first century B.C.: in Sulla's Tabularium, Pompey's theater, and Augustus's temple of Mars Ultor; it was still being used for the foundation and podium of the temple of Antoninus and Faustina in the Roman Forum in the mid-second century A.D. Its dark gray color was regularly combined with off-white travertine, but perhaps not for visual effect since most such stone masonry is thought to have been stuccoed. Of special importance for construction were the fire resistant properties of peperino, and for that reason it was employed in fire walls including those of the fora of Augustus and of Trajan.[65]

Sperone (lapis Gabinus)

Quarried, just as its name implies, near Gabii on the via Praenestina, Gabine tufa or *sperone* was first used in the piers of the Mulvian Bridge (109 B.C.). It is the stone with which the outlet of the Cloaca Maxima was arched, but it is uncertain whether these arches should be dated to the end of the second century B.C. or to Agrippa's restoration of the great drain in 33 B.C. It was certainly used in the walls of the Tabularium (78 B.C.), the Pons Fabricius (62 B.C.), in the *tabernae* of the west flank of the Forum Julium (which may date to ca. 46 B.C. or to a Domitianic restoration), and— together with *peperino*—in the towering fire walls that formed the rear curtain of the Forum of Augustus. Gabine tufa was not a particularly good building stone per se, but like *peperino* it had strong fire resistant properties that recommended its use for fire protection walls, a property which appears to have saved the Forum of Augustus, for example, from devastation during the fire of A.D. 64.[66]

Travertino (lapis Tiburtinus)

Travertine, though a calcareous sedimentary rock rather than a volcanic tufa, occurs precisely because Latium was formed by volcanoes. It was created by deposits left on the ground by hot springs that had opened on the surface during the earliest volcanic eruptions in the Alban volcanoes. It was, and still is, found in its best quality in deposits between Bagni and Tivoli. Travertine is a hard, off-white stone still used today for curb stones throughout the city of Rome. It was not used by the ancient Romans before 109 B.C., when it appears in the Mulvian bridge. By the early first century B.C. it had begun to be used in tandem with *peperino* in almost all the major architectural monuments of the era, and its use continued unabated through the Empire. It can still be seen in the tomb of Caecilia Metella, the theater of Marcellus, and the temple of Castor (among others) from Augustan times, and it was used extensively in the Flavian amphitheater.[67]

These stones—eight volcanic tufas (one, *Campidoglio,* hardly ever used) and one related sedimentary stone—provided the basic building stone of Rome and of central Italy throughout ancient times. Vitruvius, after listing a number of these stones from Latium, goes on to describe them and shows quite clearly that their strengths and their liabilities were well-known to architects of his time:[68]

> All these quarries which are of soft stone have this advantage: when stones are taken from these quarries they are easily handled in working, and if they are in covered places, they sustain their burden, but if they are in open and exposed places, they combine with ice and hoar frost, are turned to powder and are dissolved: along the sea coast, also, being weathered by the brine, they crumble and do not endure the heat.

Travertine, however, and all stones which are of the same kind, withstand injury from heavy loads and from storms; but from fire they cannot be safe; as soon as they are touched by it they crack and break up.

It is perhaps surprising, given his interest in fire resistance and the fact that it was already in use before his day, that Vitruvius never mentions Gabine tufa, but that omission aside it seems clear that the basic repertoire of building, as opposed to decorative, stone available to Roman architects was limited to these. We are nowhere given specific information about their quarrying nor any way to assess it as a business. The ancient evidence we have is concerned solely and entirely with the properties, appearance, and reliability of these local stones.

CONCRETE AND ITS TUFA MASONRY

The use made of the building stones changed radically after the development of Roman concrete (*opus caementicium*) early in the second century B.C. or possibly slightly before. The preparation and use of mortar as a bonding agent between stone blocks had long been known, and the Romans were aware that it had to be produced by mixing together sand and lime in proper proportions with water. Vitruvius specifies a mixture of three parts sand to one part lime if pit sand is used but a proportion of two to one if the sand comes from the river or the sea. In the latter case, since the sand is clearly of inferior quality, Vitruvius urges that crushed and sifted potsherds be added to the sand in a proportion of one part sherds to three parts sand before mixing with lime to produce an overall material that is better for use as a mortar.[69]

At some point, probably quite early in the development of mortar, it became apparent to builders working in Latium and Campania that the mortar they could produce by using the dark volcanic sand native to those areas yielded a bonding of remarkable strength and setting power. In Vitruvius's day it was common to attribute this property only to the sand produced around Mt. Vesuvius—hence, the particular name *pulvis Puteolanus*, also occasionally called *pulvis Baianus*—but, in fact, almost all the sand used for making mortar in Latium and Campania from the beginning of the second century

B.C. onward was of this type. Vitruvius makes a distinction between regular sand, *harena,* and *pulvis Puteolanus,* which is quite correct. What he was apparently unaware of was that there was a great deal of "pozzolana" (as it has come to be called) readily available in huge deposits along the valleys of both the Tiber and the Anio rivers very near Rome.[70] It is not possible to determine, however, whether this was merely an oversight on his part or a lacuna in his knowledge or whether Romans themselves were not yet aware of or exploiting their own vast stores of "pozzolana." It is at least possible that many of the impressive early monuments of Roman concrete architecture, such as the Porticus Aemilia built between 193 and 174 B.C.,[71] whose concrete is every bit as strong as that of buildings known to have been constructed using "pozzolana" in their mortar, were built with sand brought from nearby but which shared the remarkable properties Vitruvius ascribes to "pozzolana."

Vitruvius's description of *pulvis Puteolana* is fascinating:[72]

> There is also a kind of powder which, by nature, produces wonderful results. It is found in the neighborhood of Baiae and in the lands of the municipalities around Mount Vesuvius. This being mixed with lime and rubble not only furnishes strength to other buildings, but also, when piers are built in the sea, they set under water. Now this seems to happen for this reason: that under these mountainous regions there are both hot earth and many springs. And these would not be unless deep down they had huge blazing fires of sulphur, alum or pitch. Therefore the fire and vapour of flame within, flowing through the cracks, makes that earth light. And the tufa which is found to come up there is free from moisture. Therefore, when three substances formed in like manner by the violence of fire come into one mixture, they suddenly take up water and cohere together. They are quickly hardened by the moisture and made solid, and can be dissolved neither by the waves nor the power of water.

This remarkable bonding mortar revolutionized Roman architecture. Walls of bonded courses of cut stone could not provide anything like the sheer strength of a wall created by pouring a mixture of "pozzolana" mortar and stone rubble between elevations of facing masonry made up of cut tufa or brick or ashlar blocks, which were already in place so that they would be held in place by the concrete when it was poured and, simultaneously, provide external protection for the wall, thus eliminating the need for frames or shuttering.[73] Furthermore, since concrete will take on the form of the mold or frame into which it is poured, rather than having to be cut to shape, the plasticity inherent in concrete challenged Roman architects to experiment and devise new solutions, often arched or vaulted rather than post-and-lintel, to the point that the arch and the vault executed in concrete became one of the fundamental design principles in the repertoire of the Roman architect.[74]

This technical development came to Roman Italy at the same time that Roman builders were being exposed to the influence of the architectural grandeur of the Hellenistic kingdoms and to the extraordinary creations of the Hellenistic architects such as Hermogenes. The result was the creation of what Vituvius called in architecture the *consuetudo Italica*, the formation of the truly and distinctively Roman sort of monumental architecture, based on the strength and plasticity of cement rather than on the structural properties of cut stone dressed with cut tufa or brick masonry facings, then decorated in stucco or in precious stone like marble. The earliest surviving examples in Italy of the sort of grandiose monument that could be achieved by this new architecture must include the sanctuary of Fortuna Primigeneia at Praeneste, the reworked sanctuary of Juno at Gabii, and, somewhat later, the sanctuary of Jupiter Anxur at Tarracina, but such utilitarian constructions as the Porticus Aemilia and the Emporium are every bit as much products of the combination of the new concrete architecture with experimentation in Hellenistic and other imported building types. We should remember that Romans had apparently become remarkably good at "hellenistic" architecture early on in the second century B.C., as is evidenced by the career of Decimus Cossutius. By the time of Sulla in the first decades of the first century B.C., the *consuetudo Italica*, the adapting of Hellenistic ideas of planning and form into Roman concrete construction and concepts of decoration, had become the dominant form in Roman architecture. Roman concrete and its exploitation were what made this revolution a reality.[75]

The uses to which the traditional building stones of Rome were put in concrete architecture placed far less burden on these not very satisfactory tufas. They were reduced to serving as facings for rubble and concrete walls, becoming a form of disguising masonry rather than true building stone that contributed to the strength of the wall itself. Again, Vitruvius describes these styles of walling for us:[76]

> There are two kinds of walling; one like network, *opus reticulatum,* which all use now, and the old manner which is called *opus incertum.* Of these the reticulatum is more graceful, but it is likely to cause cracks because it has the beds and joints in every direction. The "uncertain" rough work, *opus incertum,* lying course above course and breaking joints, furnishes walling which is not pleasing but is stronger than reticulatum. Both kinds of walling are to be built with very minute stones.

Archaeology attests to the general chronology given by Vitruvius: *opus incertum,* which used small but unshaped or only irregularly shaped stones as a facing for the rubble and concrete cores of walls (fig. 3.2) is found in the Porticus Aemilia at the beginning of the second century and may have been in use as early as the restorations to various of the monuments in the Forum Romanum carried out between 210 and 200 B.C. In short, the development of *opus incertum* is contemporary with the development of Roman concrete itself.[77]

Opus incertum was in use throughout Roman Italy at the same time, as shown by its appearance in walls datable between 200 and 150 B.C. at Ostia, in house walls at Norba, in temple podia at Marzabotto, in the city walls of Pompeii and at various spots in the temples of Apollo and of Jupiter, in the orchestra and lower rows of seats of the large theater, in the tribunal of the basilica, and in the Stabian Baths of that city, and possibly at a variety of other places in Italy.[78] *Opus incertum* remained in use through the first quarter of the first century B.C. and occasionally appears later than that. But in general it gave way to the increasingly regular "network" of small shaped tufa blocks that Vitruvius calls *opus reticulatum.*

As often happens in the history of developments, the shift from *incertum* to *reticulatum* was gradual, not radical or sudden. Rather, the monuments attest to a growing tendency to face concrete walls with uniform-sized blocks of tufa laid in a diamond pattern. The

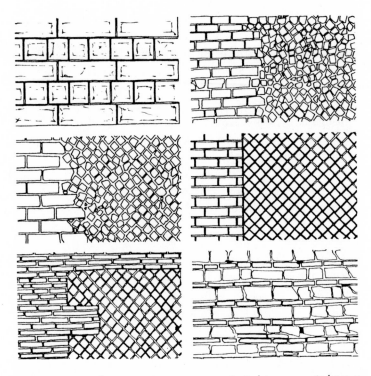

Figure 3.2 Opus quadratum, opus incertum, opus quasi reticulatum, opus reticulatum et testaceum, opus mixtum, opus vittatum (left to right, top to bottom). [Coarelli (1974) p. 342; reproduced by permission of Arnoldo Mondadori Editore]

earlier attempts, which fail to achieve uniform regularity in the lines of blocks, have been labeled *opus quasi-reticulatum* by archaeologists; there is no such term in Vitruvius. Vitruvius, indeed, is slightly misleading in his description of the two styles of masonry, since he implies that the shift from *incertum* to *reticulatum* was for him a contemporary event, when in fact the transition was complete by the middle of the first century B.C., at least twenty-five years before Vitruvius wrote.[79] Examples of this early transitional *reticulatum* can be seen at Rome in the House of the Griffins and the so-called House of Livia, both on the Palatine Hill, as well as in Livia's villa at Prima Porta, in the Sullan walls and the cella of the Hercules temple at Ostia, in the House of the Dioscuri and the second phase of the

Villa of the Mysteries at Pompeii, and in innumerable less well-known buildings at these sites and in many other Roman sites around Italy.[80] It can be all but impossible to distinguish between walls archaeologists label "late *opus incertum*" and "*quasi-reticulatum*," which simply emphasizes the fact that this was a continuum of development in masonry style, not a sudden nor a rapid change as Vitruvius seems to suggest.[81]

It is generally asserted that "true" *opus reticulatum* first appears in Rome in the Theater of Pompey, which was completed in 55 B.C. A number of its substructural passages still exist. Perhaps a better way to think of it is to say that by the time of the construction of Pompey's theater, the use of reticulate to provide an absolutely regular network of diamond-shaped blocks across the entire surface of concrete and rubble walls (see fig. 3.2 above) had been established, and it was employed regularly from that time forward.[82] In *opus reticulatum* the tufa blocks are cut to a uniform size and shaped like small rectangular boxes, flat at one end and terminating, at the other end (which was inserted into the concrete), in small "pyramids." During the construction process, these small blocks were put in position before the concrete was poured and took the place of framing or shuttering inserted with their inward-turned points bonding into the concrete and the bottoms of their bases forming the exterior masonry. By the time of major construction work in Rome under Augustus, that is, by the later 30s B.C., *opus reticulatum* had become firmly established as the preferred method of facing concrete walls, and its use spread throughout Roman Italy. Its absolute dominance for such masonry lasted only until the early first century A.D., when kiln-dried brick began to be used, first in combination with reticulate facing, then on its own. While tufa continued to be quarried and employed for foundations and substructures, and for masonry, its economic importance—never very great due to its easy accessibility and ease of workmanship—appears to have lessened. Even its importance in wall facing decreased with the rise to prominence of baked brick, although reticulate did not disappear from use. The rapid adoption of brick was the next major step in the development of Roman architecture, and brick became the central commodity in an important supply industry about which we have a fair amount of information left to us.

BRICK AND TILE

The manufacture of bricks and tiles from the mixing of clay and straw, shaped and then dried by the sun, was traditional in the Mediterranean and seems always to have been known to the Italians; certainly they were used in the Greek colonies of Sicily and southern Italy from their foundation, as well as by the Etruscans. The Etruscans may also have made use of bricks dried by fire, a sort of semibaked brick,[83] but no kiln-baked bricks are attested with certainty in Roman architecture before the early years of the reign of Augustus, and even then only in monuments or in parts of buildings that seem to have been especially exposed to humidity. The earliest example of extensive use of baked brick in a Roman building is the tomb of Caecilia Metella on the via Appia, which can be dated anywhere from 50 to 20 B.C.[84] Thus we see baked brick just beginning to enter into use at the time Vitruvius was writing his *De Architectura*. Vitruvius never specifically describes the manufacture or use of baked brick, but he clearly knew of its existence since he draws a precise terminological distinction between baked brick (*later coctus*) and unbaked or sun-dried brick (*later crudus*) when describing materials appropriate for use in city walls.[85] In his more general treatment of building materials, he does provide a discussion of sun-dried brick and how it was made, but passes over baked brick, presumably because it was made of the same materials, merely hardened in a kiln rather than in the sun (and hence not so susceptible to the time of year):[86]

> [Bricks] ought not to be made from sandy nor chalky soil nor gravelly soil: because when they are got from these formations, first they become heavy, then, when they are moistened by rain showers in the walls, they come apart and are dissolved. And the straw does not stick in them because of their roughness. But bricks are to be made of white clayey earth or of red earth, or even of rough gravel. For these kinds, because of their smoothness, are durable. . . . Now bricks are to be made either in the spring or autumn, that they may dry at one and the same time. For those which are prepared at the summer solstice become faulty for this

reason: when the sun is keen and overbakes the top skin, it makes it seem dry, while the interior of the brick is not dried. And when afterwards it is contracted by drying, it breaks up what was previously dried. . . . But most especially they will be more fit for use if they are made two years before, for they cannot dry throughout before.

It is surprising that Vitruvius never returns to discuss the differences between sun-dried and kiln-dried brick, but this could well be due to the fact that kiln-dried brick was in his day a very new commodity. The kiln-drying process eliminated both of the main problems that the author cites as affecting the strength of brick: baked brick comes from the kiln completely dry all the way through and does not contract further; hence the problem of cracks due to contraction is mostly eliminated as long as the baking has been done at an even temperature. Thus both the need for manufacture only at certain times of the year, and the need for a two-year drying process, were eliminated by the adoption of baking brick in kilns.[87] Vitruvius's word for brick (*later*, pl. *lateres*) appears as early as Plautus and the elder Cato and continued in common use as attested in Caesar, Cicero, and Varro prior to Vitruvius's own work.[88] Vitruvius is the first Roman writer to draw a verbal distinction between sun-dried and kiln-dried brick by using the adjective *latericius* specifically for sun-dried and coining the adjective *testaceus* for the baked variety.[89] Bricks came to be labeled according to their size as baked:[90] *bessales* (two-thirds of a Roman foot = ca. 19.8 cm.), *sesquipedales* (one and a half feet = ca. 44.4 cm.), and *bipedales* (two feet = ca. 59.2 cm.) (fig. 3.3).

In addition to bricks for masonry, the brickmakers produced roof, or pan, tiles (*tegula*) and the accompanying ridge, or cover, tiles (*imbrex*) essential to roofing, as well as other sorts of clay products for building and for other purposes.

During the reign of Tiberius (A.D. 14–37) baked brick was used for the first time as the primary facing masonry for rubble and concrete walls in the Castra built for the Pretorian Guards as well as in the walls of his new palace on the west summit of the Palatine, the Domus Tiberiana;[91] it appears to have come into use in building warehouses (*horrea*) for storage of shipped goods at Ostia at about

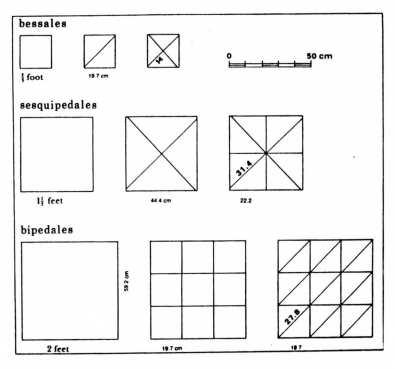

Figure 3.3 Different sizes of Roman bricks. [Adam (1994) fig. 347, p. 147; reproduced by permission of the author and of Indiana University Press]

the same time.[92] From that time until late antiquity brick remained in constant use in Roman architecture, in a variety of different masonry styles. The correct Latin name for masonry facing done entirely in baked brick was apparently *opus testaceum,* employing Vitruvius's adjective, but archaeologists also sometimes use *opus latericium,* although that should properly refer to masonry of sun-dried brick, which was not used once baked brick became readily available (see fig. 3.2 above). So extensive did the use of *opus testaceum* become that even a simple listing of examples in Rome and Italy between the reign of Claudius (A.D. 41–54) and that of Theoderic (A.D. 493–526) would require many pages.[93] In the reign of Nero (A.D. 54–68), especially after the terrible fire (A.D. 64), *opus testaceum* was employed to an overwhelming degree in Rome itself,[94] though not in the surrounding countryside of Latium nor in Ostia until later. This continued through the reign of Hadrian (A.D. 117–138). While there was much less building going on in Rome, and generally in Italy, after Hadrian's time, what was done both in Rome and, even more clearly, in Ostia from A.D. 138 until the massive projects carried out under Septimius Severus (A.D. 193–211) and his successors down to A.D. 235 was also regularly accomplished in *opus testaceum,* as were such subsequent major building projects in the capital as the city walls erected by Aurelian (A.D. 270–275), the new Curia and the Baths built under Diocletian (A.D. 284–306), and the immense Basilica Nova of Maxentius (A.D. 307–312), which was reworked under Constantine (A.D. 312–337). At its finest, under the Flavians, Trajan and Hadrian, Roman brick masonry has seldom if ever been equalled in world architecture for the extraordinary skill and elegance with which it was employed.[95]

During the same years in which *opus testaceum* was slowly coming to prominence, another type of wall facing appeared which combined the older *opus reticulatum* to cover expanses of wall face with the new baked brick used for vertical piers and quoins as well as in periodic horizontal bands. This constituted a compromise form of masonry, and its use spread—especially in Latium and at Ostia, though not so much in Rome itself—more quickly than that of exclusively brick masonry. The visual effect of this composite masonry is as if panels of *opus reticulatum* had been set into surrounding frames of *opus testaceum.*[96] We have no record of an ancient name for this masonry style; logically, if somewhat uneuphoniously, archaeologists have coined the phrase *opus mixtum* for this mixture of the two masonry techniques (see fig. 3.2 above). The earliest example of its use appears to be in the water channel (*specus*) of the Anio Novus aqueduct, which was constructed ca. A.D. 50, in the surviving stretch from Le Capannelle into Rome. In the city it is seen periodically in buildings erected before the reign of Trajan (A.D. 98–117), and it never seems to have been widely used there, but in the *suburbium* around Rome—where so many of the great villas of the Imperial period were located—it was used frequently in wall construction from the reign of Domitian (A.D. 81–96) onward.[97] At Ostia *opus mixtum* is ubiquitous at least from

Flavian times well into the reign of Trajan, only thereafter being replaced by *opus testaceum* for the rest of the second century and into the third. It was also in use at Pompeii between the earthquake of A.D. 62 and the eruption of Vesuvius in A.D. 79 and is much in evidence in remains from the time of Domitian until the mid-second century A.D. all over Campania.[98] In Campania, and particularly in Pompeii, a local variant of *opus mixtum* seems to have been invented in which *opus incertum* rather than *opus reticulatum* was employed together with brick.

There are two further masonry styles in Roman building that employed baked brick. *Opus spicatum* was a method of setting bricks into concrete in a herringbone pattern. It is most common in flooring rather than in walls, and is often used in association with the waterproof mortar invented by the Romans to use on floors near or in fountains, called *opus signinum*; it appears as a wall facing only in the western European provinces, most commonly in Gaul.[99]

Opus vittatum, another name invented by scholars but not known from ancient sources, had been used in central Italy outside Rome as early as the late second century B.C. This facing consists of horizontal rows of tufa (or other stone) or interspersed rows of tufa and brick with thick bands of mortar between each row, which reduced the quantity of facing material required. In the second and first centuries B.C. it was executed solely in stone; this first type of *opus vittatum* continued in use periodically in central Italy at places where tufa was abundant but brick had to be brought in. For instance, there are walls of tufa *vittatum* in various sections of Hadrian's villa near Tivoli and at various spots around Italy that date from almost every period of Roman construction. All-stone *opus vittatum* is also known from many parts of the western Empire.[100] In the first century A.D., a variant form of *opus vittatum* came into use more or less simultaneously in Latium, Campania (especially at Pompeii), and Gaul in which the rows of local stone are interrupted every so often by layers of brick (see fig. 3.2 above), the proportion of brick to stone varying widely from place to place. This version of *opus vittatum* became increasingly common in Roman architecture from the middle of the second century A.D. onward and by the middle to late third century was being employed even in the most prestigious and expensive buildings, presumably because of the failure of the brick supply and the necessity to turn once again to local tufas for masonry. Its use is often a good indicator of third or fourth century A.D. construction or restoration of buildings in Rome, the *suburbium*, Latium and particularly at Ostia. Its frequency of use increased in the European provinces, especially in Gaul, during the second century A.D.[101]

As baked brick took on a role in construction during the late first century B.C., and particularly as *opus testaceum* and *opus mixtum* came into extensive use in the first century A.D., the demand for brick led to the development of one of the more remarkable industries of Rome. While the brick industry functioned in many parts of the Empire, the evidence for it is most extensive and best known in and around Rome, where demand was greatest, and it is at Rome that we can consider the production of brick and tile as a true example of an ancient industry. The evidence for the industry, its organization, and its participants is almost entirely epigraphical.

Beginning near the end of the first century B.C., just as baked brick became important, its makers began from time to time impressing stamps onto the bricks and the texts of these stamps form the raw data of our information. The brick stamps from the time of Augustus until the time of Nero tended to be simple, usually just one person's name plus occasionally the name of the brickyard (*figlinae*) from which the brick itself came. Late in the first century, probably on account of the gigantic increase in demand that the brickmakers experienced after A.D. 64, the stamps tended to become increasingly elaborate and correspondingly more informative, probably because of the rapid development of organized procedure that would have been needed in the brick industry. By the end of the first or beginning of the second century A.D. the shapes of the stamps had become quite varied as had the quantities of information they might contain. In A.D. 110 for the first time so far known to us the names of the consuls of Rome for that year were included in the text of a brick stamp, thus providing an absolute date for the manufacture of bricks so stamped; this occurs periodically thereafter until A.D. 164. Brick stamps continue to appear on bricks into the reign of Caracalla (A.D. 211–217). There is an inexplicable but total hiatus in the use of stamps bearing texts between the end of the reign of Caracalla and the beginning of the reign of Diocletian (A.D. 284–306); in later antiquity they reappear, almost always bearing only the name of an emperor, all the way into the fifth century A.D. (fig. 3.4).[102]

The stamps can provide five different sorts of information, depending on their texts; no one stamp carries all five, however, so the gathering of their evidence is a laborious and specialized study. The five kinds of information that may appear on brick stamps are:[103]

1. the type of product it is, for instance, a tile (*tegula*) or, more generally, a brick/tile product (*opus doliare*);
2. the name of the clay field from which the raw material came, or of the brickyard where it was made (*figlinae*);
3. the name of the owner (*dominus, domina*) of the place, usually a private estate, on which the clay was located (*praedia*);

Figure 3.4 Examples of brick stamps, first century B.C. to fourth century A.D. [Adam (1984) fig. 146, p. 67; reproduced by permission of the author]

    4. the name of whoever was in charge of producing the brick (*officinator* or once in a while *conductor*); and

    5. the names of the consuls of the year it was produced (*COS(S)*).

The names are frequently abbreviated, sometimes drastically so (to a single letter), and while this habit hampers certain identification of the parts of the name in some instances—whether an initial represents a *praenomen*, a *nomen*, or a *cognomen* can be impossible to decide without independent evidence—and while slaves are generally connected with the names of their masters (given in the genitive case to show ownership), there is otherwise little consistency among the different stamps as to which elements of names are presented or in what order they appear.[104] In a few cases persons mentioned on the brick stamps are known independently of them as well, but these are almost always either estate owners[105] or consuls, members of the aristocracy.

What the stamps do clearly tell us is that there were two people essential to the production of brick in the Roman system: the *dominus* or *domina* who owned the estate, and hence the clay from which the brick was made, and the *officinator* who must be the manufacturer. Owners tended to be aristocrats, often of senatorial rank, and quite often female; *officinatores* came usually from the lower middle stratum of Roman society and were often freedmen or slaves.[106] The very high social status of the *domini* has been interpreted to reflect an ever increasing stranglehold on ownership of the brick industry in ever fewer and more influential hands. This led in the end to its disappearance into an Imperial monopoly, but the relative independence of the *officinatores* from the *domini* may imply that, rather than being agents tied to the estates of the *domini*, the *officinatores* often acted as independent entrepreneurs, possibly leasing the brickyards for production with the clay fields and workshops included in the arrangement. *Officinatores* do not, however, seem to have owned their *officinae*, and they do not become *domini*. It is probably overall the best suggestion to think of them rather like *institores*, or workshop managers, who were the more-or-less independent contractors responsible for the running of a number of other businesses in the Roman world.[107] In this social context, it also makes excellent sense to think of *figlinae* and *praedia* as essentially equivalent terms that indicate the brickyards located on or near the actual fields that produced the clay from which the bricks were made, and the *officina* as the actual production unit, presided over by the *officinator*.[108]

It is of particular interest that such a large number of women are attested in brick stamps, both as *dominae* and as *officinatores*. A few examples will reward closer scrutiny. In many cases these were women of the very highest aristocracy who held or had inherited landed estates and hence were *dominae* to the brickyards operating on them. A remarkable example is Flavia Seia Isaurica, who was *domina* of six separate brickyards that operated more or less contemporaneously, though on different estates, between A.D. 115 and 141. These were the *figlinae Aristianae, Caelianae, Fabianae, Publilianae, Tonneianae* and *Tur*(?). It was from the evidence of her ownership of brickyards on separate estates that Helen concluded that the word *figlinae* probably meant a "clay district," which would have been a specific location within a private estate, while the actual workshop making the bricks was the *officina*.[109]

Brickstamps are among the best pieces of evidence we have for another influential female aristocrat, or possibly two, of the mid-second century A.D., called both Domitia Lucilla and Lucilla Veri on various stamps. We know that "Lucilla Veri" (Lucilla wife of Verus) was the name used by Domitia P.f. Lucilla Minor between A.D. 145 and 155. It is possible, however, that other stamps which refer to Lucilla Veri as a *domina* who employed the slave Earinus as her agent (*actor*) might be naming Lucilla Minor's mother, Domitia Cn.f. Lucilla Maior; furthermore there are other stamps in which Earinus is listed as *actor* of "Domitia Lucilla," who might be either the mother or the daughter. Perhaps the most interesting thing shown by this is that the ownership of brickyards could and did pass, presumably by inheritance, from mother to daughter, just like ownership (and the services) of a slave.[110]

There are also attested women working as *officinatores,* whether as free entrepreneurs or directly as workshop managers in brickyards, and the female *officinator* was specifically provided for in

Roman law.[111] Children, both female and male, worked in the brickyards from a fairly early age. An inscription from Pietrabbondante in Samnium, datable to the first years of the first century B.C., records two female slaves, named Amica and Detfri, slaves of Herennius Sattius, who was a well-known tile manufacturer. The two women had signed the tile when they made it and impressed their footprints on it, one set of footprints and one signature on each side. Aubert estimates from the size of the footprints that Amica and Detfri would only have been about twelve years old, though admitting that such estimation is largely speculative. What is perhaps more surprising than the possible employment of slave children, which was common in the Roman world, is that the two girls were literate. Given their possession of this skill, it is reasonable to suppose that they may have been record-keepers or office staff or even, to some degree, managers in the workshop.[112]

The record of brick stamps, most important those that have been found *in situ* in otherwise datable architectural contexts, has contributed tremendously to the chronological study of Roman Imperial architecture[113] and at the same time permits us to trace the chronology of the individual brickyards and thence of the whole industry with unparalleled completeness in ancient history.[114] The brick industry grew on account of the intense demand generated after the fire of A.D. 64 and by the immense building programs undertaken by Nero, the Flavians, and Trajan into the early decades of the second century A.D. It reached its highpoint of development under Hadrian, who may have attempted to regulate or reform the industry in some way, since our evidence shows that in the year A.D. 123 the names of the consuls Paetinus and Apronianus were included on every stamp used in that year. This was at the same time that M. Annius Verus, himself an important *dominus* in the industry, was also city prefect of Rome and may have insisted upon meticulous use of these stamps.[115] We do not know exactly what Hadrian was attempting to accomplish, and whatever it was it does not seem to have worked, since brick stamps are never again used so extensively.

After Hadrian's reign, public and private building slowed down and so must have the heaviest demand for bricks. Through the end of the second century A.D., the brick industry seems to have shrunk. A number of the smaller brickyards disappear from the stamps altogether, either put out of business or absorbed by larger ones such as those of the *gens Domitia,* and the number of both *domini* and *officinatores* attested on stamps declines. An example of what was happening can be seen in two brickyards, the *figlinae Furianae* and *Tempesinae,* which belonged to Q. Aburnius Caedicianus. His two separate yards had flourished until the last few years of Hadrian's reign, when a number of his *officinatores* began to drift to employment in other brickyards or disappeared altogether. By the next decade, so much had the production from his holdings shrunk that the same stamps were being used to stamp bricks from both yards.[116] Brickyards seem to have come more and more often into the ownership of the Emperors; even the immense holdings of the *gens Domitia* were acquired by Marcus Aurelius, although admittedly as a result of normal inheritance, and by the time of Septimius Severus an industry that had grown and flourished as a private enterprise in which land owners developed and exploited the possibilities of their lands by letting skilled brickmakers establish, either by lease or by contract, brick workshops on them, appears to have become little more than an Imperially owned and controlled monopoly.

The abandonment of the use of stamps on brick altogether after the death of Caracalla (A.D. 217) must indicate that there was some further radical shift in the industry, but there is no evidence upon which to base speculation, since all is suddenly silent. A reform sometime during this silent period, often attributed to Aurelian (A.D. 270–275), seems to have led to a change in the terminology employed on the stamps after their reappearance under Diocletian and must indicate another reorganization of brick production, since in late third and fourth century stamps *figlinae* are called *officinae*—administrative units of some sort—while what had been *officinae,* or actual offices of brick production, come to be labeled *stationes.* The reason for these changes is not known. What is apparent is that the brick industry came to be all but completely dominated by the new system of government introduced by Diocletian, as a monopoly in which there appears to have been almost no place for the *officinator* any longer.[117] For no other ancient industry do we have so much information or so clear a chronological development.

The main question that remains about the organization of the Roman brick industry is why the bricks were stamped at all. Various suggestions can be made. Steinby has suggested that the texts were really abridged versions of the legal contract that must have existed between *dominus* and *officinator.*[118] In her interpretation, the contract implied was a typical work contract (*locatio conductio operis faciendi*) under Roman law, which would list (as do the stamps with fuller texts) the object to be produced (in this case the *opus doliare* or *figlinum*), the landowner (*dominus* = *locator*) who wants his land developed, the entrepreneur (*officinator* = *conductor/redemptor*) who accepts the contract, and the place where the work is to be carried out (*ex figlinis*). This is a useful suggestion, but if true the stamp could have been no more than a shadow of such a contract, certainly not carrying any legal weight, since nowhere does it include the *merces* or price to be paid which was absolutely required in contracts in *locatio conductio*. A further potential problem is the fact that in brickyards, it was often the *dominus,* not the *officinator,* who owned the means of production which the manager made use of, which would invalidate a work contract but would have been possible under a labor contract (*locatio conductio operarum*). These objections are cogent, and must cause some doubt.[119] Nonetheless, Steinby's suggestion does permit her to go further and hypothesize a reasonable use for the stamps: that they allowed comparison between different brick production units operating in proximity within the same *figlinae* and/or under contract to the same *dominus.* This also aids in explaining the periodic inclusion of consular dates, which would have allowed a *dominus*—or an Imperial tax assessor if the production was being taxed by the government—to find out the annual production of each *officina.*

There are other possibilities, however. Helen suggested that the stamps might have been some sort of clue to geographical identification since the words *figlinae* or *praedia* are often accompanied by a localizing adjective, such as *Marcianae.*[120] He suggests that if the origin of the clay was known to the prospective purchaser, this could have served as a "quality mark" while the presence of the names of both landowner and brickmaker would have constituted a sort of "trademark." This idea is, of course, directly in line with Helen's redefinition of *figlinae* as a clay district, and a number of objections have been raised, including that there was no particular consistency of quality among bricks from the same yards and that some parts of the clay fields themselves may have overlapped estate lines and so been under different owners.[121] Some possible corroboration for Helen's idea may be seen in the evidence that Tiber Valley stamps are found on bricks in a remarkable number of areas of the Roman world. These might have been shipped around the Mediterranean, possibly to avoid empty holds on return voyages and to supply a limited demand for high quality brick to be used in important building work in areas such as North Africa, where there may not have been equally excellent clay available. It is possible, though perhaps less likely, that these bricks were manufactured locally (in the same vicinity where they were used) but stamped with stamps leased or contracted to the local branch workshop from the main brickyard in the Tiber Valley, as seems to have been the case with clay lamps throughout the Roman world.[122] In such cases the known stamps might have served as an identification of the source of the original brick, or as some sort of promise of quality in manufacture, although given the fact that the stamps had to be impressed on bricks before the bricks were fired, the idea of any guarantee of quality would seem fraudlent at best,[123] since the quality of any individual brick could not have been known until it was determined whether or not the baking had been successful. Poorly made bricks, however, might simply have been destroyed rather than sold, in order to protect the reputation of the manufacturer and the integrity of the stamp.

The other question still under investigation about the Roman brickyards is, where were they located? It has been amply demonstrated that the *figlinae Caepionianae, Marcianae, Subortanae,* and *Ocianae* were more or less next to one another near the town of Horta close to where the Nar River joins the Tiber on the border of Umbria and southern Etruria.[124] More such locations are reportedly established by the medieval registers that list *fundi*, registers preserved at the monastery of Farfa, but this has yet to be published.[125] Steinby has suggested that, in general, the names of brickyards mentioned on the stamps might be identified with homonymous places known from the ancient topography of central Italy, and on this basis it can be suggested that the *figlinae Bruttianae* should be near the "Campus Bruttianus" and "Vicus Brutianus" of ancient Transtiberim (modern Trastevere), and the *figlinae Mucianae* near the "prata Mucia trans Tiberim" (modern Prati), but this has done little but point up the major clay districts of the ancient territory, and publication of the material from Farfa is badly needed. An even more reliable method, not so far undertaken but promising, would be to study the chemical and mineralogical composition of different clays by using small samples from stamped bricks and then comparing them to samples from likely areas until the matching compositions were found, probably using wavelength-dispersive X-ray fluorescence, which has been experimented with successfully.[126] At this point we can be fairly certain that the main clay fields, and hence the main brickyards, probably included establishments—in addition to those mentioned above in Horta, in Trastevere, and in Prati—near the via Triumphalis (where brickyards were still functioning at the end of the nineteenth century), along the via Aurelia, the via Nomentana, the via Salaria, at Tusculum, at Aricia, and in the general vicinity of Ostia.[127] But this is an area in which much more scientific research is needed.

To conclude, we have in the Roman brick and tile industry a unique quantity of documentary evidence for the organization of and participants in one of the most important supply industries that serviced the Roman building and construction trade. Clearly, the fortunes of the brick industry and its practitioners were tied to the expansions and contractions of, primarily, the immense public building programs of the emperors of the first and second centuries A.D. The land and natural resource (clay fields) essential to the business were largely owned and exploited by wealthy aristocrats, up to and including the Imperial families.[128] Interestingly, the actual brickyards themselves—that is, the means of production as well as the raw materials—were owned by the *domini*. Actual exploitation of the fields, the manufacture of bricks, was done by *offi-*

cinatores, either free entrepreneurs or skilled slaves of the land-owners, who were essentially workshop managers. Whether the stamps themselves served as abbreviated forms of the legal contracts between *dominus* and *officinator,* thus permitting levels of production to be assessed between different workshops, or as records for general inventory in the brick business that would be useful to the Imperial bureaucracy, or as some form of identifying "trademark" or "quality guarantee" or even "advertisement" remains an open question. Perhaps they served various of these functions either at different periods or at one and the same time.

Women and children were involved in the business, not just as landowners but as managers and as brickmakers. The stamps seem to have been distributed widely around the Roman world, but what implications should be drawn from that remains to be clarified. Roman brickwork itself rose to become a fine art in the architecture, especially, of the second century A.D., as monuments like the Palatine palace of Domitian, the so-called Markets of Trajan and his Baths, and Hadrian's Pantheon reveal. During the second century A.D., bricks were of very high quality, regular in size, and closely spaced with thin courses of mortar between. So refined were the techniques that it was possible for several courses of bricks to be carved so accurately that they would create standard architectural moldings, as can still be seen in the Markets of Trajan and, especially, in the theater at Ostia.[129] But the private sector of the brick industry appears to have faltered in the second half of the second century A.D., and by the time of Septimius Severus or slightly before, brick supply—and the brickyards themselves—had come under the control of the Emperor, ending up as an Imperial monopoly. Nonetheless, the skill of Roman brick masons remains unsurpassed as monuments of the early third (e.g., the Severan additions to the Palatine palace, the Baths of Caracalla), later third (Aurelian's walls; Diocletian's Curia and his Baths), and early fourth (the Basilica Nova) centuries reveal, although the supply of new baked brick available clearly dwindled as reuse of brick made much earlier (which can be dated by its brickstamps) becomes common even in major official building projects such as the Aurelianic Walls (ca. A.D. 370–375).

MARBLE AND DECORATIVE STONE

There is no hard and fast line that can be drawn between stone used for construction and stone used for decoration; what is decorative in one context or in the hands of one designer may perfectly well be used for more mundane purposes by another. Two of the local stones discussed above can be found in construction of the Republican period used intentionally in decorative contexts: *peperino* was of high enough density that it would take and preserve decorative carving and so is found in carved entablatures in various monuments, where it would then presumably have been covered in stucco; travertine seems regularly to have been regarded as a decorative stone, presumably because of its near-white color, even long after the introduction of white marbles.[130] The Romans in Italy, especially in Rome itself, were slow to adopt marble into their architecture. As far as our sources tell us, it was Q. Caecilius Metellus Macedonicus who engaged Hermodorus to build the first marble temple in Rome, dedicated to Jupiter Stator and located in the Campus Martius near the Circus Flaminius, in 146 B.C. As late as the time of L. Licinius Crassus (who died in 91 B.C.) no marble columns had ever been used in a public building in Rome, and when Crassus introduced six of Hymettian marble into the atrium of his house—columns he had imported from Greece to be used in decorating the stage of a temporary theater—he was denounced for the extravagance.[131]

But a taste for imported marble, both white and colored, was on the rise. In the first quarter of the first century B.C., L. Licinius Lucullus, consul of 74 B.C., is said to have imported into Rome a large amount of a black marble with which he had been impressed and it came to be called after him, *marmor Luculleus.* Not too long after his sack of Athens in 86 B.C., Sulla is reported to have brought to Rome marble columns, or perhaps column capitals, taken from the temple of Olympian Zeus in Athens and to have set them up on the Capitoline Hill. M. Lepidus seems to have had to endure some sharp criticism for introducing lintels of yellow Numidian marble into his house.[132] By the middle of the first century B.C., marble was becoming accepted for architectural decoration: M. Aemilius Scau-

rus is said to have imported three hundred and sixty marble columns for the decoration of his temporary theater in 58 B.C. and only
stirred up minor comment.[133] We are told that the infamous
Mamurra, Julius Caesar's *praefectus fabrum* in the Gallic campaigns
and a man renowned for his wealth (as we have seen in chapter 1),
was the first Roman to revet (i.e., veneer) the walls of his *domus* in
marble brought from the Luna quarries of Italy, and that he also had
columns of both Luna and Carystian marble in his house.[134] By the
early years of the reign of Augustus, marble had become such an
accepted part of architecture that it could be introduced into the
official building program, first Agrippa's massive reworking of the
Campus Martius, then into all official construction, most notably in
Augustus's eponymous Forum and its temple to Mars Ultor.

It seems most likely that the marble used in the second century
B.C. and the first half of the first arrived in Rome by boats on the
Tiber and was distributed from the Emporium wharf, but in Augustus's time, most likely in the 30s B.C., a new wharf was designed
specifically for delivery of building materials, including marble, on
the river bank in the Campus Martius, near the Pons Aelius.[135] The
area around this wharf became a new center for stonecutters' workshops, and the whole system delivered to Agrippa's great project the
materials needed, which included vast amounts of imported marble. Tibullus describes the scene when a huge column of imported
marble had to be pulled through the narrow and winding streets of
the Campus Martius from this wharf for delivery:[136]

> His fancy turns to foreign marbles, and through the quaking city his
> column is carried by a thousand sturdy teams.

From the 30s B.C. marble became the most admired and most
prized of decorative materials in Roman architecture, used for the
revetment of walls both interior and exterior, for the sculpted columns, capitals and entablatures of great buildings, for interior columns and decoration in fine homes, and for the highly valued *opus
sectile*—cut pieces of colored stone worked into patterns—used so
magnificently for floor covering. By the later part of his long principate, Augustus could use marble as a symbol of the grandeur he

had brought to the city of Rome, in a famous remark quoted by Suetonius:[137]

> Since the city was not adorned as the dignity of the empire demanded, and was exposed to flood and fire, he so beautified it that he could justly boast that he had found it built of brick and left it in marble.

This quotation should not be taken too literally: the real explosion of brick-faced concrete architecture was barely beginning in Rome in the age of Augustus, and it is worthwhile remembering that Suetonius puts the Latin word for sun-dried brick (*latericium*) into the princeps' mouth making no reference at all to baked brick. By the same token, the city was by no means drenched in marble revetment in Augustus's day. Yet the remark indicates the future appearance of the finest Roman architecture clearly: it would become an architecture sheathed, faced, and floored in the finest white and colored marbles and similar decorative stones, many of which had to be imported. Because it was in his day a relative innovation in Roman architecture, Vitruvius says little about marble, although he does assert that the first marble quarries in the Mediterranean from which huge blocks for building were extracted were at Ephesus,[138] and is well aware of the many uses to which the Greeks had put marble. Certainly, the colored marbles just coming into favor in first century B.C. Rome had long been in use in the eastern Mediterranean and continued in use then, for example in Alexandria where Cleopatra's palace is said to have been decorated with them.[139] While the development of the quarries at Luna provided a ready source of white marble relatively close to Rome and hence cheaper to transport by land or river, the colored marbles and granite and porphyry were all reaching Rome in ever increasing quantities throughout Augustus's reign, the difficulty and expense of such long distance shipment from outside Italy notwithstanding.

The sources of most of the decorative stones used in Roman Imperial architecture have been identified, and these magnificent natural resources of the Mediterranean basin were exploited to a remarkable extent. In geological terms, marble is a limestone that has crystallized from pressure and heat. It is produced by medium- to high-grade metamorphism of carbonate sediments and is usually found in complex crystalline deposits of igneous and regionally metamorphosed rock. Such deposits occur widely in both Greece and Turkey, as well as on the Aegean islands, especially in Thrace and in various regions of Anatolia. With a few exceptions it was quarries in these deposits that supplied the marbles of Imperial Rome.[140] The most important of the white marbles used in Rome were brought from the following quarries: Luna, near modern Carrara, Italy; Mt. Pentelikon and Mt. Hymettos, near Athens; Proconnesos, on the island of Marmara in the Sea of Marmara; Thasos, from the island of Thasos off the coast of Thrace; and Paros, from the island of Paros in the mid Aegean Sea.[141] Less common in Rome, but still quarried in Roman times, were the white marbles from the Aegean island of Lesbos, and white varieties from quarries at Heracleia under Latmos, Docimium (much more important as a source of colored marble), Ephesus, and Aphrodisias, all in modern Turkey.[142]

Colored marbles were quarried at Carystos, on the island of Euboea in Greece, noted for dark or light green bands and commonly called *cipollino* in modern times since it has been thought to resemble onion skin; Cape Taenaros, in the Peloponnese of mainland Greece, a blood red to purple marble sometimes with white veins, commonly called *rosso antico;* Chalcis, from Boeotia in central Greece, which contains red, white, and purple inclusions of different shapes, often called *fior di pesco;* Chios, an island in the eastern Aegean, noted for delicate pastels in pink, purple, and gray, often referred to as *portasanta;* Thessaly, the north central mainland of Greece, a dark green marble, sometimes called *verde antico.* Other important quarries included Verzirken, in northwestern Turkey, producing a coral-colored marble with fragments of red, pink, yellow, and white, commonly called *breccia corallina;* Teos, an island in the eastern Aegean, noted for variable marbles in black, dark green, and gray with pink, grey, and white inclusions, confusingly called *africano* though not from Africa; Iasos, from southwestern Turkey, which provided red marble with white and gray bands that often undulate through the stone; Docimium, from Phrygia in central Turkey, especially renowned for its white or yellowish stone with purple markings, commonly called *pavonazzetto;* Simitthus, modern Chemtou in Numidia, the southern part of modern Tunisia, providing a wide range of shades of marble in yellow, from ivory to deep gold, often called *giallo antico;* and on Scyros, an island in the central Aegean where a dark purple marble with white, red, and yellow inclusions was found.[143]

Among the other major types of decorative building stone employed in Imperial architecture, porphyry was quarried at Croceae, near Sparta in the Peloponnese, a dark green porphyry with lighter green inclusions, often called *Lacedaemonian* or *Laconian;* and at Gebel Dokhan, ancient Mons Porphyrites, Egypt, a deep purple with tiny white inclusions.[144] Granite was obtained primarily from Syene, modern Aswan, Egypt, a red or pink granite with darker pink or grey inclusions; Mons Claudianus, modern Gebel Fatireh, Egypt, a grey granite with grey feldspar, white quartz or black mica inclusions; and from the Troad, northwestern Turkey, grey granite with large violet and white particles of quartz and feldspar and some black inclusions.[145]

The identification of these decorative stones in architecture was until recently based almost entirely upon visual observation, but the introduction of such chemical typing procedures as stable isotope analysis, especially for the marbles, has placed the entire procedure of identification on much more scientific ground.[146] Individual studies of particular quarries, as cited in notes to the list above, have also advanced our knowledge of the individual stones, how they were quarried, how the quarrying operations were organized, who were involved in the quarrying business, and how the stones were shipped from their sources to Rome.[147]

The quarrying of architectural stones began in Egypt, perhaps as far back as the Third Dynasty (2686–2613 B.C.), when granite monoliths were already being extracted and shipped between Aswan and Giza. The techniques invented there, with some refinements and modifications added over the centuries, were still essentially those used when the Mediterranean quarries came into Roman hands. How the stone was extracted depended on the way in which it had been deposited and on how valuable it was deemed to be. The most common method, where it could be used, was to work a large, sheer face of rock either vertically or horizontally or both at once, cutting off large pieces either by cutting narrow trenches around each block or, less laboriously, hammering in iron or wooden wedges to induce the block to split itself away from the quarry face. Other methods known included outlining separation trenches with lots of cylindrical holes on three sides of the block, then applying pressure from one corner to split the block away (often called the *pointillé* technique); a combination of the wedge and the *pointillé* methods; or in exceptional cases, as at Paros, tunneling into a quarryside in order to follow and extract a particularly precious vein of stone (fig. 3.5).[148]

Interestingly, quarrying in Greece seems to have been rather more sophisticated in its instruments and in application of some of the standard extraction methods than contemporary quarrying in Egypt as early as the Bronze Age, but at the same time in Anatolia Egyptian equipment and methods were the only ones known.[149] In classical Greco-Roman times the main technical innovation in the quarries seems to have been a Roman one: the application of the pendular saw, long used for working the faces of re-cut blocks of stone, to the removing of large sheets of stone for veneer directly from the quarry face. This was being done at the Docimium quarry in Phrygia by the third century A.D.[150] The transport of the stones was accomplished, wherever possible, by water. When the stone had to be dragged overland it was most often done by sheer force of pulling the stone which was placed on sleds with runners (fig. 3.6);when columns or column drums were to be moved overland, the cut stone itself was used as a roller, set in a wooden frame to protect it to some degree from damage, with iron pincers set into the ends of the stone, and the whole then harnessed to a team of oxen (fig. 3.7).Transport costs for quarried stone were always high and remained so throughout Roman Imperial times.[151]

For reasons that have yet to be completely explained, the emperor Tiberius seems to have taken control of many of the principal sources of supply of building stone. Suetonius describes this in a brief passage:[152]

> many states and individuals were deprived of immunities of long standing, and of the right of working mines [and quarries] and collecting revenues.

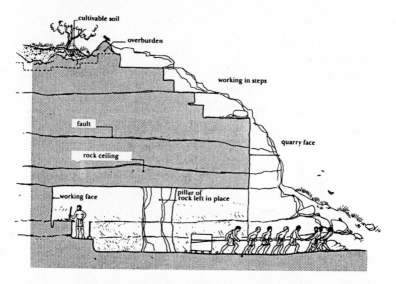

Figure 3.5 Varieties of extraction methods from a quarry, including tunneling. [Adam (1994) fig. 21, p. 22; reproduced by permission of the author and of Indiana University Press]

This has, until recently, been taken to indicate that Tiberius undertook a radical and rapid overhaul of the entire system of quarrying and transport and thus turned the emerging Roman marble trade into a partial Imperial monopoly. What is really being described is an extremely broad reform affecting not just quarries and mines, and certainly not just quarries of marble and other decorative stone, but also certain types of leasing rights and "immunities" of some unstated kinds but presumably involving production of various sorts. The remark is much too broad to build the image of an immediate and radical overhaul of the Roman marble trade upon. Rather it might better be seen as the starting point of the development of the Roman system for trading in decorative stone, a development that continued throughout the first century A.D., receiving special emphasis during the great building programs of Nero and the Flavian emperors, when the demand for marble, porphyry, and granite must have increased tremendously, just as had the demand for brick.[153]

Figure 3.6 Overland transport of stone by sled. [Adam (1984) fig. 31. p. 30; reproduced by permission of the author]

The usual historical model cited for the Roman marble trade and its organization was first proposed by J. B. Ward-Perkins. While it has been modified and continues to be, it is still the basis of all analysis of this important sector of the Roman building and construction industry in Imperial times. Ward-Perkins saw six factors as essential to the decorative stone trade:[154]

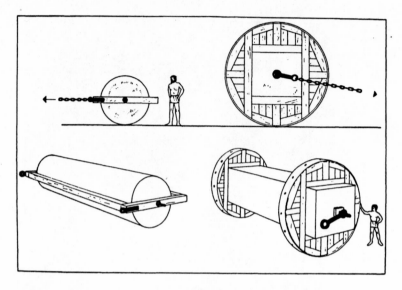

Figure 3.7 Transport using a rounded monolith as roller. [Adam (1984) fig. 33, p. 31; reproduced by permission of the author]

1. "State ownership of the major sources of supply," that is, of the marble and stone quarries, which he thought had been instituted very quickly under Tiberius. While later research has shown that this monopolization was more gradual and much less thorough than Ward-Perkins asserted, it remains an important element in the system as it was established.
2. "Rationalisation of quarrying methods," so that the quarries were administered by imperial freedmen or slaves who were accountable to the emperor but who could in some cases lease out quarrying of at least some sections of the quarry to private contractors.
3. "A completely new quarry-customer relationship," meaning that builders no longer placed orders directly with the quarry. Instead a system of stock-piling in stone and marble yards at both the production and the reception ends of the trade was established, as is demonstrated by evidence from the Marmorata quarter of Rome and at Ostia.

4. "Standardisation and prefabrication" were introduced, perhaps as a natural development from bulk production and stock-piling. Very simply, blocks of stone, columns, and other architectural members were cut and exported in standard dimensions and sometimes in a nearly finished form, thus contributing to efficiency at the quarries and at the warehouses where they were delivered, as well as determining sizes and shapes of standard architectural features beforehand.
5. "The availability at some quarries of specialised workmen" who would have known the properties and peculiarities particular to the stone being extracted from that quarry and thus could undertake finer or special types of cutting and who could, if needed, provide expert help with the stone at building sites where it was to be used.
6. "The establishment of agencies overseas" that handled both orders and shipments. From this form of organization it became inevitable that certain quarries tended to develop particular markets and provide locally desired special products, such as particular types of sarcophagi.

The evidence for the marble trade that Ward-Perkins and all subsequent scholars have employed is literary (ancient references), epigraphical (especially quarry inscriptions), and archaeological (exploration of the quarries, the depots, and the buildings in which marble was used). Many gaps remain in our knowledge, but the basic soundness of Ward-Perkins's model, with modifications as our evidence increases, has been demonstrated. Each item can be briefly discussed in light of more recent research. State ownership of at least some of the quarries certainly would have permitted the builder-emperors of the first and second centuries A.D. to have guarantees that they could obtain the fine and special stones their building programs required.[155] Here the quarry inscriptions are of inestimable importance as evidence. Early quarry inscriptions were often a sort of accounting and control system cut or painted onto blocks either at the quarries or during transport. They may tell the place of extraction (*locus*), and the workshop or gang (*officina*) responsible; on blocks intended for export a consular date might be added. Lead seals were sometimes used, and more markings might be added at the point of delivery. However, there are severe limitations to the evidence of these quarry inscriptions, just as there are to brick stamps. They represent evidence of a system of accounting that was in use only for 150 years or so, from the reign of Nero to that of Septimius Severus, and not all quarries used quarry marks at all (none are ever attested from some very important quarries, including Mt. Pentelikon, Thasos, Thessaly, Cape Taenaros, Croceai, the Troad). Of the others, while all did use the marks to some degree, it is impossible to demonstrate that they all used the same accounting and inventory system. The evidence is best at quarries from which there is a substantial number of surviving inscriptions, especially Docimium.[156] Another ongoing debate is how much of a role private contracting and contractors played in running some of the quarries.

It is apparent that an increase in production was the main reason for the Imperial takeover of quarries. We know that new quarries were opened under Hadrian and under Antoninus Pius and Marcus Aurelius, and it seems probable that the widespread adoption of quarry marks reflects the Imperial desire for accounting. Exactly when the whole system was changed at the major quarries can be debated; while the demands on the system of the immense Flavian building program would seem an obvious point to assume the change, there is evidence from certain quarries that it took place a good deal later, most likely under Hadrian, and as a sort of ex post facto response to the stress brought on by the high demands of previous decades. Certainly seeing a Hadrianic reworking of the quarry accounting and inventory system would seem to accord with the similar possibility that Hadrian tinkered with the brick industry as reflected in the brick stamps of A.D. 123. Most sensible of all, perhaps, is the suggestion that there was not one but two reorganizations and expansions of the quarry system, one fairly early in Flavian times, then another late in the reign of Hadrian.[157]

The development of indirect ordering and stockpiling is best attested at Ostia, but its actual extent is not yet known; nor has there been sufficient investigation of stockpiling at the quarries themselves. The evidence of how marble yards functioned in general, including further evidence for stockpiling as well as for the delivery of architectural elements to some extent precut, is further attested in the scattered remains of the marble yards around the modern via Marmorata at Rome.[158] The development of such standardization—production of blocks, columns and other items precut in the quarries and shipped to the marble yards—is attested by the discovery of what seem to be column shafts of preset length. But this evidence is far from straightforward. There is epigraphical evidence of orders having been placed, if not filled, for huge granite column shafts of 50 Roman feet, but the archaeological evidence is doubtful. Columns of 16, 20, and 24 feet are standard features of Severan buildings in Leptis Magna, and 40-foot columns are well-known at Rome (e.g., the columns of the Pantheon porch and those of the peristyle for the temple of Antoninus and Faustina, the latter of which are actually 39 feet and apparently had to be cut down at top and bottom, possibly as a result of damage suffered in shipping). What the evidence really seems to attest is the production and, if possible, delivery of sets of columns of uniform length, but there is no evidence at all that these were prefabricated and able to be supplied from stockpiles. Indeed there is relatively little evidence that truly immense columns, of 50 Roman feet or more, could be successfully quarried or shipped. Much remains to be investigated in this realm.[159]

There can be little doubt that the quarries came to employ groups of specialized workmen who knew the stones and the products desired: just such workshops of specialists are well attested at Docimium. We also hear of groups of stonecutters and sculptors established as overseas agencies who to a large degree determined the nature of sculpture and architecture in these precious stones wherever they worked. Indeed it would appear that in some areas, at least, the craftsmen were imported along with the stone, although local workshops must have existed too. In both these areas Ward-Perkins's model holds up exceedingly well as the available evidence increases.[160]

The final area of enterprise that directly affected architecture as well as the marble trade is that of distribution. It seems difficult, on the face of it, to place much credence in an extensive long-distance trade in stone, but that is what seems to have developed in the

Roman marble industry. Substantial blocks had been shipped by the Egyptians down the Nile from Aswan, and later, cut into obelisks and sculpture; this continued and increased. The Romans took it much further by shipping immense quantities, clearly associated purely with the Roman concept of conspicuous luxury.[161] This implies the existence not only of the technology with which such transport could be accomplished, but of the ships with which to do it. Some were owned by the state, at least by the time of Diocletian. There may have been a similar business that moved the stone from Ostia to Rome on the Tiber, called the *corpus traiectus marmorum*. Ward-Perkins long argued for an extensive shipping arrangement between the Docimium quarries, as well as others in Anatolia, and the city of Nicomedia on the Sea of Marmara, but the evidence has proven rather slight. It seems that most quarries were near the sea or near rivers sufficient to permit transport of the stone.

The main direction of marble transport and marble trade in the Mediterranean was from east to west, from Anatolia, Greece, and Egypt to Italy, with the exception of white marble, with which Italy was abundantly well-supplied by the quarries at Luna. Oddly enough, during the reign of Hadrian, the movement of white marble, too, seems to have shifted to being imported into Italy from the East as marbles such as Proconnesian and Thasian began to displace Italian Luna in architects' preference; use of Luna marble in architecture in general seems to have declined sharply at the end of the second and beginning of the third century A.D. The fortunes of other marbles seem to have risen or fallen, perhaps because of shifts in taste: the *africano* marble from Teos seems to have fallen out of favor, and the quarry to have fallen out of use, during the second half of the second century A.D., while the *verde antico* marble from Thessaly did not begin to be worked until Hadrian's reign. Such things probably have to do with prevailing fashion rather than with any exhaustion of supply at the various quarries.[162] Thus the transport of marble and decorative stone must have constituted a substantial shipping industry in and of itself, but we know surprisingly little about how it was organized or who was involved. The price of marble and other precious stones was high, so there were clear profits to be made even in so labor-intensive an undertaking. The prices as capped in Diocletian's Prices Edict of A.D. 301 demonstrate this quite clearly.[163]

In the Roman marble industry and trade in decorative stones, we see another highly developed ancient business, not as thoroughly documented in detail as the brick industry in Italy, but far more extensive and undoubtedly of far more economic impact. Marble had in early times been purchased, or ordered, directly from the producing quarries, implying that until the later first century A.D., at any rate, the designing architect and the contractor (or the supervisor from the Imperial bureaucracy, depending on the nature of the construction) had to arrange and supervise this directly. Beginning with Tiberius's reforms and proceeding through the first century A.D., it appears that the marble quarries and thus the entire industry became more and more heavily organized, possibly at direct Imperial command, and ownership of quarries began to pass into Imperial hands. The industry was probably reorganized and Imperial controls tightened at least once and probably twice, first under the Flavians and again toward the end of the reign of Hadrian. Quarries, except small or local ones, were for the most part run by Imperial freedmen and slaves but there always remained the system of leasing out the working of parts of many of the quarries to public contractors. The very existence of the system of extraction and of delivery of the stone depended on the Mediterranean-wide Pax romana, and when this deteriorated in the third century A.D. so did the Roman Imperial marble trade. But by that time it had become highly organized and in some ways remarkably modern. Supplies were prefabricated and stockpiled, either at the quarries or at the delivery points or both, based on the likelihood that the market for them was reliable. Different stones went up and down in public favor and with these shifts in taste went the fate of many of the quarries. During the first two centuries A.D., the marble trade was one of the most remarkable, most highly organized, and most expensive of Roman businesses. It must have provided a livelihood for Romans of all levels, all over the Empire. After its effective collapse in the third century A.D., it was never brought completely back to life, although exploitation of the quarries began again under Diocletian and continued into the fourth century A.D. and afterwards.

PART II

HOW THE ROMANS ORGANIZED SPACE

Four

Planning and Layout of Cities and Towns in Roman Italy

The words "city planning" imply a predetermined or patterned layout of streets, walls, buildings, and open spaces that precedes the actual creation of an urban space.[1] The Romans were well versed in the methods and principles of town planning and examples of planned Roman towns are found throughout the Empire. The Romans themselves turned to the founding of towns only as a corollary to the spread of their power and influence, first in Italy and then throughout the Mediterranean world and eventually far into northern Europe. Also, especially in Italy, Romans refounded conquered towns—sometimes moving them to a new location near the original settlement and starting again from scratch (e.g., Saepinum), at other times incorporating elements of the earlier street and building plan or plans into the Roman version (e.g., Pompeii)—and settled the newly Romanized inhabitants into spaces that were purely Roman and would ostensibly promote the spread of *Romanitas* among the inhabitants and in the environs. Describing the Roman methods employed in Britain in the first century A.D., Tacitus gives a well-known description of the process, both architectural and societal, that we know as "Romanization":[2]

> He [Agricola] would exhort individuals, assist communities, to erect
> temples, fora, houses: he praised the energetic, rebuked the indolent,
> and the rivalry for his compliments took the place of coercion. Moreover
> he began to train the sons of the chieftains in a liberal education, and to
> give a preference to the native talents of the Briton as against the plod-
> ding Gaul. As a result, the nation which used to reject the Latin language
> began to aspire to rhetoric; further, the wearing of our dress became a
> distinction, and the toga came into fashion, and little by little the Britons
> were seduced into alluring vices: to the lounge, the bath, the well-
> appointed dinner table. The simple natives gave the name of "culture" to
> this factor of their slavery.

Tacitus's rhetorical hyperbole aside, it is important that one of the
first elements that Romans, or at least the distinguished general and
governor of Britain Cnaeus Julius Agricola, felt essential in order to
create a Roman world in a far-away place was to prompt, and to
fund, the building of public, religious, and private architecture of
the Roman type: *templa fora domos.*

This remark also implies something that archaeological data
confirm: the principles of layout for planned urban areas designed
by the Romans were based upon experiments first made in the
garrisoning and colonizing of Italy—which led directly to the creation of Roman towns throughout the peninsula—during Rome's
early expansion of power within Italy. In order to make Samnites or
Oscans, just as much as Tacitus's Britons, long "to rise" to the status
of their Roman conquerors, the conquerors would make them
move into and inhabit urban spaces that were designed to look and
feel "Roman." Together with the education of the children in the
Latin language and in Roman dress, this was one of the subtlest but
most effective ways to begin the slow process of altering the world
view of subjects: anyone who speaks and dresses like a Roman and
inhabits sacred, public, and private spaces that are visually and
physically identical with those of the Romans themselves will in
time adopt and absorb Roman ways and so spread *Romanitas.* The
corollary presumption seems clearly to be that, even if the conquered natives retain a certain amount of local custom and senti-
ment, the next generation will do so to a far smaller degree, and the
same effect ultimately will be achieved.

In this chapter, once the textual evidence for city planning has been discussed, the physical evidence and examples to be considered will be drawn exclusively from Roman Italy and from the city of Rome itself. It was in Italian towns and in Rome that the Romans devised, experimented with, revised, and codified their principles and methods of planning urban spaces. Only thereafter were they exported to the far-flung provinces of the Empire. Hence, we should be able to find all the elements that Romans viewed as essential to the physical creation of a Roman urban environment, and hence to the "Romanization" of those not fortunate enough to have been born Roman, in the early foundations made in Italy as Rome's hegemony in the peninsula grew. Moreover, since the evidence for the profession and organization of architecture in the Roman world is overwhelmingly Italian, so the clearest evidence, as well as the earliest, for Roman methods and principles of urban layout are to be found there.

The principles upon which Roman site planning was carried out are described, though with omissions and anomalies, by Vitruvius. He seems to provide a fair reflection of the state of this particular area of Roman building practice at the point when the Republic was passing into the Empire, just as he does with the profession of architecture. He begins with the most basic definitions (1.3.1):[3]

> Building is divided into two parts; of which one is the placing of city walls and of other public buildings on public sites; the other is the setting out of private buildings. Now the assignment of public buildings is threefold: one to defence (*defensio*), the second to religion (*religio*), the third to convenience (*opportunitas*). The method of defence by walls, towers and gates has been devised with a view to the continuous warding off of hostile attacks; to religion belongs the placing of the shrines and sacred temples of the immortal gods; to convenience, the disposal of public sites for the general use, such as harbors, open spaces (*fora*), colonnades (*porticus*), baths, theaters, promenades (*inambulationes*) and other things which are planned, with like purposes, in public situations.

Vitruvius proceeds to work his way through each of these various areas of planning and design, including a lengthy disquisition on how to choose the healthiest place to put the city walls and hence

185

the site (1.4). He turns first, once the wall's circuit has been determined and towers and gates defined (1.5), to the laying out of the streets, both broad and narrow, within them, a procedure which might also be influenced by local climatic conditions (1.6.1):[4]

> When the walls are set round the city, there follow the divisions of the sites within the walls, and the laying out of broad streets and the alleys with a view to aspect. These will be rightly laid out if the winds are carefully shut out from the alleys. For if the winds are cold they are unpleasant; if hot, they infect; if moist, they are injurious. Therefore this faculty must be avoided and guarded against, lest there happen what in many cities is not infrequent.

Whether this principle was a governing one for street layout in Roman towns is difficult to determine, but certainly basic health and protection from harsh climatic conditions were very much of concern. Once the street grid is completed, real planning would commence (1.7.1–2):[5]

> After apportioning the alleys and settling the main streets, the choice of sites for the convenience and common use of citizens has to be explained; for sacred buildings, the forum, and the other public places. And if the ramparts are by the sea, a site where the forum is to be put is to be chosen next the harbor; but if inland, in the middle of the town. But for the sacred buildings of the gods under whose protection the city most seems to be, both for Jupiter and Juno and Minerva, the sites are to be distributed on the highest ground from which most of the ramparts is to be seen. To Mercury, however, in the forum, or also, as to Isis and Serapis, in the business quarter; to Apollo and Father Bacchus against the theater; to Hercules, in cities which have no gymnasia nor amphitheaters, at the circus; to Mars outside the walls but in the parade ground; and also to Venus near the harbor.

With a few more words on what Etruscan haruspices may require for religious foundations, Vitruvius ends his treatment of town planning and design, although he spends most of the rest of his treatise, of course, on the individual building types that will make up the city.

Although his few pages on the subject are quite brief, and deeply concerned with the salubriousness of sites selected, Vitruvius, nonetheless, provides us with a summary of all the essential elements with which one can construct a Roman urban environment. The circuit of the walls, towers, and gates are laid out first, thus defining the outer limit of the space to be planned, at least initially, and they are immediately succeeded by what many architectural historians and practicing town planners would assert is the single most important element in the entire planning process, the network of interconnecting streets, alleys, passageways, stairs (if the site is steep), and open spaces that will in a very real way define the physical form that life will take for many of the inhabitants and the appearance and visual effect the city will have. The importance of the street plan, once in place, is probably even greater than the emphasis Vitruvius places on it; his concern seems mostly to be about the prevailing winds howling down the streets if they are incorrectly or unfortunately placed.[6]

Vitruvius then turns to the major elements of city architecture: religious structures and civic buildings. Temples and their sanctuaries require books 3 and 4 of the treatise. In book 5, the various other forms of civic, public architecture are treated, in order: forum and basilica (5.1), treasury, prison, and curia (5.2), the theater (5.3–8, including lengthy digressions on acoustics and on the Greek theater building), colonnades and porticoes, especially behind theaters (5.9), baths (5.10), *palaestrae* (5.11), harbors, and shipyards (5.12). The selection of buildings treated and of those omitted is at best odd. His overwhelming concentration on temples, including very lengthy descriptions of the ancient Greek peripteral temples, which were hardly ever adopted in Italy or the Empire, and the excessive amount of space devoted to theaters, which did not even exist in many Roman cities, seems ill-judged. The same proves true in books 6 and 7, on domestic architecture, where he spends a fair amount of time describing a form that he calls the Greek house for which no archaeological evidence has ever been located anywhere in the ancient world.

Perhaps even more surprising is how much Vitruvius has omitted from the picture. Most of the elements that must have had the biggest effect on daily life for middle- and lower-class citizens of any Roman urban area are simply missing: apartment buildings (*insu-*

lae), shops, taverns, and inns (*tabernae, popinae, thermopolia, cauponae, stabula, hospitia*), markets of all kinds (*macella, emporia*), the
public fountains and porticoes that provided water and shade, all
these do not figure in Vitruvius's picture of the Roman city; even the
amphitheater disappears without trace after its single mention in
1.7, perhaps because the building type was sufficiently new that he
decided against including it; the first one known to have been built
in stone in Italy had only appeared in 80 B.C. in Pompeii, and
amphitheaters were only just becoming fashionable in the early
years of Augustus's regime.[7] The summation, not surprisingly but
regrettably, must be that Vitruvius failed to present a full picture of
the urban landscape of the Roman world, although he does provide
a clear view of the principles that guided site selection and layout.
Ultimately, he concerns himself largely with those elements most
important to the upper-class, educated, well-to-do audience who
could have read or would have been likely to encounter his treatise,
and these were, of course, the patrons who would keep architects
and builders in business. His editorial choice, although unfortunate
from the point of view of all the information that is missed, was
sensible and justifiable given the makeup of his likely readership.

Thus it is within Italy that we should look for examples of Roman
methods and experiments in town layout. Roman city and town
planning must have been influenced by two other major factors
inherent in the overall population of ancient Italy. We know only a
limited amount about one of these major influences: the towns and
cities of the Etruscans. Etruscan town plans are hardly known to us,
with the exceptions of Marzabotto, near Bologna, and Capua,
known almost exclusively from aerial photography; their plans date
to times well after Etruscan contact with Greece and presumably
with well-established traditions of city planning there. From what
little we know, the town layouts and street patterns in early Etruscan
sites appear relatively random, even haphazard;[8] these seem regularly to have been overlaid by orthogonal grid plans of the type
typical in the contemporary Greek world and almost undoubtedly
borrowed by the Etruscans from their contacts with Greek traders
and with the great Greek foundations of southern Italy and Sicily.

Although the Romans' own antiquarian traditions maintained

that Etruscan town planning was the main source of their methods, there is no evidence to support this assertion. Where the Etruscans seem to have exercised real influence on Roman concepts was in the layout and architecture of temples and their sanctuaries and the forms of domestic and funerary architecture. The roots of Italian orthogonal planning, however, can much better be traced in the planned Greek colonial foundations of southern Italy and Sicily, and the influence the Romans conceived as coming to them through the Etruscans, especially during the century or more when Rome was ruled by Etruscan royalty, came instead from the Etruscans' Greek neighbors in Campania and further south, where they had gotten it. The fact that there is little evidence of any attempt at orthogonal planning in the earliest street patterns of the city of Rome, what little we know of them, should occasion no surprise: the city's foundation would have predated the spread of such architectural influence northward. The tradition, communicated to us by Varro, that Rome was originally laid out in quarters (*quadrata*) because it was laid out on a plan for equilibrium (*quod ad aequilibrium foret posita*) is obscure in meaning at best and is impossible to demonstrate in any of the remains known to us from the archaic city. The whole tradition must be a product of antiquarian speculation centuries after the fact.[9]

Etruscan planning certainly did have an important effect on Roman sacred architecture, though here, too, the evidence is contradictory, communicated as it is only by sources centuries later. For instance, Vitruvius asserts that the front of a temple should normally face west, while five other Roman writers imply that the temple normally faced east, but another three suggest that an orientation to the south is best.[10] No one would seriously attempt to deny that the most important temple plan known to the Romans, together with its sanctuary and appointments, was that most commonly employed by the Etruscans, what Vitruvius called the "Tuscan" temple. It seems likely that Roman domestic architecture also inherited a great deal from the Etruscans, including the basic atrium plan of the single house. Varro asserted that both the word and the house design were derived from the Etruscan town of Atria at the mouth of the Po River. While Vitruvius does not corroborate Varro's remark in so many words, he does apply the adjective "Tuscan" to the noun "atrium" and thinks his meaning clear.[11]

Actual "drawing-board" town planning, then, came to the Romans from the Greeks. Although the Greek tradition, handed down by Aristotle to Diodorus and Strabo, attributed the invention or at least the elaboration of orthogonal town planning to Hippodamus of Miletus, the architect credited with laying out Athens' port Piraeus, Thurii, in south Italy, and the city of Rhodes, there can be little doubt that orthogonal planning appeared in western Asia Minor, for instance, in the city plan of Miletus (where Hippodamus might have received his training in laying out a city during his youth), immediately after the Persian Wars. The Greek tradition surrounded both orthogonal "grid" planning and the name of Hippodamus with complex philosophical speculations on the nature of the ideal city and the highest planes of geometry, but that sort of philosophical approach appears to have been ignored entirely by Roman builders. What the Romans adopted and, very quickly, adapted to their own needs was the principle of orthogonal layout, which is stunningly simple: a repeated pattern of more or less identical units (usually rectangular or square blocks) that forms a grid in which all the architecture, streets and open spaces of the city can be accommodated. There had always to be a good deal of space reserved for public building—commercial, civic, and religious—which would be easy of access to whatever docks or harbors the town might have, to gates and main thoroughfares, and to the residential sectors of town. The classic example in the Greek world is Miletus's street plan, but in fact the partially known plans of Piraeus, Priene, Olynthus, Rhodes, and Knidos are all clearly of this type. During the fourth century and afterwards, magnificent Hellenistic "showcase" cities such as Pergamon in northwestern Asia minor, the reworked plan of Rhodes in its Hellenistic "theaterlike" shape, steep Assos not far from Pergamon, and the great cities of Greek Egypt—Ptolemaic Alexandria above all—and Syria (Antioch, Seleucia, Dura-Europus) represent monumentalized adaptations of orthogonal "grid" planning to apparently unsuitable sites with remarkable results. This was the Greek tradition that informed Roman town planning.[12]

The evidence that orthogonal planning came to Italy via the Greek colonies of the southern peninsula and Sicily seems reliable. By the fifth century B.C. cities such as Paestum (Poseidonia) reveal that the grid plan with all its possibilities was well established in south Italy. Indeed such plans seem already to have been in use in the sixth century at Agrigento (Akragas) in Sicily, and during the fifth century such important cities as Naples (Neapolis), Heraclea, and Tarentum on the Italian mainland and Megara Hyblaea in Sicily (which was refounded sometime after its destruction by the Syracusans ca. 483 B.C.) all were laid out or reworked employing this system. Periodic irregularities in these cities' gridded plans, noticeable at Selinunte (Selinus) on the south coast of Sicily, are probably best explained by the fact that the orthogonal street plans were often replannings after disasters of various kinds had damaged or destroyed earlier colonies. The meeting point for this Greek system with the Etruscans who adopted it was most likely Campania, where the orthogonal system seems to have had an effect on the plan of archaic Capua. It was apparently adopted rapidly in Etruria, if the evidence from Veii and Marzabotto can carry such weight, and then passed to Rome where, while it may have had only a minor effect on the capital city itself except in outlying districts, it was adapted for use in colonies to be established throughout central Italy to act as advance scouts and as guardians of Roman expansion in the peninsula.

There are clear orthogonal elements in the street plan of Alba Fucens, founded high in the Appennines in 303 B.C. to guard a transmontane road, despite very real difficulties of topography at the site which lay in a steep-sided valley and had to accommodate the established route of the road (fig. 4.1). At Ostia, too, the essentially military nature of the *castra* foundation was clearly compatible with, and may well actually have sprung from, orthogonal principles of design and zoning restriction, whether the traditional founding as early as 338 B.C. is exact or merely an estimate. In the Roman world, street surveyor (*gromaticus*) and military engineer must often have worked side by side, if they were not one and the same.[13] Roman planning continued to develop in new foundations throughout Italy down to the Augustan period, and for the most part it seems likely that it was town plans that caused the military *castra* to take the form they did, rather than the other way around.

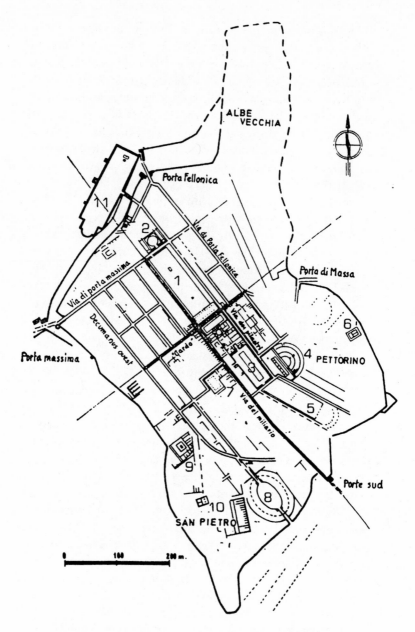

Figure 4.1 Plan of Alba Fucens. [Coarelli & LaRegina (1993) p. 68; reproduced by permission of Gius. Laterza & Figli, S.p.a.]

Frontinus tells us clearly that Roman armies adopted the standardized sort of formal encampment they would use throughout their vast empire only after overrunning the camp of the invader Pyrrhus in 275 B.C. In Italy at the Augustan foundations of Turin (27 B.C.) and Aosta (25 B.C.) alone has any real case for influence from military camp layout to town plan been arguable or sustainable, although this was clearly the usual case on the Roman frontiers for centuries. By the second century B.C., Polybius described the layout of a military camp inside its walls as resembling the appointments of a city, not vice versa.[14]

It has become a truism in the literature on the history of city planning to regard the Roman adoption and application of the orthogonal grid plan as an example of rigid forcing of an intractable principle onto topography and landscapes to which the grid was often unsuitable. Nothing could be further from the truth. In fact, the grid layout was tested and tried, adapted, manipulated, and rediscovered, in all sorts of settings, first in Italy and subsequently around most of the Empire. It was never universally applied: small towns were not forced to adopt it in most cases unless they were likely to expand or had a particularly important military or economic function.[15] Indeed, the very point that had attracted the Romans to the orthogonal plan was very likely its appearance of simplicity which masked a remarkably plastic ability to be applied, with variations and shiftings, to almost any topography, however rugged. The Greeks of Hellenistic Asia Minor and Syria knew this, and it was from their extraordinary adaptations of the system that the variability inherent in the orthogonal plan was made apparent to the Romans. We can look briefly at four examples in Roman Italy, first, Pompeii, a pre-Roman town adapted to the Roman plan; another, Ostia, a combined military and commercial settlement that developed into a major port city; then, Cosa, a purely military foundation on a difficult and previously uninhabited piece of terrain; and finally, Saepinum, a resettlement of a defeated enemy town near the original town that had been destroyed and in territory that placed its own requirements on the planning.

The city plan of Pompeii is, at first glance, surprisingly random in appearance (fig. 4.2). The sector around and to the east of the

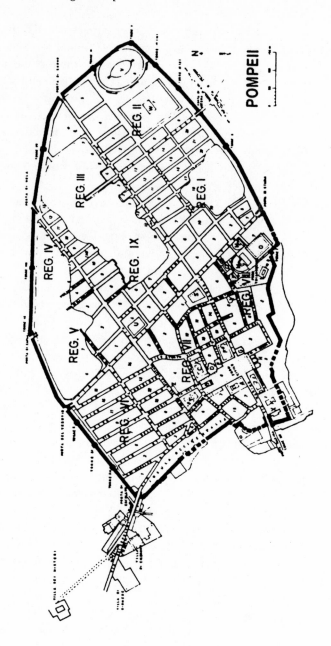

forum is not only not, so it would seem, on a direct axis with any of the other major streets through the city, it is not even entered at an exact right angle to its axis by any communicating streets. The theory has been advanced that this was the original extent of the town, thus hypothesizing a Greek town presumably attached to the Doric temple, later incorporated in the so-called Foro triangolare. Further to the east, beyond the "strada Stabiana," the entire grid of the city shifts once again, and this requires some exceedingly odd adjustments to be made in the shapes of some of the individual city blocks (e.g., the first two rows in Regions I and IX east of the "strada Stabiana" are rhomboid, and I.vii just beyond it is a trapezoid in order to adjust between rhomboid and rectangle). Either this must reflect a later adjustment to the overall street plan, or some element other than the axial orientation of the forum and its environs must have been controlling the layout. The most likely element to control, or at least have a strong effect upon, a town's grid is its walls and their towers and, especially, gates.

It has recently, and convincingly, been asserted that the apparent anomalies of Pompeii's seemingly irregular plan should not be put down to a clumsy attempt to adjust grids to include the axes of the original Greek agora and town within the later Italic walls and street plan, but that the entire plan should be looked at from the point of view of the walls. Those walls were, in all probability, laid out in the middle of the third century B.C. There is no real archaeological evidence for habitation at Pompeii except in the precincts of the Doric temple and of Apollo, west of the Forum, until this time. What the plan of Pompeii may well reveal is, in fact, a sanctuary site of Greek times, unquestionably with some dependent residents but not a functioning or planned city, which was incorporated into a city during the third century B.C. with all the street lines and grid patterns determined by the line of the walls and the placement of gates. This is consonant with what Vitruvius implies was the guiding principle behind laying out sites; furthermore, it eliminates the

---

Figure 4.2 Plan of Pompeii. [Gros & Torelli (1988) p. 59, fig. 34; reproduced by permission of Gius. Laterza & Figli, S.p.a.]

need to posit a period when the long, narrow forum of Pompeii was shaped as and served as a Greek-style agora, something for which there is no evidence at all. Even more important, this reading of the plan of Pompeii demonstrates the essential correctness of Vitruvius's information on city design and explains the variant gridded sections of Pompeii not as uncomfortable compromises or errors but as adjustments that kept the streets and neighborhoods in correct, functional, and convenient relationships with one another. That Pompeii functioned very well indeed as a prosperous Roman town is unquestioned; that it functioned in and around a city design that is a masterly example of the adaptability of the orthogonal "grid" plan to an irregular but essential line of city walls gives a new interest to its layout.[16]

Despite the legendary tradition that Aeneas first landed in Latium at Ostia, which took its name from its situation at the "mouth" of the Tiber, and despite the inscription set up in the second century A.D. at the town, the fragment of Ennius and the passage in Livy that record a foundation under Ancus Marcius, fourth king of regal Rome,[17] the fact is that the Ostia we know was founded not before the middle of the fourth century B.C. on a site never previously inhabited, although the possibility remains that there was an earlier settlement near the river founded in order to exploit the salt beds of the area.

The traditional date for the founding of Ostia is 338 B.C., which cannot be proven since we lack inscriptional or textual confirmation but seems about right. It was founded as a military *castrum* to defend the river's mouth, and the collection and transportation of salt in this area (probably already of economic importance) may well have provided a secondary but powerful economic incentive for the foundation. Ostia was established as a *colonia maritima*.[18] The plan of the *castrum* was the predictable rectangular grid with *decumanus* (main east-west street) and *cardo* (main north-south street) intersecting at its center, defining the area which became the Forum of the city as it developed (fig. 4.3). This *castrum* was planned within a rectangle of strong Fidenae tufa walls with four gates at the compass points, and it seems to have contained the town, more or less, until rapid expansion began as Rome gained more and more need for port and river harbor. To provide for the growing volume of shipping, Ostia had to grow and it did so primarily to the west of the *castrum* first, that is toward the seacoast, spreading well outside its original walls by the beginning of the first century B.C.

A new, much larger wall circuit was established early in the first century B.C., possibly by Sulla, to protect the now thriving port/harbor city. The town's early expansion westward toward the coast, rather than eastward toward Rome is interesting and also probably explains the seeming lack of a coherent street plan—certainly the lack of an orthogonal grid for the streets—west of the original *castrum*. This area was the one that grew up following the course of the river; it was essential to keep in close contact with the town's source of livelihood as the new western quarter grew, and that involved running a new street, not an extension of the *decumanus*, sharply northwestward along the south bank of the Tiber River just outside the *castrum* wall (the so-called via della Foce).[19] Probably not long afterward the line of the *decumanus* itself was extended, but southwestward toward the coastline rather than due west. This early and irregular spread to the west would dominate the subsequent topography of a large sector of Imperial Ostia in later times.

During the first century B.C. the town developed rapidly, notably with the establishment of the *pax Augusta*. The Forum had grown up, a long narrow reserved space in the best Italic tradition, where the original main roads had met. A warehouse and apartment quarter had begun to spread southward from the "Via della Foce," which followed the line of the Tiber (and led to the settlement of Region III of the town to the southwest of that road), and the *decumanus* itself now extended to the southwest, forming the south boundary of Region III and the northern boundary of Region IV. At the same time, as the first century of the empire progressed, the town began to grow eastward along the *decumanus*, with a theater installed there in Augustan times, and eventually filled in the area as far as the eastern gate (Porta Romana). Another interestingly nonorthogonal development in Ostia's plan was that the *cardo*, after it left the Forum to the south, took a bend to the east and ran southeastward rather than due south. This, too, had developed sufficiently early

197

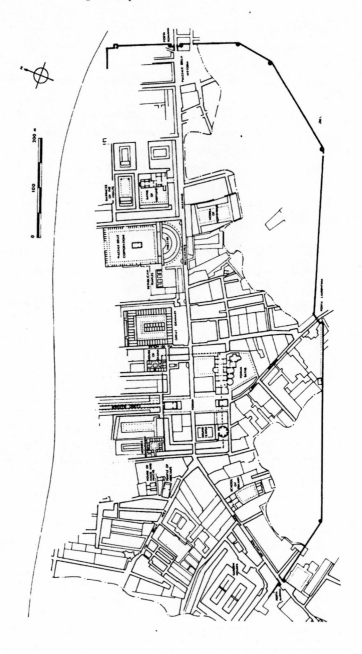

that the Sullan walls took account of it in the positioning of the south gate (Porta Laurentina). Thus Ostia developed a highly distinctive town plan that owed only its center to its original layout as a military foundation and seems to have owed the rest to the directions of its early expansion. While by no means rectilinear, the town plan is highly rational and well interconnected. As at Pompeii individual districts take on street grids of relative regularity (such as Region V) and the interconnections between the areas of the plan are worked out in remarkable but perfectly utilitarian shapes, such as the unusual form taken by the small block just north of the "five points" intersection formed where the northwest road and the southwestward-running *decumanus* both split from the original line of the *decumanus* as it left the *castrum*, at a point where a subsidiary north-south street (that upon which the Horrea Epagathiana are situated) crossed.

The great reworkings and expansions of Ostia in the Domitianic and Hadrianic periods seem to have had little effect on its street plan. Growth tended to be toward the ends of the long roads where there was space, especially near the Porta Marina, where the southwesterly stretch of the *decumanus* approached the coastline, and along the northwest road. Internally, the *insulae* (apartment buildings) and *horrea* (warehouses) that were the most constant features of the architecture at Ostia were fitted easily into mostly rectangular-shaped city blocks. Space along the riverfront was consciously and conscientiously reserved for warehouses and shipping facilities, and thus Ostia became an example of an urbanized shipping town, its plan like its cult life and society dominated by its identity as a center for receiving and dispatching goods (mainly food) and people to and from Rome.

This plan continued to function even into the fourth century A.D., when Rome fell from its position as the ruling city of the Empire, and Ostia's importance as a port collapsed. Some *insulae* seem to have been converted to elegant resort homes for the well-

Figure 4.3 Plan of Ostia. [Sear (1982) fig. 67, p. 119; reproduced by permission of the author and of B. T. Batsford, Ltd., Publishers]

to-do (e.g., the house of Fortuna Annonaria in Region V, the house of Cupid and Psyche in Region I) while others must have stood empty, slowly decaying along streets largely abandoned, and *horrea* all too often stood empty as Ostia attempted to become a fashionable seaside resort along the lines of a late antique Stabiae or Herculaneum, until silting and malaria and the continuing marginalization of Rome itself pulled Ostia down too.[20] The city plan of Ostia is a remarkable example of relatively random expansion from an original rectangular grid in which the geography of the town's river and seacoast setting and her economic needs were allowed to dictate a plan that at first glance seems random but proved to be efficient and successful for many centuries. It is typically pragmatic in a quintessentially Roman manner.

Cosa was founded on the heights above Ansedonia, which provided a natural defensive position but required remarkable adaptations of the orthogonal grid in order to accommodate the geography of a steeply rising hill that culminated in three separate summits: one at the southern corner, one at the east, and one at the northwest (fig. 4.4). Apparently these were used as cardinal points around which to run the circuit of the walls, with a sharp corner around the rocky outcropping to the east and a fairly broad turning around the outside edges of the southern corner (the substantial summit that became the sacred center, the Arx, of the city), while the northwest summit was enclosed and overlooked the road that ran up from the coast to the main gate of Cosa, a little further northward. A long, narrow rectangle of a Forum was laid out appropriate to the geography of the hill to take advantage of a low saddle between the southern and eastern high points, and it was connected to the Arx by a broad roadway. The rest of the grid, in largish rectangles, was fitted in on the axes laid down by the sides of the Forum, on a plan which accommodated access to gates in the walls on the northwest, northeast and southeast sides of the hill. This seems to reflect the original arrangement of the site, in which case it is eloquent testimony to the plasticity of the orthogonal grid as it was already being used by the Romans in 273 B.C., when Cosa was founded.[21]

In origin a Samnite foundation high in the Abruzzi Mountains, Saepinum (first called "Saipins") was destroyed by a consular army

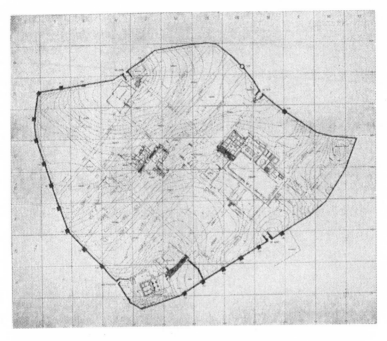

Figure 4.4 Plan of Cosa. [Brown (1961) fig. 12, subsequently revised; reproduced by permission of the American Academy in Rome]

under Papirius Cursor in 293 B.C.[22] The town site was abandoned and survivors, together with Roman colonists, were resettled in the valley below. The new town that was laid out demonstrates the adaptability that Roman designers found in the grid pattern (fig. 4.5). The choice of site had probably been dictated by the presence of a small but important sheep and cattle track that ran through the valley from Bovianum (modern Campobasso) to Beneventum (modern Benevento) and was essential to herding in the region. Founding towns across roads to protect and maintain them was not uncommon Roman practice, for the same thing had been done ten years before at Alba Fucens. But at Saepinum the rough terrain and already established route of the road dictated that although it served as the main axial street (*decumanus*) of the town, it could not have run through or even particularly near the center of the territory

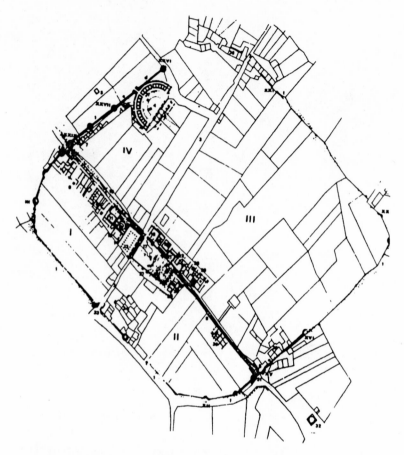

Figure 4.5 Plan of Saepinum. [Gros & Torelli (1988) p. 154, fig. 58; reproduced by permission of Gius. Laterza & Figli, S.p.a.]

enclosed by the town's walls as we know them. There is no sure archaeological evidence whether the town was walled at that early stage, but it would have been extremely unusual to leave it defense-less. No evidence of any wall course other than that of the walls now surrounding the site has been found, so it seems reasonable to assume that they retained the course of earlier defenses. In order to bring the sheep and cattle track into town as the *decumanus*, the grid had to be adjusted in several different areas of the town.

The *cardo*,[23] which entered from the so-called Porta Tammaro, the north gate, could not intersect the already well off-center *decumanus* at right angles, but this was solved by incorporating the intersection into the Forum and lining the streets at that point with public buildings including a basilica and a temple and a number of tabernae. Beyond the basilica on the *decumanus* toward the west was a *macellum* for fresh foodstuffs to be sold. Residential areas grew up off the Forum area, although whether the town ever grew to fill its circuit of walls is not certain. A theater was added to the city with an entrance to it from behind the *cavea* (seating area) incorporated into the fabric of the city walls. This could date from the time of the reconstruction of those walls in *opus quasi-reticulatum* perhaps ca. 60–50 B.C., or it could be contemporary with the addition of the western (Bovianum) gate to the walls in the first years of the first century A.D. These major projects may have been direct rewards to Saepinum for siding with Rome during the Social Wars, although this can only be argued *ex silentio;* it is doubtful that walls of *opus quasi-reticulatum* of such a degree of irregularity could date to the period of completion of the Bovianum gate, so two benefactions, one in the late sixties or fifties B.C. and another ca. A.D. 1–5 must be postulated. The town seems to have received further benefactions during the reigns of Trajan and Hadrian, possibly because of the rise to prominence of its only renowned citizen, the jurisconsult L. Neratius Priscus, who was rumored as a possible successor to the purple after Trajan. As an example of Roman town layout, Saepinum is remarkably complete and shows admirable plasticity in adjusting to the necessities of a particular local topography.[24]

Planning in the City of Rome

PUBLIC BUILDINGS AND BUILDING PROGRAMS

But what of the city of Rome itself? How did the growing Roman facility with orthogonal planning and the laying out and design of towns and cities affect, or was it in any way reflected in, the Eternal City? Here, of course, the evidence is much more abundant, but the city much larger, much more complex, and far older. In order to look for elements of planning in the city, we will have to consider certain episodes and periods in the history of its urbanization and expansion, beginning at the start with the foundation of the city by Romulus, the laying out of the wall circuit, and the creation of its *pomerium*. The very fact that Rome's foundation myth incorporates the concept of "laying out" the wall circuit for the city shows that the basic idea of *planning* an urban environment had, to a primitive degree, already been adopted in central Italy, although there was clearly a strong element of retrograde projection by the far later authors (Livy, Plutarch, Dionysius, Ovid) who provide the main sources of the foundation legend. The most complete, and probably most famous, version is Plutarch's:[25]

> [Romulus] set himself to building his city, after summoning from Tuscany men who prescribed all the details in accordance with certain sacred ordinances and writings, and taught them to him as in a religious rite. A circular trench was dug around what is now the Comitium and in this were deposited first-fruits. . . . They call this trench, as they do the heavens, by the name of "mundus." Then, taking this as a center, they marked out the city in a circle around it. And the founder, having shod a plough with a brazen ploughshare, and having yoked to it a bull and a cow, himself drove a deep furrow round the boundary lines, while those who followed after him had to turn the clods, which the plough threw up, inwards towards the city, and suffer no clod to lie turned outwards. With this line they mark out the course of the wall and it is called, by contraction, "pomerium," that is "post murum," *behind* or *next the wall*. And where they purposed to put in a gate, there they took the share out of the ground, lifted the plough over, and left a vacant space.

The rite thus described was performed "in the Etruscan manner" (*more Etrusco*) of founding a city described by Varro, who goes on to add that all Roman colonies were founded by this method.[26] There are decided oddities in Plutarch's account. The *mundus* trench, for example, cannot in fact have been dug in the Comitium—the traditional place of assembly next to the Curia in the Forum—since it is so low-lying. In order to see the intended course of the walls, the *mundus* must rather have been placed higher up, in this case most likely atop the Palatine Hill, which the tradition except for Plutarch universally regards as the actual area fortified by the first walls built around the city, a tradition now seemingly corroborated to some degree by archaeology.[27]

More significant as evidence for planning, if rather vague in spatial terms, is the *pomerium*. Plutarch's derivation of the word was apparently common among the Romans, but it does not specify what the *pomerium* really was, a problem recognized by the Romans themselves, as Varro indicates. Tacitus describes the *pomerium* of Romulus as encircling the Palatine Hill around its lower slopes, beginning to the west of the Palatine in the Forum Boarium and proceeding south to the Ara Maxima of Hercules, where it turned eastward and ran along the base of the south slope of the Palatine, along the length of the Circus Maximus, to the altar of Consus at the hill's southeastern tip. There it turned north again running between the Palatine and Caelian slopes until it reached the Curiae Veteres, in the area where the Meta Sudans and the Arch of Constantine were later erected, where it turned westward, ran over the Velia and down the slope into the Forum Romanum past the *sacellum* of the Lares. Its western side then must have connected the *imum Forum* (the inner area of the Roman Forum) to the Forum Boarium in a line running down the lower western side of the Palatine, perhaps roughly along the line of the subsequent Vicus Tuscus (fig. 4.6).

It is probably significant that the *pomerium* seems to correspond closely to the courses of streams along its route, such as the Circus Maximus brook, although exactly how it related to the Cloaca brook is not clear; nonetheless, sacred water crossings and boundaries seem clearly to be observed by it.[28] Livy discusses the *pomerium* briefly in his account of Rome's first census under Servius Tullius and provides us with the important information that, indeed, the *pomerium* was an entirely separate entity in Roman thinking from the walls, although they could follow the same course when this was convenient but could diverge from one another, and that the line of the *pomerium* could be, and was frequently, changed:[29]

> It was apparent that the City must expand, and so the king added two hills, the Quirinal and the Viminal, after which he proceeded to enlarge the Esquiline. . . . He surrounded the city with a rampart, trenches, and a wall, and so extended the "pomerium." This word is interpreted by

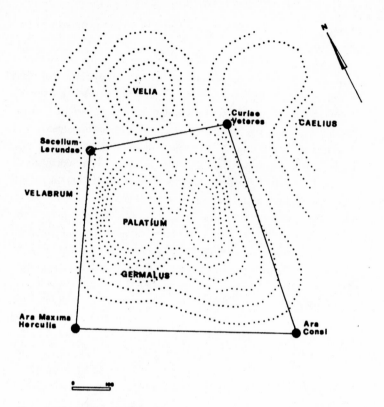

Figure 4.6 Rome: The *pomerium* of Romulus. [Gros & Torelli (1988) p. 64, fig. 36; reproduced by permission of Gius. Laterza & Figli, S.p.a.]

those who look only at its etymology as meaning "the tract behind the wall," but it signifies rather "the tract on both sides of the wall," the space which the Etruscans used formerly to consecrate with augural ceremonies when they propose to erect their wall, establishing definite limits on either side of it, so that they might at the same time keep the walls free on their inward face from contact with buildings, which now, as a rule, are actually joined to them, and on the outside keep a certain area free from human uses. This space, which the gods forbade men to inhabit or to till, was called "pomerium" by the Romans, quite as much because the wall stood behind it as because it stood behind the wall; and as the city grew, these consecrated limits were always pushed out for as great a distance as the walls themselves were to be advanced.

While the planning for the city beyond the basic establishment of a wall and a sacred boundary may have been meager at best, as was certainly the case elsewhere in Italy during the eighth century B.C.;[30] nonetheless, the concept was inherent in the ritual. In later times the *pomerium* was marked with boundary stones (*cippi*) some of which survive, so that no Roman would be unaware when he or she crossed the *pomerium*. Its sanctity was extremely important. Our sources tell us that this *pomerium*, the one established under Servius Tullius, remained in use and intact until the dictatorship of Sulla. It was subsequently expanded, according to a variety of ancient sources, fairly regularly; although only the expansions under Claudius, Vespasian, and Hadrian can be securely documented,[31] many more are suggested in the literary sources. Clearly the *pomerium* remained religiously and conceptually important at least until the construction of the Aurelianic walls. This may be taken to imply that Rome was concentrating on developing her internal street plan and public architecture from the seventh to the first century B.C. without any tremendous pressure to expand beyond the boundaries set by the old pomerial line. While the broad outlines of the city's growth as well as many of its specific developments during these centuries are known to us, elements such as the laying out of the walls and *pomerium* that imply conscious prior planning are rare indeed.

Around 390 B.C. Gallic tribes entered Rome and sacked it. Most of the domestic quarters and many sacred precincts were destroyed, and only the Capitoline, the sacred center of the city, was left unharmed. After the general and dictator Camillus had routed the Gauls from the city, Livy tells us that a proposal was made in the Senate to shift the Roman people from their mangled city to newly conquered Veii; Camillus's speech opposing this suggestion was followed by an omen observed in the Comitium, and the proposal was defeated. With the city partially destroyed, Livy continues,[32]

> people began in a random fashion to rebuild the City. The state supplied tiles, and granted everybody the right to quarry stone and to hew timber where he liked, after giving security for the completion of the structures within that year. In their haste men were careless about making straight

the streets, and paying no attention to their own and others' rights, built on the vacant spaces. This is the reason that the ancient sewers, which were at first conducted through the public ways, at present frequently run under private dwellings, and the appearance of the City is like one where the ground has been randomly appropriated rather than logically divided.

Livy's clear implication is regret that a more logical city street plan, possibly a Hippodamean or, at the least, a logically worked-out orthogonal, grid was not introduced to the city at this time, but the opportunity was missed. While orthogonal town planning was brought into Italy by the fifth century B.C., and while it could in theory have been known to Romans by 390 B.C., the likelihood is not great. The disorder of Rome's streets and buildings so regularly lamented by Livy and others seems to have bothered writers who thought about the city, who were aware of the augural layout associated with the legends of Romulus and seem to have felt that the city as they knew it ought to show more logical coherence than it did or ever had. The partial destruction by the Gauls, which is reflected archaeologically in burn layers of early fourth-century date beneath the Comitium, was adopted by Cicero, Livy, Tacitus, Plutarch, and others to explain the disordered plan they knew as Rome's by blaming it on the haste with which the city was reconstructed after the sack.[33] Whether or not an orthogonal plan was known to the Romans of 390 B.C., it was most certainly not applied to the city after the Gallic sack, and Rome arose from its ashes pretty much as Livy says it did, in traditional street patterns and building locations sanctified by custom and by time. The tale and its explanation tell us little about the advance or lack of orthogonal planning in central Italy at the beginning of the fourth century B.C., other than the apparent fact that its influence was not felt at Rome.

In fact, any form of long-range city planning in republican Rome was strongly militated against by the very organization of public building projects as censorial contracts or as contracts let out by aediles. As we have seen, censors were elected every five years but laid down their office after eighteen months; aediles turned over annually. Lower-level bureaucrats certainly existed, but they were for the most part too far down the chain of command to be entrusted with the authority or the responsiblity to pursue long-range projects for the city. The only exceptions to this unwritten rule that prevented long-range planning were the building and maintenance of roads and of aqueducts, and even these, with their more permanent boards of *curatores,* came into being only through the "rogue elephant" approach to the censorship exercised by Appius Claudius Caecus beginning in 312 B.C. But aside from these admirable elements of city services planned on behalf of the Roman people, any other conscious planning for the city had to wait until the first century B.C., and even then all too often it came to naught.[34] When the Romans came into alliance with Capua and saw its broad streets and thoroughly orthogonal, logical layout (fig. 4.7), the contrast seems to have become starkly clear, yet nothing was or could be done about it given the magisterial system that governed Rome.

As late as January 63 B.C., Cicero could contrast the images of the streets and buildings of Capua with those of Rome, to the latter's disadvantage, and expect his audience to recognize and shake their heads ruefully at the urban disaster that was the capital city:[35]

> [The Capuans] have always been proud owing to . . . the healthiness, arrangement and beauty of their city. It is this abundance, this affluence of everything, which is the origin of that Campanian arrogance which made them demand of our ancestors that one of the consuls should be chosen from Capua, and next of that luxury which vanquished by pleasure Hannibal himself, whom arms had been unable to conquer. When those decemvirs have settled 500 colonists there according to the law of Rullus, when they have set up 100 decurions, ten augurs, and six priests, imagine their state of mind, their vehemence, their ferocity! They will laugh at and despise Rome, planted in mountains and deep valleys, its garrets hanging up aloft, its roads none of the best, by-ways of the narrowest, in comparison with their own Capua, spread out on a vast and open plain and most beautifully situated.

While Rome began to increase in the luxury, size, and utility of its public buildings with the beginning of the second century B.C., there is no evidence at all of any sort of organized planning behind either utilitarian additions of tremendous importance, such as the

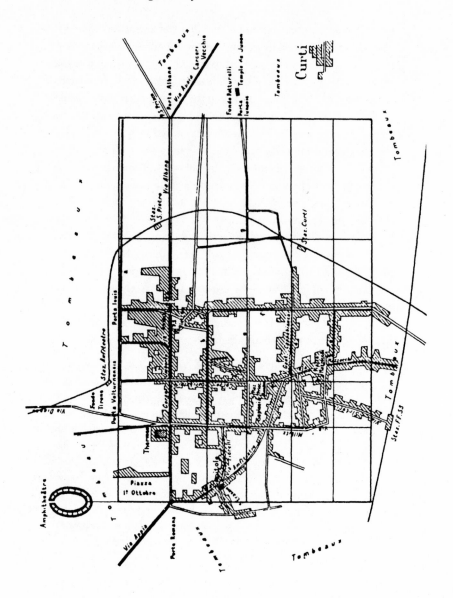

Emporium and Porticus Aemilia that transformed the Tiber docks and selling areas, or in the construction of increasingly elegant temples and porticoes, as in the Porticus Metelli and its temple(s). While the art and craft of architecture made gigantic strides in Rome, as well as all over Roman Italy and increasingly beyond, organized planning even for limited sections of the city remained unknown. It is possible to see a glimmering of some sort of organized plan in the undertakings of Sulla, which revitalized the north and west ends of the Forum with repaving, a new Curia, and changes to the Comitium in relation to the massive projects undertaken just above that area on the slopes of the Capitoline, with the magnificent structure usually thought to be the Tabularium, and beyond that the magnificently rebuilt temple of Jupiter Optimus Maximus. This suggests architectural planning similar to that of the great Hellenistic cities—Pergamon, for example—which Sulla had seen, admired, and pillaged during his eastern campaigns. With the completely redone Capitoline slope, covered by the arcaded façade of the Tabularium, as a backdrop the renewed political center in the Forum was set into a piece of real urban magnificence that must have been intentional. The opportunity afforded Sulla to rebuild the Jupiter Capitolinus temple, which loomed above and to the left of the Tabularium as one faced it from the Comitium, may not have been part of the original plan, but it all fit in nicely. It is reasonable to regard this as one of the earliest samples of true urban planning that was imposed on the face of Rome, and it had taken until the late 80s B.C.[36]

Some scholars have argued that the construction of Pompey's theater, completed in 55 B.C. with its temple to Venus Victrix (dedicated in 52), together with the porticus that ran from the theater *scena* eastward and contained among other items a Curia building, combined with his nearby *villa urbana* should be regarded as a "next step" in urban planning in Rome, but in many ways this is unconvincing. Pompey's project was one massive public complex of

---

Figure 4.7 Plan of ancient Capua. [Castagnoli (1971) fig. 18, p. 48; reproduced by permission of M.I.T. Press]

theater-temple-porticus inflicted in the middle of the southern Campus Martius; its relationship to his villa urbana is unknown, and its effect on the topography of the whole area (fig. 4.8), for instance, the Circus Flaminius, the temples of the Largo Argentina, seems to have been limited.[37]

It is only with the dictatorship of Julius Caesar that we can discern a true vision of urban replanning as a conscious and calculated element in the overall policy of a Roman leader. Some of Caesar's plans horrified Cicero, who complained that Caesar wanted to divert the very course of the Tiber.[38] Suetonius's description, although omitting a number of items that Cicero attributes to Caesar's plans, is indicative of the extent to which Caesar was planning a true reworking of Rome into a city worthy of a Hellenistic monarch, a sort of Italian Alexandria or Antioch, as his enemies feared:[39]

> In particular, for the adornment and convenience of the city . . . he formed more projects and more extensive ones every day: first of all, to rear a temple to Mars, greater than any in existence; filling up and levelling the pool in which he had exhibited the sea fight; and to build a theater of vast size, sloping down from the Tarpeian rock. To reduce the civil code to fixed limits, and of the vast and prolix mass of statutes to include only the very best and most essential in a limited number of volumes; to open to the public the greatest possible libraries of Greek and Latin books.

In fact, he intended much even beyond this. He repaved the northwest end of the Forum, eliminating the Comitium entirely, and built an entirely new Curia probably on a different orientation. Behind the new Curia he raised his own *monumentum*, the Forum Julium dominated by its temple to Venus Genetrix, sacred ancestress of the Julian family as well as the mother of Aeneas; the symbolism of this could not have been lost on any well-educated Roman. Much of the regular business and ceremonial that surrounded the Senate was transferred to the Forum Julium from the lost Comitium. Across the Forum from the new Curia, he replaced the old and battered Basilica Sempronia with a new, bigger, and far more elegant Basilica Julia (another building not completed at the

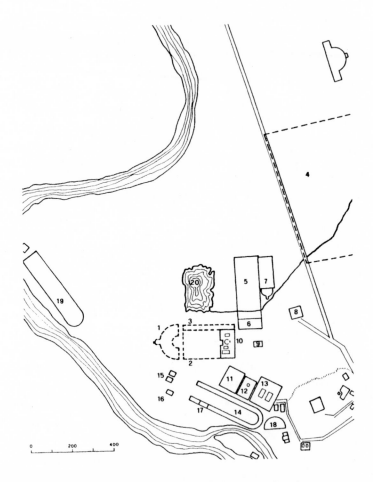

Figure 4.8 Rome: Campus Martius ca. 50 B.C., including Pompey's projects.
Key: *1*, Theater of Pompey; *2*, Pompey's porticus; *3*, Hecatostylum or porticus ad nationes; *4*, Pompey's urban villa; *5*, the Saepta; *6*, Diribitorium; *7*, Temple of Isis; *8*, altar of Mars; *9*, Temple of the Nymphs; *10*, Porticus Minucia and temples of the Largo Argentina; *11*, Porticus of Octavia; *12*, Temple of Hercules Musarum; *13*, Porticus Metelli; *14*, Circus Flaminius (shape is speculative); *15*, Temples of Neptune and of Mars; *16*, Temple of Hercules Custos; *17*, Temple of the Castors; *18*, wooden theater and temples of Apollo and Bellona; *19*, Trigarium and Tarentum; *20*, Palus Caprae. [Gros & Torelli (1988) p. 123, fig. 46; drawn by P. Monella; reproduced by permission of Gius. Laterza & Figli, S.p.a.]

time of his death). He began the theater near the Tiber Island and Circus Flaminius, which would eventually be completed as the theater of Marcellus, a plan clearly in direct competition with Pompey's theater (just as the temple of Venus Genetrix must have been a form of political oneupsmanship over the defeated Pompey's dedication to Venus Victrix). Apparently he also planned to rework various parts of the northern Campus Martius and had already begun by eliminating the ancient *ovile,* the traditional enclosure where Roman citizens came to vote, and rebuilding it as an elegantly colonnaded, huge porticus with marble colonnades a mile long on its flanks, which was to be called the Saepta Julia.[40] The first of these projects had been the Saepta and the new Forum; Cicero and Oppius were acting as his agents to purchase land as early as 54 B.C.[41] A number of these projects, including the Curia, the Basilica, and the Theater were left unfinished at Caesar's assassination in 44 B.C. and subsequently completed by Augustus.

Judging from these testimonia, there can be little doubt that Caesar was truly attempting to bring forms of urban planning to the architecture and layout of Rome. Perhaps equally notable in Suetonius's remarks is Caesar's attempted codification of the civil code. We have independent testimony of this in the remains of the so-called *Lex Julia municipalis,* which embodies the very concept of planning in its clauses dealing with Rome, and which demonstrates that Caesar's reform of Rome was to have been even more sweeping than the creation of a monumentalized city center; it was to have extended to the rules and regulations that governed city life, too.[42]

Upon Caesar's death his architectural and civic improvement programs were not so much abandoned as suspended until his adopted heir, Octavian, was firmly entrenched in power at Rome. His immense program of public building, both new construction and restorations, is documented by Augustus himself in his *Res Gestae,* by contemporary poets such as Vergil, Horace, Propertius and Ovid, by his biographer Suetonius, and by the third century A.D. historian Cassius Dio. In his epitaph, Augustus himself emphasized his restorations of sacred shrines and of civic monuments and his completion of works begun by Caesar (*RG* 19–20). Of the new monuments built during his reign he mentions the two altars vowed to him by the Senate (one to Fortuna Redux in 19 B.C., the other to Pax Augusta in 12 B.C.) on his returns from settling affairs in the eastern and the western provinces, respectively (*RG* 11, 12), and of his own buildings he points particularly to the temple to Apollo on the Palatine, the temple of Divus Julius in the Forum Romanum (*RG* 19) and the temple of Mars Ultor in his new Forum (*RG* 21). These rather bare listings from Augustus's own hand are fleshed out by the testimony of Suetonius, who is also our source for Augustus's boast that he had found Rome a city of brick and left it a city of marble. These new monuments and restorations are more than sufficient to demonstrate that the architectural glorification of Rome begun by Caesar was continued, indeed quite substantially expanded.[43]

In addition to the monuments attributed to Augustus himself, Cassius Dio records the enormous amount of new construction, including the first Pantheon, first public baths, Basilica of Neptune, and restoration, including the Saepta, undertaken by Marcus Agrippa (very much Octavian's right-hand man) in the Campus Martius, which gained an entire new planned complex of buildings in its central area, including the still relatively poorly understood monumental sundial, the Horologium Solare Augusti. In the northwestern sector of the Campus Martius, on the bank of the Tiber, Augustus also constructed his immense Mausoleum, possibly in an intentional visual relationship to the sundial and, perhaps, the Ara Pacis.[44]

Augustus encouraged others to give public and sacred monuments to the city, too. Suetonius provides an impressive list that includes the porticus of Livia and of Octavia, the porticus and basilica of Gaius and Lucius Caesar and the theater of Marcellus—all actually built by Augustus, if Suetonius is to be believed but dedicated in the names of his relatives—as well as a temple of Hercules and the Muses built by Marcius Philippus, a temple of Diana by Lucius Cornificus, the Atrium Libertatis by G. Asinius Pollio, a temple to Saturn by Munatius Plancus, a theater by Cornelius Balbus (an entirely separate building from the theater named after Marcellus) and an amphitheater, the first permanent one in Rome, built by Statilius Taurus.[45] These were splendid monuments, first, to Roman wealth, second to Augustus's desire to make Rome a city truly worthy in its architecture to stand as the center of the empire, and, third, to his very substantial success in achieving that goal. But beyond the glorification and the architectural and decorative propaganda, there was a deeper and more clearly urbanistic planning underway at the same time. Suetonius tells us:[46]

> He [Augustus] divided the area of the city into regions (*regiones*) and wards (*vici*), arranging that the former should be under the charge of magistrates selected each year by lot, and the latter under "masters" (*magistri*) elected by the inhabitants of the respective neighborhoods. To guard against fires he devised a system of stations of night watchmen, and to control the floods he widened and cleared out the channel of the Tiber, which had for some time been filled with rubbish and narrowed by jutting buildings. Further, to make the approach to the city easier from every direction, he personally undertook to rebuild the Flaminian Road all the way to Ariminum, and assigned the rest of the highways to others who had been honoured with triumphs, asking them to use their prize money in paving them.

This organization of metropolitan Rome into fourteen regions (fig. 4.9) attests a true program of planned public works, administrative, protective, and transportational.

What Suetonius does not mention, although it is attested in other sources, is that, in 26 B.C., Augustus also revived the office of the city prefect (*praefectus urbi*), a magistracy that had been allowed to lapse, and gave it broad new powers and duties. Under it Augustus placed three cohorts of troops, called the *cohortes urbanae,* who were charged with keeping order among slaves and unruly citizens. Once an able prefect was found—in fact the same Statilius Taurus who had built the amphitheater—the prefecture quickly developed into the role of a police commissioner for Rome and became a regular part of city administration from that time onward. To these urban improvement plans must be added the creation of the water board and the expansion of the aqueduct system under Agrippa, probably during his aedileship in 33 B.C., and the complete reworking of the sewer system for the city at the same time.[47] What becomes apparent is that it was Agrippa's contributions that

Figure 4.9 Rome: Augustus's 14 regions. [Gros & Torelli (1988) p. 168, fig. 63; reproduced by permission of Gius. Laterza & Figli, S.p.a.]

can really be designated as elements of "city planning." The only area of the city comprehensively redesigned in the Augustan building program was the central Campus Martius, and the responsibility there was primarily Agrippa's. The complete restructuring of public works—roads, water, sewer, fire prevention—can also be connected fairly closely to Agrippa's innovations, especially in his aedileship. Nonetheless, it is fair to assume that these innovations could not and would not have been possible without Augustus's acceptance of the concept of planning that lay behind them and they certainly required the princeps' acquiescence in their implementation. The reorganization of the city administration with services to a large degree supervised by the urban prefect and the divison of the city into fourteen administrative regions and those in

217

turn into wards with their own elected magistrates was nothing less than a revolution for the city, and the system instituted by Augustus and Agrippa became so well-entrenched that it became a quasi-official designation—Rome of the 14 Regions—that lasted at least into the fourth century A.D. This constituted, in fact, the organization of the disparate Republican city into a manageable municipality.[48]

Throughout the Imperial period, there were frequent programs that seem to have brought new attempts at urbanization to various sectors of the city much as Augustus and Agrippa had changed the face of the central Campus Martius. Indeed, the Campus itself had to be restored almost entirely after being ravaged by fire in A.D. 80, and it fell to Domitian—probably the most influential builder of all the Roman emperors—to restore most of the monuments there including building a completely new Pantheon (in turn replaced by the Hadrianic building we know today), the Saepta, the Baths of Agrippa, the Basilica of Neptune, and the precinct of Isis and Serapis. Much of this area was reworked again under Hadrian and yet again under Alexander Severus, so the details of the Domitianic Campus Martius are at best muddled, but it is significant that so many emperors chose to restore, and undoubtedly to bring their own architectural concerns, and meanings, to the area.[49]

Other sectors of the city enjoyed (or suffered) urbanistic development over the course of several different reigns. Possibly the two biggest overall projects were the development of the public entertainment complex in and around the Flavian amphitheater, which began in A.D. 70 with Vespasian's accession and was completed under Trajan with the dedication of the Thermae Traiani in A.D. 109, and the slow architectural articulation and connection of the originally independent elements that made up the Imperial Fora, a process (not a cohesive project until late in its development) that began with Julius Caesar's land purchases in 54 B.C. and was completed only when Hadrian dedicated the temple to the Deified Trajan, which capped the Forum of Trajan ca. A.D. 118–122. Both reflect major schemes of monumental urbanization of sufficient importance that they were passed on from one emperor to the next in succession until they were eventually brought to completion.

The Flavian amphitheater was Vespasian's response to the pre-

sumed outrage felt by the Roman populace to Nero's vast appropria-
tion of land in the city center for his second palace complex, the
infamous Domus Aurea, which was constructed only after the di-
sastrous fire of A.D. 64 had swept away his earlier Domus Transitoria, which apparently spread from the Palatine to the Oppius.
The Domus Aurea has lived in infamy as a result of the gaudy
descriptions of it provided by Tacitus and Suetonius, though the
battered remains beneath the Trajanic Baths on the Oppius hardly
seem to justify the exaggerations of the writers. In terms of conscious planning in the city of Rome, however, its destruction by
Vespasian is the essential element to keep in mind. The lake in the
center of its grounds was drained, and the great Flavian amphitheater (subsequently given the nickname "Colosseum" from its proximity to the immense statue of Nero, the Colossus Neronis, left over
from the Domus Aurea) was constructed over the decade of the 70s
A.D. with dedication under Titus in A.D. 80 but coming to total
completion only under Domitian.

Titus realized the possibilities of making this whole sector of the
city into a pleasure area that would always recall the benefactions of
the Flavian dynasty to the Roman populace, and so had a small bath
building constructed immediately north of the Colosseum. Domitian continued the glorification with a magnificent fountain, the
Meta sudans, which may have been the successor to a fountain of
Neronian date, and a sequence of gladiatorial schools and practice
courts to the east. It has been asserted that Domitian also introduced a triumphal arch to this complex, on the site subsequently
(and still) occupied by the Arch of Constantine, but the evidence is
disputed and inconclusive. Domitian may well have been planning
to replace the Baths of Titus with a grander scheme, but if so, his
assasination stopped the project temporarily; it was revived under
Trajan and the Baths dedicated in his name in A.D. 109. Here a
Flavian-planned pleasure area for the entertainment of the Roman
mob came to fruition and gave its character to that sector of the city
forever afterward. That the plan was sufficiently coherent and cohesive to be carried on and completed under five successive reigns
speaks well for the clarity of the original conception (fig. 4.10).[50]

On an even grander scale was the group of buildings and open

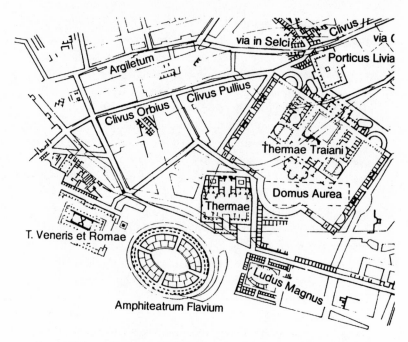

Figure 4.10 Rome: Flavian amphitheater complex. [Anderson (1985) Ill. 1, p. 500; reproduced by permission of the author]

spaces that came to be called the Imperial Fora. This complex originated as a series of individual fora surrounded by colonnades and graced with temples. Julius Caesar's, just north of the Curia and Comitium, was the first; it was apparently serviceable by 44 B.C. but only completed by Augustus. To the northeast of it, Augustus built a similar but much grander forum-temple-porticus complex that was finally dedicated and opened to the public in 2 B.C., having been under construction, probably, for nearly twenty years. These two quite similar complexes dominated the northeast side of the Forum area and were bounded on the west by the Clivus Argentarius, on the south by the Argiletum, on the east by the Vicus Longus, and on the north by a street whose name has not been preserved to us (which was removed during construction of the Forum of Trajan). There is no real evidence for assuming that with the construction of

Augustus's Forum a plan, almost a long-range blueprint, came into effect that predicted the further urbanization of the area into a sequence of Imperial dynastic and ceremonial monuments.[51]

The third element in what was to become the Imperial Fora was never even called a "forum" before the fourth century A.D.; it was vowed in A.D. 71 and dedicated in A.D. 75 as the temple of Peace, created to celebrate the pacification of the Empire by Vespasian and Titus with their conquest of Judaea, the spoils of which were housed there and displayed to the public. The temple of Peace was not a forum at all but a porticus, a quadrilateral space enclosed by colonnades on all four sides. The shrine to Pax was a sanctuary in the southeast side of the colonnade; it was flanked by a Greek and a Latin library, one on each side. Gardens or pools filled the open center, and works of art were displayed in the colonnades and, perhaps, in the gardens. It has more in common as a piece of architecture with the Porticus Pompeianae that stretched behind Pompey's theater than with the fora of Caesar and of Augustus, and it was completely separated from them physically by the Argiletum.[52] The temple of Peace was only incorporated into the sequence when Domitian eliminated a stretch of the street and converted it into his Forum Transitorium, which featured a plan of incredible architectural refinement—very likely the inspiration of his master architect Rabirius—which allowed a forum-temple-porticus complex to be fitted into the restricted space of a street with no changes at all to the Augustan Forum on one side and only the alteration of a single perimeter wall of the templum Pacis on its other.[53] Contemporary with the invention of the Forum Transitorium, Domitian also rebuilt the Forum of Julius Caesar, which may have been damaged in the fire of A.D. 80, and very likely brought it into close association with the southwest end of the Forum Transitorium, thus increasing the effect of binding the three fora and the temple into a single complex of buildings.

There is a good likelihood that Domitian had intended to crown the series of fora with a fifth member, since he seems to have been responsible for the clearing of land, and possibly for the excavation of the Quirinal slope, that opened the way for what was to become the Forum of Trajan. If so, it is probable that not much had been built there at the time of his assassination, and the complex that has come down to us is that attributed to Trajan's architect, Apollodorus of Damascus, not one designed or built by Rabirius.[54] Trajan's Forum was the largest and grandest of the five buildings, including a huge open forum with colonnades and hemicycles on either side, and a massive basilica closing the north end. The dating of the elements of the plan beyond the Basilica Ulpia—the sculpted column and its flanking libraries—is disputed, and our knowledge of the element that crowned the entire conception, the temple dedicated to the memory of the deified Trajan by his successor, Hadrian, is practically nonexistent. Whether these final elements were part of Trajan's and Apollodorus's original plan (with the dedication of the temple altered only at the last moment)[55] or a reworking mandated by Hadrian (which included changing the position of the column and converting it to serve as Trajan's tomb as well as adding the temple on to the original design)[56] is a complicated and at present insoluble problem. What is certain is that the Forum of Trajan brought the entire sequence of Imperial Fora to a spectacular conclusion (fig. 4.11).

The fora now fulfilled the urbanistic purposes devised for them as a group by Domitian: to dominate the entire sector of the city that stretched from the Flavian amphitheater on the south to the via Lata and entry to the Campus Martius on the north. In this they showed clearly the achievement of urban planning, even when it was inflicted to some degree on monuments that already existed and were not intended initially to form a group. With the construction of Trajan's Forum, the Imperial Fora became, and would remain throughout Roman antiquity, a monument to, a symbol of, and a touchstone for the might and the grandeur of the Roman Empire in the very heart of the capital city.[57]

Evidence for planned development in the capital city is relatively meager from the mid second century A.D. onward. Two items appear important: first, the fire of A.D. 192, which led to the huge reconstruction program undertaken by Septimius Severus and his successors and, second, the encirclement of the city by walls, for the first time in centuries, carried out under the emperor Aurelian in the 270s A.D. The damage done by the fire that appears to have severely damaged the city at the very end of the reign of Commodus (A.D. 180–192) is extremely difficult to assess since our sources for it are meager. We are told that the fire began in a private house, destroyed the templum Pacis and the nearby horrea Piperataria, both on the northeast side of the Forum Romanum, that it eventually ran through the entire Forum and burned at least as far as the Palatine, probably inflicting damage on the Imperial palace there.[58]

Once he was firmly established in power, Septimius Severus began the process of restoring the city, at the same time using the opportunity to add monuments that would emphasize his own political and symbolic program, such as the Septizodium erected at the southwest corner of the Palatine Hill where the Viae Latina and Appia approached the city center.[59] Other new construction under Septimius included the Castra Nova military camp, baths in Transtiberim and in Region I, extension and additions to the Palatine palace, and the huge sculpted arch erected in the Forum Romanum and the smaller porta Argentariorum in the Forum Boarium. Septimius also restored the templum Pacis and the templum divi Vespasiani after damage by the fire as well as the temple and atrium of Vesta in the Forum (actually done by his empress, Julia Domna), the Aqua Marcia, the Pantheon, the Porticus Octaviae and its temples, and the theater of Pompey. Under his successors there were constructed the Baths of Caracalla and the via Nova (Caracalla, reigned 211–217), the Sessorianum palace, Amphitheatrum Castrense and Circus Varianus on the Esquiline, the temple of Elagabalus on the Palatine, and a restoration of the badly damaged Colosseum (Elagabalus, reigned 218–222), and the Baths and aqueduct of Alexander in the Campus Martius, the temple of Dea Suria built from scratch with restorations of the temple of Jupiter Victor on the Palatine, of Isis in the Campus Martius, and of the Stadium of Domitian (Alexander Severus, reigned 222–235).[60]

Taken together, these new constructions and restorations add up to a building program, still relatively little explored and but poorly understood, as massive as any previous one and perhaps approaching most closely in scope the projects undertaken by the Flavians at the end of the first century A.D.[61] One notable element that is

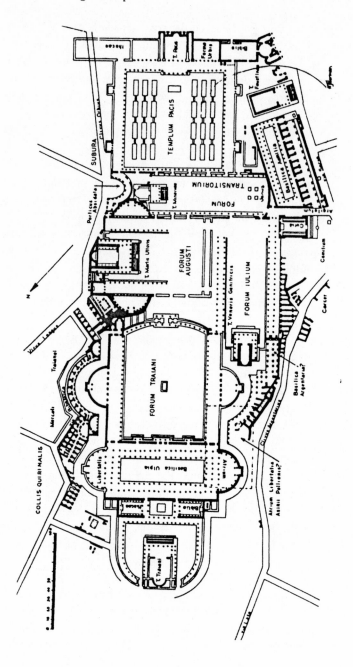

relatively well documented is the restoration of the templum Pacis, which involved the conversion of the libraries installed there by Vespasian, whose collections may well have been lost in the fire, into the office of the *praefectus Urbi,* which would remain there well into later antiquity. While the testimonia are somewhat scanty for the actual restoration, that it was done is not in doubt since the building continues to be praised and admired for at least two more centuries.[62]

What had been the Greek and Latin libraries of this temple complex prior to A.D. 192 were converted into an office and archive for the urban prefecture after the fire. This is shown clearly by the discovery of the fragments of an immense map of the ancient city incised on slabs of marble at the foot of a wall that had been a part of one of those libraries and had survived by being incorporated into the church of Sts. Cosmas and Damian during the sixth century A.D. The Forma Urbis Romae, as the map is known, had been clamped to that wall at second-storey height as a part of the reconstruction and conversion of the space under Severus.[63] This marble map was hung on a wall that divided what seems to have been a vestibule from a large hall behind it, all now incorporated into the church. It has often been suggested that the huge map must have served some sort of actual cadastral purpose related to the archive of the *praefectus Urbi.* That such an archive existed and was in effect the central records office for real estate holdings and evaluations for tax assessment in the city is generally accepted, but assigning an actual cadastral function to the marble plan would seem dangerous, since by the very nature of the volatility of property possession in a free market economy such as Rome's, its record of property holdings would have been out of date before the carving was even completed, and its scale is insufficient for any kind of realistic use for tax assessment or recording. Much more likely is that it was seen as a decorative element that symbolized the functions of the office it adorned. There is now good evidence that there was an earlier, probably

---

Figure 4.11 Rome: The Imperial Fora. [Anderson (1984) Pl. 1; reproduced by permission of the author and of *Collection Latomus*]

Vespasianic, version of the plan probably hung in the same complex, possibly on the same wall. The use of maps as decoration in Roman buildings is also attested in the Augustan Porticus Vipsania, where Agrippa is said to have hung a map of the world.[64] Another possible reason for the existence of the marble plan could have been to record for those who had reason to come to the city prefecture the extent of new and restoration building that had been done by the emperor. That there was some sort of planning, probably quite extensive planning, involved in so massive a reworking of the major sectors of the ancient city seems apparent, and the marble plan could have memorialized it. Sadly, we do not yet know enough to go much further.

The final project that must imply direct, "blueprint" planning work in the city is the erection of the immense circuit of walls around the city begun during the reign of Aurelian (A.D. 270–275) and completed about ten years later, in their initial form, under Probus (A.D. 276–282). These walls (see fig. 4.8 above) not only kept attackers out, at least in theory, but also enclosed and impressed an artificial boundary on the urban, versus the suburban, territory of the city of Rome, a sort of boundary that had not existed throughout the centuries of Rome's greatest development. To a large extent the location of the walls was determined by preexisting topography since numerous monuments already standing were simply built into them wholesale (e.g., the Castra Praetoria, the Pyramid of G. Cestius) and the gates had to accommodate the already existing courses of the great roads that led into and out of the city. In addition to their apparent defensive purpose it seems possible, though perhaps not probable, that the walls were built with the secondary purpose of making it easier to assess customs duties on goods being imported into Rome. While the planning of the Aurelianic walls was probably not extremely elaborate, since there were so many constraints on their course and openings because of the topography they crossed, nonetheless it does represent planning on a large scale for the city. The long-term effect on the urbanization of later antique and medieval Rome of these walls was probably more profound than that of almost any other ancient monument in the city.[65]

STREETS AND PRIVATE QUARTERS: RESTRICTIONS
AND REGULATIONS

Such achievements of urban grandeur, unfortunately, do not seem to have been accompanied by reliable improvements in the living conditions of city dwellers, despite the periodic evidence of attempts, or at least of good intentions, on the part of the *principes*. After the catastrophic fire of A.D. 64 and Nero's expenditures and expropriations for the construction of the Domus Aurea, Tacitus tells us that Nero attempted to bring building codes and some sort of zoning laws to Rome:[66]

> In the part of the city not reserved for the Palace, the rebuilding was not at random nor uncontrolled, as after the Gallic fire. Regulations prescribed the alignment of roads, the width of streets, and the height of houses. They stood in spacious building-plots and colonnades were added to the blocks of apartments so as to protect their street frontage. Nero undertook to construct these colonnades at his own expense, and to clear up all building sites before restoring them to their owners. Rewards were announced, in proportion to the standing and resources of individual citizens, for the completion of private houses or blocks of apartments by a given date. The marshes by Ostia were designated for the dumping of rubble, and instructions were given that the ships employed to bring corn up the river should make the return trip loaded with rubble. A portion of all buildings had to be made without timber and of stone from Gabii or Albano, which is fire proof. Water inspectors were appointed to ensure a better and more efficient service from the public supply, which had suffered from the tapping of unauthorized individuals. Each householder had to keep fire-fighting apparatus ready to hand. Party walls were forbidden, buildings must be surrounded by walls of their own. Necessity caused these measures to be accepted, and they certainly added to the city's amenities. Some, however, thought the old city had been a healthier place to live in, arguing that the narrow streets and tall buildings offered protection against the intense heat of the sun, while now the open spaces, devoid of shade, reflect the sun's rays much more intensely.

Suetonius adds a bit more information:[67]

> He [Nero] devised a new form for the buildings of the city and in front of the houses and apartments he erected porches, from the flat roofs of

which fires could be fought; and these he put up at his own cost. He had also planned to extend the walls as far as Ostia and to bring the sea from there to Rome by a canal.

These items, strange as some of them are at first reading, would seem to indicate that Nero had in mind a major revision of the methods of private construction in Rome and that fairly strict codes, ordinances, and zoning were inflicted on the rebuilt city. Certainly many of the ideas expounded by Tacitus sound surprisingly modern in their attempt to provide for protection from natural disaster.

There is little evidence left in the archaeological record to indicate that much if any of this revolutionary program was realized. Contemporary and later writers, notably Seneca, Martial, and Juvenal, indicate that there was little enough improvement in the conditions and the construction of urban *insulae* at least for the poorer strata of Roman society,[68] and only a few buildings in Rome and at Ostia carry anything like the protective balconies or porches mentioned by both authors (the so-called Casa di Diana at Ostia is one of the few; such balconies also appear along the via Biberatica in the Markets of Trajan in Rome). It takes only a glance at the fragments of the Severan marble plan that show domestic quarters of the city a century and a half after Nero's time to realize that the street pattern remained tangled in many areas and the streets and alleys themselves quite narrow and dark. Yet there is a certain regularity about the layout that might imply some form of control or regulation being exercised. The Justinianic *Digest* preserves legal interdicts that show that there were certainly restrictions on intrusions into the city streets and public squares by architectural features, at least at street level (apparently balconies could protrude),[69] and these clearly imply that there were means of controlling the openness of city streets, although we are not told how this was effected. In Tacitus's passage especially, what we find is an intent to impose planning and controls on the domestic quarters of Rome. Some parts may well have been achieved: a certain proportion of the buildings could, from that time forward, have been constructed of concrete, for example. But the extent to which we should accept the particulars of these principles and restrictions is unclear, since the archaeological record does not seem to corroborate them, and we are left with a conundrum: to what extent is the *Nova Urbs Neronis* a fantasy propounded by the literary sources, and to what extent was it actually built? What relationship, if any, did it have to the urban shape that the streets and buildings of Rome assumed from the first century A.D. onward?

The idea of imposing regulations on private building within the city was not new with Nero. Vitruvius records regulations in public laws (*leges publicae*) from before the early 20s B.C. that restricted the thickness of party walls between buildings to no more than 1.5 Roman feet. Such a restriction would have effectively limited buildings made with sun-dried brick to one storey since the walls would have been too thin to support a storey above them, and this served as an impetus to use kiln-dried brick, stone, and concrete in apartment architecture in the city. It is Vitruvius, also, who records a building regulation at Utica that dictated the amount of time sun-dried bricks had to be allowed to dry before they could be employed. The elder Pliny's remark that after the war with Pyrrhus the Romans changed from roofing with wooden shingles to roofing with tiles has been interpreted as reflecting a legislated change but could just as well simply reflect (and vastly oversimplify) a slow process of change in roofing technique brought about by the dawning realization that tiles would resist fire better than wooden shingles. Strabo tells us that Augustus had imposed a restriction of 70 Roman feet on the height of any new buildings erected on public streets, and Suetonius mentions the *princeps* reading to the Senate from books such as Rutilius's *De Modo Aedificiorum*. It is possible that Nero was doing nothing more in determining building heights, if he did so at all, than repeating and emphasizing Augustan legislation already in place.[70] While Nero's attempt at building regulations and at controlling the nature of private architecture at Rome was, so far as our sources seem to indicate, the most extensive ever, the fact that this was an important concern is indicated subsequently, too. There is evidence that Trajan again at the beginning of the second century A.D. attempted to dictate building materials and limit building height,[71] and as late as Tertullian the sheer height and ricketiness of the *insulae* of Rome was a standard *topos* for jokes.[72]

To summarize the evidence, we can see first that there was a real and recurring interest by the Imperial administration in controlling the shapes taken by the streets and domestic buildings of the city which is attested periodically in the documentary sources. Such rules and regulations must have seemed good to those charged with protecting and administering the huge city. The literary record, particularly the gibes and wisecracks of such urbane poets as Martial and Juvenal, seems to indicate that unfortunately the realization may have fallen well short of the intent unless we assume that all their remarks are nothing more than examples of a popular urban imagery employed over and over again. It remains unknown whether Nero intended to impose a precedent meant to govern building construction in the future, or was aiming primarily at controlling the immediate rebuilding mandated by the ravages of the fire of A.D. 64. Much of what is recorded by Tacitus and Suetonius, writing long after the event, may simply reflect the facts of how Nero's architects and engineers planned the task of rebuilding large tracts of the domestic quarters of the city.[73]

PUBLIC SPACE VERSUS PRIVATE SPACE: *URBS ET SUBURBIUM*

At Rome we can trace the growth of public architecture and its effect not just upon the architectural fabric of the city but also upon human topography and private space. The central areas of Rome, specifically the Forum Romanum and the Capitolium, had from the earliest times been reserved for sacred and public architecture and had been controlled open space with tabernae lining the Sacra Via. The earliest evidence of dwellings indicates that most of the rest of the urban center was open for habitation, as needed, and for commercial construction. Along the Tiber banks there were open areas for the delivery and sale of goods from earliest times. Early commercial areas are perhaps commemorated in names such as Forum Boarium (forum of the cattle-sellers) and Forum Holitorium (forum of the vegetable-sellers),[74] and there was reserved sacred space in those areas, too, such as the precinct of Fortuna and Mater Matuta *in foro Holitorio*. Another such open space for selling provisions was the area in the southern Campus Martius near the river that came to be known as the Circus Flaminius, although it never took the architectural form of a true circus, remaining simply an open area of roughly oval shape, increasingly hemmed in by the growth of sacred precincts around its perimeter.[75]

Prime residential sectors of the earlier city seem to have clustered around the Forum, that is, on the Palatine Hill to its south and in the low-lying areas below the fingers of the Quirinal, Viminal, and Fagutal in the area that came to be called the Subura. From there residential quarters spread up onto the Esquiline to the east and north and up the slopes of its spurs from the Subura.[76] Presumably space for housing was available in the low-lying Campus Martius, but it does not seem to have developed rapidly or extensively, perhaps for two reasons: its low level made it particularly susceptible to flooding by the Tiber, and it lay outside the *pomerium* with whatever problems of lack of religious sanction and divine protection that might imply.

As Rome grew, especially after the Gallic sack and the rebuilding of much of the city in the early fourth century B.C., the areas given over primarily to private dwellings seem to have remained much the same, with the primary sectors for further expansion proving to be the Caelian and Aventine hills, south and east of the Palatine and Circus Maximus, which were enclosed within the fourth-century walls. It is notable, and another strong reason why the area did not become an important residential quarter at this period, that the Campus Martius was left unprotected outside the course of those walls, thus making it even less appealing for private construction. The picture we get of residential quarters in Rome between the early sixth and the early second century B.C., then, is one of a slow spreading outward from the Forum and Capitoline to the northeast (the Subura, the Quirinal, Viminal, and Fagutal, and the Esquiline) and to the south (southwest on the Palatine and subsequently the Aventine, and southeast on the Caelian). The city's outward growth was undoubtedly a direct result of the expansion of Rome's influence and domination of Italy and increasingly of the central Mediterranean, which were reflected in an expanding population and also in an ever increasing number of and demand for religious,

231

civic, and recreational buildings to serve its needs and residences to house its people.[77]

From the middle of the second century B.C. and the introduction of hellenistic Greek modes of architectural planning, styles, materials and architects, as well as the development of *opus caementicium*—developments which came about in direct correlation with Rome's conquest of the eastern Mediterranean and increasing exposure to the civilization of the Hellenistic world—the city of Rome began to gain a very large number of public buildings in all quarters of the city. Buildings such as the Porticus Metelli surrounded, defined, glorified, and expanded an ancient sacred precinct devoted to Jupiter Stator and Juno Regina, as the subsequent Porticus Philippi did for Hercules Musarum. Such projects took up a good deal of space in the vicinity of the Circus Flaminius, in turn rather reducing its utility as a market area though increasing its ceremonial importance as, for instance, the staging area for triumphal processions.

Whatever original markets may be recalled by the names of the fora Boarium et Holitorium, the markets or docking areas there had long disappeared, replaced by the great Emporium and its associated Porticus Aemilia further south along the Tiber in the vicinity of Monte Testaccio. The filling up of the Campus Martius with temples and other public buildings had already begun but increased rapidly in the second and first centuries B.C., resulting in groups of temples such as those excavated in the area sacra di Largo Argentina, and in the filling up of more and more land with such dedications. Around the Forum the press became particularly apparent with the development of a passion for basilicas with their handsome columnar façades that lent such architectural distinction to whole areas. The first, the Basilica Porcia, was put up somewhere very close to the Curia in 184 B.C. and was rapidly followed by the Basilica Aemilia (179 B.C.) and Basilica Sempronia (170 B.C.) on either long flank of the *imum Forum,* and the Basilica Opimia set somewhere fairly near the temple of Concord at the west end of the Forum when it was rebuilt by L. Opimius in 121 B.C.[78]

With the arrival of Sulla as dictator, the glorification of the city center began in earnest and continued, if sporadically, through the rest of the first century B.C. The effect of building programs—or of random architectural gifts to the city such as Pompey's theater-temple-porticus complex in the Campus Martius—was certainly visually splendid but the concomitant must have been an increasing difficulty in finding open space and an upward spiral in city property prices (which is well attested by Cicero when he tried to buy land for Julius Caesar). With first Caesar's, then Augustus's increases in building, land anywhere near the city center began to come at a premium and was difficult to obtain for both the Forum Julium and the Forum Augustum. But the other side of the "glorification" programs, in addition to spiralling land prices, was clearly a pushing of residents out of the central quarters of Rome, a process which was to be largely complete by the end of the following century, the first century A.D.[79]

A glance at what happened in a few select quarters of the city of Rome between the reigns of Augustus and Domitian will make the picture clear. On the Palatine Hill an expensive aristocratic residential quarter had grown up, home to the distinguished political and social figures of Rome such as Marcus and Quintus Cicero, during the second and first centuries B.C. It was, therefore, no surprise when Augustus chose to have his town mansion there, but at the same time he also took over a substantial swatch of potentially prime residential real estate next door and built upon it his temple to Apollo Palatinus, complete with libraries and porticus. He appears to have expanded his holdings even more in the later part of his reign, possibly thinking of creating a true palace, but decided against it.[80]

Under Tiberius (A.D. 14–37), the mansion inhabited by Augustus was apparently no longer deemed sufficiently grand, and the whole northwest height of the Palatine was taken over wholesale for the erection of a true palace, the Domus Tiberiana, which was in turn expanded by Caligula (A.D. 37–41). Under Nero (A.D. 54–68) came far more expansion with virtually the entire Palatine Hill stripped of private residences and turned into a part of his two successive palaces, the Domus Transitoria followed by the Domus Aurea. Indeed the Neronian palaces spread well beyond the Palatine, with the Domus Aurea ultimately encompassing the areas of the Caelian, the Velia, and the Oppian hills, adding up to a huge encroachment in the very center of the Imperial city. Although after Nero's demise the Domus Aurea was first opened to the public and then dismantled, its territory was never turned back over to private developers but became in part the vast entertainment complex surrounding the Flavian amphitheater and in part remained Imperial palace when Domitian completely rebuilt the structures on the Palatine to make them his own. Thus the Palatine Hill, once entirely private residential space, within little more than a century was removed from private use entirely and taken into the Imperial domain.[81]

A similar development occurred in the area northeast of the Roman Forum, in the sector where the parallel streets Argiletum and Corneta entered the Forum. After the Gallic sack, there seems to have been no provision made, among many other items, for any sort of centralized provisions market in the city. Rather a loose agglomeration of markets seems to have grown up along the Tiber outside the porta Trigemina, where in due course the Emporium would succeed them, and in other spots all over the city. Varro tells us that at some point Rome's several widely dispersed provisions markets were brought together into a single space in the city, a space which came to be called the macellum, probably organized during the censorship of L. Aemilius Paullus and M. Fulvius Nobilior in 179 B.C. as the endpoint of a long project of bringing these provisions supply areas together that had begun after the fire of 210 B.C. The area that held this central macellum was the large square of land stretching northeast from behind the Basilica Aemilia, between the Argiletum and the Corneta streets.

"Macellum" seems to have become the usual way to refer to this district behind the basilica and at the entry to the Subura quarter by the first century B.C., according to Cicero.[82] It contained a fish market, a market for imported delicacies, meat and vegetables, and possibly for baked goods and wine. It must have occupied more or less the entire area subsequently filled by Vespasian's templum Pacis. But by the end of the first century B.C. the Roman population had so expanded that a second *macellum* was needed though not in the city center. The demand for it was on the Esquiline Hill, now a true center of residential buildings, and so one was dedicated there by Livia at an unattested point during Augustus's reign. In A.D. 59 another *macellum,* called the "Macellum Magnum," was dedicated by Nero on the Caelian Hill, implying yet again the move of residential population away from the city center to the eastern hills. After the fire of A.D. 64, which very likely destroyed the old central *macellum* since it swept right through the area in which it was located, the need for it apparently no longer existed and it was not rebuilt. Rather the land where it had stood was incorporated, first, into the grounds of the Domus Aurea and then was readily available to Vespasian for his templum Pacis.[83]

The point, of course, is that what had been commercial space providing essential goods, mainly foodstuffs, to the residential quarters along the northeast flank of the Forum Romanum—the sectors of the Subura lying closest to the city center—and to the residents of the Palatine was no longer needed by the middle of the first century A.D. Residential population had moved elsewhere around Rome. Indeed, Domitian was even able to close off completely the southwestern end of the Argiletum where it approached and entered the Forum and replace it with his Forum Transitorium; the rear part of the templum Pacis may well have had much the same effect on the lower end of the Corneta. In short, the Subura was being progressively pushed away and kept separate from the Forum area, which in the later first century A.D. had, of course, lost most of its political and administrative purpose to the Palatine bureaucrats and to the Imperial Fora anyway and was instead becoming an ever more glorious museum and shrine to Roman might, dominated at the end of the century by the immense equestrian statue of Domitian set up in its center. Construction of Trajan's Forum completed the process, leaving the Forum surrounded on its long northeastern flank by the sequence of Imperial Fora and the area reserved for entertainment around the Colosseum, on its southern flank by the Imperial Palatine and its palace, on its short west end by the temples and shrines of the Capitoline (as it always had been), and on the east by the ridge of the Velia crowned by the Arch of Titus and succeeded by the putative Domitianic arch, the Meta Sudans fountain, and the Flavian amphitheater itself. The busy bustling Forum of the Republic was no more. The residential

235

quarters of the Palatine and the part of Subura near the Forum were no more, and the space of the entire center of the city had come to be reserved exclusively and entirely for Imperial and public buildings and monuments.[84]

With residential space in the city center disappearing, two related phenomena occurred in the urban fabric of Rome, the first in the center and the second in the *suburbium*. As residental neighborhoods were forced out of the inner Subura and off the Palatine and pushed farther east onto the outer areas of the Esquiline and Caelian hills, first by the Domus Aurea and after it by the Flavian amphitheater complex, the higher and farther areas of the city atop the Quirinal, Viminal, Esquiline, and Caelian hills as well as the Aventine and the Transtiberim area bore the brunt of the expansion. But these areas, too, had a certain amount of territory reserved in them for public buildings of various sorts. With somewhat better control of the Tiber floods and because it was accessible and flat and therefore easy to build on, the Campus Martius might have been expected to take on the sort of ramshackle tenement-filled character so often attributed to the Subura, but on the whole this did not happen precisely because the Campus had already to such a remarkable degree been filling up with public monuments ever since the second century B.C. and especially during the programs carried out by Agrippa and Domitian. Little enough space was left there for apartment buildings (fig. 4.12). Thus builders continued to crowd four- and five-storey *insulae* close together wherever space was available for them farther and farther from the glorified city center.[85]

Expansion occurred into the *suburbium* of Rome, the vast territory called in modern times the Campagna romana that stretched out from the so-called green belt of private *horti* immediately encircling the city (by the first century B.C. if not somewhat earlier) on the east as far as Tibur and on the southeast to the Alban hills. This expansion had begun early when Republican leaders came to build villas in the countryside outside Rome to which they could retire for *otium,* periods of leisure away from city pressures. The building of pleasure villas in the countryside around Mons Albanus (Pompey near Bovillae and, later, Domitian at modern Castel Gandolfo),

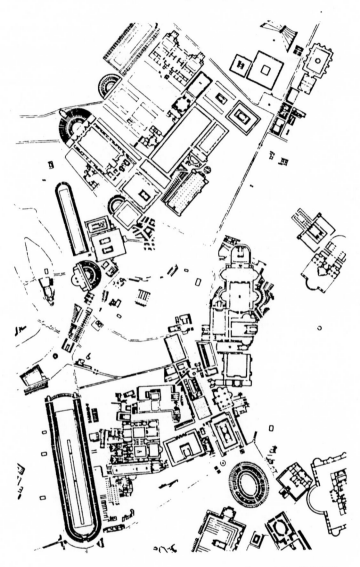

Figure 4.12 Rome: Public building in the Imperial city center. [Gros & Torelli (1988) p. 207, fig. 94; reproduced by permission of Gius. Laterza & Figli, S.p.a.]

Tivoli (perhaps Horace, certainly Hadrian), Tusculum (Cicero), and other such rural towns became a matter of social pride and standing that continued through the Imperial period, thus gobbling up a good deal of open countryside for the wealthy much as public buildings and Imperial palaces had gobbled up the center of Rome.[86] Together with the spread of the aristocratic *villae suburbanae* must have gone the outward movement of less prosperous people unable to find housing in the center of Rome or unwilling to pay the inflated prices demanded for it. It is probably no accident that the extremely rare noun *suburbium* first occurs in Latin in one of Cicero's speeches from the last year of his life, 44–43 B.C., when the expansion into the Roman surburban area was already well under way.[87]

Writing during the reign of Augustus, Dionysius of Halicarnassus says that Servius Tullius had brought the Viminal and Esquiline hills into the city proper. He then discusses the extent of Rome during his own lifetime and gives us a remarkable picture of *urbs* and *suburbium* around the time of the birth of Christ:[88]

> Farther than this [the Viminal and Esquiline] the building of the city has not yet progressed, since the gods, they say, have not permitted it; but all the inhabited places round it, which are many and large, are unprotected and without walls, and very easy to be taken by any enemies who may come. If anyone wishes to estimate the size of Rome by looking at these suburbs he will necessarily be misled for want of a definite clue by which to determine up to what point it is still the city and where it ceases to be the city; so closely is the city connected with the country, giving the beholder the impression of a city stretching out indefinitely.

This picture of the *suburbium* as giving the viewer the impression that the city ran on indefinitely and without specific identifiable division from center into countryside is stressed to an even greater degree at the end of the first century A.D., when Martial describes looking down from the Janiculum Hill across Rome and gazing southeastward toward the Alban hills, then eastward toward the hills of Tusculum, then northeastward toward Fidenae and finally northward up the Tiber toward Saxa Rubra and seeing the city stretched out unbroken before him and thus "taking the measure of all Rome."[89]

This vision of Rome as an urban/suburban continuum, or sprawl, from the Forum and Capitoline all the way out to the surrounding volcanic hills has been little understood, probably because of the addition of the Aurelianic walls in the third century A.D., which provided exactly the visual division between city and suburb that is so specifically lacking in Dionysius's and Martial's descriptions. From the construction of those walls all the way to our own century, the topographical reality of Rome has been one of a city marked off by that enclosure, surrounded by an extensive but ever emptier and more desolate *campagna* full of the crumbling ruins of antiquity. This vision, absolutely invalid for Rome at any time between the early first century B.C. and the third quarter of the third century A.D.—between the abandonment of the old fourth century B.C. wall circuit and the construction of Aurelian's defenses— was unintentionally transposed by Romantic poets and writers as well as by early topographers, who tended always to begin their descriptions on one side or the other of the Aurelianic walls, onto our inherited view of the late Republican and Imperial city. It was not so. The ancient *suburbium* was a continuous extension of the *urbs*, visually, economically, topographically, and conceptually, throughout the centuries of Rome's greatest power and influence.[90] Once this misconception is put aside, the testimony of Dionysius and Martial makes vivid sense.

But the picture must not be overweighted. While the great aristocratic and then Imperial villas and pleasure gardens were certainly a major factor in the *suburbium,* they were by no means the whole story. The picture of the area that we receive from modern archaeological surveys and from the older descriptive studies of Ashby and Lanciani, as well as from the distribution of traces of roads and byways, foundations and cisterns, and of stamped bricks throughout the Campagna from ancient times, is one of an area well-supplied also with smaller private villas (*villae rusticae*), small and middle-sized farms, way stations along the highways interspersed with innumerable funerary monuments (especially near the city outside the *pomerium*), and of innumerable byways, small lanes and paths that turned off the main roads leading to farms, vineyards, smallholdings, and similar establishments. The area by the end of the first century B.C. may in fact have been fairly densely populated and distinguishable from the city primarily by the occurrence of funerary monuments and by the lack of multistorey *insulae* (which seem never to have reached as far from the city center as the line that Aurelian chose for his walls anyway).[91]

The monumentalization of the city center and the increasing disappearance of living space within the city throughout the first century A.D. can only have aggravated the situation and increased the movement toward the suburbs. As Nero brought the countryside into the city (*rus in urbe*) so in fact if not in literary conceit there must have grown up a sort of townscape in the surrounding countryside, an *urbs in rure*.[92] It is likely that this situation remained well into the third century A.D., although it is certainly correct that during the second century more and more land was bought up by aristocrats and successful members of the Imperial bureaucracy, particularly when, for example, Trajan passed an ordinance that seems to have required those standing for high offices in Rome to buy land in Italy, and their obvious and logical response was to purchase villas and estates in the *suburbium* close to Rome. The urban/suburban continuum remained a real fact of the economic and physical topography of the city until the reign of Aurelian. After the construction of the Aurelianic walls, the Imperial estates appear to have overwhelmed the *villae rusticae* and small holdings, and the *suburbium* to have passed for the most part into Imperial hands.[93]

Five

Architecture, Space, and Society in the Roman World: Public Architecture and Shared Space

At this point it is essential to turn to the evidence of Roman architecture itself and to investigate questions about public and private space, and the intersection between them, in order to discuss the relationship between Roman architecture and society. Those questions will be different, though interrelated, for public and for private buildings and space, and so will be pursued in separate chapters, with the public aspects of Roman architecture explored first. The main questions that need to be asked concerning public architecture and the use of public space in the Roman world are: (1) How were the major forms of public architecture—sacred, municipal, and recreational—set within the urban fabric both of Roman towns in general and of the city of Rome itself? And (2) how were they made accessible, visible, yet separate from other forms of public building and from private and commercial architecture and space?

Public buildings in Roman architecture fall into the three broad categories mentioned above: religious or sacred, municipal or civic, and recreational or entertainment. It is traditional in architectural scholarship to separate sacred architecture from all other forms and regard it, as Vitruvius did, as the highest form of the art. While this division may serve well within the theory of architecture and its decoration, it is not one germane to studying architecture within and as a reflection of its society. It is also usual to lump civic and recreational architecture together under the general label of "public buildings," but again it is essential for this study to remember that a basilica, as a random example, served a societal function very different from that of a bath building, and the categories will be more useful for our purposes if kept separate from one another.[1] I am here intentionally separating certain types of small-scale commercial architecture from other forms of "public" building, although it is obvious that commercial buildings were intended for the use of a wide range of people and were therefore "public" by definition, although for the most part privately owned. But the ways in which these buildings related to individual Romans in their daily existence must have been quite different from the ways grander but more distant public buildings did, since these commercial buildings were made up of individual, often private or leased, spaces in which people dealt individually in buying and selling, rather than on a broader social scale.

Religious Architecture and Sacred Space

The various types of religious, administrative, and recreational architecture created by the Romans have been surveyed frequently by historians of Roman architecture.[2] Nonetheless, there are some observations that are germane to this investigation, such as the distinction between civic or administrative and recreational or entertainment building types and where they tended to fit within Roman cities. There is also an interesting contrast between which forms of public building served multiple purposes or functions within Roman society and which were limited to one use, more or less. Next we should turn to the streets, open spaces, piazzas, doorways, arches, and other such determinants of movement and boundary, the importance of which, as MacDonald has asserted, is overwhelming, central, and essential to the definition of all forms of space within any Roman, or indeed any human, architectural context, hence the importance of planning and design, of the layout of urban spaces.[3] Furthermore, it is how the individual architectural elements fit into the design or layout that dictated what space was available to people and organizations for their lives and their functions, and it is that element in public and private Roman architecture that we need to consider. One final point should be kept in mind and will be discussed again: the very distinction between "public" and "private" itself was a rather different one for the Romans, as attested by the very "public" nature of most of the major spaces in, for instance, the typical upper-class Roman's *domus*.[4] The absence of a clear distinction, a distinction that we have come to assume in our own times, between place of work and place of residence, is inherent in many Roman architectural forms. The terms "public" and "private" are essential to this discussion since there are no clearer terms to employ that do not smack of sociological jargon, but the Romans had a much more fluid and interactive idea of them than we do, and this should be kept always in mind as we proceed.

If we continued to follow Vitruvius's lead, we would regard religious architecture and sacred precincts in Roman cities as completely distinct from all other forms of space. But a look at the sources beyond Vitruvius will show that temples and shrines were by no means isolated areas reserved solely for religious expression and to serve as the houses of the gods, nor does Vitruvius himself ever say that they were. Instead, they could and did serve a sometimes bewildering variety of purposes that were both public and private. Indeed, the private side of Roman temples and shrines—the observance of personal devotions—while fairly apparent, is poorly documented in our sources. That this was a regular and essential element in religious observance in the Roman world is attested to by the vast number of *ex-voto* dedications that have been excavated at temples and shrines throughout the Roman world, eloquent evidence of the conviction of the faithful that a vow had been fulfilled or that the god had appeared in a dream.[5]

Some public functions of the temple are obvious: religious ceremonies and festivals. Others, while not perhaps immediately apparent, do not occasion much surprise. Roman temples served as landmarks within the street pattern of cities and towns and provided clearly visible (because raised on substantial podia) and accessible spots for arranging to meet. Indeed they must have been essential to the stranger attempting to find his or her way around a Roman town of any size, especially in a major city like Rome itself, since there were no street signs or other clearer directional guides easily available.[6] Temples also often gave their names to particular neighborhoods and so, in popular parlance, became tied with the economic activities of their area; for instance, booksellers were to be found in Martial's Rome near the templum Pacis, and in the later Empire wine was sold in the porticoes of the temple of Sol.[7] Vitruvius emphasizes the importance of temples being clearly visible within any sort of urban context:[8]

> If the nature of the site interferes, the aspect of the temple must be so altered that the greatest possible part within the walls of the city may be visible from the temples of the gods. Also, if a sacred temple is raised along the riverside, as by the Nile in Egypt, it ought to seem to regard the banks of the river. Likewise if the edifices of the gods are about the public thoroughfares, they are to be so arranged that the passersby can look aside, and make their reverence in full view [i.e., of the temple's façade].

Temples were also used for official civic business, such as meetings of the Senate in Rome, as locations for trials, and as seats of city offices and their archives (e.g., the censorial records stored in the temple of the Nymphs in Campo at Rome or the public treasury maintained by the quaestors in the precinct of Saturn). Temples that lacked a full frontal staircase—such as the temple of Castor in the Roman Forum and that of Venus Genetrix in the Forum of Julius Caesar—were particularly associated with political and legal functions since their "rostrate" façades were designed for and used as public speakers' platforms. We also know of temples containing collections of art on public display and having public libraries within their precincts[9] and making these available to the literate and appreciative stratum of Roman society.

Temples were also, quite blatantly, employed for purposes of propaganda, both political and personal. A particular favorite, it would seem, among politically motivated temple foundations was the goddess Concordia. She was given temples, or her temples were restored with great flourish and display, with some regularity to celebrate the ostensible resolution of political or other conflicts. The first in Rome was vowed in 367 B.C. by M. Furius Camillus as a commemoration of the passage of the Licinian laws, thus celebrating the legal "concord" between patricians and plebeians, though it may not have been built. Later it was constructed or reconstructed by L. Opimius after the murder of G. Gracchus to commemorate the supposed end of discord among the Roman people, and it was restored by Tiberius in 7 B.C. as part of his triumph after the German campaigns, when "concord" was reestablished on the northern borders. Another temple to Concord, on the Arx, was vowed by L. Manlius while a praetor in Gaul in 218 B.C. and completed two years later; this temple could have had some relationship to Hannibal's invasion of Italy, demonstrating the continuing "concord" of the Romans in the face of their most serious threat. A third temple to Concord was built by Augustus's wife Livia somewhere in Rome, and the much-debated building of Eumachia on the Forum at Pompeii may well have imitated this, since it was dedicated to *Concordia Augusta et Pietas*. Further, we are told that a temple to the "new concord" (*Concordia Nova*) had been decreed by the Senate in 44 B.C. in honor of Julius Caesar and his accomplishments in uniting the Roman people, but this was apparently never even begun. All these dedications to Concordia constitute more or less blatant political propaganda, intended to deliver a message as if it were sanctioned by the gods.[10] Equally propagandizing were such dedications as the temple to Hercules erected in the Forum Boarium in 142 B.C. by Scipio Aemilianus Africanus to celebrate his triumph and the destruction of Carthage with a dedication to the Romans' favorite "strong-man" deity.[11]

The temple dedications in the Imperial Fora were especially propagandizing. Caesar placed a temple to his own family's ancestry, which he traced back to Aeneas and his divine mother Venus, in his Forum (which Cicero bluntly calls "Caesar's *monumentum*"). The temple to Mars Ultor in Augustus's Forum recalled both the avenging of Caesar's murder—since the vow had been made the night before the Battle of Philippi in 42 B.C.—and the recovery of the

Parthian standards negotiated in 20 B.C., which were given their own shrine within or immediately next to the temple. At the same time the temple and the sculptural decoration of the Forum connected Mars and his son Romulus, through the mythology of the god's adoration of her, to Venus and her son Aeneas, thus neatly placing Augustus's own family (that of the Julii) parallel to the line of kings and heroes descended in Roman thinking from Romulus. The temple to Peace celebrated the peace inflicted by the Roman victory over Judaea in A.D. 70, suggesting that the emergence of Vespasian as ultimate successor to Nero had brought peace after the civil wars and power struggles of the year A.D. 69. Domitian placed his patron deity, Minerva, above the Forum Transitorium, and Hadrian attempted to symbolize the legitimacy of his questioned adoption by and succession to Trajan by his addition of the temple to Deified Trajan, dedicated in Hadrian's own name, to Trajan's Forum. It would be difficult to conceive of more baldly propagandistic religious foundations than these.[12]

In considering temples and shrines as parts of the overall architectural fabric of Rome and of Roman cities and towns throughout the Empire, we find that the two functions that were probably the most significant, that most affected the daily existence of the inhabitants of Roman urban spaces, were the two most directly related to their extraordinary visibility. These would have been (1) their ready identifiability as landmarks to which people could come for appointments and meetings, by which one could direct strangers through the maze of streets that made up city and town, and which could be used as nicknames for areas of city or town, and (2) their usefulness in disseminating political and personal propaganda through their dedications, their decoration, and their placement, to every level of the populace that could, to whatever degree, comprehend their messages. While many temples were undoubtedly founded from the purest of devotional reasons, it is symptomatic that Roman authors consistently emphasize ready visibility and equally ready politicization as characteristic of Roman temple architecture within the urban context. Even the temple to Jupiter Optimus Maximus was first dedicated in the midst of tremendous political upheaval surrounding the expulsion of the Etruscan kings from

Rome, and its major restorations under Sulla and Q. Lutatius Catulus after 83 B.C. and under Domitian after A.D. 80 were equally
propagandizing (as presented to us), and at the same time and in
each of the three events, the temple's dominating position high atop
the Capitoline Hill is emphasized since it was the most obvious and
essential of all the architectural landmarks of Rome.[13]

Municipal Architecture and Civic Space

Nonsacred public architecture in Roman cities and towns is treated
relatively briefly by Vitruvius in Book 5 of his treatise. He begins
where his audience would have expected, in the absolute political,
and sometimes physical, center of the Roman town, its Forum. He
shows the particular nature of the Roman forum in contrast to the
Greek agora and emphasizes the essential dimensions and the need
for surrounding colonnades:[14]

> The Greeks plan the forum on the square with most ample double
> colonnades and close-set columns. . . . But in the cities of Italy we must
> not proceed on the same plan, because the custom of giving gladiatorial
> shows in the forum has been handed down from our ancestors. For that
> reason more roomy intercolumniations are to be used around the spec-
> tacle (*circum spectacula*); in the colonnades . . . shops (*tabernae*); and
> balconies (*maeniana*), rightly placed for convenience and for public
> revenue, are to be placed on the upper floors. The dimensions of the
> forum ought to be adjusted to the audience (*ad copiam hominum*) lest
> the space be cramped for use, or else, owing to a scanty attendance, the
> forum should seem too large. Now let the breadth be so determined that
> when the length is divided into three parts, two are assigned to the
> breadth. For so the plan will be oblong, and the arrangement will be
> adapted to the purposes of the spectacles.

PORTICUS AND COLONNADES

It is significant that Vitruvius opens his discussion of public buildings not with a building, in the truest sense of the word, but with a
colonnaded open space. Surrounded open spaces were essential
and basic to Roman public architecture, indeed to Roman city
architecture of every kind. Colonnades, arcades, porticoes, and
columnar porches defined space and provided an architectural fa-

çade and boundary to these piazzas, and they were regularly used, as the colonnades of the fora of Pompeii and Ostia demonstrate.[15] The provision of a colonnaded appearance around the Forum Romanum seems to have involved a good deal of ingenuity over several centuries. The desire for it probably explains the colonnaded *tabernae veteres* that fronted the via Sacra and the creation of the arcades in front of the basilicas on both the northeast and southwest sides of the Forum, the Basilica Aemilia and its successors and the Basilica Sempronia and its successors, respectively. But in Imperial times, there was only one true colonnade in the Roman Forum: the colonnade in front of the Senate house that was variously called Atrium Minervae or Chalcidicum.[16] As noted, the basilicas had arcades—not colonnades—along their forum façades; in both buildings the piers between the archways of these arcades were decorated with engaged Tuscan columns and the passageways behind the façades functioned as walkways indistinguishable from those behind colonnades. Interspersed among these arcades and colonnades and shopfronts were the columnar porches of the temples that faced onto the central forum, which would have varied and enlivened the architectural frame, not simply continued it visually.[17]

In due course, the four-sided colonnade, which enclosed open space with vistas of columns—the true *porticus*—became an important factor in Roman architecture of every kind. It was adopted to surround temples (e.g., the Porticus Metelli, Porticus Philippi and their various successors, and the Porticus Liviae, all at Rome, and the colonnaded surround to the precinct of Apollo at Pompeii) and appropriate expansions behind the stage buildings of theaters, which is the context in which Vitruvius discusses them (such as the Porticus Pompeianae in Rome or that behind the Large Theater at Pompeii, the Piazzale delle Corporazioni at Ostia, which in addition surrounded a temple [fig. 5.1]). In general *porticus* were used as multipurpose enclosures in all manner of Roman contexts (e.g., the building of Eumachia on the Forum at Pompeii).

A *porticus* has the effect of turning every architectural context in which it was used into a visual simulacrum of a Roman forum while providing definition to open space as well as shelter for people,

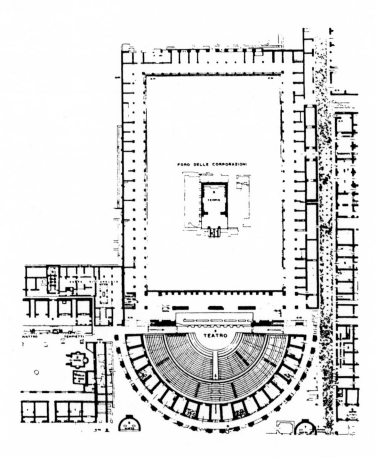

Figure 5.1 Ostia: the porticus called Piazzale delle Corporazioni and environs. [Gros & Torelli (1988) p. 226, fig. 110; reproduced by permission of Gius. Laterza & Figli, S.p.a.]

works of art, library collections, shrines, meeting places, and so on. The *porticus* was a basic form in Roman architecture, inspired by and in turn informing the Roman concept of the city center, the forum. What Vitruvius is describing is really the open forum at the center of the city surrounded by its *porticus*. When he actually introduces the *porticus* into his fifth book, he does so in the context of theater porticoes, but goes on to cite examples of all the different kinds, and to discuss their wide-ranging importance to architecture.[18]

BASILICAS

Vitruvius proceeds rapidly to deal with a few civic (administrative) buildings—the basilica, treasury (*aerarium*), prison (*carcer*), and senate house (*curia*)—which, together with such buildings as municipal offices and records archives, may be considered from the archaeological evidence. Of the administrative building types, the basilica and the senate house were the two essential buildings for the functioning of government, law, and administration in every Roman city and town, and they are always present in the urban fabric, almost invariably next to the town forum. A basilica, as Vitruvius describes the one he himself designed and constructed at the colony of Fano (5.6–10), was basically a rectangular hall, sometimes apsidal, and generally having one or occasionally two interior colonnades all the way around the interior space, which thus formed aisles between external and internal colonnades or between the internal rows of columns (when there was more than one). Basilicas were roofed, usually with a clerestory so that light was admitted into the central open rectangle of the building through the clerestory windows.

The placement and purpose of basilicas are made equally clear by Vitruvius:[19]

> The sites of basilicas ought to be fixed adjoining the fora in as warm a quarter as possible, so that in the winter, business men may meet there without being troubled by the weather. And their breadth should be fixed at not less than a third, nor more than half their length, unless the nature of the site is awkward and forces the proportions to be changed. When the site is no longer than necessary, the committee rooms are to be placed at the end of the basilica.

Vitruvius mentions commercial and social intercourse taking place in basilicas; to this sort of function was added, quite early on, the convening of law courts, for which purpose it became common to erect a tribunal for the presiding magistrate at one end of the basilica. There is no direct precedent from Greek architecture for the

Roman basilica, although some have been suggested without much conviction, nor is it at all certain where basilicas were first built in the Roman world.[20] The first basilica known in Rome was the Basilica Porcia, built by the elder Cato in 184 B.C. probably between the Clivus Argentarius and the Curia, near the location of the still-preserved Carcer, on ground subsequently occupied by one part of the Forum of Julius Caesar. It was apparently very small, since it could be built on ground previously occupied by just four shops and two (probably private) atrium houses, and it was destroyed in the funeral conflagration lit in the Curia itself by partisans of Clodius, in 52 B.C., and never rebuilt.[21]

After the Basilica Porcia, the three earliest basilicas known to us archaeologically seem to be the often rebuilt Basilica Aemilia (Paulli) in the Roman Forum, whose earliest architectural form is impossible to reconstruct, the Basilica Sempronia across the Roman Forum from it, which was entirely obliterated by the Basilica Julia, and the basilica on the Forum at Pompeii, which represents the earliest example known to us by its physical remains.

The Pompeiian basilica was probably built during the last quarter of the second century B.C., certainly before the first century B.C. Its façade was constructed in tufa and opened directly onto the Forum (see fig. 4.2). Its main hall consisted of the typical long central rectangular hall with an interior colonnade all the way around the rectangle (forming the "nave"); the columns were constructed of shaped brick. A tribunal rose at the far end of the long axis of the building from the Forum, though apparently not one intended for a magistrate's use, since the base for an equestrian statue erected directly in front of it would have interfered hopelessly with any sort of judicial proceeding.[22] If this basilica was roofed over its nave at all, a point that is disputed, it must not have been with the usual clerestory system, but rather with a single gable oriented along the long axis of the building, since there seem to have been continuous windows set high in the walls of the side aisles, a two-storey front to the tribunal, and no stairs anywhere in the building to provide access to a second storey.[23] Despite the oddity of the roofing system, Pompeii's basilica provides a good early example of the location and nature of such buildings. Graffiti found scratched on the columns and doorposts of the building indicate that it was used primarily for commercial purposes such as banking and stockbrokering and may have contained offices for public magistrates as well (by analogy with those of the Basilica Porcia at Rome), as well as areas reserved for the drawing up of contracts, leases, and other such commercial forms, both public and private.[24] Clearly Vitruvius's precept of direct accessibility from the Forum was observed at Pompeii.

Probably the most influential, and certainly the grandest, of Imperial basilicas, the Basilica Ulpia, was designed by Apollodorus of Damascus to close off the northwest end of Trajan's Forum (see fig. 4.11) and built in the early second century A.D. Its principal entrance was on the long flank that was turned broadside to the open space of the Forum and took the form of a triumphal arch with three bays. The basilica's interior had a lengthy central nave surrounded by two full rectangles of colonnades, thus creating that rarity a five-aisled basilica. The columns were of gray granite in the nave but of imported marbles—*giallo antico, cipollino, pavonazetto*—around the aisles, with capitals and plinths of white marble; in addition, the walls of the entire building were revetted in white Luna marble, while the roof was covered with gilded bronze tiles.[25] This basilica housed a major library—the Bibliotheca Ulpia—which may well have consisted, at least in part, of censorial records moved there from the defunct Atrium Libertatis. Certainly the evidence of an inscribed fragment of the Severan marble plan indicates that in some way it succeeded to the functions of that earlier complex. In addition, the Trajanic Forum and basilica were the single most important locale in Imperial Rome for legal proceedings, especially prestigious ones, a function they took over from the Forum of Augustus and continued to fulfill well into later antiquity.[26]

Smaller towns throughout Roman Italy and the Empire also constructed basilicas directly accessible to their fora. Of Italian towns whose plans we have considered, Ostia, Cosa, Saepinum, and Alba Fucens join Pompeii in revealing this arrangement. The dual functions that the basilicas served—municipal and commercial—seem to have rendered them essential, or at least they were thought essential, to the design of the center of any truly Roman town and so they are ubiquitous in the archaeological record. Much public life must have centered around them: banking and other financial arrangements, contracting and leasing, legal business (whether courts met in them or not), magisterial functions (in those that had tribunals), consulting of municipal and legal archives (at least in those, like the Basilica Ulpia, that contained or were connected closely to libraries and record offices), and public business in general of the broadest definition. The fact that the basilica continues so vigorously as a building type into very late antiquity—and in due course gave its basic architectural form to the early Christian churches of the converted Roman world—attests to its importance in Roman architecture and civic design.[27]

SENATE HOUSE AND PLACE OF ASSEMBLY

Other important forms of civic architecture included by Vitruvius in Book 5 are the senate house (*curia*), treasury (*aerarium*), and prison (*carcer*). Beyond these types specifically mentioned, we should also look briefly at the evidence for outdoor places of assembly (*comitia*), municipal offices (*secretaria*), and archives or record offices (*tabularia*). For most of these our prime examples must be drawn from the remains of the city of Rome itself; occasionally other examples are known, but it is at Rome that these types of civic building are best documented.

The Senate house that still stands in the Roman Forum is a rebuilding by Diocletian of a much earlier structure. On its exact site stood the *curia* built by Julius Caesar and Augustus and a successive *curia* constructed by Domitian. The original Roman Senate house—the Curia Hostilia—was attributed by tradition to King Tullus Hostilius and seems to have stood on a different axis just to the north of the later one. An unpopular rebuilding of it by Faustus Sulla, son of the dictator, after the Clodian conflagration of 52 B.C. cannot be located, but it, like earlier unattested reconstructions, probably stood on the spot of the original.[28]

Vitruvius lays down the basic design clearly:[29]

> the senate house is to be built with a view to the dignity of the municipality or city. If it be square its height must be one and a half times its

width; but if it be oblong, let the length and breadth be added together
and let half of the total amount be given to the height under the ceiling.

His description fits the example in the Roman Forum well enough
and is equally applicable to the rare examples securely identified
elsewhere in the Empire. The Roman Curia is a tall, rectangular
building of brick and is approached by a long, high flight of stairs.
A senate house served one purpose and one purpose only: a location for meetings of the Senate. It had to be a consecrated *templum,* and the one at Rome seems to have had a colonnade—the
previously mentioned Chalcidicum or Atrium Minervae—which
contained a quantity of fine bronze statuary. The high flight of
steps leading to the entranceway must have provided a dramatic
and fitting venue for the pronouncement of senatorial decrees and
decisions to the assembly and people, and its design in concert
with the place of assembly (*comitium*), both in Rome and elsewhere, notably at Cosa and at Paestum, was certainly not acciden-
tal.[30] Here again, the civic sense of design is implied. The *comitium* was designed as an excavated stepped circle with the Curia
dominating it (originally on a north-south axis),[31] which thus
doubled the effective height of the senate house since the people
looking toward it would have stood at the bottom or on the steps
of the *comitium,* well below.

In addition to the circular place of assembly itself, the zone of the
comitium contained a speaker's platform (*rostra*), and a variety of
specially sanctioned religious and other monuments had to be accommodated within its sphere, most notably the Volcanal, the *lapis
niger* (which may have been a commemorative "tomb" for Romulus), the Puteal libonis, a sacred fig tree (*ficus*), and the Maenian
column, a typical commemorative dedication of the sort erected
around the assembly place.[32] More functional were such important
comitial items as the tribunal of the praetors and the benches (*sub-
sellia*) of the plebeian tribunes which were located there.[33]

During the Republic all sorts of official political and diplomatic
events took place in the *comitium,* including voting by the Roman
people and the official reception of foreign embassies (at the
Graecostasis, a point where any non-Roman had to stop and wait

for the agreement and invitation of the Senate to pass). But the *comitium* in Rome was superseded during the first century B.C. For purposes of voting it was replaced by the Saepta Julia in the Campus Martius on the initiative of Julius Caesar during the 40s B.C., in the same period when the Curia itself was probably moved to its current location. But as a site for the enactment of the drama of government or diplomacy before the people, the complex of Curia and *comitium* in Republican Rome must have been highly effective, and certainly it was regularly imitated elsewhere.[34] Such political drama must, to a great extent, have disappeared under the Empire, and what there was of it would have been enacted, it would seem, largely in the Imperial Fora as they were built.

TREASURY AND PRISON

The treasury (*aerarium*) and prison (*carcer*), though mentioned by Vitruvius, are practically unknown to us from Rome itself. One example of each survives, more or less: the treasury during the Republic was located beneath the temple of Saturn in the Forum, while the prison for traitors and political prisoners also stood near the Forum, at the foot of the Capitoline Hill between the temple of Concord and the Senate house (see fig. 5.2). The treasury beneath the temple of Saturn no longer exists, probably because it was located beneath the front steps, which have since disappeared. About all we know of it is that it had a single entryway—either a door beneath the steps opening onto the Forum from the temple's side, or a staircase descending downward from the midst of the frontal stairs to the temple—and that public documents of various kinds were affixed to its exterior (and to the temple's). The treasury at Pompeii could be analogous to that at Rome and is partially preserved beneath the front stairs of the temple of Jupiter on the Forum. A staircase descending to it from the middle of the temple's stairs, which divided in two halfway up to accommodate entry to the treasury, led to several vaulted chambers.[35]

The prison, the only public one in Rome, still exists in part, beneath the church of S. Giuseppe dei Falegnami, and was vividly described by Sallust at the time of the incarceration in it of the Catilinarian conspirators in 63 B.C.:[36]

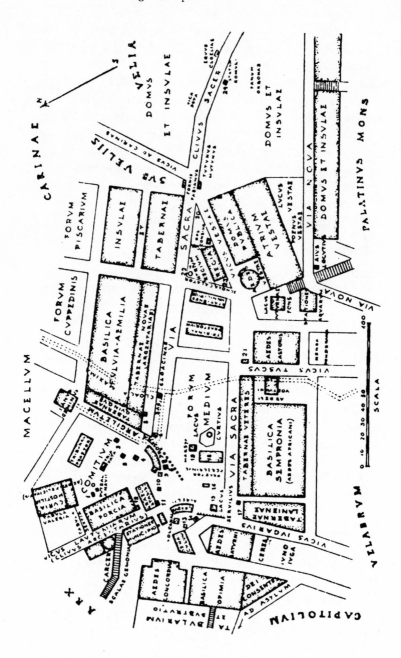

> After setting guards, he [i.e., the consul, Cicero] personally led Lentulus to the dungeon while the praetors performed the same office for the others. In the prison, when you have gone up a little way towards the left, there is a place called the "Tullianum," about twelve feet below the surface of the ground. It is enclosed on all sides by walls, and above it is a vaulted roof of stone. Neglect, darkness, and stench make it hideous and fearsome to behold. Into this place Lentulus was let down, and then the executioners carried out their orders and strangled him.

Lentulus had to be "let down" into the subterranean part of the prison through a hole in the vaulted roof of the chamber, the only means of ingress in antiquity (today it is accessible by a staircase). The chamber was excavated into the hillside and then lined with large blocks of peperino that defined a chamber about 7 meters square. The prison may have taken advantage of ancient tufa quarries in the side of the Capitoline, the *Lautumiae*, which gave their name to that area of the city (e.g., *in lautumiis*). At some later time in antiquity, but before the first century B.C., an upper chamber was built atop the Tullianum, and the whole came to be known as the Carcer. The upper chamber is trapezoidal. Here were imprisoned many famous political prisoners of the Romans, including Jugurtha and Vercingetorix and, according to later Christian tradition, Saints Peter and Paul during the reign of Nero. It was still in use during the fourth century A.D. and was preserved because of its association with early Christian saints and martyrs. Whether it served in any way as an architectural model for prisons elsewhere in the Roman world is extremely dubious, but the archaeological evidence for prisons anywhere in the Roman Empire is slight.[37]

MUNICIPAL OFFICES, ARCHIVES, AND PUBLIC LIBRARIES

Vitruvius fails to mention two other important forms of administrative architecture, municipal offices (*secretaria*) and archives or records houses (*tabularia*), nor are they extensively documented in the archaeological record, but literary and epigraphical testimonia help

---

Figure 5.2 Rome: The inner Forum during Republican times. [Lugli (1946) Pl. 3; reproduced by permission of G. Bardi Editore]

to provide some sort of general picture. Essentially, municipal offices—both in Rome and in smaller cities and towns—were accommodated wherever they could most conveniently be located, or wherever there was space. After 184 B.C., the tribunes of the plebs used the Basilica Porcia (see fig. 5.2) as the center of their activities, and at least parts of it seem to have come to be considered the "offices" of those tribunes until the basilica's destruction in 52 B.C. It would seem likely that similar municipal offices were located in shops (*tabernae*) and sometimes in larger rooms in or near the great basilicas facing onto the Forum (Aemilia/Paulli and Sempronia/Julia), and inscriptions from the basilica at Pompeii would appear to confirm this.[38] A late inscription attests that, at least in the fourth century A.D., one of the *tabernae* that flanked the Forum of Julius Caesar, immediately behind the Curia and accessible from it, served as the Secretarium Senatus, which by that time meant a courtroom used for trials involving senators. It is reasonable to assume that this was one of the purposes for which the Forum Julium was designed with lines of "shops" on either flank, and that these were for all the Imperial period the public offices of the Senate and its various committees.[39]

Under the Empire, the offices of municipal authorities seem to have moved and expanded or contracted depending upon their relative importance. The offices of the city prefect (*praefectura urbana*), originally not a major magistracy within the city of Rome, were located on the Oppius Hill by the fourth century A.D. and probably long before. But as the power and importance of that office grew during the second century A.D., so, it would seem, had its need for space. After the fire in A.D. 192, the urban prefect appears to have moved his central office and, probably, the prefecture's main archive, into what had been the Greek and Latin libraries that flanked the actual sanctuary to Peace in Vespasian's Temple of Peace (see fig. 4.11). Thus the office and archive of the *praefectus urbi* was perhaps the most powerful and influential administrative office in Rome by the early third century A.D., and it came to be located in a magnificent *porticus,* admittedly rebuilt after damage by fire, where it could not help but be associated with the "golden days" of the ostensibly happy and prosperous reign of Vespasian. The library rooms would clearly have been perfect to serve as record offices for the prefecture, since they would have been built for the storage of documents in the first place, and the surrounding porticoes of the Vespasianic precinct seem to have had at least some rooms opening off behind the colonnades which could have served as offices for the prefecture as its duties and, inevitably, its bureaucracy grew.[40]

It also seems likely that we know where the censors—the real official record-keepers of Rome during the Republic and for most of the first century A.D.—had their municipal offices, at least during the Republic, and their archives, although the exact location of the building they used is disputed. It was called the atrium Libertatis—the "atrium of Freedom"—and Livy provides the most detailed evidence when he describes the actions of the censors of 169 B.C., who had been accused of irregularities in their administration of the census:[41]

> The censors immediately mounted to the Hall of Liberty (*in atrium Libertatis escenderunt*), and, having there sealed the public accounts and closed the account room and sent away the public slaves, declared that they would transact no public business until the judgment of the people upon them had been passed.

The importance of the census records, clearly being stored in the atrium Libertatis at this time, was that they were often the crucial evidence in questions of citizenship and tax ratings. Their place of storage must have taken its name from the fact that one of the most essential acts of manumission was the listing of the newly freed person on the census rolls, a ceremony that would presumably have taken place during the Republic at the *atrium* whose name commemorated the ceremony. We know that the census, at least in the early Empire, was actually taken in the Villa Publica, and Livy's tale makes it clear that the atrium Libertatis was not only the archive for the censors but also their office.

This may have changed when the building was massively restored in 39 B.C. by Asinius Pollio, and it seems certain that it had been superseded by and perhaps its archives taken into the holdings of the Basilica Ulpia and its *bibliotheca* by the early second century A.D. The word *Libertatis*, clearly inscribed as a naming label, appears on a fragment of the Severan map of Rome that shows one of the apsed ends of the Basilica Ulpia, while all other reference to it disappears during the reign of Domitian, when the censorship itself was reduced to a meaningless formula. It would make sense that its archives might have been absorbed into those of Trajan's great hall of justice in his basilica. The actual census records from earlier times could have been stored, if they were preserved at all, in some of the *tabernae* of the so-called Markets of Trajan, which were located on the slope of the Quirinal directly behind the eastern apse of the Basilica Ulpia, storage in the Basilica or its immediate vicinity would seem unlikely because immediate accessibility to such old records would not have been important. A public slave could be sent to fetch what was wanted whenever the need arose.[42]

While the fate of the censorial archive after Domitian must remain theoretical—extrapolated largely from a single fragment of the marble plan—its location during the Republic in the atrium Libertatis along with the censors' offices is securely attested. The physical location of the *atrium* is not absolutely known, but it must have stood above the area of the *comitium* and Curia since Livy says the censors had to climb up to it, implying most probably either that they had to ascend the Clivus Argentarius (which ran up the slopes of the Arx from the Curia northward, eventually leading toward the Campus Martius) or that they actually had to climb the Clivus Capitolinus toward the summit of that hill. If one of the apsed ends of the Basilica Ulpia was anywhere near the original location of the *atrium,* then most probably it was near the highest point reached by the Clivus Argentarius, which would place it very near the rear wall of the Forum of Julius Caesar and its temple to Venus Genetrix in the 40s B.C. This location for the *atrium* would seem to be confirmed by the testimony of the elder Pliny, who says that a fountain of the Appiades was located in the atrium Libertatis after its rebuilding by Asinius Pollio, and by a remark of Ovid, who twice asserts that the Appiades were to be found as near neighbors to Venus Genetrix. These passages can be variously interpreted, however, and Purcell would now identify the atrium Libertatis with the building on the slope of the Capitoline usually thought to have been the Sullan Tabularium.[43] Wherever it was located, the atrium

Libertatis provides a good example of the kind of building where both municipal offices and the archives and records of a particular public office might have been. Clearly, the architectural form of such buildings could differ, since the office of the censors of the Republic was an "atrium" in some sense, whereas those of the Senate seem to have been located in *tabernae* (shops) and those of the city prefecture in the libraries and rooms of a great *porticus* (the templum Pacis).

The subject of the location of records houses and archives and their architecture is one that must be deduced from scattered and often random information. Two inscriptions attest that during the time of Sulla a large record office was built by Quintus Lutatius Catulus (completed during his consulate in 78 B.C.) in which were to be filed the official archives of Rome. Lucius Cornelius (see chap. 1 and fig. 1.1, above) served as *praefectus fabrum* during Catulus's consulate and so may well have been responsible for this building. Another inscription attests that the Tabularium, as it was called, was restored by the emperor Claudius in A.D. 46, but it is never mentioned anywhere in our literary record. The findspots of the two inscriptions led nineteenth-century topographers to identify the Tabularium with the massive lower stories of the building atop which Michelangelo built the Palazzo del Senatore in the mid sixteenth century, a complex that had been used during medieval times as a storehouse for salt and altered in various ways under Popes Boniface IX (ca. 1400), Martin V (ca. 1427), and Nicholas V (1453) before Michelangelo carried out his commission. If this was the Tabularium completed in 78 B.C., then the original must have been a tremendously complex building, and a testimony to the extraordinary skill in architectural design of its architect, whether L. Cornelius or another.

As originally designed, the complex rose up the Capitoline at the northwest end of the Forum Romanum, thus providing, as the Palazzo del Senatore still does, a massive architectural backdrop to the inner Forum (*imum Forum*) and to the temples of Saturn and Concord (and, eventually, of the Deified Vespasian), which sat in front of it (see fig. 5.2). Its façade on the Forum had arcades whose arches were framed in Doric columns and entablatures (which still

261

survive) and above this were perhaps two more stories now lost. Access to it was steep and difficult, and its interior design was very complicated. The Tabularium was notable for its thick walling, probably intended to protect records from damp and fire, and for its division into at least nine separate chambers, perhaps the archives themselves, placed at different levels. Whether this was the Tabularium or some other complex, it does seem to have been intended for storage, and its proximity to the Capitoline Hill with its sacred center and to the Forum, Rome's Republican political center, make it highly likely that it was some sort of major—indeed essential—archive where important historical documents were kept as safe as possible. It was also an architectural masterwork that contributed (as it still does to some extent, even in its much altered state) a great deal to the architectural grandeur of the Forum and that served as a constant visual connector—not to mention a symbolic one—between the political and sacred centers of the city. Symbolically, certainly, its identification as the Tabularium would seem highly suitable to its architecture and topography.[44]

An almost entirely Imperial phenomenon was the rise of public libraries (*bibliotheca,* pl. *bibliothecae*) in Rome and, soon thereafter, in Roman cities throughout the Empire, including notable examples preserved in whole or in part at Athens, Ephesus, and Timgad, and possibly at Pompeii. The architectural form of libraries varied a good deal in detail but most often consisted of two rooms either facing each other or next to one another and identifiable because of tall niches let into the walls where the cupboards to hold the papyrus scrolls would have been set. The first public library in Rome was dedicated in 39 B.C. by Asinius Pollio, at Augustus's behest, in his reconstruction of the atrium Libertatis. It was succeeded by several later libraries at various sites: the temple of Apollo on the Palatine Hill, dedicated in 28 B.C.; the Porticus of Octavia, 23 B.C.; the temple of the Deified Augustus, after A.D. 14; the Tiberian palace on the Palatine, ca. A.D. 14–37; the templum Pacis of Vespasian, dedicated in A.D. 75; Basilica Ulpia in Trajan's Forum, called the Bibliotheca Ulpia, ca. A.D. 104; and flanking Trajan's Column (the so-called Bibliotheca Divi Traiani because of the association with the temple of the Deified Trajan), ca. A.D. 118–120. All these were parts of larger complexes, sometimes temples, sometimes multipurpose public buildings, and only the low courses of the Bibliotheca Divi Traiani remain for us in the extant archaeological record, although the libraries of the temple of Apollo on the Palatine are relatively well documented.[45] The great Imperial bath complexes seem often to have accommodated libraries, at least to judge from their architecture; also a late antique biography of the emperor Probus asserts that the collection of the Bibliotheca Ulpia— presumably located in the Basilica Ulpia, a library which may itself have consisted largely of the holdings previously housed in the Bibliotheca Asinii Pollionis, formerly in the atrium Libertatis—had been transferred by the fourth century A.D. to the Baths of Diocletian.[46] Despite their apparent importance and popularity, we have relatively little information left on the public libraries of ancient Rome, and even less about their collections, patrons, architecture, and relative importance in either official or unofficial contexts. It is a sad *lacuna* in our knowledge.

ARCHES AND FOUNTAINS

The last important structures that belong to municipal forms of Roman architecture are the commemorative monuments with which ancient cities were frequently embellished. In the context of public architecture, these must include especially the triumphal and the commemorative arches and the grand public *nymphaea* (fountains) that were erected for purposes of ceremony, memory, and propaganda by official bodies or by individuals functioning in some official capacity. To be sure, individual and familial commemorations in architectural form, especially private tombs, were equally important, and will be considered in the next chapter but as public commemorative monuments these two categories are typical and quintessentially Roman.

The origin of the Roman tradition of constructing freestanding arches across streets and passageways may stem from the earlier technique of inserting vaulted gateways into fortifications, and certainly the earliest arches known to us, both in Rome itself and in the provinces, seem to have served as gateways into precincts of one kind or another. Livy tells us about the earliest arches known to have been put up in Rome, those constructed by Stertinius in 196 B.C. to commemorate his triumph and surmounted by gilded statues but otherwise undecorated. They stood as entrances to the precinct of Fortuna and Mater Matuta just below the Capitoline Hill on the vicus Iugarius.[47] Soon thereafter, in 190 B.C., Scipio Africanus built an arch directly commemorative of his triumphal celebration somewhere near the Clivus Capitolinus. Livy's brief description is informative:[48]

> Publius Cornelius Scipio Africanus, before he left the city [to set off to his proconsular provincial command], constructed an arch on the Capitoline, facing the street by which one climbs the Capitoline, with seven statues of bronze and two equestrian figures and two marble basins before the arch.

The Latin term Livy employs for these early freestanding vaulted spans is *fornix,* which seems to have been interchangeable with the more common *arcus,* from which English derives the word "arch." It is clear that these early arches in the city were erected near the traditional parade route taken by generals celebrating triumphs upon the successful conclusion of military expeditions abroad but not directly across it and hence avoided being overtly triumphal; they commemorated triumphs rather than flaunting them to the public. After 190 B.C., freestanding arches in Rome were often erected across the triumphal route, such as the arch of Calpurnius (fornix Calpurnii), also erected on the slope to the Capitoline, that of the Fabii (fornix Fabianus), built in 121 B.C., and the arches of Augustus (built in 19 B.C.) and Tiberius (A.D. 16); the last three stood at the corners of the inner area of the Roman Forum (the *imum Forum*). Other arches seem to have been erected for purely commemorative, not triumphal, purposes, such as the arch of Drusus (arcus Drusi) built on the Appian Way. In the Forum of Augustus, dedicated in 2 B.C., arches to both Drusus and Germanicus were built on either side of the temple to Mars Ultor and these appear to have signaled the start of a new idea in the creation of freestanding arches, that they could be erected just about anywhere in the city and to commemorate any suitable deed or person. After Augustus's reign it remained important to connect arches to the route of the triumph, but was no longer by any means essential, and the list of Imperial arches erected all over the city becomes gigantic.[49]

Important examples put up during the first century A.D. certainly included the arch of Claudius across the via Lata, which was voted by the Senate in A.D. 51/52 to commemorate his conquest of Britain nine years before;[50] Nero's arch in the middle of the Capitoline Hill, which was erected in A.D. 62 but dismantled soon after his suicide in A.D. 68 and must be reconstructed on the evidence of coins;[51] the still extant though heavily restored arch of Titus built at the high point of the via Sacra after Titus's death in A.D. 81 to commemorate his capture of Jerusalem eleven years before;[52] and several arches erected by Domitian and mostly pulled down after his death, most of which are little known except for the securely recorded arch at the foot of the road up the Palatine Hill and a rebuilding in triumphal freestanding form of the Porta Triumphalis (triumphal gateway), which marked the beginning of the traditional route of triumphal processions.[53] Trajan, Hadrian, and Marcus Aurelius certainly erected examples during the second century A.D. in every section of the city, and two arches from the early third century—from the reign of Septimius Severus—survive, as does a later one erected by the emperor Gallienus. The tradition was still current in the fourth and fifth centuries, as the extant arch of Constantine and various later examples recorded in our sources reveal.[54]

These magnificent arched structures must have constituted a major element in the decoration of the main streets and roads of the city. They appear to have become important landmarks in Imperial Rome, ones that could be easily located and referred to, rather in the manner of the most visible temples and sanctuaries. At the same time, they served to reinforce the great deeds of triumphant generals and, as time wore on, more specifically the grand military accomplishments of the emperors, and thus were every bit as much politically motivated as were the most blatant of the religious dedications in the Imperial Fora, for example. In the same way, commemorative arches such as that of Drusus on the via Appia served to recall important figures of the past to the minds of those moving about in, entering, or leaving the capital city of the Empire. But beyond these political and commemorative functions, the freestanding arches also marked important gateways and passages in the city and thus formed an integral part of the working of the street pattern. Hence it is hardly surprising that they were often recorded as notable items in lists of city buildings such as the fourth century A.D. regionary catalogues. Triumphal and commemorative arches were eminently visual landmarks in the rabbit warren of Rome's streets just as much as they were political or propagandizing symbols. The same seems to have been true of arches erected elsewhere, for example, in Orange, St. Rémy, Carpentras, and Aix-les-Bains in Narbonese Gaul, at Timgad in Algeria, at Medinaceli in Spain, as well as at Cosa, Aosta, Susa, Rimini, and Ancona in Italy.[55]

Also important in the context of the official appearance given to the streets and neighborhoods of Rome and of Roman towns and cities were fountains (*nymphaea*). These were often glorifications of *castella,* the collection or end points of aqueduct lines from which water brought into city or town was dispersed to the neighborhood, and it is hardly surprising that the idea occurred to decorate such important—and necessarily large—features by the play of the very water they distributed. Two examples still partially extant from ancient times in Rome can be cited, as can two later and still functional versions of the same idea. The so-called trophies of Marius are, most likely, the remains of the elegant fountain erected as the endpoint of the Aqua Julia in what is now the Piazza Vittorio Emanuele and called the Nymphaeum Alexandri because it was built by the emperor Alexander Severus. It is mentioned in the regionary catalogues for Region V and appears on a medallion struck during Alexander's reign. From the medallion and the battered remains, we can reconstruct a two-storey fountain with an upper storey consisting of a central niche containing statuary framed by columns and two flanking niches with trophies. The lower storey appears to have been embellished only with architectural decoration, and a triangular basin stood in front. Somewhere on or next to the fountain there may have been a statue of a recumbent water deity. This fountain must have dominated the angle at which the via Labicana intersected the via Tiburina Vetus and thus have constituted a major decorative, as well as life-giving, element of that area of Imperial Rome.[56]

That gigantic fountains could be made part of important monuments of official architecture, too, is certainly implied by the presence of the collection point of the Aqua Marcia between the Forum of Augustus and that of Trajan, in the so-called Terrace of Domitian. Here, Domitian seems to have enshrined the new terminus point of the Marcia in a huge *nymphaeum* when he cut the actual line of the aqueduct during his unfinished projects in the areas of the Forum of Julius Caesar and Forum of Trajan, and the fountain must have loomed impressively over that area. It may never have been completed; if it was it can only have functioned for a decade or two, since the orientation and subsequent construction in the Forum and Markets of Trajan certainly indicate that it was eliminated in Trajan's and Apollodorus's massive project.[57] Such large and elegant fountains continued to be built in the Renaissance and Baroque periods at the endpoints of the city's aqueduct lines: both the Trevi fountain and the Aqua Paola or "Fontanone" (on the Janiculum) are later variations on the Roman *nymphaeum*.

Architecture for Entertainment and Space for Recreation

When he has completed his treatment of "official" buildings, Vitruvius turns his attention to architecture intended for entertainment: theaters and baths—mostly private (*balneae*) rather than public (*thermae*) since the latter were a very new innovation in his time and the term "thermae" was perhaps not yet in use—and their associated exercise grounds (*palaestra*).[58] While often interesting, the treatment here is erratic and omits a very great deal. It will be better to consider the evidence from known Roman towns if we are to proceed further. Vitruvius aside, we can list the kinds of recreational buildings that were usual in public architecture in Roman towns. Those that occur with some regularity include the amphitheater, bath, circus, concert hall (*odeum*), library, stadium, and theater, of which Vitruvius omits altogether the amphitheater, circus, concert hall, library, and stadium.

BATHS

It is significant that Roman towns can and do occur, although clearly not large or important ones, without other buildings for recreation than baths (*thermae* and *balnea*). Baths were of tremendous hygienic importance to the Romans, it is true, but they were equally important socially since they were meeting and gathering places patronized by all classes and both genders of Romans. Baths were the most successful of all the building types devised by the Romans and came to possess the same plethora of uses and functions as the temple and the *porticus*.[59] This multiplicity of function was not shared by the other forms of recreational building, which tended rather to accommodate only one specific type of entertainment, often spectator rather than participatory. Cisterns and latrines Vitruvius obviously considered too lowly for inclusion in a manual of architecture—he would have regarded them simply as necessities of engineering—but they too are never missing and the hydraulic sophistication they imply was, of course, a very important element in Roman construction.

The importance of bathing itself to the Romans is attested frequently, for instance, by Cicero when he describes having a good bath as the first thing he will do when he arrives at his Tusculan villa at the end of a seven-day journey, by the younger Pliny as one of the proudest features of his Laurentian villa, and by Apuleius in his evocation of the ritual of bathing in second century A.D. north Africa.[60] Such baths were private *balnea*; there were very few bathing facilities in city or town houses, much less in apartment complexes or tenements. For the great majority of Romans, bathing was a public act—as to a great degree was evacuation of waste—and public bathing establishments, which came to be called *thermae* only during the reign of Augustus, enjoyed architectural design and quality of construction that was generally above the norm for public buildings and was periodically luxurious. Baths, both public and private, were also characterized by extraordinarily advanced engineering and decoration.

The Romans derived much of the hydraulic engineering of their bath buildings from Greek heating and water distribution systems that they presumably knew from examples in the Greek colonies of Sicily and southern Italy. These technical systems were greatly elaborated in the early baths built by Romans in the area of Campania and especially in the cities and towns around the Bay of Naples, where many thermo-mineral baths were built in Republican times to take advantage of the natural hot water and mineral springs of that actively volcanic region. These early thermo-mineral baths seem to have had an important effect on Roman taste quite early on, for Campania's baths became an immensely popular curative resort in the early years of the Republic. But the basic technical designs were most probably of Greek origin.[61]

In Campania, baths were often graced with gymnasia and exercise grounds (*palaestrae*), although, according to Vitruvius, exercise grounds were rare.[62] Perhaps he meant outside Campania; certainly by the second and first centuries B.C., the Roman towns of Campania were filled with baths of all sizes and levels of sophistication, both in engineering and in architecture, many of which featured the extra amenities of gymnasia and/or exercise grounds. At Pompeii, for example, three bath complexes dating from the second and first centuries B.C. contained *palaestrae* (the Republican Baths of Region VIII, ca. 100–80 B.C.; the Stabian Baths of the second century B.C.; and the Forum Baths of ca. 80 B.C.), while a fourth complex including exercise ground—the Central Baths—was under construction at the time of the eruption of Mt. Vesuvius in A.D. 79. These are instructive examples of the growing size and elaboration of city baths in Roman Italy, and the concept quickly spread, it would appear, to Rome herself, throughout Italy, and into the provinces as they came under Roman sway. Such baths show a clear separation of functions between exercise ground and bathing chambers proper: the *palaestra* was an open courtyard with attached rooms and *exedrae;* the *balnea* consisted of a row of vaulted rectangular rooms, often arranged in a line, with at some point a domed circular room, highly heated, which served as the sweat room (*laconicum*). The main entrance to such "Pompeiian" style baths was through the exercise ground; the actual bathing facilities were sometimes (e.g., the Stabian Baths) separated into men's and women's sides.[63]

This "Pompeiian" type of bath complex remained influential far into Imperial times and examples are known from all over the Roman world. One of the best excavated and best documented is the Forum Baths at Ostia, dating from the reign of Antoninus Pius (A.D. 138–161) and rebuilt at least twice. In that establishment an elaborate hall-like vestibule ran the width of the complex and must have served as a depository for clothing, a conversation area, an indoor exercise room, and so on (it also contained a large latrine). The actual bathing rooms, heated to a variety of different temperatures, stretched parallel to the vestibule and included a sun-room (*solarium*), sweat room (*laconicum* or *sudatorium*), a pair of warm rooms (*tepidarium,* pl. *tepidaria*) possibly of different temperatures, and a hot room (*caldarium*) with three cold plunge pools on three sides. All these bathing rooms looked out, through windows of various sizes and shapes, onto the exercise ground, which presumably was planted as a garden in addition to providing space for exercise and recreation. The bathing rooms all had a southerly exposure so that they could take advantage of the heat of the sun when possible; an extensive heating system ran beneath them (and can still be entered). The floors of the rooms were suspended on brick piers (*suspensurae*) forming a "hypocaust" system for heating, and in the hottest rooms clay piping ran up through the walls (still preserved in a few places) showing that they and possibly even the domed ceiling of the sweat room could have radiated steam heat upon the bathers.

Nonetheless, the sophistication of Ostia's Forum Baths cannot disguise the fact that they are in essence a sophisticated and elegant elaboration on the basic Pompeiian style of bath complex.[64] So elegant and sophisticated were baths of this kind by the late first and early second centuries A.D. that they were frequently celebrated by Imperial poets. The architectural decor and sheer ostentation of the Baths of Claudius Etruscus, a distinguished private establishment probably located on the Quirinal Hill in Rome and noted for the extraordinary use of imported marbles in its architectural decoration, are described in the most glowing of terms by Martial, during the reign of Domitian (A.D. 81–96):[65]

If you do not bathe in the warm baths of Etruscus, you will die unbathed, Oppianus. No other waters will so allure you. . . . Nowhere is
the sunlit sheen so cloudless; the very light is longer there, and from no
spot does day withdraw more lingeringly. There the quarries of Taygetus
are green, and in varied beauty vie the rocks which the Phrygian and
Libyan has more deeply hewn. The rich alabaster pants with dry heat,
and snakestone is warm with a subtle fire. If Lacedaemonian methods
please you, you can content yourself with dry heat, and then plunge in
the natural stream of the Virgo or of the Marcia [aqueducts], which
glistens so bright and clear that you would not suspect any water there,
but would fancy the Lygdian marble shines empty. You don't attend, but
have been listening to me all this time with a casual ear, as if you didn't
care. You will die unbathed, Oppianus!

Martial's description is strikingly echoed by the planning, appointment, and elaboration of the Forum Baths at Ostia.

As the great public bathing establishments, the *thermae*, began to
appear in Rome during the Imperial period, the bath complex
became, both architecturally and socially, one of the most important
features of Roman life. It was for these grand Imperial public baths
that the Latin word *thermae* was employed, keeping them quite
distinct from the smaller and less elaborate *balnea,* whether public
or private. Not that baths labeled *balnea* disappeared under the
Empire; on the contrary the term continues to appear throughout
the history of construction in the city and throughout the Empire.[66]
Thermae came to be the term applied specifically to the huge Imperial complexes only slowly, and confusion periodically enters the
terminology. I shall employ it, for the sake of clarity, only in reference to the Imperial bath complexes of the city of Rome.

The first of these was the Baths of Agrippa, begun possibly as
early as 25 B.C. in the Campus Martius, for which the Aqua Virgo
aqueduct was constructed to supply the copious amount of water
required. Cassius Dio tells us that Agrippa gave these *thermae* to the
Roman people in 12 B.C. in his will, and the elder Pliny tells us that
they contained magnificent statuary and paintings (the latter set
into the walls) and that the walls themselves were elaborately stuccoed or decorated with encaustic.[67] Other Imperial *thermae* are

attributed, by our sources, to Nero, Titus, Trajan, Commodus, Septimius Severus, Caracalla, Alexander Severus, Decius, Diocletian, Maxentius, and Constantine, and remains of a number of these still exist, the most extensive being those of Trajan on the Oppius, Caracalla east of the Circus Maximus and below the Caelian Hill, and Diocletian on the northeast end of the Quirinal and Viminal ridge.[68] A good choice to study as an example of the type is the Baths of Trajan (fig. 5.3).

Of the sheer size and magnificence of the architecture of Trajan's *thermae* there can be no doubt. The space for the complex was obtained only through the fluke of the destruction of Nero's Domus

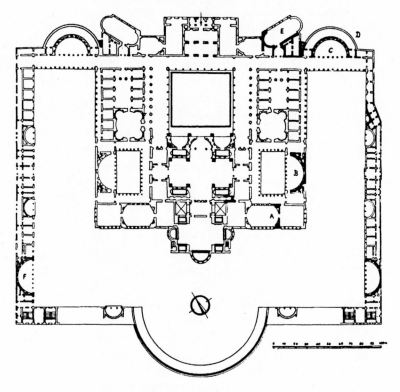

Figure 5.3 Rome: Ground plan of the Baths of Trajan. [Anderson (1985) ill. 2, p. 503; reproduced by permission of the author]

Aurea, which had previously covered the Oppius with one of its wings. The need for baths there probably stemmed from the site's proximity to the Flavian amphitheater and its gladiatorial schools, an area of public entertainment that may very well have quickly outstripped the facilities for bathing provided for that sector by the small *thermae* hastily erected by Titus and dedicated in A.D. 80.[69] Trajan's huge complex completely superseded, and may have either incorporated or submerged, Titus's. It was set upon a gigantic concrete platform over the filled-in remains of the Neronian palace. Upon the platform was designed an immense rectangular precinct some 250 m. by 210 m., surrounded by an exterior circuit wall into which a variety of other features were inserted, most notably an impressive semicircular *exedra* on the southwest side. Around the inside of the courtyard wall was built a variety of elaborately shaped rooms including half-domed apses, *exedrae* with niches, small rectangular rooms resembling shops (*tabernae*), and on the northeast side, two almost basilical small halls. It is likely indeed that the two semicircular *exedrae* on the northeast side that flanked the main entrance just beyond the basilical hallways were libraries (*bibliothecae*) judging from their architecture. Other hemicyclical *exedrae* off the sides were probably fountains (*nymphaea*) and the shoplike rooms perhaps equipment rooms, club and meeting rooms, and so on. The huge southwest *exedra* may simply have been added to emphasize the main axis of the building at its exterior or could conceivably have contained some form of seating and thus served as a theater or concert hall (such spaces are known in baths, e.g., the Baths of Caracalla).

The central bathing block of the complex is highly elaborate, designed as a mirror image of suites of rooms flanking the central northeast-southwest axis from the main entryway. The axial symmetry begins in the central block of rooms, which consists of a nearly square open area, an elaborately vaulted central space of cruciform shape, and a second cruciform-shaped room after it, this one with an apse at the end recalling in miniature the huge semicircular apse beyond it in the outer circuit wall. Beyond the central line of rooms, the repetition is nearly exact in the parallel lines of rooms on either side of the central axial chambers, as the plan reveals.

273

Presumably bathers could proceed down either side of the block and then back through the central halls, or vice versa, depending upon their bathing temperature preferences, needs, and wants. From the central block, bathers could exit to the courtyard area and there indulge in exercise, sport, or any of the other distractions provided in the many rooms and areas of the *palaestra*.[70]

What is striking about baths from the perspective of Roman society and its architecture is that they were clearly able to fulfill multiple purposes. When the list of amenities beyond simple bathing and exercise—meeting rooms, lecture halls, performance areas, libraries, collections of statuary and other works of art, fountains and other elegant architectural decor to admire—is taken into account, it becomes possible to view the Imperial *thermae* as a recreational equivalent of the Imperial Fora and *porticus* which, as we have seen, served such a variety of political, ceremonial, religious, and official purposes for the Romans. This may be the secret behind the tremendous success of the *thermae* as architectural forms in the Roman world: they were perfectly suited to be multipurpose recreation centers and thus fulfilled not one but a spectrum of societal needs, requirements and desires.[71] In a famous passage, written in the middle of the first century A.D. describing a private bath, Seneca criticizes the sheer volume of noise that occurred in baths; while his picture of a bathing establishment is pejorative, it does bring a vivid sense of the variety of activities that took place in them, whether small private or large public examples, and the extraordinary heterogeneity of social contact that characterized them:[72]

> I have lodgings right over a *balneum*. So picture to yourself the assortment of sounds. . . . When your strenuous gentleman, for example, is exercising himself by flourishing leaden weights; when he is working hard, or else pretends to be working hard, I can hear him grunt; and whenever he releases his imprisoned breath, I can hear him panting in wheezy and high-pitched tones. Or perhaps I notice some lazy fellow, content with a cheap rub-down, and hear the crack of the pummeling hand on his shoulder, varying in sound according as the hand is laid on flat or hollow. Then, perhaps, a professional comes along, shouting out the score. . . . Add to this the racket of the man who always likes to hear

his own voice in the bathroom, or the enthusiast who plunges into the swimming-tank with unconscionable noise and splashing. Besides all those whose voices, if nothing else, are good, imagine the hair-plucker with his penetrating, shrill voice,—for purposes of advertisement— continually giving it vent and never holding his tongue except when he is plucking the armpits and making his victim yell instead. Then the cake seller with his varied cries, the sausageman, the confectioner, and all the vendors of food hawking their wares, each with his own distinctive intonation.

Beyond the various activities here described for a relatively small bathing establishment, the immense *thermae* of Trajan accommodated committee meetings, lectures, possibly musical and staged performances, all manner of exercise and sports in the *palaestra* surrounding the bathing block proper, halls for the display of statuary and painting, and very possibly libraries too. In short, *thermae* such as Trajan's were capable of becoming, and did become, central public entertainment complexes which could and did accommodate all manner of requirements and *desiderata* attractive to the Romans. Since they were open to both genders, at the most convenient times of the day and for a very small entrance fee, their burgeoning popularity throughout the Roman Empire was understandable and, perhaps, inevitable.[73]

The Baths of Trajan may have been conceived some time before they were built. It is possible, but by no means certain, that it was Domitian who started the project of filling in the remains of the Oppius wing of the Domus Aurea and had conceived of such a grand *thermae* as an appropriate capstone to the public entertainment area he had devised around his father's amphitheater (which Domitian, in fact, completed). It can be argued that the architectural design of the building is rather like the conceptions we associate with Rabirius, but there can be no doubt that the actual building was completed under Trajan. Indeed Cassius Dio states unequivocally that Apollodorus of Damascus was the architect, and St. Jerome indicates that it was a fire in A.D. 104 that destroyed this section of Nero's palace, although it was probably abandoned well before that. The Baths were dedicated in A.D. 109, however, and a mere five years might seem a rather short period of time for the entire project to have been completed. But if the concrete platform was already in place prior to A.D. 104, the chronology would seem easier to accept.[74]

The main points of interest in the thermae Traiani must be the grandeur and careful planning revealed by the architecture itself and the multiplicity of functions provided for within the architectural concept of them. In this, Trajan's Baths provided the model upon which all the subsequent Imperial baths were based, and they remained the single most important *thermae* in Rome well into the latest years of antiquity. Their importance as an architectural model is manifested by all subsequent large bath complexes, notably those of Caracalla and of Diocletian in Rome, as well as examples spread throughout the Empire from the second century A.D. onward. We can presume that their importance to the daily functioning of society and culture among Romans throughout their Empire was also apparent. Indeed, Trajan's Baths must be regarded as one of the central monuments of Roman Imperial architecture and as a major source of information about the nature and habits of the Roman society contemporary with them. Certain social details are made clear by our sources; for instance, Saint Jerome maintains that in Trajan's time these baths were used by women as well as men—but even more indicative are the implications to be drawn from the sheer variety of forms of recreation and entertainment offered in them. Baths became the great gathering places, and thus a central social and cultural fact, of the lives of Romans during the Empire.[75]

CIRCUSES AND STADIA

Spectator sporting events were immensely popular among the Romans and the architectural elaboration of settings for them attests to this. The circus was a long narrow racetrack building curved at one end with seating on both long flanks and at the curved end, a design intended for chariot racing, whereas the stadium although similar in shape was shorter and thus could accommodate races other than high-speed chariot contests, for example, foot races, as well as other forms of track and field events. Both were adapted from Greek models and had very long traditions in central Italy.

According to Livy, it was the Etruscan kings who laid out and founded the first circus in Rome, the Circus Maximus, in the valley between the Palatine and Aventine hills, and it became the model for all subsequent circus buildings throughout the Roman world. The popularity of horse racing was always great among Roman sporting events and grew as the Imperial period stretched into late antiquity, but throughout Roman times the attraction of these events is manifest in frequent testimonia from ancient literature. The basic plan of the Roman circus is often illustrated, but is best preserved in the fourth century A.D. Circus of Maxentius built as part of his great private villa on the via Appia. The circus consisted really of four closely related elements: the race track proper, the starting gates (*carceres*) installed at the rectangular narrow end of the track, the central island called the *spina* along and around which the race had to be run and upon which the lap recorders (*metae*) were located, and the seating area (*cavea*) on the three sides of the racetrack that did not contain starting gates. In Rome itself, architecturally formalized circuses other than the Circus Maximus were not built—and presumably not needed—until Caligula began one in the area called the campus Vaticanus (Vatican field) on the west bank of the Tiber. This was actually constructed primarily under Nero, and its main east-west axis lay directly beneath the basilica of St. Peter; the obelisk that stood upon its *spina* is the same one that was moved to the middle of St. Peter's square by Pope Sixtus V in 1586 and still stands there. The Vatican circus was probably unnecessary; at any rate it appears to have fallen out of use by the early second century A.D., when the area became a graveyard. In short, the Circus Maximus, on the whole, served Rome's need for a public chariot racing course quite sufficiently. Maxentius's relatively well-preserved private circus shows how little the architectural form had been refined or changed over the centuries; except for construction techniques and mechanical refinements, it is essentially indistinguishable from the architecture of the Circus Maximus.

The description of the Circus Maximus as it was in 7 B.C., preserved to us by Dionysius of Halicarnassus, sums up its architecture and public conveniences quite well:[76]

The Circus is three stades and a half in length and a half plus four plethra in breadth. Round about it on the two longer sides and one of the shorter sides a canal has been dug, ten feet in depth and width, to receive water. Behind the canal are erected porticoes three stories high, of which the lowest story has stone seats, gradually rising, as in the theatres, one above the other, and the two upper stories wooden seats. The two longer porticoes are united into one and joined together by means of the shorter one, which is crescent-shaped, so that all three form a single portico like an amphitheater, eight stades in circuit and capable of holding 150,000 persons. The other of the shorter sides is left uncovered and contains vaulted starting-places for the horses, which are all opened by means of a single rope. On the outside of the Circus there is another portico of one story which has shops in it and habitations over them. In this portico there are entrances and ascents for the spectators at every shop, so that the countless thousands of people may enter and depart without inconvenience.

Ovid tells us that both genders and all social classes frequented the races and mentions specifically the free mingling of men and women spectators as if this were an unusual feature.[77] The term "circus" was occasionally, and somewhat confusingly, applied more broadly to open oval-shaped spaces that could be used for occasional races but were not primarily race courses. The best-known example of this is the Circus Flaminius, which opened out near the Tiber and gave its name to the region of Rome that contained the theater of Marcellus and the Porticus of Octavia. It will be discussed in more detail when we consider markets and public squares, to which category it more properly belongs.[78]

The Roman stadium took the elongated shape of the circus, probably because it was intended as the location for, among other events, foot races, but it was always shorter than the circus and lacked the central *spina*. There was usually some sort of stadium connected with the great Imperial *thermae,* and a feature in the shape of a stadium was included in the Imperial palace on the Palatine under Domitian though it may well never have been used formally and could have been considered as much decorative, perhaps a garden area, as functional. The only major independent stadium built in Rome was the one Domitian constructed in the

Campus Martius, where it provided the outline and foundations for the Piazza Navona (elements of the seating area and its substructures still remain). But sporting events other than chariot races never seem to have enjoyed the rabid popularity of the chariot races or of the gladiatorial *ludi*—for which the amphitheater was created—and hence *stadia* remained only occasional and derivative architectural forms, of secondary importance and influence.[79]

AMPHITHEATERS

Unquestionably the most popular, most important, and most characteristic type of building devoted to spectator sports in the Roman world was that uniquely Roman creation, the amphitheater. Its very name tells about its form: it is designed like two Roman theater buildings placed facing each other so that the semicircular seating areas of both (the *caveae*) seem to join at their ends, with a completely ovoid—rather than half ovoid—orchestral space in the middle of the encircling tiers of seats, and no stage or scene building whatsoever. The intent of the Latin word *amphitheatrum* aside, however, the origin of the amphitheater is mysterious, and in fact its popularity was limited almost exclusively to the western, Latin-speaking, half of the Roman Empire, since very few examples indeed appear in the Greek-speaking regions of the Roman world at any time. This in no way implies any lack of popularity for gladiatorial contests and the other blood sports that were staged in amphitheaters in the eastern Empire; however, such events were held in the (often venerable) theaters of the formerly Greek cities of the eastern Empire, which were regularly converted to accommodate them, and the amphitheater never spread there.

Gladiatorial contests are often thought to have arrived in Latium and Rome from Etruria and Campania around 264 B.C., when they are first mentioned in historical sources (but in funerary context).[80] There is, however, quite a body of evidence that such games (*ludi*) were held from quite early times in the Roman Forum, either in the open area without an architectural setting or, perhaps more likely, in a temporary "amphitheater" of wood, which could be put up for specific *ludi* and then removed so as not to clutter up the central Forum, but which may have influenced the architecture of amphitheaters a good deal earlier than is often conceded.[81] That the building type was highly popular in Campania at a fairly early date is without doubt, and it is clear that Campanian cities and towns had permanent stone amphitheaters long before these were built at Rome, which was indeed quite slow to adopt them. The oldest securely dated amphitheater surviving in Italy is that at Pompeii, which was built, or at least begun, in 80 B.C., although it is possible that others were built in stone even earlier, though this cannot be proved (e.g., the amphitheater at Cumae). Pompeii's amphitheater is a fine example of the early stone type. It is an ellipse with ovoid arena and *cavea*. It is nestled into the walls of the town at their southeast angle, and lacks both the elaborate substructural vaulting to support the seating and the complex system of passageways beneath the arena that can be seen in Imperial amphitheaters still preserved in Rome (the Flavian amphitheater), Puteoli and ancient Capua. Rather the slope for the seating is provided by packed earth upon which the seating was raised. In smaller Roman towns, this was the usual practice; indeed at Alba Fucens, the amphitheater was excavated out of a steep slope, with the debris gained from the excavation used to build up the slope needed to support the seating on the opposite side.[82] Entry for spectators to this type of amphitheater was by staircases from the exterior walls (as at Pompeii) or from the level of the arena (as at Alba), and the participants and officials for the *ludi* must have entered through the main axial gateways directly into the arena.

At Rome, the tradition of holding gladiatorial games in the Forum or other open public spaces—whether in true wooden amphitheaters or not—continued until the late first century B.C. The first amphitheater mentioned in the city is one built by C. Trebonius Curio in 53 B.C., which seems really to have consisted of two theaters that could be brought together, thus a literal *amphitheatrum*. The first permanent stone amphitheater, however, was that built by Statilius Taurus in 30/29 B.C. in the southern Campus Martius near the Capitoline Hill, which was destroyed by the fire of Nero in A.D. 64. Suetonius reports an amphitheater begun by Caligula near the Saepta Julia in the central Campus Martius that was abandoned after his death in A.D. 41, and Nero is credited with a wooden amphitheater put up in A.D. 57, which can hardly have been intended to be permanent, despite its rather elaborate decoration. It was left to the combined effects of the fire of A.D. 64 and the accession of the Flavians to the purple to provide the capital city with a truly magnificent amphitheater.[83]

So well known is the Flavian amphitheater—called the "Colosseum" only after A.D. 1000 because of its proximity to Nero's Colossus—as symbol of Imperial Rome's might and brutality as well as of Roman persecution of the Christians and other religious sects thought to be dangerous, that it hardly needs description. Its construction was begun in A.D. 70, when the lake (*stagnum*) in the center of the grounds of Nero's Domus Aurea was drained to accommodate it. The architecture of the building is remarkable primarily for the truly labyrinthine system of vaulted ramps and stairways that both sustained the *cavea* and controlled ingress to and egress from the seating, and for the extraordinary substructural maze of passageways and lifts that ran beneath the arena and presumably served the decorative and dramatic needs of the spectacles given. The amphitheater was dedicated with one hundred days of games in A.D. 80, but apparently only finally completed—perhaps by the addition of the top storey of the *cavea* and perhaps completion of the substructural passageways, although this is not certain—in the first years of Domitian's reign. It became and remained the central location for gladiatorial spectacle in Imperial Rome and must have witnessed a great deal of slaughter, although it is notable that not a single Christian martyrdom can, in fact, be securely assigned to the building at any time in its history (although Christians certainly were martyred in amphitheaters elsewhere, e.g., St. Januarius at Puteoli).[84]

Around it Domitian and Trajan devised a massive public entertainment complex that included gladiatorial training schools (the ludus magnus, ludus matutinus, ludus Gallicus, and ludus Dacicus, each of which trained gladiators for specialized forms of gladiatorial combat), important and often propagandizing decorative features (e.g., the meta Sudans fountain, the Colossus Neronis with its portrait head altered, possibly a Domitianic arch), and the Baths of Titus and of Trajan immediately adjacent. Thus in truth the Flavian amphitheater became the new center of Rome in human topography, the point of concentration—between the amphitheater itself and the Trajanic Baths—of much of what the city had to offer to its everyday citizens when they were not going about their jobs or at home. Given this fact, it is hardly surprising that it became so firmly fixed a symbol of the might of the "Eternal City" during the Empire.[85] Amphitheaters were a phenomenon of Empire to a very great degree—at least their rise to popularity was—and it is worth recalling that they are mentioned just once, and that in passing, by Vitruvius. At the beginning of the Empire, in the age of Augustus, the amphitheater barely existed in the consciousness of Roman architects, and seemed—at least to a relatively conservative author like Vitruvius—hardly worthy of comment. Had Vitruvius written seventy-five years later, this silence would not have been possible.

THEATERS AND CONCERT HALLS

Probably the biggest surprise in Vitruvius's fifth book is the extraordinary number of chapters devoted to the theater and its architecture. As noted above, this is to some extent deceptive since one long chapter (5.9) is in fact devoted to the *porticus,* which had a much larger role in Roman public architecture than serving just as *ambulacra* behind stage buildings, but Vitruvius clearly sees the theater as an especially important type of public architecture. For our purposes, we can use the Roman theater (*odeum*) as a specimen through which to consider how a single-purpose (for the most part)[86] and architecturally quite distinct building type, clearly derived from Hellenistic Greek models, was integrated into the urban fabric. In fact, the entire organization of Vitruvius's chapters on the theater is unexpected. He begins (5.3) with a treatment of the topographical requirements for siting a theater, in which he recommends following the same principles for selection of a healthy location that he had previously recommended for the city walls. The theater's seating area (*cavea*) is not to open to the south or it will be too sunny for the spectators. Setting the *cavea* into a hillside will make it easier to build the foundations. The shape of the whole building must be such that the voices of the actors will carry properly to all points. Passages between seats are to be spacious. After this bare list of essentials, Vitruvius turns back to the question of sound (5.3.6–8) and continues to wax theoretical about the nature of the voice and the passage of sound until the end of the chapter. This subject, rather than theater architecture per se, is at the basis of the somewhat unexpected chapter 5.4, which is a dissertation on sound and harmony derived, perhaps, from Aristotle, and the subject of harmony in turn leads to a chapter on how to control the sound in a theater by the use of bronze vases set under the seats of the *cavea* with their mouths open toward the stage building (*scaena;* its facade is designated *scaenae frons*) for resonance (5.5). Oddly enough, no archaeological evidence of the use of bronze vases in this way has ever been found, but ceramic pots and jars used in exactly the manner prescribed by Vitruvius are known from archaeological excavations.[87] He returns to actual theater architecture only in 5.6, which describes the parts of the building (*cavea, orchestra, scaena*) and the geometry required by the plan of a Roman theater. Having at long last considered the Roman theater building, Vitruvius then digresses again, this time to the Greek theater building and its architecture (5.7) presumably by way of comparison. But his real concern returns in 5.8, which is once again on the subject of sound, more specifically on acoustics and how to plan for them in either Roman or Greek theaters. Chapter 5.9 brings us to the consideration of porticoes and colonnades behind the stage buildings, the last chapter connected with the theater. It is interesting to note, at the start, that the archaeological evidence does not confirm Vitruvius. No Roman theaters are known that fulfill all his criteria, and there is much scholarly debate over the degree to which the theaters we do know demonstrate developments from or total rejections of the Vitruvian scheme, an interesting ongoing discussion that lies outside the parameters of this study.[88]

What is pertinent to the question of how Romans planned public space within their cities and towns is not the design of the theater itself, but where theaters were located in urban contexts. If we look at a selection of towns outside Rome, first, we find that their location in cities that had permanent stone theaters before the middle of the first century B.C., and hence before one was built in Rome, seems to have been determined by their derivation from and architectural dependence upon the Greek theater. To simplify, possibly oversimplify, a complicated element in Greek architectural planning, Greeks built their theater *caveae* into hillsides, and this topography determined where the theater would be located much more than any other single aspect. This is clearly true in the great theaters of Sicily—Taormina, Syracuse, and Segesta especially—and the principle was handed on to the towns of southern and south-central Italy, Samnite, Oscan, and Etruscan as well as Greek.[89] Stone theaters of the second century B.C. are known at Pompeii, Sarno, and Bovianum Vetus (modern Pietrabbondante) and all observe the rule. Pompeii's "theatrum maius" is the best known of these and makes the best example. The theater is on the south edge of the town plan, set into a modest slope (the best available within the city walls' circuit). It was necessary, in fact, for the *parodoi* (entrance gangways at either side of the stage building that led into the *orchestra*) to be excavated out so that they sloped downwards into the *orchestra*, thus showing that the Pompeians felt it essential to increase the slope in order to accommodate their large theater properly.

It is interesting to note that until after A.D. 62 the Forum at Pompeii was not provided with *maeniana* (galleries or balconies) above colonnades, which Vitruvius (5.1.2) prescribes as essential for fora in which gladiatorial games and spectacles are to be given. Perhaps they simply were not needed given the population of the town; however, it is also possible that Pompeii's big tufa theater was used instead as the location for such shows, at least until the construction of the amphitheater there ca. 80 B.C. Of course, with a permanent theater already available in the town, there was no particular reason for the citizens of Pompeii to have to stand through such spectacles in their forum anyway, and perhaps they did not do so.[90] In the Latin towns nearer Rome, the earliest permanent theaters display much less direct use of Greek principles of design and construction and are in general closer to the Roman theater as described by Vitruvius. A good example is the theater at Tusculum, probably built sometime in the first half of the first century B.C. This more tightly enclosed "Roman" design seems to have been taking hold throughout Italy at that time: Pompeii's "theatrum maius" was reconstructed after 80 B.C. more along those lines than it had been previously. But the new "Roman" type seems still to have been controlled topographically more by the need for a hillside into which its *cavea* could be set than any other consideration. The theater at Tusculum is set directly into the steep slope that rose behind the Forum area of the town.[91]

At Rome the situation for theater building was anomalous. Permanent theaters built of stone or concrete had long been banned within the city by decree of the Senate. Although theatrical performances were exceedingly popular in the city, the city elders apparently considered them a hellenizing and therefore effeminate indulgence. In 151 B.C., when the censors undertook to build a permanent theater in the city, the senator P. Cornelius Nasica moved, and the Senate voted, that it be dismantled and that Romans should always watch plays standing rather than sitting, so that they would not sink into Greek-like effeminacy.[92] This statute must not have been in place, or at least not being enforced, for very long: in his aedileship, sometime before 100 B.C., L. Licinius Crassus adorned a (presumably wooden) theater he had built with columns of Hymettian marble, and when Aemilius Scaurus was aedile in 58 B.C., he built a theater noted for its incredible luxury and excessive decor that seems to have stood untouched for several years. With the ban already broken in this way, Pompey apparently saw no reason not to proceed with his own theater, but he did it in a remarkable way that would form a precedent ever afterward. Pompey placed his theater on completely flat ground in the southern Campus Martius immediately to the west of the Area Sacra di Largo Argentina. The *cavea* was raised on soaring vaults of *opus caementicium* faced with *opus reticulatum*. A shrine to Venus Victrix, as well as other shrines, were raised atop this towering *cavea,* and it must have been matched to the east by the height of the stage building,[93] behind which the immense Porticus Pompeianae stretched all the way to Largo Argentina (see fig. 4.7).

The *porticus* must have been intended to bind this immense construction into the general street plan of that area of the city, but it is an open question to what extent this succeeded.[94] Yet the placement ar d form of this theater's successors—the theaters of Balbus and Marcellus, both close by—show that its method of construction and placement became the rule at least in Rome itself. It is possible and has been proposed that, in addition to a shift in topographical requirements for placement of theaters, Pompey's theater was important not only in that it brought the theater as a building type permanently into the architectural fabric of the city, but also because it connected the theater to and made it part of a temple precinct and sanctuary, and that this in turn suggested similar symbolic uses to the Augustan architects and planners who built the theaters of Balbus and Marcellus while at the same time allowing them to be incorporated as significant structures into the urbanization of the southern Campus Martius.[95] Writing in the early first century A.D., Strabo provides a description of the three theaters that certainly suggests such a conscious incorporation of them into the district's increasing monumentalization:[96]

> The later Romans, and particularly those of today and in my time, have . . . filled the city with many beautiful structures. In fact, Pompey, the Deified Caesar, Augustus, his sons and friends and wife and sister have outdone all others in the zeal for building and in the expense incurred. The Campus Martius contains most of these. . . . The works of art [architecture?] situated around the Campus Martius and the ground, which is covered with grass throughout the year, and the crowns of those hills that are above the river and extend as far as its bed, which present to the eye the appearance of a stage-painting—all this, I say, affords a spectacle that one can hardly draw away from. And near this campus is another campus [the campus or circus Flaminius] with colonnades round about it in very great numbers, and sacred precincts, and three theaters, and an amphitheater, and very costly temples in close succession to one another, giving the impression that they are trying, as it were, to declare the rest of the city a mere accessory.

Here Strabo binds the three theaters into the urban fabric of the city by emphasizing the connecting colonnades that would have organized them as elements in the greater urbanization of the area. To what extent their interconnection and interdependent symbolism would have been apparent to the middle- or lower-class Roman seems to me debatable, but to the more educated citizen of Augustan Rome their integration into the general Augustan propaganda inflicted on the city plan would have been clear. They are symbols for us not only of the Augustan program and its tremendous effect on both the public spaces of Rome and their architecture, but also of the limited, educated, aristocratic audience toward which this message and its architecture were directed. They represent the absolute antithesis of domestic or quotidian architecture, the opposite of private space.

Related architecturally to the Roman theater was the concert hall (*odeum*). These were not frequent and are generally known only in large or prosperous cities: we know of examples in Rome and Athens, for instance, and perhaps the best preserved example is the one misnamed the "Small Theater" at Pompeii. Very simply, an *odeum* was a Roman theater building reduced in size and covered with a roof. So apparent was this plan's derivation from the theater that, in fact, the concert hall at Pompeii, which stands immediately next to the large theater, was called—in its dedicatory inscription— not an *odeum* but a *theatrum tectum*, a roofed theater. Such buildings were employed for musical performances, recitations, and (perhaps) rhetorical contests and exhibitions. The one attested in Rome was built by Domitian in the Campus Martius and was probably adjacent to and contemporary with his Stadium, an initially surprising juxtaposition except that both buildings were elegant examples of architecture created for the tastes in entertainment of the relatively well-educated minority of Rome's population. Nothing of Domitian's *odeum* survives today. The comparatively small number of concert halls throughout the cities and towns of the Roman Empire—when compared to the numbers of baths or amphitheaters—attests to the same relatively limited appeal of the entertainment offered in them.[97]

Six

Architecture, Space, and Society in the Roman World: Quotidian Architecture and Individual Space

I n this chapter we must seek the answers, insofar as the evidence can provide them, to two broad sets of questions about Roman architecture and its connection to Roman society, both relating specifically to the domestic and commercial architecture that would have formed the physical context of daily life for the average Roman:

1. How do the different forms of private architecture reflect the society of the Romans, in towns and the countryside as well as the city? How did this private architecture relate to and coexist with public buildings?
2. What was the nature of the point at which public and private architecture intersected, that is, the quotidian commercial buildings so much a part of everyday life in any society— shops, inns, bars, warehouses, and markets—that are all too easily ignored in favor of the grander forms of architecture? How did this architecture connect with both public and private forms and with the overall shaping of space for living in the Roman world?

Domestic Architecture and Private Living Space

Since the discovery of the impressively preserved ruins of Pompeii and, to a much lesser extent, Herculaneum in Campania, the study of Roman domestic architecture has been dominated by the evidence from those sites because they constitute a rare cache of data for the domestic scene of Roman towns at a specific point in time: August 24–26, A.D. 79. For the various forms and sizes of the atrium house, these two sites are indeed unique resources. But it must be kept in mind that the housing appointments in the Vesuvian cities do not reflect domestic architecture either in the great cities of the Empire, especially Rome itself, or in the rural countryside. In fact, the domestic architecture of the Italian countryside is very poorly documented indeed since so few villas or farms have been excavated; this is an area of archaeology still in its infancy, although much can be expected.[1]

Domestic architecture in larger Roman cities is best documented at Ostia, and the Ostian evidence seems in many ways confirmed by both the scattered archaeological material and the literary evidence for Rome itself. What we need to look at for our purposes are the two major forms of domestic architecture known to have been in use in the Roman world—the atrium house and the multiunit apartment building—as evidences of family and social structure within the urban contexts in which they were built.

THE ATRIUM HOUSE

Vitruvius is once again our most important textual source for the atrium house (*domus*) though not for the apartment building (*insula*). He devotes his sixth book to domestic architecture, and his seventh to its decoration. The only design for human habitation he discusses is the *domus*; apartments and multifamily dwellings he does not seem to think worthy of consideration in this context. Houses known from Pompeii and Herculaneum illuminate his descriptions. Certain features were standard; others could and did vary.

To start from the beginning, one entered an atrium-style house from the street door through a long, narrow corridor called the *fauces.*[2] This passageway led the visitor directly into the atrium, which was the "public" or "business" center of the house. Vitruvius distinguishes five forms of atrium, which he calls Tuscan (*atrium tuscanicum*), Corinthian (*atrium corinthium*), tetrastyle (*atrium tetrastylon*), displuviate (*atrium displuviatum*), and testudinate or roofed (*atrium testudinatum*).[3] These terms describe the different manners of roofing the central rectangular or square hall of the Roman house. The atrium has an opening (*impluvium*) in its roof that is answered by a collecting and reflecting pool (*compluvium*) in the center of the floor. A Tuscan atrium is one whose impluviate roof is supported on beams carried across the atrium, that is, the roof is not supported by columns inside the room. This is the commonest form of atrium at Pompeii and Herculaneum, and there are many classic examples, such as Casa dei Vetti, Casa del Fauno, Casa di Sallustio at Pompeii, and Casa Sannitica at Herculaneum.[4] Corinthian atria had a number of columns surrounding the central *impluvium/compluvium* opening, a system often used in secondary atria of very large houses, such as the Casa del Menandro, where the atrium opening onto the baths was surrounded by nine columns, and the Casa della Fontana Grande at Pompeii. This system served for the central atrium in the Casa dei Dioscuri and the Casa di Epidio Rufo, also at Pompeii.[5] The four-columned, tetrastyle, atrium was second in popularity only to the Tuscan; it featured columns set only at the corners of the *impluvium*, and is used in, among many examples, the Casa delle Nozze d'Argento, the Casa dei Ceii, and the Casa della Grata Metallica, all at Pompeii.[6] The displuviate atrium, in which the roof sloped outward from the *impluvium* toward the street, rather than vice versa, and water was shed into pipes and collected in external tanks, is very little known, and Vitruvius himself did not recommend it. An example seems to have stood in the *praedium* of Julia Felix at Pompeii, where the central columns in an impluviate room are higher than the surrounding walls, but it is a highly unusual design.[7] Finally the roofed or testudinate atrium was just that: a central room roofed over without an opening, relying on windows for light. This was probably the oldest atrium form and was commonly in use for smaller, simpler, humbler houses; examples include two houses (I.xiv.6/7 and VI.xi.12) at Pompeii, as well as the Casa di Giulio Polybio and, although it is difficult to believe because of the sheer size of its atrium, the Casa del Chirurgio, again all at Pompeii.[8]

After providing the various proportions appropriate for atria, Vitruvius lists the other main divisions of space within the house. The atrium should have *alae* ("wings") to right and left, spaces which in aristocratic houses came to be the place for the various secretaries, assistants, and clerks who helped the master (*dominus*). At the far end of the atrium from the *fauces* was placed the *tablinum,* a sort of grand alcove in which the master received visitors and clients. Distributed around the atrium, often on two stories, were bedrooms (*cubicula,* that is, small rooms for personal uses of various kinds, including sleeping), storerooms, and dining rooms (*triclinia*).

Frequently houses were surrounded on three sides by their neighbors in the block; if a house did occupy an entire block its rear façade almost always opened onto a secondary street or an alley, and most of it was blank or had only tiny windows heavily barred. Clustered along the main façade so that they would open onto an important and busy street were often shops (*tabernae*), either owned by the *dominus* and run by him or sublet to shopkeepers. The number of shops depended, obviously, on the width of the house façade. When the frontage was not used for shops, the space gained on one side of the *fauces* might contain the winter dining room, entirely enclosed and heated by a brazier; it would then be answered by a doorkeeper's cell (*cella ostiarius*) on the opposite side of the entrance. At the other end of the atrium, the large rectangles that flanked the *tablinum* were often very fancy *triclinia,* one at least very open and airy for summer use and possibly both designed with different wall decorations to distinguish them; or the other might be enclosed to serve as the winter *triclinium* if there were not one at the front of the house. That was the sum of the true atrium house.

Changes and adaptations introduced into the scheme were generally ways of expanding the house, by the incorporation of a second atrium, for instance, or eventually by the inclusion of a garden (*hortus*) or in the more elegant houses a peristyle courtyard surrounding a formal garden (*peristylium*). The Casa di Sallustio is a good example of such expansion, eventually taking over a house next door and so having the original large atrium/garden house with all its appointments plus the smaller atrium and peristyle of the adjacent property. Much the same expansion can be seen in the Casa del Fauno, which eventually featured two large peristyle, or quasi-peristyle, gardens as well as two atria side by side.[9] Of course, the best-known of all examples of the atrium/peristyle sequence in the upper-class house at Pompeii is the Casa dei Vetti, with its handsome peristyle of columns and formal rectangular garden, now beautifully replanted and regularly beseiged by visitors. Vitruvius describes elaborate halls, which he calls *exedrae,* if they were apsed and had a bench, or *oeci,* if they were large formal rooms added to extremely elaborate houses. *Oeci* could be of four types: Corinthian (surrounded by columns), tetrastyle (columns only at the four corners), Egyptian (designed like a basilica, two-storey and rectangular with a central nave and side aisles with promenades above the single-storey side aisles, which were lined with windows), or Cyzicene (long broad halls featuring gigantic windows overlooking formal gardens).[10] These large halls might often supplant the *tablinum* or sometimes a *triclinium,* providing an even grander setting in which the *dominus* might present himself to clients and callers. As time went on a number of the larger atrium houses gained private baths as part of their elegant appointments, too, as seen in the Casa del Menandro (see fig. 6.1 below).

These atrium houses, particularly as Vitruvius describes them, were clearly the town homes of the well-to-do, not the dwellings of the humble, and yet there is much evidence at both Pompeii and Herculaneum that some of the largest and finest houses periodically fell on hard times and had to be partitioned into apartments, or at the very least have separate exterior staircases added so that their upper floors could be rented out, as was certainly the case at the Casa Sannitica and the Casa del Bicentenario in Herculaneum by A.D. 79. Graffiti attest that sections in the *praedium* of Julia Felix, the *insula* of Arriana Pollana (where the new owner had taken over and converted the once-elegant Casa di Pansa), and a variety of other houses in Pompeii were for rent.[11] Sections of large houses or even entire smaller houses were sometimes converted into shops or

workshops, for example, the laundry or fullery (*fullonica*) of Stephanus at Pompeii. In general there seems to be a fairly regular
shifting, at least in Pompeii where the evidence is sufficiently extensive to judge, between what was deemed the finest domestic real
estate and what was considered less good. It is important to keep in
mind, too, that most of the examples I have given represent housing
that, at least at some period, was of the very highest social and
economic level in the Vesuvian cities. There were many more mid-
dle- to lower-class houses, some with *atria* but many little more
than single shops with a room atop for sleeping, and these were the
living space of the humble majority of those who inhabited Pompeii
and Herculaneum. It is essential that we pay some attention to them
and their domestic spaces.

URBAN CONTEXT: THE INSULA OF THE MENANDER AT POMPEII

Since the atrium and atrium/peristyle houses of Pompeii and Herculaneum are well known and readily visited, I would like to turn
now to questions of the urban setting, or context, in which they
existed and the social structure implied (or blatantly expressed) by
the spaces and shapes inhabited by the families who lived in these
houses.[12] To look at the urbanization of such housing, I intend to
take a "walk" around a single block (*insula*) of Pompeii, the so-
called insula of the Menander, where the famed Casa del Menandro
is located (fig. 6.1). The word *insula* represents a problem for us
today and seems to have been ambiguous to the Romans themselves. It was the term regularly employed to indicate a city block—
as in the "insula of the Menander"—but could also be used to
indicate any building that contained more than one dwelling,
whether that building occupied a full city block or not. This dual
usage must be kept in mind.

The numbering system adopted by archaeologists at Pompeii
assigns a number to every entryway in every city block, starting
from the north corner of the block, proceeding counter-clockwise
around the *insula* numbering the entrances sequentially, including
entrances to no longer extant upper stories that had separate staircases leading directly in from the street and back and side doors of

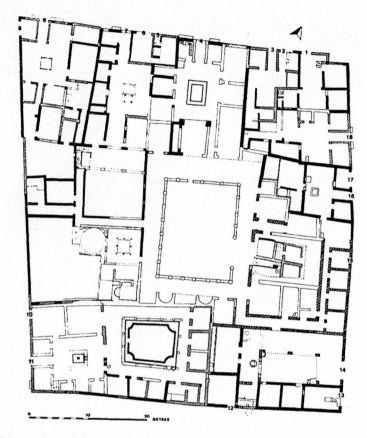

Figure 6.1 Pompeii: Insula of the Menander, Regio I.x. [Ling (1983) fig. 6; reproduced by permission of the author]

houses whose main entrances may be all the way across the block. By simply proceeding around this particular block, numbered I.x, we can get a good sense of the shapes that domestic space took in a single area of Pompeii.[13]

At the northern corner of the block, number 1 was a *taberna,* probably a downstairs workshop with a dwelling above reached by a staircase; the back section contained a kitchen, a relative rarity in small dwellings of the *taberna* type, and three rooms. Number 2/3 was of similar design, but contained (at no. 2) a bar (the *caupona* of

294

Coponia) with front and back rooms that were internally accessible from the dwelling next door (no. 3), presumably inhabited by the proprietor, whose home had three rooms at ground level and stairs to a second floor, of which nothing is preserved. Number 4 was the grand front door to the Casa del Menandro, which led into the main atrium then back through an open *tablinum* to a huge peristyle garden; stairs at the front of the atrium led to a second storey that contained at least 12 *cubicula,* 4 storerooms, and possibly more. In addition, off the west side of the peristyle, there were a private bath complex reached through a small Corinthian atrium, a kitchen, and a garden with 2 service rooms and cellars beyond, and off the east side a second, very extensive, service area with separate atrium and yard and 9 rooms on the ground floor and beyond it (toward the east corner of the block) another bath. This huge mansion, ca. 1700 square meters, filled much of the central area of the block. Next to its front door number 5 was the exterior entrance to a staircase up to a small set of rooms, supposedly a brothel (a usage advanced on little evidence), above the room entered through number 6, which was a *taberna* apparently set up as a fullery. Number 7 was the door into the *fauces* of the Casa del Fabbro, a typical smallish atrium house that consisted of atrium and peristyle with a *tablinum* flanked by 2 *triclinia,* 6 rooms, and a staircase to the second floor at the back; a line of 3 *cubicula* ran to the right of the atrium.[14] Number 8, at the corner of the west side of the block, led into yet another smallish atrium house, the Casa di Minucio, which consisted of an atrium, a secondary back courtyard, and an upper storey.

Around the corner, number 9 was the front of a tiny one-room *taberna,* and then there were no more doors until the far end of the south flanking street—just the blank south wall of the Casa di Minucio and then of the bath and kitchen complex of the Casa del Menandro, until numbers 10 and 11 opened at the far south corner, both leading into the atrium/peristyle Casa degli Amanti, which was a middle-class but prosperous dwelling with the peristyle colonnaded on two levels and anywhere from 10 to 13 *cubicula* (depending upon how certain rooms are interpreted) around both atrium and peristyle. The entrance at number 10 may imply a shop, but if so it communicated with the atrium.[15] After the next corner and facing onto the eastern street only one door, number 12, opened in its entire length. This entered a single room with stairs up to one above, possibly an office of some kind. On the fourth and final side of the block, number 13 opened immediately: a bar (*popina*), another single room with stairs to living quarters above. Numbers 14–17 were side entrances into, first, the stableyard (14), then the service area (through a shop, 16) and its atrium (15) and through another shop (17), of the Casa del Menandro. The last doorway on this street and in the block (18) led into the Casa di Aufidio Primo, a simple atrium plan with a backyard and a second storey, and 5 *cubicula* downstairs.

Looking back over the *insula,* we get a fair picture of the sort of context in which the inhabitants of Pompeii must have lived. The huge mansion house, the Casa del Menandro, consumed most of the real territory of the block, and it was one of the most elegant in all Pompeii, probably owned by the family of the Poppea who married Nero. Nevertheless, its front entrance was flanked by a bar and a fullery. Farther to the left of the mansion's front door were two small "live-over" shops, one a tavern and to its right the mansion was flanked by the two fairly modest houses, the Casa del Fabbro (about 310 square meters floor space) and Casa di Minucio (ca. 270 square meters). These were small and rather old-fashioned dwellings, atria with a very modest attempt at a peristyle (Casa del Fabbro) and merely a small garden (Minucio). Indeed the presence of a tool chest gave its name to the Casa del Fabbro (cabinetmaker), and the Casa di Minucio has been identified as a weaving establishment set into an old house because loom weights were found there.[16] Neither house, however, has revealed any clear signs of a working manufactory, so these explanations may well be fanciful. Somewhat grander, but still extremely humble in comparison to the Casa del Menandro, the Casa degli Amanti featured a true and rather elegant peristyle and some 470 square meters of ground-floor space with some attractive wall painting in the atria and cubicula. There was one more house in the block, the very small (ca. 120 square meters) but fine Casa di Aufidio Primo, a true atrium plan with tiny backyard but quite elegantly decorated. There were at least three more shops or working locations in the block (nos. 9,

12, and 13), and possibly two more if the numbers 14 and 17 were rented out by the owners of the Casa del Menandro.

The first and strongest impression all this gives is the notable lack of discrimination between the wealth and leisure obviously attested by the Casa del Menandro, the middle- to upper-middle-class comfort of the Casa degli Amanti, the humbler but refined Casa di Aufidio Primo, the Casa del Fabbro, and, if it was still a dwelling, the Casa di Minucio, and the clearly poor working-class accommodations atop their businesses at numbers 1, 2/3, and perhaps 5/6. It seems quite clear that there was little perception that this was unusual.

Throughout Pompeii the blocks "read" in much the same way, with what (to us) would be the most noxious forms of business and commerce, for example, fulleries with their vats of urine, and noisy *cauponae* and *popinae* with potentially rowdy crowds of drinkers hanging about, set immediately next to the houses of the wealthy and the respectable middle class, and smaller homes slipped in here and there between mansions and brothels and workshops. It is a very socially heterogeneous mixture. When other examples are adduced, for instance, the famous Casa del Labirinto, a magnificent rich house in which a bakery with no less than four mills was located—enough to run a business from and far in excess of what could have been consumed in the house[17]—it becomes striking how economic activity and high social standing could be mixed in a Roman town.

The great excavator of Pompeii and Herculaneum, Amedeo Maiuri, analyzed this social and economic mix as a sign of deterioration after the damage of the earthquake in A.D. 62, and classified all houses and house-connected spaces at Pompeii in a hierarchy with the patrician house at the top and shops/workshops at the very bottom.[18] The model simply does not work. It makes assumptions about what was taking place in the minds of the residents of these heterogeneous town blocks for which there is no evidence whatsoever, and it must be dispensed with. Rather, the multiple levels of society being mixed together in such places seem to have been regarded as the normal way of things in Roman cities to at least some degree. It is fairly likely that the entire residential space available on the Palatine Hill during the second and first centuries B.C. was not taken up exclusively by the mansions of the well-to-do, but that smaller homes and shops were interspersed, much as was true (and remains so but to a lesser degree) in Rome and, especially, Naples into modern times.[19]

Two points about the design of the atrium house should be made and this can be done by looking, first, into the pages of Vitruvius and then at the examples in the Pompeiian city block just described. First of all, it is fairly clear that the Roman atrium house reflects the society that built it. Roman society was deeply influenced by distinctions of social rank (except, apparently, in town, or city block, planning), and the houses reflect this. Vitruvius says that that is intentional, that houses were purposefully designed in just this way:[20]

> We must go on to consider how, in private buildings, the rooms belonging to the family, and how those which are shared with visitors, should be planned. For into the private rooms no one can come uninvited, such as the bedrooms (*cubicula*), dining rooms (*triclinia*), baths (*balineae*) and other apartments which have similar purposes. The common rooms are those into which, uninvited, people can come by right, such as vestibules (*vestibula*), courtyards (*cava aedium*), peristyles (*peristylia*), and other apartments of similar uses. Therefore, magnificent vestibules and alcoves (*tabulina*) and halls (*atria*) are not necessary to persons of common fortune, because they pay their respects by visiting among others, and are not visited by others. But those who depend on country produce must have stalls for cattle and shops (*tabernae*) in the forecourt . . . and other apartments which are for the storage of produce rather than for elegant effect. Again, the houses of bankers and farmers of the revenue should be more spacious and imposing and safe from burglars. Advocates and professors of rhetoric should be housed with distinction, and in sufficient space to accommodate their audiences. For persons of high rank who hold office and magistracies, and whose duty it is to serve the state, we must provide princely vestibules, lofty halls and very spacious peristyles, plantations and broad avenues finished in a majestic manner; further, libraries and basilicas arranged in a similar fashion with the magnificence of public structures, because, in such palaces, public deliberations and private trials and judgements are often transacted.

Something of what Vitruvius is getting at may be seen if we look at the location of the service quarters in the houses of our *insula*. In the Casa del Menandro (fig. 6.2), these quarters—shaded in the plan— are scrupulously placed off the peristyle and accessible only through extremely narrow corridors that would clearly tell anyone who looked that this was the entrance to slaves' territory.

At the Casa degli Amanti the servile rooms are entirely in a line with narrow doorways on one side of the peristyle; the servants would be seen as little as possible and not interfere with the grander workings of the house. Significantly, it is far more difficult to identi-

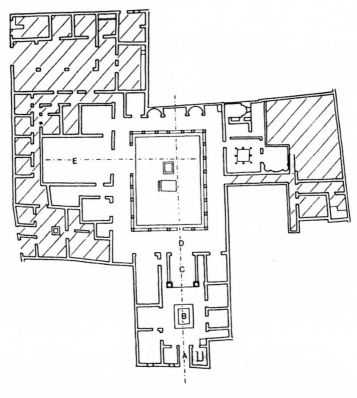

Figure 6.2 Pompeii: Casa del Menandro. [Wallace-Hadrill (1994) p. 40, fig. 3.1; reproduced by permission of the author and of Princeton University Press]

fy servants' quarters in the smaller houses; a servant may well have functioned from the small room opening to the right off the *fauces* in the Casa del Fabbro, but there is no way to be certain.[21] Small rooms to the left of the *triclinium* might appear to be servile in the Casa di Minucio, but again there is no confirmation. But if the demonstrable examples are compared to the situation in other Pompeiian houses (e.g., the Casa dei Vetti, the Casa del Principe di Napoli) the same phenomenon is clear: the servants, although essential, were marginalized by the way the space of the *domus* was designed, and their humble status emphasized. The reverse side of this, and the one that must have been much more important in the minds of the architects who designed these houses, was that the grand rooms and passageways, public and private, should emphasize and reinforce the dignity and importance of the *dominus,* above all, and secondarily the pride of the entire family. This can certainly be seen in the Casa del Menandro, where the person entering could see the magnificent peristyle garden all the way from the narrow *fauces,* and where in fact there was a *tablinum* on that axis in which the master might receive the visitor. However, upon reaching that point, the visitor would find instead that he or she had to continue and move around the peristyle, because in fact the *dominus* possessed a most impressive basilical *oecus,* located on a cross axis from the longitudinal one and to the left, which had to be approached in order to see and speak to the head of the household. This is planning of a subtlety worthy of, and indeed reminiscent of, that employed in the sight lines of the Domus Flavia in the Palatine palace.[22]

Perhaps even more tellingly "Roman" in the layout of these houses is the fact that there is really hardly any of what we would call "private" space in the Roman atrium house and that the very language of public architecture is used by Vitruvius to describe the house. The basilicalike halls and so on are clearly derived from public architecture, just as the peristyles cannot help but recall the ubiquitous *porticus* and colonnades that gave architectural definition to so much of Roman public space. The atrium, with its collection of family death masks, was the public center of the house and in every way intended as such; it was meant to impress with the

sheer family pride and weight of tradition that the *dominus* represented in the flesh.[23] Beyond it the *tablinum* initially, and the *oecus*
later in the most magnificent houses, served as the place in which
the head of the household presented himself. But beyond these
clearly public rooms, such areas as the peristyle, the dining room or
rooms, the library if there was one, even the several *cubicula,* which
served all manner of purposes, were rooms into which guests might
be invited, places into which friends, colleagues, or valued clients
might be brought allowing yet a further penetration into the functioning of the family.

Thus the house and its parts had to be made very clear to the
visitor. Although there was no exclusively private space as we might
now define it, there was a progression in the degrees to which
outsiders might be allowed into the house and thence into contact
with the family. The so-called private sections of the house were
never visually closed off from the visitor; the sight line of most
atrium/peristyle houses led the eye straight into the peristyle garden and so to the heart of the *domus* (e.g., Casa dei Vetti, Casa del
Menandro). The real message Vitruvius is giving is precisely that
there was not a division in the Roman household between public
and private but between business (*negotium*) and entertaining (*hospitium*). It is an axiom of Roman architecture that Romans did not
seek privacy for what we consider such extremely private, even
embarrassing, human functions as bathing and defecating, but undertook them by choice in group settings. There is no reason to
expect their houses to defy or contradict the basic tenets of their
world view.[24]

THE PALACE

A conspicuous lack of what modern Westerners would label "privacy" or "private space" within the plan of living areas was carried to
its furthest extension in the immense palaces constructed, first in
Rome and subsequently at various spots around the Roman world,
by the Emperors. The aggrandizement of the habitation of Rome's
first citizen (*princeps*) began with Augustus. Despite his propagandizing contention that he lived like a normal citizen, his elegant
house on the Palatine Hill was regularly expanded and reworked

until it certainly deserved the designation "mansion." Essentially the *atrium* plan but expanded to tremendous height and elegance, as well as bound closely to the elaborate precinct of Apollo he had built adjacent to it, this *domus*, at least by virtue of historical hindsight, points the way to the extravagances of domestic architecture to come.[25] It was succeeded by the mansion laid out atop an extensive concrete platform on the north edge of the Palatine looming above the Forum.

Very little is known of this complex, although the name "Domus Tiberiana" occurs often in our sources and the location is confirmed by them. It was apparently altered under Tiberius's successor, Caligula, and extensively under Nero, when it must in some way have been joined to his first palace whose remains are known on the eastern and southern sides of the Palatine, the Domus Transitoria.[26] The first Neronian palace was in fact merely a grandiose extension of the Domus Tiberiana, as its name implies, that connected the Palatine complex with Imperial property on the Esquiline Hill to the east, including the elaborate Gardens of Maecenas, as both Tacitus and Suetonius attest. Beyond the two small fragments of it which were built into the substructures of Domitian's Palatine palace we know nothing whatsoever about its architecture, although in extent it must have been gigantic. Since it was destroyed in the fire of A.D. 64, the fact is often forgotten that it must have been nearly as extensive, if not perhaps as overwhelming, as the much-maligned Domus Aurea that succeeded it.[27]

We have spoken of Nero's second palace before (chap. 1) and its undeniably overwhelming effect on central Rome and on subsequent Imperial architecture. Sadly, however, we must admit once again that we really know very little of its architecture, although theories based on the descriptive passages in our sources abound, as do attempts to reconstruct the battered remains on the Oppius beneath the platform of the Baths of Trajan into something commensurate with what we are told existed in that palace. Certainly the Domus Aurea must have incorporated the Domus Tiberiana and much of the rest of the Palatine within its parameters, but how this was done remains utterly enigmatic. Perhaps they were relatively unimportant in Severus's and Celer's design. It is also possible that the Domus Aurea was never completed; certainly its destruction began relatively soon after Nero's suicide in A.D. 68, when Vespasian drained its central lake to accommodate the Flavian amphitheater.[28]

Only the immense Domus Augustana, built by the architect Rabirius for the emperor Domitian on the Palatine Hill, is known to us through archaeological remains that permit any sort of assessment of its architecture. The immense complex of rooms was laid out around two parallel axes, oriented roughly north-south. In the more westerly of these main axes were public meeting rooms, a fountain garden which perhaps served as a waiting area for those coming to see the emperor, and an elaborate banquet room. Along the more easterly axis were larger rooms and gardens culminating in the multistorey *triclinium* that, in turn, opened into the Imperial viewing box over the Circus Maximus. Again oriented roughly north-south (parallel to the two main axes) was a simulacrum of a stadium but one which appears to have been intended for a formal garden more than for a race course, and later extensions, especially those under Septimius Severus, eventually covered the entire southern and eastern slopes of the Palatine with outbuildings of the palace. For sheer, almost incredible, grandeur this palace is unmatched anywhere in the Roman world, and despite their badly damaged state, the remains on the Palatine can still give some sense of the multistoried magnificence of it.

But there is nothing whatsoever that is identifiably "domestic" about this palace. It is an architectural showpiece clearly intended for public ceremonies and spectacle. Whatever appointments there were for private habitation must have been hidden away or carefully kept from view and from ready access by the multitudes who would have seen and, presumably, visited this public palace. Although its architectural origin is to be found in domestic buildings, there is little if anything left in its own architecture that is at all homelike.[29] Perhaps the best sense of the palace, how it affected those who saw it, and how public a "house" it was intended to be (the site for "thousand table" banquets, not family dinners!), is provided by a description given by the poet Statius, written in A.D. 93 or 94, when it was new:[30]

303

An edifice august, huge, magnificent not with a hundred columns, but with as many as would support heaven and the gods, were Atlas eased of his burden. The neighbouring palace of the Thunderer [temple of Jupiter on the Capitoline] views it with awe, and the powers rejoice that thou [i.e., Domitian] hast a like abode. Nor wouldst thou hasten to ascend to the great sky; so huge expands the pile, and the reach of the far-flung hall, more unhampered than a plain, embracing beneath its shelter a vast expanse of air, and only lesser than its lord; he fills the house. . . . Libyan mountain and gleaming Ilian stone are rivals there, and much Syenite and Chian and the marble that vies with the grey-green sea; and Luna also, chosen but to bear the pillars' weight. Far upward travels the view; scarce does the tired vision reach the summit, and you would deem it the golden ceiling of the sky. Here when Caesar has bidden the Roman chieftains and the ranks of knighthood recline together at a thousand tables, Ceres herself with robe upgirt and Bacchus might strive to serve them.

The Palatine palace continued as the central official residence of the emperor as long as the emperor remained in Rome, periodically refurbished and expanded, and was always a stunning public show-place. But it is doubtful that its "homey" qualities were ever intended to be considered. Later grand palaces—such as that of Diocletian at Split (Spalato)—took their cue from the Palatine complex and became grand official "residences" constructed for administrative and display purposes more than for domestic appointments or convenience. How the emperors lived in them, or whether they did so any more than was absolutely necessary, we do not know.

APARTMENTS AND APARTMENT BUILDINGS

The forms of domestic architecture other than the palaces, the atrium mansions, and single houses of the aristocrats and well-to-do (or at least the financially comfortable) that must concern us are the abodes available to the rest of the urban population, which were far more modest and for the most part rented rather than owned. Probably the most ubiquitous was also the most humble: the simple dwelling on the floor above a *taberna*, corresponding in size to the establishment beneath it and usually inhabited by the propietors of the business. The examples at numbers 1 and 2/3 in Insula I.x at Pompeii, which we surveyed, are very typical. Other than these shop/dwellings, there were essentially three types of home available in a Roman city, and they seem to have varied a good deal in size and cost.

First are the so-called strip houses, which are usually assumed to have been common although neither Pompeii nor Ostia has produced many examples. These are quite simple, consisting of a property in which a *taberna* opens onto the street with a stairway on one side to a second storey, often consisting of one or two apartments of varied shapes, and a corridor (much like the *fauces* of the atrium) opens on the other, which led to a narrow passageway running straight to the rear of the property. Off this passage opened several rooms one after the other and a small courtyard or light well. An example known from Herculaneum is the so-called Casa del Papiro Dipinto at IV.8–9;[31] such apartments resemble nothing so much as the plan of the old-fashioned railroad pullman car. Strip apartments of this kind were sometimes inserted into originally sizeable atrium houses that had been divided up into apartments and/or commercial establishments.

Such reworked houses represent the second type of dwelling available in Roman cities and towns to potential renters of various economic levels. A particularly vivid example is the Casa a Graticcio in Herculaneum, which had been converted through extensive employment of the wattle-and-daub *opus craticium* denounced by Vitruvius into a complex with a *taberna* opening onto the street next to the original *fauces*, a porter's cubbyhole and bedroom opposite it, behind which were an apartment or workshops or a combination of the two lit by three small courtyards. A staircase inserted into the first of these, partially masked by a partition in *opus craticium*, led to the upper floor which had been divided into two separate residential spaces, one apartment at the rear reached by this staircase, and another facing onto the street reached by its own exterior staircase. The building appears to have been in a state of transition in A.D. 79 and suggests the variety of social classes that could be accommodated in tight spaces in a Roman town. The front upstairs apartment was noticeably more spacious and grand than that behind it, even

305

including a hearth for cooking and a large room that opened onto a balcony. Its second-floor partner was smaller and much more modest, while such accommodation as there was on the ground floor (which is difficult to determine given the condition of the house after the eruption of Vesuvius; all but the porter's sleeping cell may have been in the process of being converted to workshop space at the time of the disaster) was poor and mean.[32] The situation in the Casa a Graticcio is typical of the fate of many substantial atrium houses in the Vesuvian cities and is attested also in Ostia and Rome.

The third type of normal domicile was the *insula* or multiple-unit apartment building. As we have seen, *insula* was the term regularly employed to indicate a city block, but at the same time it appears in both legal texts and inscriptions as the term appropriate to buildings that hold more than one dwelling. The two fourth century A.D. Regionary Catalogues that survive—strange lists of buildings, both famous and humble, in the fourteen regions of Rome during the reign of Constantine—make the problem a great deal more complicated by offering the information that there were either 44,200 or 46,602 *insulae* in the city of Rome at that era, for which gigantic number there is no possible way to find the space within the Aurelianic walls if *insula* here means either a city block or a freestanding apartment building without party walls, as it was defined by Festus and the legal writers.[33] The word may well have had an extremely broad application in the legal texts and in the Regionaries, indicating little more than any sort of multiple-unit dwelling, not specifically the high-rise apartment building known to us primarily from the excavations at Ostia.[34] If so, this helps in dealing with the problems presented by the testimony of the Regionary Catalogues but leaves us without a proper Latin word for the typical apartment building. Hence, I shall continue to use *insula* occasionally to refer to the multistorey Ostian type of apartment building for conevnience' sake—despite having used it previously to refer to a city block—while recognizing that this is a far too limited definition of the term.

Vitruvius knew of the multistorey apartment buildings in Rome by his time and seems distrustful, as well as mildly contemptuous, of them. Nonetheless, it is from his testimony that we must start:[35]

Public statutes do not allow a thickness of more than a foot and a half to be used for party walls. But other walls also are put up of the same thickness lest the space be too much narrowed. Now brick walls of a foot and a half—not being two or three bricks thick—cannot sustain more than one storey. Yet with this greatness of the city and the unlimited crowding of citizens, it is necessary to provide very numerous dwellings. Therefore since a level site could not receive such a multitude to dwell in the city, circumstances themselves have compelled the resort to raising the height of buildings. And so by means of stone pillars, walls of burnt [baked or kiln-dried] brick, party walls of rubble [and concrete], towers [high buildings] have been raised, and these being joined together by frequent board floors produce upper stories [of apartments] with fine views over the city to the utmost advantage. Therefore walls are raised to a great height through various stories, and the Roman people has excellent dwellings without hindrance.

Despite the doubts he expresses, Vitruvius has here encapsulated the nature of the Roman apartment building and the examples excavated at Ostia confirm his basic description but refine the details. Of course, the evidence from Ostia is almost all a good deal later than Vitruvius's description and so shows refinements and developments not known to him.

At Ostia the basic plan of a high-rise building of three to five stories with apartments of ever decreasing size and cost as one proceeded higher was subject to a variety of modifications of plan. The two most useful ways of categorizing the *insulae* would divide them into classes based, first, on the number and disposition of the shops (single row, two rows back to back, three or four rows grouped around a courtyard, shops mingled with apartments on the ground floor) or, second, on the uses to which the ground floors of the various *insulae* were put (shops, apartments, manufactories, workrooms).[36] To take one Ostian example as typical, though by no means universal, may help to make the use of space in the *insula* clearer. The Casa di Diana (I.iii.3) faces onto the via di Diana east of the Capitolium temple and northeast of the Forum (fig. 6.3).

On the ground floor, *tabernae* opened onto the street on two sides of the building (4, 6, 8–11, 15, 16), two of them with a second room each behind the first (5, 7). The residential area of the apart-

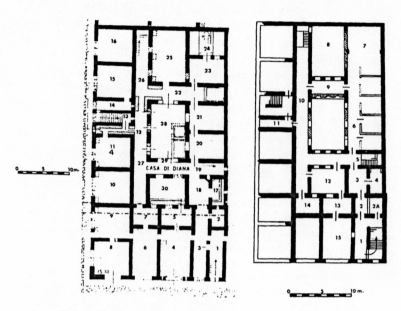

Figure 6.3 Ostia: Casa di Diana. [Packer (1971) plans 2 & 3; reproduced by permission of the author]

ment building was entered through *fauces,* the primary one (3) on via di Diana and secondary ones (12/13, subsequently blocked up, and 19) among the side street shops. Entering from via di Diana the resident or visitor encountered a porter's lodge (2) and a communal latrine (17) before passing through a vestibule (18) and reaching the central courtyard (28) which contained a cistern to provide water for the inhabitants. The courtyard was surrounded by a corridor (22, 26, 27) and several sets of rooms, some independent (20, 21), others interconnected, including one group of three (23, 24, 25) from which the largest room (25) was later blocked off (perhaps when 24 was altered to contain a Mithraeum at some point), and another (30) that was at some time connected with the back rooms of the two via di Diana shops (5, 7) but had been converted, it would appear, into a stable.

Access to the second floor was by staircases, two opening onto the surrounding streets (1 and 13, though 13 was later blocked off to permit internal access only) and at least one more (26) for internal access only. On the second floor, which has been less thoroughly studied and is less well preserved, the sets of rooms seem clearly to have been grouped into apartment units of various sizes: we can be fairly certain that two apartments facing onto the via di Diana and lighted by windows onto it were of three (12, 13, 15) and two (14 and successor) rooms in size, respectively. The forms of the apartments along the west side of the second floor are not known but the rooms from which they were made up were rectangles of more or less similar size with street windows. What appears to be a spacious single room (8) at the north end with three openings onto the light coming in from the courtyard was in fact not space to be used on the second floor at all; it was rather the upper part of a large two-storey room. The apartment on the northeast side of the second floor (6, 7) seems to have been a long narrow set of rooms opening off a straight corridor that led to the main room of the apartment at the back, in fact one type of *cenaculum medianum*.[37] We do not know anything of the building above the second storey.

Several points about the uses of space may be raised from looking at this apartment building. First, it must be noted that the apartments vary a good deal both in size and in availability of light. Presumably the most expensive ones were on the ground floor, closest to both the water cistern (which itself was a later addition to the apartment house, not part of its original amenities) and the latrine. But clearly the combination of rooms into particular apartments could be changed as circumstances and finances dictated (e.g., the periodic reworkings that seem to have taken place in 23, 24, and 25, or between 30 and 5 and 7). On the second floor, the most pleasant of the apartments must have been rooms 12, 13, and 15, although the exact relationship of 12 to 13 and 15 as well as to 14 and successor is completely unclear and could have changed over time (indeed, 13, 15, and the successor to 14 might have shared access to 12). The 6 and 7 complex of four small and one large room could well have been rented out to more than one family, or to a large extended kin group. The Casa di Diana *insula* is remarkable for having, at least in one of its later incarnations, provided a water cistern and a latrine (it is reported that evidence for an earlier pre-cistern fountain has been found, but this has not been pub-lished) and so was presumably quite a desirable building in which to live both as originally designed and even more so after its ameni-ties were substantially improved. The multiplicity of staircases also attests to the convenience of the tenants being of concern to de-signer and landlord.

The *cenaculum medianum,* possibly exemplified in the Casa di Diana by apartment 6, 7 on the second floor, was the most common form of apartment in Ostia's *insulae.* The term *cenaculum* occurs in the legal writers of the *Digest* as the term for the spaces into which an *insula* was divided, and is regularly so defined. Hence, it is presumably the general term for an "apartment." The designation *medianum* refers to a particular and very common design of *cenaculum.* Other clearer examples include, especially, the carefully geometrically planned and balanced apartments of the Garden Apartments complex, those in the Casa dei Dipinti, the Casa di via della Fontana, and the Casette tipo complex. Such apartments con-sisted of a series of small rooms (*cubicula*) that opened off a long hallway or room (*medianum*) that ran along one outer wall and was pierced by a series of windows that provided the main light source for the entire apartment; at one or both ends there was a larger room (*exedra*). Of those examples, the most remarkable are the Garden Apartments, one of the most highly developed apartment com-plexes known to us from the Roman world.

The Garden Apartments (located at III.ix.13–20) are perhaps the clearest example known to us of "drawing board" or "blueprint" construction in Roman architecture. Built after the Hadrianic reor-ganization of Ostia, this complex makes highly inventive use of the irregular space available to its builder by reducing what was in essence a very rough trapezoid of land into a development of two long rectangular blocks divided up into four rigidly symmetrical apartments on the ground floor, which looked out onto gardens that filled out the uncouth remaining space of the open area. Thus they had no commercial frontage whatsoever and are supposed to have been relatively "high rent" properties. The odd shape of the plot was disguised by the varying widths and depths of the struc-tures that were run up around the gardens, while the inner rectangle and its gardens were completely geometrically regular. The planning of proportions and light, of open spaces and entrances, was remarkable for its geometrical sophistication in the central block of apartments, a plan of one section of which is highly revealing (fig. 6.4).

A look at the plan shows that these apartments had some luxurious appointments, as well as elaborate geometrical layout, incorporated into them. The *medianum* seems to have been two stories high as were the two rooms at either of its ends (the smaller one perhaps a dining room [*triclinium*], the larger an *oecus* or some sort of substitute for a *tablinum*). All three spaces were lit by two rows of windows, placed one above the other. The putative bedrooms (*cubicula*) opening off the *medianum* were usually only one storey high, which allowed additional *cubicula* to be incorporated into the second storey, which was reached by a private internal staircase. This generic apartment plan, a development of the so-called *casette-tipo* plan, was repeated throughout the remarkably carefully planned and precisely executed complex.[38]

In most, probably all, Roman *insulae*, the *medianum* was jointly held common space within the apartment. This is shown by the famous legal example commented upon by Ulpian that states that if a number of people inhabit the same apartment and some damage is done by anything that has been tossed or poured into the street from a window, they can all be sued for damages as a group (*in solidum*) since it would be impossible to determine who did the evil deed. If, however, a number of persons share the apartment but inhabit separate sections of it, a suit can only be brought against the person who inhabited that part of the apartment from which the object was tossed or liquid was poured. Another example states that if someone rents an apartment to several people and keeps a part of the space for himself, everyone including the owner is responsible for damage done, and although it is possible to start proceedings against one individual in the apartment if the object or liquid came from his or her private window, if it was thrown or poured from the windows of the *medianum*, then everyone living in the apartment is regarded as equally liable.[39] These passages attest not only to the nature of the rentals of apartments in Rome, a subject upon which

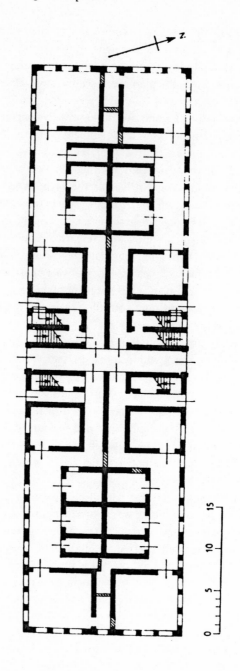

there has been much useful study, but to the nature of communal space within them—which in turn clearly implies that apartments did not have to be rented out solely to related families and kinship units—but that the owner or his rental agent had a fair amount of flexibility in determining to whom they would rent. Other requirements and niceties of renting an apartment, as well as the overall nature of the Roman rental market, are attested in the legal sources in substantial if sometimes confusing detail.[40]

With the evidence of Ostia and of the legal writers available, it is time to consider the situation in Rome itself. Vitruvius has already provided the essential evidence that Rome was turning increasingly into a city of high-rise apartment buildings by the 20s B.C., but examples from archaeology are relatively few. *Insulae* at Rome are known (1) on the slope of the Capitoline Hill just to the left of the staircase that leads to S. Maria in Aracoeli, (2) incorporated into the Aurelianic Walls at Porta S. Lorenzo, (3) built into the church of SS. Giovanni e Paolo, (4) beneath the modern Galleria Colonna on via del Corso, and (5) on via Giulio Romano, though none is in any way complete. Those beneath Galleria Colonna have yielded the most extensive ground plan.

In general *insulae* at Rome seem to confirm the evidence from Ostia since they contain shops with small apartments immediately above, larger apartments lit by rows of windows, probably of the *medianum* type, and perhaps even examples that can be read as "strip" apartments, but the evidence to be recovered from archaeological excavation in these mundane buildings in so busy and vigorous a modern city is inevitably limited.[41] Two other sources of information more valuable in determining the urban spaces available to Roman apartment dwellers in antiquity are the literary record, especially the letters of Seneca and the poetry of Martial and Juvenal, and the fragments of the Severan marble plan that show the streets and apartment complexes of Rome shortly after A.D. 200. The fragments of the Severan map reveal tremendous diversity

---

Figure 6.4 Ostia: Plan of the ground floor of the central block of apartments in the Garden Apartments complex. [Pavolini (1983) p. 157; reproduced by permission of Gius. Laterza & Figli, S.p.a.].

among the various habitations they show, reminiscent of a mixing together of Pompeii and Ostia and expanded to a much larger scale. The fragments confirm the information provided by the Regionary Catalogues that *insulae* were far more numerous than atrium-type houses in the city, and they further reveal vast numbers of *tabernae* of every sort along the street frontages. The main areas of habitation shown on the remaining fragments are a reasonably representative sample of residential quarters of the city: the Esquiline east of the Porticus Liviae along the clivus Suburanus, the streets of houses and shops on the Janiculum (fig. 6.5), and the area on the Viminal along the vicus Patricius.

All three reveal a schematic diagram of the urban texture of Rome at the beginning of the third century A.D. that emphasizes the importance of *insula* and *taberna,* apartment buildings and shop-fronts, interspersed apparently at random with the larger single houses of the wealthy (or ones that had been subdivided into apartments; the scale of the plan does not permit such fine distinctions to be observed). This is the picture we would have expected from Ostia and, secondarily, Pompeii and Herculaneum, and it is precisely the picture that the marble plan confirms.[42]

From the archaeological evidence, we can turn to the testimony of Romans who lived in the *insulae* of the Imperial city. Two complaints, among many, seem to be overwhelmingly common: the flimsiness and combustibility of the apartment buildings, and the noise and innumerable inconveniences that had to be endured by those living in them.[43] The poorer the apartment dweller, the higher in the structure he had to live (the opposite of a situation frequent in our own time when top-floor apartments are often the largest and most expensive) and the flimsier its construction was likely to be. Perhaps Juvenal, in his well-known Third Satire, paints the most vivid picture of life in and around the *insulae* of Imperial Rome:[44]

> Who at cool Praeneste, or at Volsinii amid its leafy hills, was ever afraid of his house tumbling down? Who in modest Gabii, or on the sloping heights of Tivoli? But here we inhabit a city propped up for the most part by slender flute-players: for that is how the bailiff patches up the cracks in the old wall, bidding the inmates sleep at ease under a roof ready to

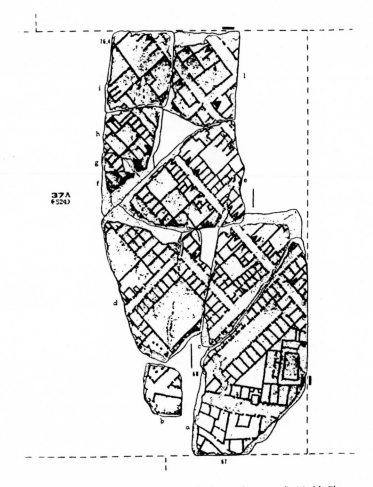

Figure 6.5 Rome: Residential quarter on the Janiculum as shown on the Marble Plan. [Gros & Torelli (1988) p. 205, fig. 92; reproduced by permission of Gius. Laterza & Figli, S.p.a.]

tumble about their ears. No, no, I must live where there are no fires, no nightly alarms. Ucalegon below is already shouting for water and shifting his chattels; smoke is pouring out of your third floor attic above, but you know nothing of it; for if the alarm begins in the ground floor, the last man to burn will be he who has nothing to shelter him from the rain but the tiles, where the gentle doves lay their eggs. . . . If you can tear

315

yourself away from the games of the Circus, you can buy an excellent house at Sora, or Fabrateria or Frusino, for what you now pay in Rome to rent a dark garret for one year. . . . Most sick people here in Rome perish for want of sleep, the illness itself having been produced by food lying undigested on a fevered stomach. For what sleep is possible in a lodging? Who but the wealthy get sleep in Rome? There lies the root of the disorder. The crossing of wagons in the narrow winding streets, the slanging of drovers when brought to a stand, would make sleep impossible for a Drusus—or a sea calf. When the rich man has a call of social duty, the mob makes way for him as he is borne swiftly over their heads in a huge Liburnian car. He writes or reads or sleeps as he goes along, for the closed window of the litter induces slumber. Yet he will arrive before us; hurry as we may, we are blocked by a surging crowd in front, and by a dense mass of people pressing in on us from behind: one man digs an elbow into me, another a sedan-pole; one bangs a beam, another a wine cask, against my head. My legs are be-plastered with mud; huge feet trample on me from every side, and a soldier plants his hobnails firmly on my toe. . . . And now regard the different and diverse perils of the night. See what a height it is to that towering roof from which a potsherd comes crack upon my head every time that some broken or leaky vessel is pitched out of the window! See with what a smash it strikes and dints the pavement! There's death in every open window as you pass along at night; you may well be deemed a fool, improvident of sudden accident, if you go out to dinner without having made your will.

Of course, Juvenal's picture is a conscious exaggeration for his own satirical purposes, but the vivid detail of life at the top of an *insula* and the innumerable difficulties involved probably rang all too true to those who might have heard it in Juvenal's own time and who lived in apartment buildings, even the best accommodations in the best buildings. With the sarcasm and cynicism removed, what Juvenal has painted is a clear and convincing picture of the usual inconveniences and dangers of life in a heavily populated city and in the urban texture of the *insula,* seen both as apartment building and as city block.

VILLA AND FARM

Outside the cities and towns, rural private architecture was determined almost entirely by function. Rural habitations ranged from the vast suburban villas of the wealthiest citizens, such as those that surrounded Rome during the Imperial period, to modest farmhouses. The battered remains of the great villas can still be seen in the Campagna, especially to the east of Rome. They were often of some architectural splendor, at least in their main blocks, and clearly intended to impress other wealthy and important visitors, while at the same time providing places for the rest and relaxation (*otium in rure*, "leisure in the country") often espoused by Roman writers. However, none of these villas is known to us as a whole.

The grand villa located at Sette Bassi, near the fourth milestone of the ancient via Latina, provides a good example of the type, although a precise "type" of the aristocratic suburban villa can hardly be hypothesized, since each varies in notable ways from the others. Until 1952, however, one important piece of ancient architecture survived on the site, and it gave some indication of the grandiosity incorporated into the central block of the villa. This was a wall rising two stories and faced with extremely fine brickwork, pierced by two rows of three windows each, which must have formed part of a grand structure. The wall collapsed during a severe rainstorm and little is left today. What there is, however, reveals that the central architectural feature of the villa was a complex of three large "blocks" of buildings which recall to mind in their plan a large residential complex of near-palatial size more than any sort of working farm. The wall that survived to 1952 seems to have belonged to a central hall (*aula*) around which the rest of the elegant buildings grew up. It must have been quite grand, as it was entered through a doorway divided into three by pillars which was approached from a garden courtyard beyond a colonnaded walkway. The remainder of the central block of buildings of the villa complex surrounded, and probably faced onto, this courtyard, and so would have been dominated by the central hall. Beyond this central block of buildings around the courtyard, there were traces of typical farm buildings and storehouses, as well as a branch aqueduct which brought fresh water into the villa, probably from the nearby Anio Novus aqueduct.

The Sette Bassi villa was built within twenty years of A.D. 150, as has been demonstrated conclusively by its brick stamps, and is

317

widely regarded as one of the finest examples of architecture from the reign of Antoninus Pius, who ruled A.D. 138–161. It was a luxury establishment, meant to impress and to provide all the amenities of comfort and citified elegance and convenience, to aristocrats who cared to vacation in the countryside near Rome. Many other such complexes are known to us, most now consumed by the suburban development of the Campagna subsequent to World War II, and Sette Bassi remains typical of them.[45]

What Sette Bassi was not, however, was a rural habitation typical of the farm or other smallholding that might be possessed and worked by a Roman farmer and his family. For evidence about such middle- and lower-class rural architecture, we must turn to remains far less impressive, though no less meaningful. While working rural villas and farms have been excavated throughout the Roman Empire, notably in Britain and France, relatively few such establishments have been uncovered in central Italy. One of the very few such sites near Rome is that of several small villas located along the route of the ancient via Gabina, which have only been partially published. Nonetheless, the via Gabina farm villas—especially that labeled site 11 by the excavators—provide a good picture of the growth of a small landholding into a family farm of moderate size in the Campagna east of Rome. The excavators divide the architectural history of site 11 into two main phases which are then subdivided as the farm developed (fig. 6.6).

The first phase is dated to the Republican period. In it the central farm villa consisted of a small *domus* with a long hall placed before a series of three rooms and opening, to the south, onto a long narrow courtyard. The courtyard in turn was flanked by working and functional rooms of the farm. To the west of the courtyard and *domus* was a second north-south line of small workrooms that opened onto an enclosed garden (*hortus*) further to the west. During phase two, which began during the early Empire, the *domus* was expanded and altered to a standard *atrium* plan with *impluvium* and one of the line of rooms at the rear (north) end converted to use as a *triclinium*. The original front courtyard was enclosed to form the *atrium* itself, but the walled *hortus* to the west with its line of working rooms separating it from the villa proper remained much as before, though

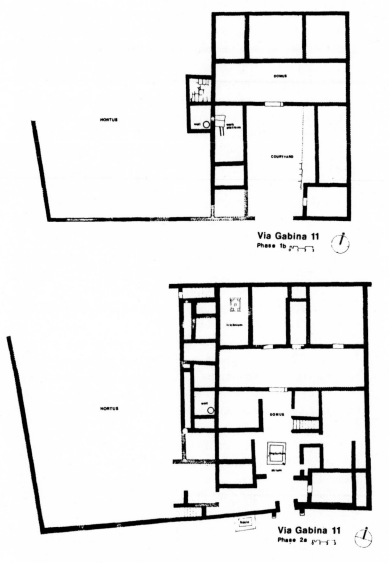

Figure 6.6 Latium: Via Gabina, villa at site 11. Plan of the first (Republican) and second (Imperial) phases. [Widrig (1986) pp. 143 & 147, figs. 3 & 9; reproduced by permission of the author]

enlarged and elaborated. Clearly the small family farm of the Republican period had grown and could be converted into a solid middle-class villa. Its economic success apparently continued into the first centuries of the Empire, when the working rooms that had separated garden from house were converted to a bath complex and a formal pool was inserted into the middle of the garden, but by the early third century A.D. the entire farm and villa appear to have slipped into decay and were abandoned.[46]

What we observe at site 11 on the via Gabina is typical of the development of successful landholdings in rural areas throughout the Roman world. Initially a small and simple residence that was intimately integrated with the functional requirements of a family farm—where the animals may well have been stabled in the rooms off the courtyard, in direct connection with the areas for human habitation—slowly grew more prosperous, and the functional requirements of the working farm could be separated from the *domus.* In imitation of town architecture, the living quarters were refurbished, probably in the reign of Augustus, into an *atrium* plan, and in the first centuries of the Empire—as the farm continued to be successful—certain architectural pretensions that allow it to resemble a luxury villa in miniature (such as baths and ornamental pool) were added, while the farming operations were either moved completely away from the *domus,* or ceased altogether (if, for example, the villa changed hands and became the suburban residence of an urban family).

Such expansion and elaboration of the basic family farm was by no means a usual occurrence. Often such basic agricultural complexes appear to have remained architecturally the same over many decades and generations; site 11 on the via Gabina would appear, in fact, to have enjoyed signal economic success and expansion throughout its existence. What it does provide, in the immediate vicinity of the capital, is a good example of the so-called *villa rustica,* the country villa that originated in a simple family farm. Such simple farms must have been the nucleus of rural life in many parts of the Roman world, and their continuing investigation has brought forward much new information about the rural nature of Roman middle- and lower-class society. Their architecture, in all honesty, is, as this example shows, deeply affected by building types, styles, and trends typical of domestic architecture in the cities and towns, which demonstrates the truism that architectural preferences tended to be disseminated outward from Rome and the other urban centers of the Roman world into the countryside.[47]

Funerary Architecture: Tombs in Urbs *and* Suburbium

A distinct element of private architecture in Roman cities and towns was the agglomeration of family tombs that tended to grow up along the main roads leading into and out of the urban areas. The reason for this suburban phenomenon was hygienic rather than superstitious: the ancient Laws of the Twelve Tables forbade burial or cremation within the sacred boundary (*pomerium*) of Rome, but the fact that such special persons as Vestal Virgins could be interred in their *atrium* in the Forum Romanum or the emperor Trajan in the base of his Column indicates that there was no absolute religious prohibition or taboo involved but a general principle of health and cleanliness.[48] Outside the city boundaries of all Roman towns and cities throughout the Empire there was little apparent legal or administrative control over burials. Hence imposing cemeteries grew up along the via Appia outside Rome, at the so-called Isola Sacra near Portus, outside both the Roman Gate and the Laurentine Gate of Ostia, and outside the Herculaneum Gate at Pompeii, and these are typical of such cemetery "suburbs." Inevitably they became a visual feature of the topography of city and town, and hence of architectural importance, while at the same time they were of clear and obvious social and familial significance both to the people who erected them and to all who entered or exited city or town through their midst.[49]

If we investigate the tomb suburbs of one of these urban areas briefly, a number of features come to light. There were in fact two major cemetery suburbs just beyond the walls of Ostia proper during Imperial times: that outside the Roman Gate (*porta Romana*), where the tombs of the well-to-do and upper middle class lined the via Ostiensis as it headed toward the capital, and that to the south of town, outside the Laurentine Gate (*porta Laurentina*),

which contained the tombs primarily of local craftsmen and trades-
people; a third major cemetery, the "Isola Sacra," was located to the
west, at Portus, and was also used primarily by the working classes.
Yet none of the three cemeteries near Ostia contain tombs of the
aristocratic class of Ostian society, that is, no tombs of magistrates
or other major public officials of any real distinction have been
found in any of them. Since the majority of truly elaborate burial
sarcophagi and funerary reliefs have come from Acilia, farther to the
east, perhaps an aristocratic cemetery there should be hypothesized, but there is no proof for this. The burials stretch in date from
the late Republic to the fourth century A.D. and so reflect the busiest
centuries of Ostia's history and, just as at Rome and Pompeii, the
layout of the cemeteries appears to reflect an almost complete lack
of any sort of control over their development. There is no progression within any of these cemeteries by date of the burials or by type
of tomb constructed; rather all types and dates are mixed in together willy-nilly.[50]

The types of tombs attested in the Ostian cemeteries are typical.
Throughout the Republic, cremation seems to have been the preferred method of interment with the ashes simply placed in a small
urn which was then buried along with a few personal possessions of
the deceased. Such burials did not carry inscriptions. Tombs with
real architectural features begin to appear, particularly at the Laurentine Gate cemetery, toward the end of the Republic and in Augustan times. These were either simple rectangular enclosures with
walls faced in *opus reticulatum* or slightly larger enclosures that
encompassed a large, usually inscribed and/or sculpted monument
of travetine or tufa in its façade. This latter type of Augustan period
tomb is intriguing, for it constituted a public statement which could
be seen and read by the traveler along the road as well as a commemorative monument to a distinguished—at least in his or her or
their family's estimation—ancestor who was in turn presented as a
benefactor and good citizen of Ostia. The tomb of C. Cartilius
Poplicola, which still stands in part outside the porta Marina to the
west of Ostia, is an excellent example of the type.[51]

The more elaborate type of tomb known as the *columbarium*,
which had been popular at Rome for some time, began to appear

in the Ostian cemeteries in the mid first century A.D. and soon became widespread. A typical *columbarium* consisted of a rectangular tomb covered with a barrel vault. Ash urns were set into niches provided for that purpose in the interior masonry of the walls, rather than being set on the ground. Such family tombs remained the most popular type in Ostia at least into the middle of the second century A.D., and this is the type well-known from the Trajanic and Hadrianic sections of the Isola Sacra cemetery at Portus. Whereas the exteriors of earlier tombs had usually been fairly plain, the *columbaria* tended to be heavily decorated inside and out. Decorative brickwork on façades was common, and relief plaques often showing the professions of those interred were set above the doorways as were ownership inscriptions. Pilasters were sometimes added to the fronts in contrasting colors to the walls, and the whole ensemble was often quite elaborate and visually striking.[52] These *columbaria,* then, were almost small houses for the dead, a sort of familial residence for one's ancestors, complete with doors and windows, elegant decoration in stucco and paint, and sometimes even with mosaics on the floor. Thus the cemetery "suburbs" of Ostia must, to the traveler, have brought the residences and the people of the town to mind. When larger or more elaborate tombs, especially those with reliefs and inscriptions, were present, a clear statement of the importance both of the town and of its major citizens was being made, a statement that must have been difficult to ignore.

These related phenomena—the cemetery "suburb" and the socially communicative tomb—occurred everywhere in the Roman world. Examples are occasionally gently, and probably unintentionally, humorous. Outside the Beneventum Gate on the southeast side of Saepinum there still stands, reconstructed from fragments, part of the tomb of C. Ennius Marsus. The tomb was built in imitation of the Mausoleum of Augustus (see below) as a circular drum raised upon a nearly square base. At each corner of the square a stone lion crouched with its teeth bared; on the face of the cylinder turned toward the road was a handsome inscription recording the career of Ennius Marsus. So grandiose is the design of the tomb that the inscription's text renders it unintentionally hilarious: this quasi-Imperial mausoleum was built to contain the ashes of and commemorate a man whose highest accomplishment was to have served as "mayor" of Saepinum, as well as on any number of civic committees, after a thoroughy undistinguished military career. Indeed so mundane was his career that, apparently, neither Marsus nor his stonecarver could find sufficient material to fill out the rectangle allotted to the inscription and so space for the final line and a half is left blank. Marsus may be characterized as a sort of Saepinate "Pooh-Bah"—a "Lord High Everything Else" of a small mountain town in the Abruzzi—but the point of his monument is that this was a career worthy of commemoration and, by implication, of emulation, one that should be and was recorded for posterity. It was by no means an isolated tomb; on the contrary it was surrounded by quite a substantial cemetery "suburb" of which it formed the single largest and therefore most readily noticeable monument. But in its original context, the tomb of Marsus must have been remarkably similar in concept and function to that of Cartilius Poplicola at Ostia's Marine Gate: it celebrated a "distinguished" citizen of the town who was surrounded by tombs that invoked not only the population but also the domestic, private architecture of the town in which all these citizens lived. And this, I suspect, was all part and parcel of its purpose.[53]

At Rome itself, the major arterial roads approaching the city from all sides were lined with tomb "suburbs" of very grand type, and many of the inscriptions and the foundations of quite a number still survive.[54] Within the urban context of the city, though outside the sacred boundary (*pomerium*), the most obvious use of tombs as sociopolitical statements were made by the mausolea first of Augustus and then of Hadrian, across the Tiber. Both still stand though in battered and reworked form. Augustus based his family mausoleum, it would appear, equally on the tumulus tradition of Etruria and the great princely mausolea attested for the Hellenistic kingdoms of the Greek eastern Mediterranean. It served as the burial place for the ashes of most of the emperors and their immediate families through the end of the first century A.D., except such disapproved figures as Nero and Domitian; Nerva was the last

Emperor to be interred there. While Trajan's ashes, most unusually, were permitted interment in the base of his sculpted Column in the forecourt of the temple of the Deified Trajan erected by Hadrian,[55] the model of the Augustan mausoleum was apparently too potent a symbol to be ignored, and so Hadrian created a much larger and more elaborate version of an Imperial mausoleum on the bank of the Tiber at the campus Vaticanus, which still survives as Castel Sant'Angelo. The architectural model is directly that of Augustus's tomb, and the message of both topography and architecture seems to be the same: a declaration of the grandeur and nobility that characterize the Imperial household and family. On the very grandest scale, then, the mausolea of Augustus and Hadrian were intended to deliver—though on an empirewide and monumental scale—essentially the same message that was delivered by the little mausoleum of C. Ennius Marsus at Saepinum: that in such tombs lay the ashes of the men and their families who made and kept Rome, Italy, and the Empire great, powerful, rich, and safe.

Of course, the Imperial mausolea were unique in being removed from the overall context of a cemetery (although in fact an important cemetery grew up somewhat behind Hadrian's Mausoleum during the second century A.D., the one excavated beneath St. Peter's Basilica), which made their political symbolism more starkly clear.[56] But travelers approaching Rome on one of the major arterial roads, such as the via Appia or via Latina, would quickly have found themselves wrapped around with funerary monuments that provided a likeness of domestic architecture and with commemoration of citizen and family. The tomb of the Scipios, for example, would have been clearly apparent just outside the porta Capena and just before the via Latina joined the Appia as both approached Rome. The renown of the family made it famous, while its conspicuous location and its unusual architectural form, almost like a huge catacomb but with a rather grandiose façade incorporating statues of famous Scipios, and location insured its high visibility. Thus the history of famous Romans was enclosed in an architectural context that recalled the domestic architecture in which all Romans lived, and the architecture of the cemetery "suburb" could deliver its message.[57]

Quotidian Architecture: The Intersection between Public and Private Space

To conclude this investigation of "Romans in space," we ought to consider what must have been to the "average" inhabitant on the streets of Rome or any Roman town (a person who by definition could not have existed except in statistical fantasy) the most important of all architectural forms. These were the everyday forms of architecture that determined his or her space: the shops, bars, taverns, cookshops, bakeries, and inns, that is, the *tabernae,* where a great deal of everyday life was lived. These mundane places constituted the daily parameters, just like the streets and intersections and fountains and piazzas, of normal human life in a Roman city or town, not the grand structures seen or visited occasionally but humble spaces providing essential needs and amenities that were entered and used over and over again. We hear of them constantly yet there has been very little consideration of them as architecture or topography, either in terms of building or in relation to human space.[58] Such architecture may best be called "quotidian," since it was the architecture of daily, and of everyday, existence.

The exact date of origin of the *taberna* is not known. Certainly prototypes of such shops were in existence as simple architectural units consisting of one room with a wide entryway and, perhaps, a second room above or behind added onto public buildings in both the Hellenistic Greek and the Roman worlds as early as the third century B.C., when a street of *tabernae* selling luxury goods is attested at Capua. They precede the development of the *macellum,* which we see coming into existence in Rome itself between ca. 210 and 190 B.C. and developing into a form of organized market building thereafter. Indeed, we are told that there were *tabernae circa forum* in Rome much earlier, as early as the reign of Tarquinius Priscus, and while no archaeological evidence has survived to show us the architectural nature of them, there is no real reason to doubt that some form of shop existed at an early period along the long flanks of the Roman Forum. Various names for the rows of shops on either side of the *imum Forum* are attested; by the later third century

B.C. those along the southwest side were called the tabernae Veteres, while the corresponding group fronting the Basilica Aemilia on the northeast flank was called variously tabernae Argentariae Novae, tabernae Novae, or occasionally tabernae Plebeiae. Thus the via Sacra in the Forum Romanum came to be lined with shops probably specializing in luxury goods, and there were also apparently shops featuring valuable goods in the region between the Forum Boarium and the Tiber by the late third century B.C., since they were there to be destroyed by fire in 192 B.C.[59]

From that time onward the *taberna* became the single most ubiquitous, if least celebrated, feature of the urban environment not just in Rome but throughout the Roman world. The evidence for them is legion at every archaeological excavation of an urban center however modest. In Rome the spectacular Markets of Trajan give vivid testimony to the importance of the *taberna* as an architectural element in the high Empire, as do the fragments of the Severan map, which attest to hundreds of them along streets in all quarters of the city. The streets of Pompeii, Herculaneum, and Ostia give even more eloquent testimony to the sheer number of such establishments. They dominated the main arteries, side streets, even alleyways of Roman cities and towns.[60]

It is interesting to note that by the last half of the first century B.C., the shop proprietors of Rome—the *tabernarii*—seem to have served in rhetorical conceit and undoubtedly in political discussion as a symbol, almost a synonym, for the whole population of the city. The aristocracy regarded them as society's dregs and blamed many ills upon the public's habit of "hanging out" in *tabernae*.[61] The architectural form of the *taberna* had become just as ubiquitous in the urbanization of the Roman world as the shopkeeper had in Roman literature and discussion. Whatever the reasons for the phenomenal proliferation of *tabernae,* it is simply a fact of the archaeological record that they constituted one of the dominating features of every Roman town and city and hence were the single most important determinant of the shapes of space available to the great majority of residents in those towns and cities. There is no obvious explanation for the tremendous success of the *taberna,* but as an architectural form it is as definitive of Roman architecture and its development as were *opus caementicium* and kiln-dried brick to the history of Roman construction.[62]

Livy gives us a vivid portrait of this phenomenon, set supposedly in the early fourth century B.C. but resonating much more sharply with the subsequent development and spread of the *taberna*. The historical setting is the arrival of Camillus at Tusculum in 382–381 B.C.; the topography described is applicable to the face of every Roman town and city from at least the third century B.C., if not earlier, to the very end of Roman antiquity:[63]

> Camillus set up his camp before the gates, and desirous of knowing whether the same aspect of peace prevailed within the walls that was displayed in the countryside, entered the city and beheld the doors open, the shops with their shutters off and all their wares exposed, the craftsmen all busy at their respective trades, the schools buzzing with the voices of the scholars, crowds in the streets, and women and children going about amongst the rest, this way and that, as their several occasions called them.

The central feature in this portrait of a normally bustling Roman town is not forum or basilica, temple or shrine, bath or theater, atrium house or apartment building, but a street lined with *tabernae*—both retail shops and workshops and apparently also providing space for schools to meet—in and out of which the whole population, women and children as well as men, moved constantly.

Given this basic fact of Roman urban life, it would seem clear that the ownership of shop property must have been a very profitable form of real estate investment, and such investment is attested for the well-to-do. However sarcastic Cicero may have enjoyed being at the expense of shopkeepers and their customers, he was himself an investor in such quotidian properties (at Puteoli and through an agent) and sounds thoroughly satisfied with the return he was making on his investment.[64] Thus funds from the upper classes fueled the spread of the *tabernae* and their adoption and adaptation to every imaginable type of use. The simple architectural form was, of course, infinitely adaptable. In its smallest shape it could house small retail businesses (providing storage for goods

and/or living quarters in the room above or behind the shop itself),
small workshops staffed by one or two people, and streetfront food
and drink shops. If the *taberna* could obtain a contiguous room or
two, it would serve for a variety of purposes, such as food and drink
bars in which one could sit or stand and consume the merchandise
on the premises in some comfort (e.g., *popinae* and *thermopolia*),
bakeries selling their own bread (with the baking ovens and flour
mills in the attached rooms), fulleries for cleaning clothes with
sufficient space for the various vats and drying racks needed, even
small hostels or inns with a very few dormitorylike communal
rooms might be so accommodated.

It is possible to provide a good example of each of these. The
thermopolium of the via di Diana at Ostia offers an excellent example
of a largish food and drink shop that had room not just to sell its
wares at its marble-covered bar but to display some of them, to store
the merchandise, and eventually even to provide a small open
garden for enjoyable eating and drinking at the back of the property
(fig. 6.7).

The fine bakery nearby in via dei Molini had acquired at least
three sizable rooms, a streetfront for selling the baked goods, a

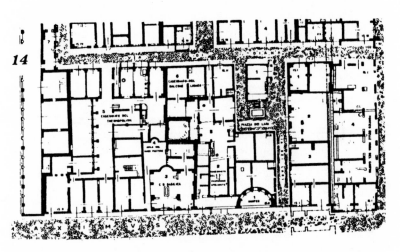

Figure 6.7 Ostia: Thermopolium in via di Diana and environs. [Pavolini (1983) p. 101; reproduced by permission of Gius. Laterza & Figli, S.p.a.]

room with a large baking oven, and a third with several mill wheels permanently installed in it (it is quite likely that, in addition to baking and selling bread, the bakery could double as a cookshop for local *insula*-dwellers who did not have cooking facilities in their *cenacula* and would bring the prepared food to be cooked). A particularly vivid example of a fullery that had expanded to meet demand is that of Stephanus in Pompeii (I.6.7): it was installed in an abandoned house that had been damaged during the earthquake of A.D. 62 and converted to laundry use; what would have been rental shopfront space had become the vestibule for the retail side of the cleaning business and the series of vats and drying racks stretched behind through what had been the rooms of the house. A small inn that would stable the patrons' livestock, too, was the *stabulum* of Hermes at Pompeii (I.1.6–9); it had absorbed four separate doorways of the street and the areas behind them to provide a few guestrooms (presumably there were more on the second storey), a bar, a dining area or two, and a back garden for its clients in addition to stable area.

These are simply random examples of the sort of adaptations and purposes to which these expansions and elaborations on the basic type of the *taberna* could be put; they can be multiplied many times over with examples from Ostia and Pompeii, not to mention other sites.[65] Indeed there is evidence in a number of instances that the commercial space originally confined to the *taberna* or *tabernae* opening onto the street at the front of a once-imposing house could take over the whole, converting it into something entirely different, a large commercial property. This process is clearly demonstrated in the history of the Casa di Sallustio at Pompeii (VI.2.4), where a large and elegant atrium house probably of the third century B.C. in time expanded to take in the atrium/peristyle house next door and to include a small, oddly shaped, but pleasant garden of its own at the back. Later the *caupona* to the northwest of the *fauces* of the house appears to have become associated with the bakery next to it, and the *caupona* was also given an entrance through its rear wall directly into the atrium of the house, probably during the first century A.D. At this point the best explanation for what had happened to this once elegant house is that it had been converted into a substantial *hospitium,* a hotel or inn. The chronology of the wall painting preserved in the house corroborates this. Its location, not far inside the Herculaneum gate of Pompeii and on the main street toward the Forum, was a good one for such a business venture into the ancient travel "industry"; clearly both *caupona* and bakery had thrived, and in due time the entire house was converted to this commercial usage.[66]

While the *taberna* in all its myriad of functions seems to have been universal, showing up everywhere around the Roman town or city and providing everything from housing to manufacturing space, and while there is little if any evidence for planned zoning of commercial quarters in Roman cities and towns, nonetheless we do find that certain areas of towns and cities became, de facto, associated with certain types of activities which might lend both their names and, sometimes, their personalities to those sectors. Our best evidence of this process comes from Rome itself, simply because the evidence is fullest for the capital city. We have mentioned earlier that the Romans themselves assumed that the names Forum Boarium and Forum Holitorium referred to very early market areas along the Tiber that had been replaced, even though it is difficult to determine why that location would have been particularly desirable for selling cattle or vegetables.

In a famous passage from his play *Curculio,* Plautus surveys the Roman forum and tells what was available—not just commercially but also in terms of social class—in each area:[67]

> I'm going to tell you where you can find people of every kind. After this it won't call for any great exertion whatever kind of fellow you want to meet, good or bad, honourable or the reverse. Now, for perjurors, try the Comitium. Liars and braggarts, by the shrine of Cloacina: rich married wastrels in stock by the Basilica. A good supply of harlots, too, if not in prime condition: also men for hire-purchase. In the Fish market, members of dining clubs, in the Lower Forum, respectable and well-to-do citizens out for a walk: flashier types, in the middle Forum, along the canal. By the Lacus Curtius, bold fellows with a tongue in their head, and a bad purpose in mind—great slanderers of other people and very vulnerable to it themselves—By the Old Shops, the money changers—loans negotiated or accepted. Behind the Temple of Castor—but you'd

331

better not trust yourself there. In the Vicus Tuscus, homosexuals, very versatile, turn and turn about.

Commodities, in short, of every imaginable kind were for sale in and around the *tabernae* of the Roman Forum at the end of the third century B.C. It was probably never particularly surprising to find such a wide variety of items available in one relatively small area: Martial tells us that, until Domitian closed it off by incorporating that part of the street into his Forum Transitorium, the stretch of the Argiletum that ran along the side wall of the Forum of Augustus and approached the Forum between the Forum Julium and the Basilica Aemilia (or Paulli), which was just next to the area of the original *macellum* and still in the late first century A.D. sported numerous fruit and vegetable stalls, was noted as an important area for book-sellers, but that it was equally well known for easy availability of prostitutes.[68]

We know of some other distinct shopping districts in Rome, but these could and did change over time. As we have already seen, the major foodstuffs market (*macellum*) of the city was organized in the area just northeast of the Forum, behind the Basilica Aemilia and bounded by the streets Argiletum and Corneta, probably beginning ca. 210 B.C. It had fallen out of use by the mid-first century A.D. when it was destroyed in the fire of A.D. 64 and not replaced, since it had already been superseded by the *macella* on the Esquiline and the Caelian. But these organized and architecturally distinct *macella* were by no means the only, or even the most common, type. It is important to conceive of ancient Rome as a truly Mediterranean city where open spaces could be and were converted to all sorts of uses, by no means the least of which was a regularly scheduled market day, possibly weekly or even daily. This seems to have been the nature of the Circus Flaminius in the southern Campus Martius. It was not architecturally a circus at all; rather it began as a roughly oval-shaped open area that came in time to lend its name to an entire district of Rome, and in due course was hemmed in by temples, porticoes, and walls of many kinds. The reason for the regular occurrence of the phrase *in circo flaminio,* and variants of it, may lie in the fact that the area, the so-called Flaminian Fields, was used for all sorts of essential functions including games, the staging of triumphal processions, and regular markets. Market days in the ancient Roman world, even in its greatest city, must have been very much like market days in Mediterranean towns to this day: people streamed into a central open area or areas of town bringing with them goods of every kind, probably largely agricultural produce, to sell. The inhabitants knew in advance when this was to occur since it was a regular event and one that was both relied upon and loved. Had the Circus Flaminius been built into a true circus with race track and permanent seating it could not have fulfilled the myriad functions that our sources attest. But if we think of it as an important open space in Rome at least up to the end of the first century B.C. that lent its name to an entire district of the city, its nature is no longer so puzzling.[69]

We know in a somewhat general way of other specialized commercial areas of the city. While early on there may have been potteries in the vicinity of the Forum and the Argiletum, these seem always to have gravitated away from the developed areas out to the less densely inhabited quarters. By the first century B.C. pottery was being manufactured in the city exclusively on the Esquiline and in the Vallis Murcia, somewhere in the valley occupied by the Circus Maximus. During the Empire, however, manufacturies of lamps and pottery are attested on the east slope of the Janiculum, on the modern via Gallia between the ancient Viae Appia and Latina to the southeast of the city center, and possibly in the vicinity of what is now the Lateran basilica. Brickyards within the city were few but were clustered mostly on the via Nomentana to the northeast and in the Campus Vaticanus, where the essential clay fields were located. Transtiberim (Trastevere) seems to have been the locale in particular of leather shops and leather workers and of specialized decorative artists of various kinds, the *eborarii* and *citrarii*.[70] There were two major areas for marble working and warehousing: the *statio marmorum* and the immense number of marble workers' shops that surrounded it in the western Campus Martius between the Stadium of Domitian (modern Piazza Navona) and the Tiber near Augustus's Mausoleum, and the great warehouse area just north of the Emporium on the Tiber near Monte Testaccio, which is commemorated in the modern name of the street "via Marmorata."[71]

Aside from these specialized areas, there were various streets or quarters of the city which, according to the testimonia left to us, were particularly full of workshops and retail outlets of various sorts. The areas most frequently mentioned as of this polyglot commercial character are no particular surprise—the Subura, Circus Flaminius, and Trastevere we have already mentioned; also bustling with making, buying and selling were the Velabrum and the streets around the Circus Maximus, the vicinity of the theaters of Marcellus and Balbus, and the Saepta Julia—and the specific streets most regularly mentioned as quotidian commercial centers are the Argiletum, the vicus Tuscus, the vicus Longus, and the via Sacra itself.[72]

Lastly, there are recorded to us a number of streets that seem to have taken their names from trades or shops that tended to congregate along them, and it seems reasonable to assume that indeed at some point in time, at least, they had been the centers for these very businesses and manufactures.[73] Here again, the main point of this topographical information must be to make us realize how intimately and inextricably shops and workshops were bound up in the urban texture of ancient Rome. The businesses and artisans gave their names, their character, and ultimately their very identities to the most heavily used streets and spaces in the city, the shopping and market districts and the streets that allowed access to and from them. In such venues, architecture became an accurate and functional component of daily life, and thus can provide us with a reflection of Roman middle- and lower-class society.

Thus the humble *taberna* and its many architectural and functional adaptations should in fact be viewed as one of the most significant determinants of the nature of human space in Rome and in the cities and towns of the Roman world. Of equal, or nearly equal, importance must have been the open areas—whether called *fora, circus,* or any other term—in which regularly scheduled markets were held but which also could and did serve a myriad of other functions. Finally the streets large and small—*viae* and *vici*—that ran through city and town connecting where people lived and often worked with where they acquired the goods essential to survival must be seen as primary determinants of human space in Roman urban contexts. Shops, open spaces, and streets can be seen, metaphorically, as the framework that held together the quarters of public and private architecture, that brought individuals into a physical relationship with the features of the urban landscape and allowed them to move through it from one to another. Indeed, like the people of many Mediterranean towns and cities to this day, ancient Romans of the lower and middle classes must have lived their lives primarily in the streets. They were constantly moving in and out of, and functioning in the architectural context of, the shops, markets, open squares, and colonnades that characterized those streets. It was also from the streets that they gained access, as needed or desired, to such amenities as they could afford: gardens, amphitheaters and theaters, circuses, baths, basilicas, temples and sanctuaries, fora. But the most important context for them was the street,[74] and the most common single feature along those streets was the *taberna*.

In all urban environments, not just Roman ones, it is the quotidian architectural elements that tell the most about the physical parameters that surrounded people who lived there. A suitably mundane example may convince: the spread of the *taberna* throughout Roman Italy preceded only slightly the development and spread of two items that quickly became essential to the diet of all who lived there, baked bread and vintage wine. The supply and distribution of these items constituted a tremendous breakthrough in the dietary habits and in the health of Romans during the third and second centuries B.C., and the availability of them was tied directly to the *taberna* from which—in their guises as bakeries and baked goods shops, as cookshops for privately prepared food, as wine bars and taverns, as inns and hostelries—they were sold. Wine and bread became the staples of the Roman diet; the *taberna* became a central feature of Roman life, neither specifically public nor specifically private, but universal and unavoidable except for the extremely wealthy, in short, quotidian. Cicero was merely reflecting a long-standing situation when he described the essentials of life for the unrefined working Roman man and woman: "there is no baker or cellar at home; the bread is from a bakery, the wine from a wineshop."[75] And this was true, and is attested both by literary and epigraphical testimonia and by archaeological remains, throughout the Roman world. For the *taberna* was arguably the most adaptable of all the myriad multipurpose building types created by Roman architecture. Besides all the commercial functions we have already mentioned, it provided housing for a large percentage of the humble working people of that world, and both its adaptability to need and its limitations on room and privacy must have become part of the patterns, largely unconscious, by which Romans conceived of, organized, lived in, and defined their spaces. The importance of the *taberna* in Roman architecture and in Roman society can hardly be overestimated. It is a fitting, if humble, spot at which to conclude this investigation, since it represents the point at which Roman society and Roman architecture intersected and determined the shapes and spaces in which the great mass of Romans, all over the Empire, lived their lives.

Notes

Chapter 1: The Roman Architects

1. On the inappropriateness of this distinction to ancient architecture and architects, see esp. Burford (1972) 101–102 and MacDonald (1982) 123. But see Martin (1989) esp. 49–52.
2. Plautus, *Mostell.* 760 and *Mil.* 915; Vitruvius 10.16.3–4 and 7. Pref. 15; Pliny, *NH* 34.42.148 and 36.18.83. Cf. Pearse (1974) 98.
3. On Apollodorus: Procopius, *Aed.* 4.6.13 and Cassius Dio 68.4.1; for ancient praise of Trajan's Forum: Pausanias 5.12.6 or Ammianus Marcellinus 16.10.15–16. Vitruvius tells his own story about the armaments (1. Pref. 2) and the basilica (5.1.6); his work on water pipes is attested by Frontinus, *Aq.* 25.1.
4. On the more limited scope of the architect in private building, see Martin (1989) 49–50; also 50–52 on the evidence from Cicero's letters. Martin is perhaps too categorical when she remarks that Roman architects "were designers, not builders" (49, n. 21), but she is considering only private construction and points out quite rightly that in Roman law architects are not connected with contracts in *locatio conductio operis*, while contracting builders were.
5. The only other surviving manual of architecture from pagan Roman times is that of M. Cetius Faventinus, *De Diversis Fabricis Architectonicae*, probably compiled in the third century A.D., which appears immediately after the text of Vitruvius's *De Architectura* in various manuscripts, and represents little more than an abridgement of Vitruvius's manual. See Plommer (1973) esp. 1–5.

6. The text of Vitruvius upon which I rely most regularly is that of the ongoing Budé series' publication of introductions, texts with French translations, and exhaustive commentaries for each of the ten books of the *De Architectura.* Where those texts are not yet available, I have turned to the texts of Fensterbusch (1964), Ferri (1960), and Granger (1931, 1934), i.e., for books 2, 5, 6, and 7. English translations throughout are those of Granger, unless otherwise noted.

7. Granger's translation of *fabrica* as "craftsmanship" is admirable, but his translation of *ratiocinatio* as "technology" makes no sense. Vitruvius himself states, quite clearly, that "*ratiocinatio* is that which is able to point out and to explain things that have been made in accord with (correct) technical skill and method" (Vitruvius 1.1.1). Granger's mistranslation was pointed out by Torrence (1994) 5, n. 12; the Latin reads: *Ratiocinatio autem est quae res fabricatas sollertiae ac rationis proportione demonstrare atque explicare potest.* For detailed explication and discussion of the terms, see Fleury (1990) 66–69.

8. An excellent study of Vitruvius's meaning and intentions in choosing these nine areas of learning is provided by Goguey (1978). See further: Fleury (1990) 69–71; also Geertman (1994), esp. 10–14.

9. Vitruvius 6. Pref. 4. Rawson (1985) 117, states: "To the Romans these were the *artes liberales,* suitable for a free man, or rather for a gentleman (any kind of technical instruction was of course excluded)."

10. Varro included architecture, as well as medicine, among his "nine disciplines" (Vitruvius 7. Pref. 14). See Geertman (1994) esp. 11–24.

11. See Goguey (1978) 103–109; Torrence (1994) 10–17; Geertman (1994) 12–13.

12. Here Vitruvius appears to echo sentiments earlier asserted by Cicero in his *De Officiis* (1.61–72). That this is derivative from Cicero and also accords well with the moral ideology espoused by the regime of the emperor Augustus, to whom Vitruvius dedicated his treatise, is clearly established by Fleury (1990) 83.

13. As Fleury (1990) ix and n. 4, points out, Vitruvius is very likely drawing this example from personal experience; see Frontinus, *Aq.* 25.1, 2, which suggest that he was in part responsible for introducing a new calibration of pipe size for water being brought into the city during the expansion of the water system directed by Marcus Agrippa. On Vitruvius's knowledge and use of Lucretius's poem, see Merrill (1904).

14. On Vitruvius's concept of the architect's "authority," see Gros (1989) 126. On Vitruvius's concept of a cultivated person, see Schrijvers (1989b) 50, who suggests that Vitruvius has based his concept of the ideal architect on Aristotle's prescription for the cultivated man, even to the extent of rendering several of Aristotle's terms into Latin; cf.

Torrence (1994) 25–27 and Novara (1994). The question to what extent Vitruvius's ideal concept of the architect is original has been discussed for some time; important contributions to the subject include Novara (1983) and Fleury (1990) lxxxvii–xc. Novara (1983) also delves into Vitruvius's motives for writing his treatise, a subject that has been further developed by Sallmann (1984) and Gros (1994b).

15. Briggs (1927) 32, long ago noted the frustrating gaps in the information Vitruvius provides. For an appreciation of Vitruvius's manual as the work of a professional craftsman, see Burford (1972) 26–27.

16. SHA *Vita Alexandri Severi,* 44. Teachers of architecture are also mentioned in the infamous price edict of Diocletian (A.D. 301), where it is decreed that they are to receive more per capita than teachers of reading and arithmetic, but only half the amount prescribed for teachers of Greek, Latin, rhetoric, and law: Briggs (1927) 32–33.

17. Burford (1972) 102–103.

18. E.g., the Cossutii (Rawson [1975] 38–41), the Cornelii (Martin [1989] 51), possibly the Vitruvii (Palmer [1983] 354–361). On these architects, see further below.

19. Briggs (1927) 32 asserts the generally more practical nature of Roman architectural training than Greek, but the evidence is meager at best. Cf. Coulton (1977) 15.

20. This tripartite model for avenues to employment is proposed by MacDonald (1977) 37, who implies that it was strictly observed, i.e., that architects were tracked into one system or another. The evidence does not support the latter assumption.

21. Cicero: *ad Q. Frat.* 2.6(5).3; Gellius: 10.10.2; Plutarch: *Mor.* 498 E (*An Vitiositas*); see Pearse (1974) 100–101 for further examples. On ancient architects' *paradeigmata* (drawings) in general, see Coulton (1983) esp. 456–459 and MacDonald (1982) 137–140. Probably the best example of what an ancient architect's plan may have looked like is the well-known mosaic plan of a Roman bath building (Carettoni et al. [1960] vol. 1, p. 209; Reynolds [1996] 39–40 and fig. 1.31). For the battered and fragmentary remains of a builder's sketch plan (questionably identified as a plan for the porch of the Hadrianic Pantheon) preserved on paving slabs in front of Augustus's Mausoleum, see Haselberger (1994), esp. 279–296; also Haselberger (1995).

22. Vitruvius 1.6.12 and 3.5.8 on the illustrations of the *De Architectura;* cf. the commentary on the latter passage by Gros (1992) 174–177. An excellent general discussion of illustrations in Greek architectural treatises and in Vitruvius is provided by Coulton (1983) 459–462; cf. Haselberger (1989). See Vitruvius 1.2.2. and 1.1.4 for the three types of plans and their names, and the commentary on 1.2.2 by Fleury

(1990) 109–110. The same three types of drawings are listed in Cetius Faventinus 1.288.6–8 (Plommer [1973] 40–41).

23. Cf. Sear (1990) and Gros (1994c).

24. Vitruvius 1.4–7. Cf. Fleury (1990) xciv–cxiv and commentary to 1.4–7 (123–193). In private building, however, the choice of site must usually have been that of the landowner, and the building site had to be specified in the contract (Martin [1982] 19, 27); presumably here the architect could only advise or warn, depending on the individual circumstance. Actual survey of land, as opposed to design of buildings to be put upon it, was carried out by *agri mensores* (measurers of land) who, by Imperial times, had been formed into a division of the bureaucracy. The *agri mensores* were not architects but surveyors, and their duties and methods are well-documented in the *Corpus Agrimensorum*, a collection of surveyors' manuals and handbooks dating from the first to the fourth centuries A.D., of which the text preserved therein of Hyginus Gromaticus is typical (Hyginus Gromaticus, *Constitutio limitum*, esp. 165–167, in C. Thulin, ed., *Corpus Agrimensorum Romanorum* [Leipzig, 1913]). See Dilke (1971) and Reynolds (1996) 25–28. In cities, or at least in the city of Rome, there was a separate official body of surveyors referred to as the *mensores aedificorum* (measurers of buildings), a body of professionals similar to but distinct from the rural surveyors (Reynolds [1996] 29–38).

25. Indeed Vitruvius repeatedly denounces architects who seek out commissions rather than waiting for clients to come to them (esp. at 6. Pref. 5).

26. Vitruvius, at 10. Pref. 1–2, urges that Rome adopt a law used at Ephesus by which the architect had to forfeit from his own pocket if the project ran more than 25 percent over the original estimate. Vitruvius maintains that this law would make those who commissioned buildings and those who built them more honest and scrupulous.

27. On these points, see Novara (1994) and Fleury (1994), the former dealing with Vitruvius's determination to provide a useful work, and the latter with *De Architectura*'s place among the mechanical treatises known from antiquity.

28. See Vitruvius 6.8.9 about decisions on materials to be used; 5.6.7 and throughout book 7 about the architect's role in obtaining building materials. Pearse (1974) 101–102 marshalls a variety of secondary sources that corroborate Vitruvius's statements and implications.

29. Martin (1989), esp. 49–57.

30. Vitruvius cites the example of Metagenes, son of Cherisiphron. Coul-

ton (1977) p. 163, n. 68, adduces further Greek examples of the custom; also see Coulton (1983) 459.

31. Cicero, *De Officiis* 1.151, where he ranks architecture with medicine and teaching and assigns all three to the lower ranks of Roman society. At the end of the first century A.D., the poet Martial placed architects at the same social rank as heralds (*praecones*), calling them both professions to which despairing fathers should assign their thick-headed, or perhaps hard-headed (in the sense of practical), sons (5.56.10–11). It is fair to wonder how seriously Martial's implied sarcasm should be taken as evidence, however; he may not mean that architecture is an appropriate field for stupid sons, but for tough-minded, practical young men.

32. Gros (1983b) is essential reading on this topic, as is Schrijvers (1989a). On the varying social and class levels attested for architects in the Roman world, see Rawson (1985) 88–89.

33. Lists of the names of known architects of the Roman world have been published periodically in the last two centuries, but their usefulness is all too often compromised by the pro-Hellenic or anti-Hellenic bias of their compilers. These include Promis (1873), De Ruggiero (1895), G. N. Olcott, *Thesaurus Linguae Latinae Epigraphicae: A Dictionary of the Latin Inscriptions*, vol. 1 (Rome 1904), s.v. "architectus," Toynbee (1951), and Calabi Limentani (1958). By far the best list compiled so far, although difficult to obtain and presented in a manner that can be confusing for the user, is Pearse (1974) 179–187. For comment on some of these lists and their philosophical problems, see MacDonald (1982) 122–123; for comment on their scholarly strengths and considerable drawbacks, see Pearse (1974) 171–178.

34. Coulton (1977) 15; also Clarke (1963) 14.

35. Coulton (1977) 25–26, 164, n. 72; Torrence (1994) 32–35.

36. Fleury (1990) xl–xlii.

37. On the questions of Vitruvius's use of compilations and abridgements of these Greek sources, see Gros (1982) 673–675.

38. See Lawrence (1983) 161–167 on the sanctuaries at Samos and Ephesus and their architects and on Priene, 249–252. For a controversial discussion of Ictinos, see Carpenter (1970) 111–158; but cf. Burford (1963) 25–26, and McCredie (1979) 71–73. See Lawrence (1983) 240–241 for the tholos at Delphi. Cicero, *De Orat.* 1.62, confirms Vitruvius and the well-known construction inscription for the arsenal at Piraeus, *IG* II² 1668; see also Jeppesen (1958) 69–102 and Lawrence (1983) 341–342. On Hermogenes and his influence, see Stampolides (1990). On the temple at Teos, see Lawrence (1983)

282. For the Mausoleum at Halicarnassus, see Lawrence (1983) 252–254 and Jeppesen (1958) 103–144.

39. The dependence of Vitruvius's third book upon Hermogenes was asserted, and the evidence for it investigated, by Gros in two detailed articles (1975), (1978). This has been reinforced by Tomlinson (1989), esp. 72–73; also see Gros (1990) lxv–lxvii. On the range of our sources for Hermogenes, see Kreeb (1990) 103–111.

40. On this controversial passage, see Gros (1978) 687–703 and Gros (1992) 107–121; cf. Schwandner (1990) 85–100, who asserts that this took place at Pergamon.

41. Tomlinson (1989) 73. Also Torrence (1994) 31–32 and 36–37.

42. Tomlinson (1989) 71–73. The tradition of such architectural treatises went back at least to the time of Socrates (Xenophon, *Memorabilia,* 4.2.6–10); see Coulton (1977) 24–25.

43. The most important study of Hermodorus is that by Gros (1973), to which must be appended his subsequent article (1976a). Gros (1973) 158–160 suggests that Vitruvius did not have direct access to Hermodorus's writings, but only secondary sources for them, especially Septimius and Varro, whom Vitruvius does mention (7. Pref. 14).

44. Velleius 1.11.3–5 does not specifically name the temple but does assert that it was encircled by the Porticus of Metellus, which in Velleius's own time (*nunc*) was called the *porticus Octaviae.* A fair amount of controversy has arisen over this passage, since the porticus of Octavia—which was built by Octavian's sister shortly after 23 B.C. to complete work begun by her deceased son Marcellus (Ovid, *Ars amat.* 1.69–70) and to make it a memorial to him (Livy, *Epit.* 140; also Suetonius, *Aug.* 29.4 and Cassius Dio 49.43.8)—enclosed not only the temple of Jupiter Stator but also the temple of Juno Regina. For discussion of what Hermodorus may have built in this complex, see the articles by Boyd (1953) and Morgan (1971); cf. Gros (1976a) 393–397, and Horsfall (1988) 13. Remains of the temple of Juno Regina may still be seen on the via di Portico d'Ottavia, now incorporated into the church of S. Angelo in Pescheria. An inscription on the propylon of the porticus identifies it as a Severan rebuilding, and the same may be true of the temple remains. A fragment of the Severan marble plan (Carettoni et al. [1960] pl. 29; Rodriguez Almeida [1981] pl. 23) also shows the temples of Jupiter Stator and Juno Regina, and the plan of the former revealed there, also of Severan date, is that of a *peripteros sine postico* and hence not Hermodorus's original design as described by Vitruvius (3.2.5). See Richardson (1992) 216–217 and 225–226.

45. On the arrival of new materials, notably Pentelic marble, from Greece, see Gros (1976a) 393. More generally, for a discussion of the impact

of the triumphing generals upon Roman architecture in Italy, and especially in Rome itself, after 146 B.C., see Coarelli (1968), esp. 302–305, and Gros (1978c), esp. 35–39.

46. Both these attributions to Hermodorus are asserted by Gros (1976a) 379 (Mars temple) and 389 (*navalia*). Little else is known of the temple to Mars except that it was in the general vicinity of the Circus Flaminius; the date is assigned from that of Callaicus's triumph over Lusitania, and Gros speculates that in this temple Hermodorus may have attempted to use native Italian materials rather than marble. Cicero, *De Orat.* 1.62 connects Hermodorus to M. Antonius's *navalia;* Gros equates this with a temple of Neptune attested in the Circus Flaminius, an identification that is difficult to accept.

47. The three other Romans mentioned by Vitruvius (7. Pref. 14) as producing technical treatises on architectural subjects—Fufidius, Varro, and P. Septimius—are nowhere attested as practicing architects.

48. The essential scholarly source on Cossutius and his descendants is Rawson (1975), which should be supplemented by Torelli (1980) and Schrijvers (1989a) 17. For the temple of Olympian Zeus, the best summary remains Wycherley (1964), now supplemented by Thompson (1987) 2–3.

49. Torrence (1994) 47 and n. 63.

50. *IG* III 1 561 (*IG* II–III² 4099). See Rawson (1975) 37 and n. 9.

51. Rawson (1975) 38–39. For Campanian Cossutii in the second century B.C., see *ILLRP* no. 712 (of 105 B.C.). An L. Cossutius is attested by two dedications made on Delos between 150 and 125 B.C. and a Cossutius son of Cossutius held a priesthood on the island of Ios, noted for the blue-grey marble that was quarried there in antiquity. M. Cossutius is named as *naumarchos* in the Isis cult at Eretria in Euboea (*IG* XII Suppl. 557).

52. Rawson (1975) 37–38. An Italic origin for the family of the Cossutii is also accepted by Torelli (1980) 319. For the two COSSVTIVS inscriptions, probably scratched into the concrete with a workman's trowel, see Campbell (1938) 205. Gros (1976a) 397 suggests that Cossutius may have been the supervising architect of Antiochus's glorification of Epiphaneia, but that he worked from a base in Italy and brought teams of Latin-speaking workmen to Syria (and to Athens?) with him.

53. On Antiochus's *Romanitas,* see Torrence (1994) 51–52; on his years as an *obses* in Rome, see *Der Kleine Pauly,* vol. 1 (Stuttgart 1964) col. 389, s.v. "Antiochos 5" (W. Sontheimer); also *CAH* viii² (Cambridge, 1989) 287 (R. M. Errington), & 340 (Ch. Habicht). On the specifics of Cossutius's work on the Olympieion, see Wycherley (1964) esp. 170–172, and Thompson (1987) 2–3.

54. This suggestion was made by Downey (1961) 102.
55. Rawson (1975) 38–41.
56. The location of this temple *ad Mariana* has puzzled many topographers (e.g., Platner & Ashby [1929] 259). The most likely solution is that proposed by Richardson (1978a) 245 that the *Mariana* mentioned by Valerius Maximus (2.5.6) consisted of Marius's house on the Sacra via (Plutarch, *Marius* 32.1 and 35.2), apparently preserved in Valerius's time, and the nearby Honos et Virtus temple on the lower slopes of the Velia (Richardson [1992] 190).
57. Attested by inscription, *CIL* 11.1831, from a triumphal arch at Arretium (Arezzo), which does not mention the architect.
58. This suggestion was first proposed by Gros (1976a) 407; cf. Torrence (1994) 41–42. On Marius's anti-Hellenic bias, see Sallust, *Jug.* 85.12–13.
59. A point noted by Richardson (1978a) 245.
60. On Scaevola, see Broughton (1952) 2.7. Richardson (1978a) 246 not only accepts the identification of Mucius with Q. Mucius Scaevola, but identifies him as the father-in-law of the younger Marius who helped Marius and his son with provisions during their escape from Rome in 88 B.C. (Plutarch, *Marius* 35.5–7). Oddly, Schrijvers (1989a) 18 seems unaware of Richardson's identification of the architect Mucius with Q. Mucius Scaevola.
61. Schrijvers (1989a) 18 for the suggestion about the freedman or client of Scaevola; also Torrence (1994) 45. Unfortunately, this intriguing possibility remains pure speculation. My suggestion that the architect Mucius might have been a free architect of *ingenuus* status attached by family association to Scaevola is strengthened by comparison to the case of L. Cornelius (see Molisani [1971] 3–4).
62. On this entire argument, see Richardson (1978a) esp. 246; note also Horsfall (1988) 16.
63. The entire issue of senators and money has been comprehensively explored by D'Arms (1980), (1981).
64. Cicero, *ad Q. Frat.* 3.1.2.
65. Cicero, *ad Att.* 4.16.8 on the reused columns and Paullus's involvement in the work. See Frank (1924) 67 on the two separate phases of reconstruction. On the funding provided by Caesar in or after 54 B.C., see Plutarch, *Caes.* 29; Appian, *BellCiv* 2.26. On the entire question, see Richardson (1979) 213–215; cf. Richardson (1992) 54–56, and H. Bauer, "Basilica Aemilia," in Steinby (1993b) 183–187.
66. Molisani (1971), esp. 1–2; *AE* 1971, 61. The inscription, preserved in very good condition and now displayed on the southeast wall in the atrium of the Ospedale Fatebenefratelli on Tiber Island, was discovered on the via Prenestina; see fig. 1.1. The Latin text reads:

L.CORNELIUS.L.F.VOT. / Q.CATVLI.COS.PRAEF.FABR / CENSORIS.ARCHI-
TECTVS. The syntax of the Latin beginning with the name of Quintus
Catulus clearly implies that he is to be taken as both consul when
Cornelius served as *praefectus fabrum* and censor when Cornelius was
architectus.

67. Molisani (1971) 2, n. 5, lists a number of parallel examples, including
ILLRP nos. 346, 379, 417, 434, 474, 1187, etc. This omission of the
nomen hardly ever occurs during the Imperial period.

68. Molisani (1971) 3. On the career of this Catulus: *RE* XIII, 2 (Stuttgart,
1927) cols. 2082–2094 (F. Münzer), and Suolahti (1963) 464–469.

69. Tacitus, *Hist.* 3.72.

70. The Catulus inscriptions: *CIL* 1².736, 737 = 6.1313, 1314. Claudius's restoration: *CIL* 6.916 = 31201. Military diplomata: *CIL* 16.35,
159, *AE* 1974.655. For a good general treatment of the sources for the
building and the remains on the Capitoline identified with it, see
Richardson (1992) 376–377; for excellent photographs, see Nash
(1968) 2.408. The generally accepted identification of the remains
beneath Palazzo del Senatore as those of the Tabularium has recently
been challenged by Purcell (1993) esp. 135–142.

71. Tacitus, *Hist.* 3.72 is again the main source for all these events. Other
testimonia include, for the fire in 83, Plutarch, *Sulla* 27.6; Cicero, *Cat.
III,* 9; Sallust, *Cat.,* 47.2; for the rebuilding begun by Sulla, Valerius
Maximus 9.3.8. Richardson (1992) 222–223 suggests that, rather
than marble columns or Corinthian capitals from Cossutius's work in
Athens, Sulla may have brought Doric elements from the original
Pisistratid temple, since Jupiter Capitolinus was rebuilt in its original
Doric order.

72. More testimonia that confirm Tacitus's account include, on the assignment to Catulus, Cicero, *Verr. II* 4.69 and Suetonius, *Jul.* 15; on
Catulus's dedication, Livy, *Peri.* 98; Plutarch, *Poplic.,* 15; Pliny, *NH*
19.23 and Suetonius, *Aug.* 94.8. Since Tacitus confirms that Catulus's
name was still inscribed above the doors of the temple in A.D. 69, it
would appear that the honor voted to Julius Caesar in connection
with his triumph of 46 B.C.—to have his name inscribed there (Cassius Dio 43.14)—was not carried out. See Richardson (1992) 223.

73. Molisani (1971) 8. On *ingenui,* see *OLD,* s.v. "ingenuus," 906–907.

74. These are the hypotheses posited by Molisani (1971) 8–9.

75. Molisani (1971) 6–7 collects and summarizes the evidence; only
twelve examples of *praefecti fabrum* are known in the epigraphical
record prior to the time of Augustus, so the evidence is meager at best.

76. Cf. Dobson (1965) esp. 61–65, who notes that in the first century
B.C., such prefects are attested to have served under Varro, Murena,
Caesar, Cicero, Pompey, Ti. Nero and M. Brutus, and M. Antonius, in

345

an immense variety of secondary capacities, only occasionally connected to construction or building; this is corroborated by Purcell
(1983) 156–157.

77. Thus Molisani (1971) 7–9.

78. The military element in Cornelius's career is assumed by Schrijvers
(1989a) 16 and seems likely indeed.

79. The inscriptions are *CIL* 6.148 = 14.5 = *ILS* 3776, and *CIL* 6.30703.
Pearse (1974) 179 expresses doubt about whether the final terms
represent profession or surname; Martin (1989) 51 accepts that "for
these men, construction seems to be a family enterprise." Whether
they should be connected with the earlier L. Cornelius is uncertain,
however.

80. On the Cornelii, see further Martin (1989) 51, n. 34; on the various
Vitruvii, see Thielscher (1961) cols. 420–425 and Ruffel & Soubirain
(1962) 133–143.

81. Cf. the list of sources for architects in Pearse (1974), divided into lists
of civilian (179–185) and military (185–186) examples, from all
over the Roman world in the later Republican and Imperial periods.
The majority of these testimonia are too meager to provide any basis
for hypothesis or conclusion, and many cannot be securely dated.

82. Cicero, *ad Att.* 2.3. For the majority of the Ciceronian passages discussed below I am indebted to Schrijvers (1989a) 15, who follows
Pearse (1974) 16 in asserting that Cyrus's *praenomen* was Vettius (*ad
Att.* 2.4) and that it was adopted by Chrysippus. See also on several of
these Ciceronian passages: Pearse (1974) 16–22, Martin (1989) 49–
51, and Torrence (1994) 58–68.

83. Pearse (1974) 175 would make Cyrus a *libertus,* but fails to explain
his reasoning. Martin (1989) 50, n. 25 is rightly cautious.

84. Cicero, *ad Q. Frat.* 2.2. Torrence (1994) 60 suggests that Quintus's
use of the word *officium* in this letter implies that a tacit but agreed
contract existed between Cyrus and the Ciceros, but this may stretch
the meaning a bit. An unquestioned expectation of dutifulness toward themselves would seem to be more what Quintus and Marcus
expected from Cyrus.

85. Cicero, *Mil.* 17–18.

86. Pliny, *NH* 36.24.103. See also the comments on this tale by Gros
(1983b) 448.

87. Cicero, *ad Fam.* 7.14. On the association between Cyrus and Chrysippus, see Pearse (1974) 16–17, 21, and Schrijvers (1989a) 15.

88. Cicero, *ad Att.* 12.29.

89. Treggiari (1969) 134, who suggests that Chrysippus may have been
responsible for the plan of the Basilica Julia and for some or all of the

rest of Caesar's public works. The evidence for this is slight. For a contrary opinion, see Pearse (1974) 21–22.

90. Cicero, *ad Att.* 14.9.
91. Cicero, *ad Fam.* 7.14.
92. Cicero, *ad Att.* 14.3. See Pearse (1974) 17–18 on Corumbus's social status. Torrence (1994) 63 discusses the terminology used for the building trades in this letter and its possible significance.
93. Cicero, *ad Fam.* 7.20.
94. On Numisius, see Cicero, *ad Q. Frat.* 2.2.1; on Cluatius, Cicero, *ad Att.* 12.36. On these two men, cf. Schrijvers (1989a) 15–16. On Diphilus and Caesius, see Cicero, *ad Q. Frat.* 3.1.2–5, and Pearse (1974) 19.
95. Cicero, *ad Q. Frat.* 3.1.5; see Martin (1989) 55–56, esp. n. 53.
96. Cicero, *ad Att.* 13.35.1. Shackleton-Bailey (1965–70) ad loc. (p. 381) speculates that this man's name was probably Caecilius or Pomponius and that he was a Greek who acquired the name upon becoming a Roman citizen, but there is no proof for this. As mentioned above, Treggiari (1969) 134 thinks this architect may be Vettius Chrysippus, but this has not been generally accepted. On Caesar's building program in general, see Suetonius, *Jul.* 44; Appian, *BellCiv* 2.102; Cassius Dio 43.49; also see Stambaugh (1988) 43–45.
97. Cicero, *De Officiis* 1.151.
98. See Treggiari (1969) 135; Molisani (1971) 8–9; Pearse's (1974) list of architects, 171–187.
99. In addition to the examples cited by Cicero, we find the occasional datable inscription that attests a slave architect: during the time of Julius Caesar one Hospes, slave of Appia, is designated *architectus* of an unknown building in Caiatia; *CIL* 10.4587.
100. Cf. Gros (1983b), esp. 425–431.
101. We should note such episodes as Cicero's inspecting and measuring for himself a newly built road (*ad Q. Frat.* 3.1.2). In the same letter he mentions that Quintus Cicero appears to have drawn up, or at least contributed to, the plans of various of his building projects (*ad Q. Frat.* 3.1.3–5). See Martin (1989) 54.
102. Cicero, *ad Q. Frat.* 3.1.2–5. See chapter 2 for further discussion of this incident.
103. Horsfall (1988) 16: "The free Roman architect could be and probably was a tremendous snob."
104. Verona: *CIL* 5.1.3464 (L. VITRVVIVS L. L. CERDO / ARCHITECTVS), which is found inscribed on the so-called Arch of the Gavii. Thilbilis: *CIL* 8, Suppl. 2, 18913 (M. VITRVVIVS MAMURRA ARCVS S. P. F. The abbreviated phrase can be expanded to "s(ua) p(ecunia) f(ecit)."

105. Thielscher (1961) esp. cols. 420–425 and 441–446. A connection between Vitruvius and Mamurra had already been hypothesized by Münzer (*RE* 14.1 [Stuttgart 1928] cols. 966–967) but not an actual identification of the two men as one. Catullus's vituperation against Mamurra is especially obvious, e.g., at 29.11–14, 20–24, at 41.4, and at 57.3–5. On Mamurra's wealth, see Cicero, *ad Att.* 7.7.6 (late December 50 B.C.); for the last datable reference to him, Cicero, *ad Att.* 13.52.1 (late December 45 B.C.), and Shackleton-Bailey (1965–70) at 7.7.6 and at 13.52.1. For later references to Mamurra, Horace, *Sat.* 1.5.37; Pliny, *NH* 36.48 (on Mamurra's expensive house); Suetonius, *Jul.* 73.4; and it is probably his memory that is attacked by Martial at 9.59.1–3 (see Palmer [1983] 347–349).

106. A point raised in its favor by Coarelli (1989) 185.

107. Shackleton-Bailey (1965–70) at 13.52.1; see Baldwin (1990) 431 & n. 43.

108. Ruffel & Soubirain (1962) 133–143; see Fleury (1990) xi–xii.

109. Fleury (1990) ix–x.

110. Vitruvius on his own poverty: 5.1.10, 6. Pref. 4–5, and 10. Pref. 1. On the stipend: 1. Pref. 2–3, and Fleury's (1990) commentary on that passage (pp. 62–64). Rawson (1985) 86 and Fleury (1990) xvi, n. 27 note the incongruity of identifying the poor architect with the notoriously wealthy Mamurra; Baldwin (1990) 431 makes the same point: "the spendthrift of poems 29.11–19 and 41.4 does not consort very well with the penny-pinching monetarist architect."

111. Thielscher's suggestion provoked a lengthy and detailed refutation from Ruffel and Soubirain (1962). Since then it has been rejected by the contributors to *Der Kleine Pauly* in the articles on "Mamurra," vol. 3 (Stuttgart 1969) col. 940 (H. G. Gundel) and "Vitruvius (2)," vol. 5 (Stuttgart 1975) cols. 1309–1313 (K. Sallmann), as well as by Palmer (1983) 343, Rawson (1985) 86, Fleury (1990) xvi, and Baldwin (1990) 431. Only Purcell (1983) 156, who calls the argument "convincing," seems to accept the identification; Coarelli (1989) 185, while finding "numerosi elementi a suo favore" (most of which he fails to enumerate) regards it as yet to be proven.

112. Pliny, *NH* 16.1 (trees), 35.1 (painting), 36.1 (stone). Frontinus, *Aq.* 25.1 and 25.2.

113. See Plommer (1973) esp. 1–2.

114. Servius, *ad Aen.* 6.43; Sidonius Apollinaris 4.3.5 and 8.16.10. On these passages, see Ruffel & Soubirain (1962) 131, and Fleury (1990) x.

115. See Fleury (1990) x–xi. "Pol(l)io" as the author's *cognomen* was summarily rejected by Granger (1934) xvii–xviii. For "Cerdo" at Verona: *CIL* 5.1.3464, which certainly cannot refer to our author, since Cerdo

is designated a freedman of Lucius (*L. l.*) on the inscription, whereas our Vitruvius states that he is freeborn of a freeborn father (6. Pref. 4).

116. See the lists in Thielscher (1961) cols. 420–425, and Ruffel & Soubirain (1962) 174–176.

117. The best summary of the arguments for and against his presence at Massilia is Callebat & Fleury (1986) 289–290, who conclude that, despite discrepancies between Caesar's and Vitruvius's descriptions, it is still a good possibility that Vitruvius was an eye-witness to that seige.

118. Ferri (1960) 87 would date the seige of Larignum to spring 58, Thielscher (1961) cols. 434–435 to winter 57–56, while Jeppesen (1989) 31, Baldwin (1990) 432, and Fleury (1990) xv all seem to lean toward the first years of the Civil Wars.

119. See Jeppesen (1989), esp. 32, who would keep Vitruvius in Caesar's army through the campaign in Pontus and the battle of Zela.

120. E.g., Thielscher (1961) cols. 427–428.

121. Purcell (1983) 156–157, although the only real parallel to an architect/engineer in such a position that he cites is an *architectus armamentarius,* attested at Rome a good deal later, during the reign of Domitian (*CIL* 6.2725 = 37189). The argument is reconsidered, and the essential correctness of conceiving of Vitruvius as a member of the *apparitores* asserted, by Gros (1994b).

122. Frontinus, *Aq.* 25.1 and 2. See Callebat (1973) x and 163–167. For the connection of Vitruvius specifically to Agrippa's aedileship of 33, see Palmer (1983) 353 & n. 58.

123. On the issue of the basilica at Fanum, especially important discussions are provided by Ohr (1975), Alzinger (1989), and Deli (1992).

124. The scholarship on this point has been enormous. Baldwin (1990) 425–430 and Fleury (1990) xvi–xxiv both summarize the major points of contention clearly and arrive at the same conclusion that I draw. It should be noted, however, that this majority point of view was accepted neither by Sir Ronald Syme, "Imperator Caesar," *Historia* 7 (1958) 182, who placed composition of the first book after 27 B.C., nor by Rawson (1985) 86–87, who would place the beginning of publication in the 40s B.C. and regard Vitruvius as a late Republican, rather than an Augustan, author. Much odder is the undocumented remark of Hodge (1992) 13, that "Vitruvius Pollio . . . lived in the early first century A.D."! Surely this is a slip; no ancient evidence exists for such a bizarre dating of Vitruvius.

125. Puteoli: *CIL* 10.1614. Cumae: *CIL* 10.3707.

126. Terracina: *CIL* 10.6339. Formiae: *CIL* 10.6126.

127. Gros (1983b) 436–437. On Cocceius Nerva, see *RE* 4,1 (Stuttgart 1900) s.v., "Cocceius (12)," cols. 130–131 (F. Groag). Horace, *Sat.*

1.5.50–51 mentions Nerva's rich Campanian villa at Caudium near Capua on the via Appia.

128. Strabo, *Geog.* 5.4.5.

129. Gros (1983b) 436; Martin (1989) 57–58; see Laserre (1967) 108, n. 3. This assumption seems in part confirmed by Cassius Dio 48.50.3.

130. Gros (1983b) 438; Martin (1989) 57. On the remains at and around ancient Cumae see Amalfitano, Camodeca, & Medri (1990) 164–165, 177–179, 294–297.

131. Pearse (1974) 179–186.

132. Amianthus: *CIL* 6.10395 = *Inscr. Ital.* XIII.1,23, line 39 = Pearse (1974) no. 10, p. 180. Tychichus: *CIL* 6.8726 = *ILS* 7733 = Pearse (1974) no. 5, p. 180.

133. Ti. Claudius Eutychus, probably Julio-Claudian: *CIL* 6.9151 = Pearse (1974) no. 7, p. 180. Rusticus of the first half of the second century A.D.: *CIL* 6.8725 = Pearse (1974) no. 4, p. 180. Anicetus, dated after A.D. 161: *CIL* 6.5738 = Pearse (1974) no. 2, pp. 179–180. Narcissus, perhaps a freedman of Septimius Severus, who worked at Leptis Magna: Pearse (1974) no. 53, p. 182.

134. Brunt (1980) 82 and n. 9 asserts three important points in the evidence for the social standing of Roman architects: (1) Vitruvius exalts, perhaps even exaggerates, the profession, which was after all one for men who had to earn their living; (2) over half the civilian architects attested epigraphically were slaves or freedmen; and (3) Cato and Vitruvius do *not* suggest that gentlemen were their own architects. Opposed to his reading of the evidence, on all three points, he cites Richardson (1978a) 245–246. See also Horsfall (1988) 15–16.

135. *CIL* 10.8093 = *ILS* 5539.

136. Palmer (1983) 350.

137. Pliny, *NH* 36.24.102.

138. Pliny, *NH* 36.42; the translation given here is that of D. E. Eichholz in the Loeb edition: D. E. Eichholz, *Pliny. Natural History,* vol. 10 (London & Cambridge, Mass., 1962) 33.

139. Pearse (1974) 179 calls them "surely legendary." On the Augustan reworking, see Richardson (1976).

140. *CIL* 10.841 = *ILS* 5638a.

141. *CIL* 10.1443; cf. 1444, 1445, and 1446 = *ILS* 5637 and 5637b. Numisius is mentioned below and in much smaller lettering than the Herculanean magistrate L. Annius L. f. Mammianus Rufus, who paid for the building (or at least the orchestra).

142. Macrobius, *Sat.* 2.4.9.

143. Frontinus, *Aq.* 116–117, says specifically that the administration of the aqueduct system included *architecti, libratores,* and *plumbarii,* who

were specialists responsible for particular aspects of the construction, maintenance, and repair of the system.

144. This is argued convincingly by Pearse (1974) 42–47; cf. 103.

145. See Weaver (1972) 299–306, followed by Pearse (1974) 104 and 179–180. Examples from Rome include: Anicetus Verna (*CIL* 6.5738), Rusticus (*CIL* 6.8725), Tychicus (*CIL* 6.8726), Eutychus (*CIL* 6.9151), and Amianthus Nicanorianus (*CIL* 6.10395).

146. E.g., C. Iulius Posphorus (*CIL* 6.8724), Alcimus (*CIL* 6.33763), and C. Octavius Fructus (*AE* 1953, 57). Note also that *nomina* such as "Rabirius" are certainly not those of Imperial freedmen or slaves, and so must attest intentional appointment from the higher social classes.

147. The last speculation is Pearse's (1974) 104, who admits the total lack of supporting evidence for any such competitive placement system in Imperial architecture.

148. Tacitus, *Ann.* 15.42. The translation is based upon that of the Loeb edition, J. Jackson, *Tacitus,* vol. 4 (London & Cambridge, Mass., 1937) 278–281, as emended by MacDonald (1982) 26.

149. The case for this is made very well by MacDonald (1982) 125–126, who rightly emphasizes Tacitus's choice of words in employing *magister* "to mean architect-in-chief or master of the works." A number of sources that ought to know better, however, label Celer "architectus Neronis," e.g., *PIR²* II.619.

150. MacDonald (1982) 126.

151. *Domus Aurea:* Suetonius, *Nero* 38.1; Cassius Dio 62.16–18. Avernus canal: Pliny, *NH* 14.61. On praiseworthy architectural projects of Nero, see Suetonius, *Nero* 9, 19.2, 31.3, and 41.2.

152. Tacitus, *Ann.* 15.43. Again, the translation is taken from the Loeb edition, J. Jackson, *Tacitus,* vol. 4 (London & Cambridge, Mass., 1937) 280–283. The existence of the porticoes and of the new requirements for buildings, i.e., of Nero's attempts to inflict a fairly rigorous building code on the city, is also mentioned by Suetonius, *Nero* 16.1, who, immediately after describing these items and in the same sentence, mentions the planned canal from Lake Avernus to Ostia.

153. De Ruggiero (1895) 646–647 assigns him to *ingenuus* status because of the omission of a *cognomen;* see Pearse (1974) 176.

154. Notably MacDonald's (1982) 126–127, which waxes altogether too rhapsodic in its last paragraph, taking inference too far.

155. *CIL* 6.14647; cf. 34085. The text, inscribed—oddly enough—on the abacus of an ancient column capital, reads CELERI NERONIS AVGVSTI L., but the letters seem a good deal more recent than the capital (MacDonald [1982] 126, n. 12). Nonetheless, it cannot be completely disregarded, though seriously questioned, and is mentioned by both

Calabi Limentani (1958) 575 and Pearse (1974) 174.

156. Martial, 7.56. The translation is that of the Loeb edition: W. Ker, *Martial. Epigrams,* vol. 1 (London & Cambridge, Mass., 1947) 463. The epigram can be dated to A.D. 92 or 93 (Lugli [1960] 181–183). For a general appraisal of Rabirius as architect, see Mansuelli (1982b) 223–224.

157. *Ep.* 8.11. These hyperbolic descriptions are discussed in the intellectual context of their time by Onians (1990) 8, who connects their language and Rabirius's architecture to the philosophical thinking of Quintilian: "Domitian, who commissioned the palace, also encouraged the writing of such descriptions. Rabirius would have known that his work would be described in hyperbolic language and this can only have stimulated him in his project for a vast complex which is indeed more like a range of lofty mountains in scale, substance and profile than any previous building. Non-objective rhetorical language was apparently already having an effect on the way buildings were designed."

158. Martial, 10.71. Again the translation is that of the Loeb edition: W. Ker, *Martial. Epigrams,* vol. 2 (London & Cambridge, Mass., 1950) 209. The epigrams of Book 10 were written after Domitian's death in A.D. 96; how long after is disputed (Lugli [1960] 182–183).

159. Both De Ruggiero (1895) 645 and Calabi Limentani (1958) 575 assign Rabirius to freed status without evidence. This is refuted by Pearse (1974) 176.

160. For fine descriptions of the remains and of the architecture implied by them, see MacDonald (1982) 52–69, and Finsen (1969); for archaeological investigations since MacDonald wrote and for discussion of the topography of the remains, see Richardson (1992) 114–117. An attempt to deny Rabirius's responsiblity for the Palatine complex (Wataghin Cantano [1966]) may be dismissed. The sheer size and grandeur of the palace are well indicated by the inflated description of a banquet hall there provided by Statius (*Silvae* 4.2); for a negative ancient viewpoint, Plutarch (*Poplic.* 15.5) calls the palace "a disease of a building, and a desire, like Midas's, of turning everything to gold or stone."

161. Seven inscriptions (*CIL* 6.8640, 8647, 8648, 8649; 15.1860; *ILS* 1630, 1775) favor *Augustiana,* while five others employ *Augustana* (*CIL* 6.2271, 8651; 15.7246; *ILS* 4270, 8694). There seems no good reason for this discrepancy.

162. On the all but incredible extent of Domitian's architectural program for the city of Rome, see Anderson (1983a), accepted by Jones (1992) 79–98; also Torelli (1987) esp. 578–582.

163. On these characteristic elements, see Lugli (1938), Blake (1959) 162,

Leon (1971) 273–280, Koeppel (1980) 16–17, MacDonald (1982) 128, and Anderson (1984) 55. The warning of Leon should always be kept in mind when dealing with these details of architectural decoration: they tend to recur as decorative features in architectural entablatures of the Severans, at the beginning of the third century A.D.

164. Forum Transitorium: Anderson (1984) 133; Jupiter Capitolinus: MacDonald (1982) 127–128, and Blake (1959) 102; Venus Genetrix and Forum Julium: Anderson (1984) 55–56; the Alban villa: Blake (1959) 134. Jones (1992) 79–98 accepts all these attributions; MacDonald (1982) 127–128 also seems to favor them.

165. Anderson (1983a). Also see Jones (1992) 79–84.

166. On Domitian's and Rabirius's possible connection with the Baths of Trajan: Anderson (1985), accepted by Jones (1992) 94, but note the questions raised by DeLaine (1988) 20. On the Forum and Markets of Trajan, Anderson (1984) 147–151. The possibility that these projects were begun under Domitian and Rabirius was previously suggested by Paribeni (1943) 129–139.

167. The most important discussions of Apollodorus include Paribeni (1943), Bianchi-Bandinelli (1958), Heilmeyer (1975), MacDonald (1977) 55–51 and (1982) 129–137, and Ridley (1989). A recent dispute over whether or not he was responsible for the plan of the northwest end of Trajan's Forum—the complex of Column, libraries, and temple that eventually stretched beyond the Basilica Ulpia—has reopened this question; cf. Claridge (1993), who builds on, but criticizes, Anderson (1984) 154–159 and Boatwright (1987) 74–98, although reaching similar conclusions. *Contra:* Packer (1994) esp. 165–167.

168. Procopius, *Aed.* 4.6.12–13. It must be the same bridge that Cassius Dio describes (68.13), although Dio does not specifically attribute it to Apollodorus.

169. While it is tempting to think that Rabirius remained in his position as late as A.D. 104, there is no real proof, although it does seem likely that he was still working in the city at the time of Trajan's accession in 98. Certainly quite a number of public and Imperial officials seem to have remained in office from Domitian's reign well into Trajan's; see Waters (1969).

170. On the date of the resumption of building in Rome during Trajan's reign, see Bloch (1944) 339 and (1947) 36, 45; also Leon (1971) 47–49 and Anderson (1985) 506.

171. For this grandiose view of Apollodorus's influence, see Bianchi-Bandinelli (1950) 211–218, which is an amplification of an earlier article entitled "Una problema di arte romana: Il 'maestro delle imprese di Trajano,'" *Le arti* 1 (1938–39) 325–334. No ancient source

actually mentions the Markets. Cassius Dio (69.4) expressly credits the Forum and the Baths to Apollodorus.

172. SHA *Hadrian* 19.13.

173. Cassius Dio 69.4. The translation is that of the Loeb edition: E. Cary, *Dio's Roman History*, vol. 8 (London & Cambridge, Mass., 1968) 430–433. See the extended comments on this passage in MacDonald (1982) 132–136.

174. We do not know what odeum is referred to here, unless it is a completion or a reconstruction of that built by Domitian in the Campus Martius, near his Stadium (Suetonius, *Dom.* 5), as has been frequently suggested, e.g., MacDonald (1982) 132; Richardson (1992) 276.

175. Given the known location of the temple, this must refer to the Flavian amphitheater immediately adjacent to it; there was no theater in the vicinity. See Richardson (1992) 409–410.

176. Suggested by MacDonald (1982) 135 & n. 45, and now widely accepted.

177. On the Hadrianic phase of the temple of Amor et Roma, see Richardson (1992) 409. For photographs of what remains, see Nash (1968) 2.496–499. MacDonald (1982) 136 notes the ambiguity in the passage, and rejects outright the story of Hadrian's execution of Apollodorus; the comprehensive study of the tale by Ridley (1989), esp. 558–565, demolishes any factual basis that could be credited to it once and for all.

178. The list is given by MacDonald (1982) 134 & n. 40 with references and some merited skepticism.

179. This is asserted most determinedly by Heilmeyer (1975) although the possibility of Apollodorus's involvement in the Pantheon had earlier been suggested by Bloch (1947) 116. It is doubtful, however, that Apollodorus enjoyed favor for very long, if at all, once Hadrian became emperor, and the Pantheon seems to have been under construction for the entire first decade of his reign, judging from the datable brick stamps found in its fabric (Bloch [1947] 14–19, 102–117); but see Haselberger (1994) 296–303: "Exkurs zur datierung des Pantheon," who attempts to date the beginning of its construction somewhat earlier. Apollodorus's participation in its creation must have been minor at best, nor does the architecture of the building really accord as well with other buildings attributed to him (despite the comparisons suggested by Heilmeyer [1975] 335–341) as it does with other creations often attributed to Hadrian himself, e.g., the various domed buildings at the villa near Tivoli.

180. In a letter to the younger Pliny during his governorship of Bithynia, Trajan wrote that most of the architects practicing in Italy at the time came from Greece (Pliny, *Ep.* 10.40). Unfortunately, the epigraphical

evidence is insufficient either to confirm or to deny this; perhaps Trajan was thinking of Apollodorus (and whatever workshop he may have brought with him to Rome)?

181. Pliny, *Ep.* 9.39. The dating of the later letters of Pliny is disputed, but the most widely accepted suggestion is that they were published ca. A.D. 108–109; see W. M. L. Hutchinson in the introduction to the Loeb edition of Pliny's letters (London & Cambridge, Mass., 1952), xvi; cf. R. Syme, "The Dating of Pliny's Latest Letters," *CQ* 35 (1985) 176–185, reprinted in A. R. Birley, ed., *Sir Ronald Syme, Roman Papers,* vol. 5 (Oxford 1988) 478–489. On Mustius, see Martin (1989) 40.

182. The main textual sources are the passage of Cassius Dio (69.4) quoted above (Venus and Rome) and SHA *Hadrian* 19.9 (temple of Deified Trajan), 19.10 (Pantheon), 19.11 (Mausoleum and Pons Aelius). See further the list given by Richardson (1992) 455.

183. Cassius Dio 69.3.2.

184. SHA *Hadrian* 14.8.11.

185. SHA *Hadrian* 19.12.

186. SHA *Commodus* 17.5; see Pearse (1974) 45.

187. P. *Oxyr.* 3.39. no. 412, lines 59–68. For discussion of the so-called bibliotheca Panthei built by Julius Africanus, see Lundström (1912) and the response by Boëthius (1930); also Richardson (1992) 59.

188. Burkert (1992). This intriguing suggestion cannot be regarded as proven.

189. In his *De Aedificiis;* Briggs (1927) 50–52. See further Pearse (1974) 185.

190. Procopius, *Aed.* 1.1.23–26; the translation is taken from the Loeb edition: H. Dewing and G. Downey, *Procopius,* vol. 7 (London & Cambridge, Mass., 1954) 10–13.

191. The suggestion is made by MacDonald (1977) 53–56 in an excellent brief treatment of Anthemius. See also Huxley (1959) on Anthemius's mathematical achievements and renown.

Chapter 2: The Organization of Building in Ancient Rome

1. The only satisfactory general treatments of Roman building contracts are those by S. Martin (1982), which deals specifically with building contracts in Roman law, and (1989) esp. pp. 19–41. I am deeply indebted to her excellent studies throughout this chapter.

2. The singular importance of the contract system in Roman building, as in many other areas of endeavor during the Republican period, is clearly demonstrated by Badian (1972) esp. 11–21, and corroborated by Brunt (1990) esp. 357–360. The evidence for contractors in both

public and private building during the Republic is collected by Pearse (1974) pp. 1–31.

3. These are collected and analyzed by Martin (1982) esp. 15–27; see also Martin (1989) 22–39.
4. *ILLRP* 518 = *ILS* 5317.
5. *ILLRP* 465, 465a, 466 = *ILS* 5799.
6. Cato, *De Agr.* 14.1–15. Goujard (1975) 24–25 for text and translation into French and 164–169 for commentary on the passage.
7. Cicero, *Verr. II* 1.50–58.
8. On the antiquity of *stipulatio,* see Watson (1965) 1–6.
9. See the discussion in Martin (1982) 15.
10. The text in Latin reads: "Insulam intra biennium illo loco aedificare spondes?" "Spondeo." Obviously the question would be revised to suit the specifics of the job being contracted in each case.
11. See Martin (1982) 15–16 and (1989) 22–29.
12. For building site, see *Digest* 13.4.2.5, and Martin (1982) 17; and for completion date, *Digest* 45.1.73 pr., and Martin (1982) 18.
13. Martin (1989) 20–21.
14. Martin (1982) 19 and (1989) 29, esp. nn. 36 and 38.
15. Martin (1989) 30.
16. Ulpian 17 *ad ed.* = *Digest* 6.1.39, confimed by Paul 34 *ad ed.* = *Digest* 19.2.22.2.
17. Paul 2 *ad ed.* = *Digest* 50.16.1. On liabilities during the term of the contract, Martin (1989) 89–102.
18. Such a *probatio,* though an interim one, seems to be described by Cicero, *ad Q. frat.* 3.1.1–2, as we have seen in chapter 1, above; see also Martin (1989) 54. For a detailed discussion of *probatio operis,* see Martin (1989) 103–113.
19. Cato, *De Agr.* 14.1–5. I quote the translation of W. D. Hooper and H. B. Ash in the Loeb edition: *Marcus Porcius Cato, On Agriculture* (London and Cambridge, Mass., 1936) 28–31.
20. I employ the texts as edited by A. DeGrassi, *ILLRP* nos. 465 and 465a (pp. 262–264). The via Caecilia was built by L. Caecilius Metellus, consul in 117 B.C. It turned off from the via Salaria, which ran north from Rome, at the 35th milestone (as the inscription records) where the Salaria crossed the river Farfarus, then ran through Amiternum to the Adriatic. These contracts for repairs to it are from the early first century B.C., possibly during the dictatorship of Sulla.
21. See Badian (1972) 136, n. 7 on this unusual term.
22. *ILLRP* 518 = *ILS* 5317. The earliest, and still the most comprehensive, study of it is Wiegand (1894). Also Pearse (1974) 13.
23. Wiegand (1894) 679, who is followed by Pearse (1974) 13 and

n. 103. *Contra:* Badian (1972) 136–137 and nn. 6, 8, accepted by Brunt (1990) 363 without discussion.

24. Cicero, *ad Att.* 12.18.1. Pearse (1974) 20.

25. Cicero, *ad Att.* 12.36.2. On the whole story of Tullia's *fanum,* see Shackleton-Bailey (1965–70), vol. 5, 404–413.

26. See examples given in Pearse (1974) 22–27.

27. Martin (1989) 46; also Rawson (1976) 85–100. For an intriguing essay on the whole question of city versus country property as investments for wealthy Romans, see Garnsey (1976).

28. On repairing Quintus's house in Rome and supervising his property at Arpinum, see Cicero, *ad Q. frat.* 2.4.2 and 3.1.1–2.

29. *Insulae: ad Att.* 12.32.2 and 15.26.4. *Tabernae: ad Att.* 13.45.2–3, 13.46.3, 14.9.1; also Martin (1989) 46, 50. On Cicero's rental property in general, see Frier (1978) esp. 4–5.

30. On the need to maintain a small staff of repairmen, see Varro, *Re Rust.* 1.17.3; also the passage of Ulpian contained in *Digest* 33.7.12.5 on the organization of larger estates. In general on the question of contracting for skilled builders, see Burford (1971) 59–60; Pearse (1974) 27.

31. Pliny, *NH* 9.79.168. Rawson (1976) 100–101.

32. Plutarch, *Crassus* 2.4–5. The translation is that of the Loeb edition: B. Perrin, *Plutarch's Lives,* vol. 3 (London and Cambridge, Mass., 1916) 317.

33. Crassus's interest in the whole scam is often thought to have been rapid rebuilding and resale of the torched property. For further comment, see Loane (1938) 81–82 and Martin (1989) 47 and n. 15.

34. Slaves: *CIL* 6.6363–6365 and 6283–6285. Freedmen: *CIL* 6.6354 and 9405. *Faber,* whose status cannot be determined: *CIL* 6.9412–9415. See More (1969) chap. 4; Martin (1989) 64.

35. Gardens: Tacitus, *Ann.* 12.59; Richardson (1992) 204. Amphitheater: Suetonius, *Aug.* 29.5 and *Cal.* 18; Tacitus, *Ann.* 3.72; Strabo, *Geog.* 5.3.8; Cassius Dio 51.23, 62.18; Richardson (1992) 11, who would locate it "east of via Lata near the south end of Piazza SS. Apostoli." See also Martin (1989) 64, n. 95.

36. See D'Arms (1980) 155–156; Martin (1989) 65.

37. Some examples are Pliny, *Ep.* 2.17, 5.6, 9.7; see Martin (1989) 47.

38. Meiggs (1973) 68–69, 76, 134, 139, 595. Martin (1989) 47–48.

39. Polybius 6.13.3. The two primary studies of the administration of public building during the republic are Strong (1968) 97–103 and Pearse (1974) 1–16.

40. Livy 4.22.7; Pearse (1974) 1.

41. This is asserted strongly by Badian (1972) 15–16 and accepted by Pearse (1974) 1–2.
42. Livy 6.32.1. It is notable that the terms Livy employs to describe this event are specifically contractual—the letting of the contract is referred to as *locatum faciundum*—although such terminology is perhaps anachronistic, reflecting legal usage in Livy's own day rather than in 378 B.C., as was suggested by Frank (1933) 102; but *contra*, and in defense of Livy's accuracy in employing this terminology, see Badian (1972) 15–16.
43. See Suolahti (1963) 57–66 on censors' letting of public contracts. On censorial building contracts, see Strong (1968) 97–100 and, especially important, Astin (1990) 22–24, 31–35.
44. Festus 120L. Further see Boëthius (1945) 94–95; Astin (1990) 23.
45. Frontinus, *Aq.* 5. The translation given here is that of Ashby (1935) 49. The other important sources for the tale are Livy 9.29, Diodorus 20.36.4, and Eutropius 2.9; the shenanigans of Appius are used as an *exemplum* of double-dealing by Cicero (*Cael.* 34). That it was Appius Claudius's co-censor, G. Plautius, who had actually identified the springs from which the aqueduct was to be drawn is confirmed by *CIL* 11.1827.
46. Frontinus, *Aq.* 6; also Astin (1990) 23. The two men were Curius Dentatus and Fulvius Flaccus; Dentatus died soon after his appointment as *duumvir,* and Flaccus completed the aqueduct on his own. Frontinus, incidentally, gets both the date of commencement of construction on the Anio Vetus and the name of one of the consuls of the year, wrong; see Ashby (1935) 54–55 and n. 7, confirmed by Broughton (1952) 1.198.
47. Livy, *Epit.* 20; Festus 89 M. On the history and form of the Circus Flaminius, see Wiseman (1974) and (1976); also Richardson (1992) 83, and A. Viscogliosi in Steinby (1993b) 269–272.
48. Frank (1933) 24 provides a list of these references. Badian (1972) 27–29 and esp. 31 emphasizes, rightly, that there is evidence for more building work in Republican Rome than that let by the censors and that it was normal practice for various magistrates, notably the aediles, to let building contracts.
49. For Camillus's temple, see Livy 5.23.7. For Carvilius's temple, see Livy 10.46.14.
50. Livy 7.28.5. See Strong (1968) 99.
51. Livy 40.44.10.
52. The references are often little more than brief notes and sometimes difficult to date precisely, but we can probably include Livy 10.33.9 (307 B.C.), 10.23.12 (296 B.C.), 10.31.9 (295 B.C.), *Per.* 19 and 24.26.19 (246 B.C.). Similar references from sources other than Livy

for such public projects up to the Second Punic War include Varro, *L. L.* 5.15.8, and Pliny, *NH* 18.286 (241 B.C.). This list is from Pearse (1974) chap. 1, n. 14, who notes that Livy and the other authors tend to use the vocabulary we associate with contracting and suggests that it is therefore reasonable to assume that these projects were all let out on contract to private builders.

53. Livy 33.42.10.
54. Livy 35.10.12. Further see Etienne (1987) and Richardson (1992) 143–144 for the Emporium; Richardson (1992) 311–312 for the two *porticus*.
55. Livy 35.41.10.
56. Dionysius of Halicarnassus, *Ant. Rom.* 3.67. Strong (1968) 97.
57. Plutarch, *Cato,* 19; Livy 39.44.8. Strong (1968) 98, Badian (1972) 36–37, and Pearse (1974) 4–5.
58. Livy 40.46.16 for the money allocated, and 40.51.1–7 for the various building projects, including the aborted aqueduct and the basilica.
59. Dionysius of Halicarnassus, *Ant. Rom.* 3.67.5 (quoting C. Acilius).
60. Livy 40.44.8–10 for vow and appointment of *duumviri*, and 42.10.5 for the dedication.
61. Livy 43.16.2. See Pearse (1974) 5–6 and n. 43.
62. Strong (1968) 97–98.
63. Appian, *BellCiv* 1.28.125; Velleius 1.15.3.
64. E.g., in 184 B.C. Cato let the contract for the basilica, while Valerius took sole responsibility for contracting for road paving; Dionysius of Halicarnassus, *Ant. Rom.* 3.67. For the mutual letting of contracts in 169 B.C., see Livy 44.16.9.
65. *ILLRP* 518 = *ILS* 5317.
66. On Gaius's public works, see Plutarch, *C. Gracchus,* 6.3; Appian, *BellCiv* 98. Strong (1968) 100 emphasizes the importance of these examples.
67. On the Capitoline temple, see Valerius Maximus 9.3.8 and Tacitus, *Hist.* 3.72.; also Pliny, *NH* 7.138; Richardson (1992) 222–223. For the Tabularium, see *CIL* 6.1313, 1314 = *ILS* 35, 35a = *ILLRP* 367, 368; Richardson (1992) 376–377. On Sulla's plans for the Forum, see Van Deman (1922).
68. A good example, if highly rhetorically colored, is the injustice arranged by Verres in 74 B.C., during his praetorship, to defraud the heir of the deceased contractor who had accepted the last contract for maintaining and repairing the temple of Castor in the Forum; Cicero, *Verr. II* 1.3.
69. On the theater, see Plutarch, *Pompey,* 42.4, 52; Cassius Dio 39.38.1–6; Richardson (1992) 383–385. On Venus Victrix, see Gellius 10.1.7; Tertullian, *De Spect.* 10; Richardson (1992) 411.

70. On Caesar's Forum, see Anderson (1984) 39–64, esp. 39–47; cf. Ulrich (1993) esp. 52–56, 80. On the Saepta, see Richardson (1992) 340–341, also 98, on its assumption of functions formerly located at the Comitium.

71. Cicero, *ad Att.* 13.35.1; the translation is that of Shackleton-Bailey (1965–1970), 5.220–221 (no. 330). Shackleton-Bailey suggests a date of ca. 9 July for the letter's composition.

72. On the city plan, see also Cicero, *ad Att.* 13.20.1; also Duret & Néraudeau (1983) 46–47 and Stambaugh (1988) 43–45. For a general statement of what Caesar was doing to redefine the public works administration, see Strong (1968) 102.

73. Suetonius, *Aug.* 29; see Shipley (1931).

74. Suetonius, *Aug.* 29.4–30.1; Strong (1968) 103; Stambaugh (1988) 48–66.

75. Cassius Dio 53.22.1–2. See Pearse (1974) 40.

76. Cassius Dio 49.16.

77. Frontinus, *Aq.* 98–99; Cassius Dio 48.32.3. Further see Ashby (1935) 11–12; Evans (1982).

78. On the number of staff on Agrippa's water board, see Frontinus, *Aq.* 115. For other evidence concerning the vastness of Agrippa's staff, see *CIL* 6.537; *CIL* 8.14564 and 14580. See Roddaz & Fabre (1982); also Bruun (1991) 190.

79. Suetonius, *Aug.* 37. Roads: Cassius Dio 54.8. Water: Frontinus, *Aq.* 100–101, 104, 106, 108, 125, 127. See further Bruun (1991) 141–142.

80. Strong (1968) 104–105.

81. *CIL* 6.3154–3155.

82. Tacitus, *Ann.* 15.43; Suetonius, *Nero* 16, 38, 39.

83. *CIL* 6.9034. See Robinson (1992) 21.

84. Pearse (1974) 32, 40; Brunt (1990) esp. 355–356.

85. On Frontinus's life, see Grimal (1961) vi–xvi; Birley (1981) 69–72; Bruun (1991) 10–11; Hodge (1992) 16–18; and Evans (1994) 53–56.

86. Frontinus, *Aq.* 98.3–99.1 *(familia publica);* 116.3–4, 117.1–3 *(familia Caesaris).* The text of Frontinus I employ is that of Grimal (1961). See also Aubert (1993) 174 and n. 34. Both Ashby (1935) 24 and Bruun (1991) 190, n. 3, speculate that the number would not have been exactly 700, which seems to represent 50 water workers for each of the 14 regions into which Augustus had divided the city of Rome in 7 B.C. (Suetonius, *Aug.* 30; Cassius Dio 55.8.7), because those regions were of very different sizes. But even if large regions required more than 50 men, in point of fact this could have been balanced by

assigning fewer men to the smaller or outlying regions. There seems no real reason to doubt Frontinus's accuracy.

87. Frontinus, *Aq.* 117; Brunt (1980) 84–85. Bruun (1991) 190–191 demonstrates that the epigraphical record supports Frontinus's list.

88. In the senatorial decree of 11 B.C. (Frontinus, *Aq.* 100.1) the *curator aquarum* is supposed to be allotted only one architect, but elsewhere Frontinus regularly mentions more than one (e.g. at *Aq.* 119.3). Perhaps the number was increased during the first century A.D.. See Bruun (1991) 193–194, and Evans (1994) 63–64.

89. N.B., Frontinus, *Aq.* 101.2, where the *apparitores* are said not to have been doing their job. See Purcell (1983) 129, 131; also Brunt (1980) 84, who asserts that all such "office staff" were free or freed.

90. Frontinus, *Aq.* 25, where the *libratores* and *plumbarii* are mentioned as if of equal status with *architecti*. Bruun (1991) 193 classifies *libratores* as members of the servile *familia aquarum,* rather than as free 'or freedmen, but does not explain his reason for this; he does not mention the *plumbarii*.

91. Frontinus, *Aq.* 119.3.

92. Frontinus, *Aq.* 96.

93. Frontinus, *Aq.* 119.4: *aestimet . . . quae per redemptores effici debeant, quae per domesticos artifices;* also 124.4: *redemptores . . . ad rivos reficiendos.*

94. On the maps, see Frontinus, *Aq.* 17.2–4. Earlier in his career, Frontinus had written a monograph on mapmaking, called *De arte mensoria,* which survives in fragments in the *Corpus agrimensorum* (C. O. Thulin, ed., *Corpus Agrimensorum Romanorum* [Leipzig 1913]). The best discussion of Frontinus's mapping of the aqueducts is Evans (1994) 58–61.

95. Pearse (1974) 41–42 and nn. 72 and 73.

96. The statistical method for calculating such information proposed by Thornton (1986) and embellished by Thornton & Thornton (1989) is largely useless (see the review of the latter in *AJA* 94 [1990] 515, and the comments of Bruun [1991] 197, n. 34).

97. Brunt (1990) 354: "Rome relied on private contractors working for profit . . . for the construction and upkeep of public buildings." He provides an excellent overview of the evidence for the *publicani* of Republican times, pp. 357–360.

98. Pliny, *NH* 36.24.107.

99. Livy 23.48.10 (*qui redempturis auxissent patrimonia*) describes the men. The contract story follows immediately at 23.49.1–4.

100. For the senate's action, see Livy 25.3.12; the individual *publicanus,*

25.3.9. On the whole story, and especially the senate's action, see Badian (1972) 18–19; also Pearse (1974) 3–4.

101. Some examples include Luke 5:27 and 19:1; Matthew 9:9; Mark 2:16.

102. The best modern treatment of the whole phenomenon of the Roman *publicani* is Badian (1972). His first chapter (pp. 11–25) provides an essential introduction to the subject. Also see Brunt (1990), who accepts most of Badian's work and extends the study of *publicani* into the Empire.

103. See Frank (1933) 183–185 for a chronological list of these contracts.

104. Livy 39.44.5–8; Plutarch, *Cato* 19.

105. Badian (1972) 37. *Contra:* Pearse (1974) 4–5.

106. Livy 39.44.1.

107. Livy 43.16.1–16, esp. 1–4.

108. Livy 43.16.2.

109. Badian (1972) 49. This was also the view of Finley (1973) 49–50 and was accepted by Pearse (1974) 6.

110. Livy 35.10.12 (Emporium), 35.41.10 (portico for timber dealers).

111. Livy 45.15.9.

112. Badian (1972) 37, 70.

113. Pearse (1974) 9 provides the best and clearest description I have encountered of these associations.

114. Polybius 6.17.2–5. The translation is that of the Loeb edition: W. R. Paton, *Polybius, The Histories*, vol. 3 (London and Cambridge, Mass., 1923) 307–310.

115. Pearse (1974) 10 and n. 72.

116. Appian, *BellCiv* 1.23; Plutarch, *C. Gracchus* 6.3–4.

117. This was the view of Wiegand (1894) 679. *Contra:* Badian (1972) 68, who would see them as additional sureties, despite the very clear statement that Blossius would serve in that role himself. On Blossius, see Martin (1989) 53, 131.

118. Cicero, *Verr. II* 1.49.127–128. On the legal and contractual implications of this episode, see Martin (1989) 53, 132.

119. Cicero, *Verr. II* 1.50.130 for the name; 1.52.137 for the equestrian relations; 1.58.151 for the description *homo de plebe Romana*; also Martin (1989) 132–133.

120. Cicero, *Verr. II* 1.57.150.

121. This is suggested by Pearse (1974) 11–12, based on his reading of Cicero's remark (*Verr. II* 1.57.150) that Verres had not gotten around to carrying out his *probatio operis* until four years after the date initially fixed for completion, and *hac condicione, si quis de populo redemptor accesisset, non esset usus.*

122. *ILS* 6085.49. Also Cicero, *Phil IX* 7.16 and *Phil XIV* 14.38.

123. Frontinus, *Aq.* 96. The translation is that of the Loeb edition: C. E. Bennett, *Frontinus. The Stratagems and the Aqueducts of Rome* (London and Cambridge, Mass., 1940) 425.
124. Frontinus, *Aq.* 119.
125. Badian (1972) 127, n. 33; Pearse (1974) 16.
126. Cicero, *ad Q. frat.* 2.4.2: *Redemptori tuo dimidium pecuniae curavi.* On Marcus's own projects, see *ad Q. frat.* 2.5.1.
127. Cicero, *ad Q. frat.* 2.6.3: *Res agebantur multis structoribus. Longilium redemptorem cohortatus sum; fidem mihi faciebat se velle nobis placere.* Further see Pearse (1974) 22–23 and Martin (1989) 53–54.
128. Longilius's social rank is established, insofar as possible, by Pearse (1974) 22. The *forma* is mentioned by Cicero, *ad Q. frat.* 2.5.4.; cf. 2.2.1–2. Pearse (1974) 23 suggests Numisius or Cyrus as the architect; Martin (1989) 54 mentions Cyrus.
129. Cicero, *ad Q. frat.* 3.3.1 and 3.2.3. Apparently there had been delays, since Marcus had told Quintus that he hoped everything would be done by the previous winter (*ad Q. frat.* 2.4.2).
130. Pearse (1974) 23. He does not explain how he arrives at this conclusion.
131. Cicero, *ad Q. frat.* 3.1.1.
132. I follow Pearse (1974) 23–24 in his analysis of the situation described in this letter. Treggiari (1969) 99 labeled Cillo a "master contractor (and) labourer" and asserts that he "held the contract and was in charge of operations," neither of which is stated or implied in the letter. Martin (1989) 55 and n. 51, is cautious. Shackleton-Bailey (1980) 205 suggested that Cillo was a freedman who continued to work with his former fellow slaves as an explanation for the term *conservos.* This seems both reasonable and helpful.
133. Cicero, *ad Q. frat.* 3.1.5. I accompany the majority of scholars here in considering Nicephorus a *servus;* see Shackleton-Bailey (1980) 206, Martin (1989) 55, n. 53, and the various references they give. Treggiari (1969) 107 and Pearse (1974) 25 both assume he was a *libertus,* presuming that a slave could not contract with his master. But that is a disputable contention, and the evidence of other *vilici* points toward the opposite conclusion.
134. Cicero, *ad Q. frat.* 3.1.1–2. This analysis of the situation is Martin's (1989) 54. *Contra:* Pearse (1974) 19–20, who deemed Diphilus an architect, as did Shackleton-Bailey (1980) 203. Loane (1938) 86 thought Caesius an architect who was also serving as *redemptor,* a suggestion rejected by Martin (1989) 54–55, n. 48.
135. On these points, see Martin's excellent summary (1989) 56–57. For an ancient depiction of pouring *opus caementicium,* see Adam (1984) 87 (the tomb of Trebius Iustus); especially important discussions of

this building material and its implications for Roman architecture are Rakob (1976) and Lamprecht (1984).

136. Narcissus: Tacitus, *Ann.* 12.57; Cassius Dio 60.33.5. On the unusual nature of his role and appointment, see Brunt (1980) 85.

137. Horace, *Ep.* 2.2.72–73. The translation is mine; the Latin text reads:

    festinat calidus mulis gerulisque redemptor
    torquet nunc lapidem, nunc ingens machina tignum.

138. I am indebted for this list, and for much of the relevant information, to Pearse (1974) 31–38.

139. In addition to the inscriptions discussed, other Imperial examples that mention *redemptores* are: IRT 275 (M. Vipsanius Clemens), *CIL* 9.3650 (C. Albius Torquatus), *CIL* 11.4127 = *ILS* 6027 (Q. Parfidius Primus), *CIL* 6.9794 = *ILS* 7672 (P. Cornelius P. l. Philomusus), *CIL* 6.33873 (Q. Casius Artema), *CIL* 10.3821 = *ILS* 3662 (Lucceius Peculiaris), *CIL* 6.9852a, b (P. Turpilius A. l. Phronimus and P. Turpilius A. l. Niger), and *CIL* 9.4694 (P. Mucius Nedymus).

140. See chap. 1. The inscriptions are *CIL* 10.3707 from Cumae, and *CIL* 10.1614 from Puteoli; also see Strabo, *Geog.* 5.4.5. Cocceius may have founded a family firm; *CIL* 10.6697 mentions a Cocceius involved in the building trade during the reign of Hadrian.

141. *CIL* 14.2091.

142. *AE* 1940.16 = *ILTunisie* 732. See Pearse (1974) 35 for the dating; Martin (1989) 58–59 on the Latin usage.

143. *CIL* 15.7150. On the games, Tacitus, *Ann.* 13.22.

144. *CIL* 10.1549. On *contubernium*, see De Ruggiero (1895) s.v., *contubernium*.

145. *CIL* 14.3530 = *Inscr. Ital.* IV, 1, no. 611 = *ILS* 3512. See *CIL* 14, p. 364 where Dessau discusses the original find spot. Also see Martin (1989) 58.

146. *AE* 1925, 87. First reported at *NSA* 1924, 348. Loane (1938) 83, n. 84, called him "a former slave in the imperial household," but this is not stated on the inscription. It is just possible that he was the son of a *libertus* of Claudius, but this is doubtful. The old-fashioned translation of *intestinarius* as "cabinet maker" can be dispensed with.

147. *CIL* 6.9034. See Martin (1989) 59.

148. *CIL* 6.607. On the reliefs, see Castagnoli (1941); Coarelli (1979) 266–267; Steinby (1983) 220; Kleiner (1992) 196–199. On the possibility of a precursor to the Arch of Constantine being represented, see Frothingham (1912) 378–380; the identification has been rejected by almost all contemporary commentators (e.g., from

Walton [1924] to DeMaria [1988] 294–295) but has recently been reasserted on the evidence from testing of marble samples from the monument (Pensabene [1988]) and from recent soundings beneath, and investigations of the internal fabric of, the monument by the Istituto Centrale del Restauro (Steiner & Melucco Vaccaro [1994]). The debate continues: much of the alleged evidence for this precursor to the Constantinian arch has now been refuted by Panella et al. (1995). For the identification of the family with Q. Haterius Antoninus, see Coarelli (1979) 266–269.

149. Martin (1989) 60.

150. Pearse (1974) 39. This difference between the *publicani* of the Republic and the *redemptores* of the Empire in all fields of contracting is well emphasized by Brunt (1990) 361–422, who asserts convincingly that private contractors continued to function in the Roman system well into the time of the Severans, if not beyond, but became more restricted in function and in latitude throughout the Empire because of the encroachments of, and supervision by, the Imperial bureaucracy.

151. Frontinus, *Aq.* 117.

152. Pearse (1974) 55–56.

153. Pearse (1974) 57. See further Dilke (1971).

154. *Tectores:* Varro, *Re Rust.* 3.2.9; Vitruvius 7.10.2; Ulpian in the *Digest* 13.6.5.7. *Structores* as builders: Cicero, *ad Att.* 4.3.2; *Phil.* 1.12. *Structores* and food: Petronius, *Satyr.* 35.2.

155. The best discussion of *fabri* and *fabri tignariorum* is that of Martin (1989) 62–72, which I follow here. On the training of *fabri,* see Cicero, *Planc.* 62; Columella 11.1.5; Vitruvius 2.1.6; and the *Digest* 17.1.26.8.

156. Seneca, *Nat.* 6.30.4.

157. Gellius 19.10.2–4. The translation is that of the Loeb edition: J. C. Rolfe, *The Attic Nights of Aulus Gellius,* vol. 3 (London and Cambridge, Mass., 1928) 387.

158. On ancient evidence for architects' models, see Benndorf (1902); Ettlinger (1977) 109; Packer (1996) chap. 7, esp. n. 2.

159. *CIL* 6.6283–6285 and 6363–6365 (slaves); 6354 (freedman).

160. Martin (1989) 64 and n. 94.

161. Onesimus = *CIL* 6.9034; Thallus = *CIL* 6.148, 10299 and 30703; Haterius Euagogus = *CIL* 6.9408. On the *collegium,* see More (1969) and Pearse (1974) 100–123. My treatment is deeply indebted to Martin (1989) 65–68.

162. On the *collegium* at Ostia, see Meiggs (1973) 319–321; Pearse (1974) chap. 5; Martin (1989) 67–68.

Chapter 3: Supplying the Roman Building Industry

1. The essential research on labor supply in the Roman world is the work of P. A. Brunt (1971), (1974) and, focussed specifically on public works and the building industry, (1980). Brunt's analyses have been seriously challenged only once, with little success, by Casson (1978), and are now widely accepted as definitive. Brunt's work deals primarily with the evidence for the city—(1974) and (1980) are exclusively concerned with Rome—yet also surveys the remainder of Roman Italy (1971). The urban evidence is also treated by Treggiari (1980), who generally confirms Brunt's analyses.

2. This is the figure accepted by Brunt (1971) 376–388, esp. 383, and it has been asserted frequently both before and since; cf. Anderson (1991) 9 and n. 33; also Purcell (1994) 648–650. Other readings are certainly possible.

3. The post-Augustan population of Rome must be surmised from evidence such as estimates of population in other Imperial cities like Ostia (cf. Packer [1967] 80–83) or from dubious textual evidence such as the fourth century A.D. regionary catalogues (cf. Hermansen [1978]).

4. Sallust, *Cat.* 37.4–5, 7. The translation is that of the Loeb edition: J. C. Rolfe, *Sallust* (London and Cambridge, Mass., 1921) 62–65.

5. E.g., Suetonius, *Aug.* 42; Appian, *BellCiv* 2.120. See comments by Brunt (1974) 90, and the admirably balanced discussion of Purcell (1994) 650–654.

6. The discussion that follows is based directly on Brunt (1974) 87–90, and (1980) esp. 92–97. *Contra:* Casson (1978) esp. 46–48, effectively countered by Brunt (1980) esp. 84. See Skydsgaard (1983) who takes Brunt's side.

7. Frontinus, *Aq.* 96.

8. Ibid., 123.

9. Cato, *De Agr.* 39.2.2–3 and 5.2, in which the landowner is strongly advised not to keep excess hands, but to hire them on for special needs, including building.

10. On slaves attached to building contractors, see Loane (1938) 79–85, Brunt (1980) 93, and Martin (1989) 43–44. These slaves were often, perhaps usually, skilled workers rather than unskilled laborers: see Ulpian (28 *ad ed.*) = *Digest* 13.6.5.7 who mentions a slave *tector.*

11. *Digest* 45.1.137.3. The translation here is that used by Brunt (1980) 87, who also offers a convincing analysis of the passage which I have followed.

12. On free vs. slave labor in construction, and on the episodic nature of demand for building workers, see Martin (1989) 69–71. Brunt

(1980) 96, discussing how such free laborers were hired, suggests that the contractor "could well have kept down the wages of workers from the *plebs frumentaria* to the level that would give them an essential supplement to the grain doles and *congiaria* supplied by the public purse."

13. The evidence, such as it is, for hiring of nonslave labor in Roman Italy is treated by Garnsey (1980b) and Skydsgaard (1980), and their evidence offers convincing confirmation for Brunt's views. Whittaker (1980) has analyzed the limited evidence from Africa, Asia, and Gaul. By far the most convincing demonstration that Brunt's model for the hiring of nonslave labor is applicable well beyond Rome itself is provided by Curchin (1986) in his analysis of hiring practices in Roman Hispania.

14. Tiberius Gracchus: Boren (1957–58), also Brunt (1974) 90. Cicero: *ad Att.* 14.3.1, and Brunt (1974) 90; *contra* Casson (1978) 47, the legitimacy of whose objection on this passage is conceded by Brunt (1980) 81.

15. Suetonius, *Vesp.* 18. The translation is that of the Loeb edition: J. C. Rolfe, *Suetonius,* vol. 2 (London and Cambridge, Mass., 1914) 310–313. For the dispute over interpretation of the passage, see Casson (1978) esp. 47–50, and Brunt (1980) esp. 81–84; also Skydsgaard (1983) esp. 225–226.

16. Cassius Dio 66.10.2. The translation is that used by Brunt (1980) 81.

17. Brunt (1980) 91–92, who summarizes: "We cannot expect inscriptions to reveal unskilled labourers who could have worked for daily hire."

18. The evidence of the jurists is collected and discussed by Brunt (1980) 88–91.

19. Pliny, *NH* bks. 12–17: 12, plane trees; 13, trees of Asia and Africa; 14, vines and wine; 15, olive and fruit trees; 16, forest trees; 17, cultivated trees. On his various errors and confusions, see Meiggs (1982) 24–25. Strabo, *Geog.* bks. 5–6. Vitruvius 2.9. N.B. also, Polybius's description of Cisalpine Gaul (2.15–16), which gives further information about forests in that area. Meiggs's magisterial study (1982) of timber in the Mediterranean world is the essential source on this topic, to which I am indebted throughout this treatment. On the Italian forests, see Meiggs (1982) 243–247.

20. Livy 9.36.1; the translation is Meiggs's (1982) 246. See also Florus 1.12.3.

21. Strabo, *Geog.* 5.2.5; the translation is that of the Loeb edition: H. L. Jones, *The Geography of Strabo,* vol. 2 (London and Cambridge, Mass., 1922) 353.

22. Meiggs (1982) 286–292.

23. Mentioned by Theophrastus, *HP* 5.8.1, as well as by Pliny, *NH* 16.71. Cf. Meiggs (1980) 190–191. Meiggs's article on sea-borne trade in timber to Rome (1980) is an important corollary to his book.

24. The trees of Liguria were praised by Strabo, *Geog.* 4.2 (202); the Sila forest is described by Dionysius of Halicarnassus, *Ant. Rom.* 20.15.

25. Dionysius of Halicarnassus, *Ant. Rom.* 1.37.4; the translation is that of Meiggs (1982) 243. Dionysius seems to be supported by Strabo, *Geog.* 6.4.1 (286). However, *contra:* Brunt (1971) 128–129, who thinks these descriptions wildly exaggerated.

26. Vitruvius 2.9.15–16.

27. Pliny, *NH* 16.76.200; the translation is that of the Loeb edition: H. Rackham, *Pliny, Natural History,* vol. 4 (London and Cambridge, Mass., 1945) 519, with the erroneous "deck of the Naval Sham Fight" corrected to "bridge of the Naumachia."

28. Meiggs (1980) 191–192; also (1982) 249.

29. Tacitus, *Ann.* 13.31.8; Calpurnius Siculus 7.23.

30. Cassius Dio 55.8.4.

31. Meiggs (1982) 219. Also essential to understanding the use and working of wood in Roman architecture is Adam (1984) 91–105; a good general survey of the evidence is Richmond (1961). One of these early huts, called the "Casa Romuli," was restored in its original form as a shrine during the time of Augustus: Vergil, *Aen.* 8.654; Vitruvius 2.1.5; Dionysius of Halicarnassus, *Ant. Rom.* 1.79.11; Cassius Dio 54.29.8. Also Boëthius (1978) 22–23.

32. For the Pons Sublicius: Pliny, *NH* 36.100, and Richardson (1992) 299. Forum Boarium temples: Gjerstad (1953–73) vol. 4.1, 399; Richardson (1992) 155, 246. Capitoline temple: Vitruvius 3.3.5 (on the wooden architraves); Gjerstad (1953–73) vol. 3, 108–190 and vol. 4.1, 168–207; Boëthius (1978) 111–112; Meiggs (1982) 221; Richardson (1992) 221–224.

33. Livy 5.41.7. On the lack of archaeological evidence: Boëthius (1978) 75–94; on the possible anachronism: Meiggs (1982) 221–222. Vitruvius 2.1.1–7 provides a general summary of the development of construction techniques and styles during the early centuries of Rome.

34. In general, Meiggs (1982) 223–227 on these developments. On the *porticus inter lignarios,* see Livy 35.41.10 and 40.51.6, and Richardson (1992) 314 and 143–144; for the form of the basilica: Boëthius (1978) 149–150.

35. On the development of concrete, see Rakob (1976) and Lamprecht (1984). For the development of the basilica: Boëthius (1978) 150–156. On the restorations of Jupiter Capitolinus: Tacitus, *Hist.* 3.72; Plutarch, *Poplic.* 15.3–4; Richardson (1992) 222–223.

36. Vitruvius 2.9; Seneca, *Ep.* 90.9; Juvenal 3.254–256.
37. Meiggs (1982) 241. On the beauty of Italian fir trees, see Vergil, *Ecl.* 7.66.
38. For use of oak, see the *Lex Puteolana* (*ILS* 5317), which specifies its use for posts, lintels, and corbels, and calls for fir in boards and in supports for the roof tiles of the porch. Cf. Vitruvius 2.9.5, who specifies fir and elm for their strength in relatively long beams, oak, and cypress for shorter lengths. He barely mentions pine, except for use in building rafts (2.9.14). Meiggs (1982) 241–243; also Adam (1984) 91–94.
39. Horace, *Odes* 1.14.11. See Meiggs's discussion (1980) 192.
40. See Sidonius Apollinaris 5.441–445.
41. Cassiodorus, *Var.* 16–18; 20. *Contra:* Winter (1974) 185, who asserts that the destruction of readily accessible forests in Italy caused the importation of wood from North Africa, Spain, and other areas of the Mediterranean, on no sound evidence whatsoever.
42. Meiggs (1982) chap. 12, pp. 325–370, which unfortunately mixes together evidence for the Greek and the Roman timber trades indiscriminately. Adam (1984) 94–105.
43. Attested by both Dionysius of Halicarnassus, *Ant. Rom.* 20.15.2 and Strabo, *Geog.* 6.1.9 (261). Cicero, *Brutus* 85, attests contractors who purchased a lease from the Roman state to tap pitch from the pines of the Sila forest in Calabria.
44. Cicero, *De Lege Agraria* 1.3; the translation is Meiggs's (1982) 327. The second, briefer, reference appears in 3.15: "You sell the Scantian forest. It belongs to the Roman people: I oppose."
45. For a good discussion of this evidence, see Meiggs (1982) 329 and n. 12. For the Urso charter, see Hardy (1912) 36, clause 82.
46. On all these technical aspects of timber for building, see Adam (1984) 91–94 (on finding, felling, and shipping trees), 94–104 (on cutting and shaping the wood), 104–105 (on the assembly of beams, trusses, supports, frames, etc.). For such operations on Trajan's Column, see Adam (1984) fig. 293 (p. 92); also Meiggs (1982) figs. 15A, B, 16A, B. Also of interest are the funerary stele of the carpenter Gaius, from Autun, that shows the carpenter's tools (Adam (1984) fig. 204, p. 96), the tomb relief from Florence that shows the more important tools of the timber worker (*ILS* 7540, illustrated in Adam [1984] fig. 217, p. 100), and a relief from Gaul showing how a huge tree trunk was dealt with by hand (Adam (1984) fig. 200, p. 95). Further ancient representations of woodworking are given by Adam (1984) figs. 203, 205, p. 96; 215, p. 100; 220, p. 101; and 223, p. 102.
47. Livy 29.1.14. During the First Punic War, we are told, Roman losses were so heavy that there was no time to wait the usual period for the

wood to season (Pliny, *NH* 16.192). On various methods of season-
ing, see Meiggs (1982) 350.

48. On Pisa and Genoa, see Strabo, *Geog.* 6.1–2 (202); Ravenna, Strabo,
Geog. 5.1.6–7 (213); Aquileia, Strabo, *Geog.* 5.1.7–8 (214); Salona,
Strabo, *Geog.* 5.1.8–9 (215); on the *negotiator materiarius,* see *CIL*
3.12924.

49. *Digest* 32.55.

50. For the various Pompeiian terms, see *ILS* 6417b, 6419d; also *CIL*
4.951: *lignarii.* For the *materiarii* and the street called from them, see
CIL 6.975 = *ILS* 6073. The street was located in Regio XIII, near the
Emporium (Richardson [1992] 425). Cf. Plautus, *Miles* 915–921,
where *materiarii* are clearly suppliers of timber. In general, see Meiggs
(1982) 359.

51. On Salona, see *CIL* 3.12924; Florence, *CIL* 11.1620; *Abietarius, CIL*
6.9104; also Festus 25L.

52. SHA *Pertinax* 1.1; the translation is that of the Loeb edition: D. Magie,
The Scriptores Historae Augustae, vol. I (London and Cambridge,
Mass., 1922) 315.

53. On this dedication by the Ostia *collegium,* see Meiggs (1973) 328,
595.

54. *Pace* Meiggs (1982) 364–370, who does precisely that, q.v., based
primarily on the information in Diocletian's infamous Price Edict of
A.D. 301. It is not a good idea to generalize from this late and very
specific edict to the Roman system in general.

55. The snugness of fit between the stones, especially at the joints, was of
such great importance to the strength of a cut-stone wall that the
technique known as *anathyrosis,* in which surfaces were drafted at the
edges and the inner parts hollowed to avoid even the smallest possibility of a projection in the planes where the blocks met, was developed quite early on in Greek architecture and passed on to Italy
through the Greek colonies of Sicily and Southern Italy. See Lugli
(1957) 1.81; Blake (1947) 104.

56. The basics of sand and lime mortar are described by Vitruvius 2.4–5.

57. The term *opus quadratum* is derived from Vitruvius (2.8.5: *sed cum
discesserunt a quadrato,* "but when they depart from squared masonry"); a common English equivalent for *opus quadratum* is "ashlar"
masonry. *Opus siliceum* is a modern term derived from a line of Martial
(9.75: *Non silice duro,* "not with hard silex") and employed primarily
by Lugli (1957) 1, esp. 45.

58. On Alba Fucens's foundation, see Livy 10.1.1; Velleius 1.14.5; for
examples of polygonal masonry at the site, see Lugli (1957) 1.105–
111. Other examples cited by Lugli (1957) 1 include Cosa, Praeneste,
Ferentinum, Segna, Aletrium, Cora, Norba, Anxur/Terracina, and

Circeii (111–154); his inclusion of Pyrgi in this group is dubious, however.

59. Blake (1947) 71–78 on Etruria, and 78–92 on southern Italy and Sicily, provides a good variety of examples.

60. An excellent general discussion of Roman stone quarrying, with illustrations, is given by Adam (1984) 23–41.

61. The original research on Roman tufa was the work of Frank (1924), which is still indispensable. On *cappellaccio,* Frank (1924) 13–14, also 17–19; Blake (1947) 23–26; Lugli (1957) 1.245–252; Coarelli (1994) 364, 367.

62. Vitruvius 2.7.1; for the linking of the *Rubrae* quarries with *Grotta Oscura,* see Frank (1924) 26–27 and Lugli (1957) 1.253. On *Fidenae,* see Frank (1924) 17, 21–22; Blake (1947) 26–27; Lugli (1957) 1.253–255, 257–258. On *Grotta Oscura,* see Frank (1924) 17, 19–21; Blake (1947) 27–29; Lugli (1957) 1.255–257. On the use of these tufas in the "Servian" walls, see Lugli (1957) 1.258–266. For color illustrations of both, see Coarelli (1994) 364, 367.

63. On *Monteverde,* see Frank (1924) 28–32; Blake (1947) 29–31; Lugli (1957) 1.311–313; Coarelli (1994) 364, 367. On *Anio,* see Frank (1924) 26–28; Blake (1947) 31–34; Lugli (1957) 1.309–311. For the name *lapis Pallenses,* see Vitruvius 2.7.1; also Lugli (1957) 1.309.

64. On *Campidoglio,* see Frank (1924) 26; it is not mentioned by Blake or Lugli, but is taken into account in more recent treatments, including Adam (1984) 24, Pisani Sartorio & Steinby (1989) 59–61, and Coarelli (1994) 364, 367.

65. On *peperino,* see Frank (1924) 22–24; Blake (1947) 35–38; Lugli (1957) 1.303–305. For the quarries at *Alba,* see Vitruvius 2.7.1. On its use in fire walls, see Anderson (1984) 74 (Forum of Augustus); Blake & Bishop (1973) 12 (Forum of Trajan).

66. On *sperone,* see Frank (1924) 24–25; Blake (1947) 38–39; Lugli (1957) 1.306–308. It is not mentioned by Vitruvius.

67. On travertine, see Frank (1924) 32–33; Blake (1947) 44–48; Lugli (1957) 1.319–326. Vitruvius knew it (2.7.2).

68. Vitruvius 2.7.2; the translation is that of Granger (1931) 106–109.

69. Vitruvius 2.5.1. Adam (1984) 69–79 provides a fine technical discussion.

70. See Pisani Sartorio & Steinby (1989) 73.

71. On the Porticus Aemilia, see Richardson (1992) 311; Coarelli (1994) 330–331.

72. Vitruvius 2.6.1; the translation is that of Granger (1931) 101.

73. Probably the best description, with remarkably fine illustrations, of construction in *opus caementicium* is that of Lamprecht (1984) 21–40. Also excellent is the description given by Adam (1984) 79–90;

see Lugli (1957) 1.363–444, which provides innumerable examples; also Blake (1947) 324–352, and especially MacDonald (1982) 154–155 and 161–162.

74. On the importance of Roman concrete to the development of arches and vaulting in Roman architecture at this time, see Lugli (1957) 1.335–359 on arches and vaults in *opera quadrata* and compare to 1.659–693 on arches and vaults in concrete. For an evaluation of the effect of concrete on architectural design in general during the Imperial period, see MacDonald (1982) 164–171.

75. On Cossutius and on the concept of *consuetudo Italica,* see Vitruvius 7. Pref. For a good discussion of this concept and its realization in Italy, see Boëthius (1978) 136–215; see also the brief discussion of the influence of the development of concrete on architecture in Gros (1978c) 14–15.

76. Vitruvius 2.8.1–2; the translation is that of Granger (1931) 111. For good illustrations of both types of tufa masonry, see Lamprecht (1984) figs. 17b, c, d, e (p. 28); for illustrations with excellent description and discussion, see Adam (1984) 139–141 and figs. 294–299 for *opus incertum;* 142–146 and figs. 301–316 for *opus reticulatum.* Also see Ling (1985) 22–26.

77. Lugli (1957) 1.449–469; Blake (1947) 249–251. On the restorations in the Forum, see Livy 36.27.1 and 37.11.16.

78. Lugli (1957) 1.468–469; Blake (1947) 228–249 for examples in Italy outside Rome.

79. This was pointed out by Blake (1947) 227.

80. See the examples offered by Lugli (1957) 1.503–505, and by Blake (1947) 251–253.

81. On this problem of distinction, see Adam (1984) 142–143 and figs. 303, 305 and 306, which demonstrate the difficulty all too clearly.

82. For good illustrations of true *opus reticulatum,* see Lamprecht (1984) figs. 17 d and e (p. 28); Adam (1984) figs. 306–310 (pp. 144–145).

83. On sun-dried and semibaked brick in Italy, see Blake (1947) 277–281.

84. Lugli (1957) 1.587. For the problems of dating the tomb, see Holloway (1966) 171–173. Other baked-brick construction of the period includes limited sections of the theater of Marcellus, the Augustan Rostra and Domus Publica in the Forum, the Pyramid of Gaius Cestius, and various other tombs; Lugli (1957) 1.588.

85. Vitruvius 1.5.8.

86. Vitruvius 2.3.1–2; the translation is Granger's (1931) 88–91.

87. See the remarks of Aubert (1994) 218 and n. 52.

88. Plautus, *Truc.* 303–306; Cato, *De Agr.* 14.4; Caesar, *BellCiv* 2.9–10; Cicero, *De Div.* 2.99; Varro, *Re Rust.* 1.14.4.

89. Vitruvius 2.8.16–20: *parietes laterici* and *structura testacea*. The distinction seems to have become standard: it is adopted by Vitruvius's contemporary Q. Curtius Rufus (*Hist. Alex.* 7.3.8) and subsequently by Pliny (*NH* 35.170–174 and 36.47) and various late authors (quoted by Blake [1947] 276–277).

90. For the majority of architectural purposes, these large tiles would be cut into smaller triangular or square bricks: Adam (1984) 159 and fig. 347. Several different measurements for the Roman foot have been advanced: Bauer (1983) 136, n. 33; cf. Rakob (1984) 222–23 (the Hadrianic foot), and Zimmer (1984).

91. Lugli (1957) 1.589–590, who refers to the baked-brick wall of the Domus Tiberiana as facing onto the Clivus Victoriae. As has recently been shown, this identification of the Clivus Victoriae is incorrect; see T. P. Wiseman, "Clivus Victoriae," in Steinby (1993b) 288. Also see Richardson (1992) 78–79 (Castra Praetoria) and 136–137 (Domus Tiberiana); also on the Castra Praetoria, see E. Lissi Caronna, "Castra Praetoria," in Steinby (1993b) 251–254.

92. The *horrea* of Hortensius (V.xii.1) and the *horrea* in the "Semita dei Cippi" (V.i.2), Lugli (1957) 1.596.

93. Lugli (1957) 1.595–621 provides such a list, all but unannotated. The examples mentioned here are from his list.

94. Boëthius (1960) 129–185.

95. For superb photographic examples, see Adam (1984) figs. 344–346, 348–356 (pp. 156–162); also Pisani Sartorio & Steinby (1989) 76–81.

96. See the examples in Adam (1984) figs. 330–341 (pp. 152–156); also Pisani Sartorio & Steinby (1989) 75.

97. Notably in Domitian's Albanum villa at modern Castel Gandolfo (before A.D. 96) and subsequently at the Villa "degli Scozzesi" near Marino (ca. A.D. 100), in Trajanic walls of the Villa dei Gordiani, in Hadrianic walls at the villa Le Vignacce, in the Antonine villas of the Quintilii and Sette Bassi. Lugli (1957) 1.523–524.

98. Lugli (1957) 1.524–526.

99. Adam (1984) 156–157 and figs. 342–343, which provide two examples of *opus spicatum* walling from France.

100. See the list given by Lugli (1957) 1.641–643. A well-known example of *opus vittatum* entirely in stone is the facing of Hadrian's Wall in northern Britain (Adam [1984] figs. 328, 329, p. 151).

101. Lugli (1957) 1.643–655 with a few illustrations. An excellent example is the house of Fortuna Annonaria at Ostia; the western apsed room had been reworked, probably in the late third century A.D., entirely in "textbook" *opus vittatum:* Meiggs (1973) 254; Stambaugh (1988) 171. Wallace-Hadrill (1994) 23 mistakenly dates this apsed

room to the second century with the rest of the house. Its facing, however, is notably different.

102. Anderson (1991) 1–2; Steinby (1978) cols. 1496–1504; also Steinby's popularizing summary in Pisani Sartorio & Steinby (1989) esp. 85–87.

103. Here I follow, with minor revisions, the useful summation of Aubert (1994) 219.

104. Wiseman (1979) esp. 221–224. He is followed by Aubert (1994) 220–222.

105. A good case in point is the *dominus* M. Annius Verus, who was also the city prefect (*praefectus urbi*) of Rome during the reign of Hadrian; see Bloch (1947) 206 and 325; Anderson (1991) 1.

106. Steinby (1978) cols. 1519–1524, counted 181 *domini*, including 67 senators, 47 women, and 1 (anomalous) Imperial slave (see also Helen [1975] 22–23, 94; and Aubert (1994) 223–224). The numbers Steinby provides for the *officinatores* (cols. 1516–1519) are 1325 names, 1076 with a *nomen* and 249 with only a *cognomen*. As Helen (1975) 23 pointed out, the majority appear to be freedmen or slaves.

107. Here I am following the excellent summary of Aubert (1994) 222–232. On the *domini* as monopolizers: Bloch (1947), contested by Helen (1975). For an example of an industry, in some ways rather like the brick industry, in which *institores* functioned quite independently, see Harris (1980) on the lamp industry, and for evidence of similar arrangements, Aubert (1993) and (1994) 201–321.

108. This was first suggested by Helen (1975) 33–88. Although there are some difficulties, acknowledged by Helen himself (e.g., p. 75), his suggestion has been accepted by N. Purcell, in his review of Helen's monograph, *JRS* 71 (1981) 214–215; Bodel (1983) 3, who in n. 14 suggests that these "brickyards" be compared to the modern usage of "vineyards" in the wine industry, "which often implies not only the land under cultivation, but also the winery where the grapes are pressed"; Champlin (1983) 258; Anderson (1991) 2. More circumspect is Aubert (1994) 237–238. Steinby (1986) 156–157 has suggested that Helen's idea be extended even further to imply an administrative unit within the brick industry.

109. Helen (1975) 57, 75; Setälä (1977) 119–121.

110. Earinus with Lucilla Veri: *CIL* 15.1049, 1050; also *CIL* 10.8046.5. Earinus with Domitia Lucilla: *CIL* 15.1047–1048. See Setälä (1977) 107–108, and Aubert (1994) 230 and nn. 95, 96.

111. Ulpianus (28 *ad ed.*) = *Digest* 14.3.7.1: "Parvi autem refert, quis sit institor, masculus an femina, liber an servus, proprius vel alienus." See Helen (1975) 112–113.

112. The inscription was published by A. La Regina, "Rivista di epigrafica

italica," *SE* 44 (1976) 284–288. See Aubert's careful discussion (1994) 224–226, which I follow here. On Herennius Sattius, see *CIL* 9.1588, 10.1272, 5204.

113. The pioneering work of Bloch (1947) remains the basic source for the importance of brick stamps to the chronology of Roman architecture. Note the use of brick stamps in all three of Blake's books (1947, 1959, and 1973); in Lugli (1957) 1.563–570; and how their utility for architectural and archaeological dating had already been understood prior to Bloch's work by Thomas Ashby: Anderson (1991) 9–11.

114. Steinby's contribution here has been enormous, especially her survey of the brickyards' chronologies (1976); also see Helen (1975) 76–82, and Champlin (1983).

115. This summary is based primarily on my preface to the publication of Thomas Ashby's brickstamps: Anderson (1991) 1–2. On the year A.D. 123, see esp. Bloch (1947) 320–327; Boatwright (1987) 22 and nn. 13–15.

116. Steinby (1978) col. 1515; Anderson (1991) 1 and n. 6.

117. Steinby (1986) 110, 117–118, 156–157. Her article is the basic work on this period in the brick industry. Also see Aubert (1994) 238. The only stamps to appear in late antiquity that bear a name other than one of the emperors are *CIL* 15.1639, 1640, 1709 and *S.* 614, 615, all of which mention "Severianus magister," otherwise unknown to us, and date from the reign of Constantine (A.D. 312–337).

118. Steinby (1982) esp. 232–233; also Steinby (1986) 100, 106–107, 149–150; and Steinby (1993a) esp. 140–142.

119. They are raised by Aubert (1994) 232–233.

120. Helen (1975) 33–88; also Champlin (1983).

121. Cf. Steinby (1982) esp. 232–233; and Aubert (1994) 232, 236–238.

122. Anderson (1991) 4. On the signed lamps (called *firmalampen*), see Harris (1980) and, for examples from Cosa, Fitch & Goldman (1994); on the possible applicability of the distribution system for such lamps to the distribution of brick, see N. Purcell's review of Helen and Setälä (*JRS* 71 [1981] 214).

123. On the remarkable distribution of Tiber Valley brick stamps, see Steinby (1981) and, for specific areas of delivery, Wilkes (1979) and Buora (1985) on Dalmatia, and Tomber (1987) on Carthage. The problem of how such a heavy commodity as brick could have been shipped profitably has never been fully addressed, but in general see Burford (1960) and Anderson (1991) 3–4, the latter also for the suggestion of name recognition playing a part in the diffusion of stamped bricks from Rome.

124. Helen (1975) 76–82; reinforced with further evidence by Champlin (1983) 258–259 and n. 3.

125. Steinby (1978) cols. 1507–1508, who attributes the still unpublished study to Huotari.
126. By using X-ray fluorescence, G. Olcese (1993) has compared products from the *figlinae Domitianae* to those signed by the Domitii with important results.
127. Anderson (1991) 3; also Steinby (1978) cols. 1507–1508.
128. See Champlin (1983) on the connections of Trajan and his family with the *figlinae Marcianae* specifically and with the brick industry in general.
129. It was also possible for standard architectural moldings to be cast and then inserted as decoration in walls; bricks of different colors were sometimes alternated for decorative effect (as can be seen at Ostia in the Horrea Epigathiana and the Caseggiato del Larario); and sometimes brick was even painted to provide a more even red texture and make the other decorative elements stand out (e.g., on the façade of Trajan's Markets, where the contrast was with Tuscan bases and capitals of travertine flanking the arched windows on the second storey). See Packer (1968b), (1969), and (1988).
130. Blake (1947) 50. Blake goes too far in implying that travertine's use as a decorative stone ended with the introduction of white marble. In cases where strength against the elements was required—or perhaps where there was a taste for simplicity of materials—travertine continued in decorative use, for example, in the façades of the theater of Pompey, the Flavian amphitheater, and the stadium of Domitian in the Campus Martius.
131. Metellus Macedonicus: Velleius 1.11.5; see Boëthius (1978) 139. L. Licinius Crassus: Pliny, *NH* 17.6 and 36.45.
132. Lucullus: Pliny, *NH* 36.49–50. Sulla: Pliny, *NH* 36.45. Lepidus: Pliny, *NH* 36.49.
133. Pliny, *NH* 36.5.
134. Pliny, *NH* 36.48. On this passage, see Fant (1988b) 149, who suggests that Mamurra may have been instrumental in the early exploitation of the gigantic Luna marble deposits which were aimed at supplying Caesar's intended building program.
135. Blake (1947) 51. The archaeological evidence is available in Colini (1938) 272–273. Further see Etienne (1987) on the topography and development of the entire district.
136. Tibullus 2.3.43–44; the translation is that of J. P. Postgate in the Loeb edition: F. W. Cornish, J. P. Postgate, and G. W. MacKail, *Catullus, Tibullus and Pervigilium Veneris* (London and Cambridge, Mass., 1912) 265.
137. Suetonius, *Aug.* 38.3; the translation is that of the Loeb edition: J. C. Rolfe, *Suetonius,* vol. I (London and Cambridge, Mass., 1914) 167. The same boast is recorded by Cassius Dio 56.30.3–4.

138. Vitruvius 10.12, 13, 14. See Monna & Pensabene (1977) 134.
139. Lucan, *Pharsalia* 10.3. See Gnoli (1971) 3 on discoveries of onyx and purple porphyry in excavations at Alexandria.
140. Herz (1988) 7–8. The major exceptions were Numidian marble from the Chemtou quarries in modern Tunisia, and Proconnesian marble from the island of Marmara in the sea of Marmara off northwestern Turkey.
141. I list here only the most important of these marble sources and include the briefest of descriptions of their appearance, together with the frequently used Italian names for them where these are common. I follow Dodge (1988) 67, 77–78. For a much fuller listing that includes all known sources, major or minor, see Dodge & Ward-Perkins (1992) Appendix 1, pp. 153–159.

    For color photographs of Luna marble, see Borghini (1989) 248; also Dolci (1980) and (1988) for information on the quarry. For color photographs of Mt. Pentelikon, see Borghini (1989) 251. For Mt. Hymettos, see Borghini (1989) 249; see Langdon (1988) on the quarry. For Proconnesos, see Borghini (1989) 252; see Monna & Pensabene (1977) 147–174. For Thasos, see Borghini (1989) 253. And for Paros, see Borghini (1989) 250.
142. For Lesbos, Borghini (1989) 158–159; for Ephesus and Aphrodisias, see Borghini (1989) 247; also Monna & Pensabene (1977) 89–101.
143. For marble from Carystos, see Borghini (1989) 202–203; for Cape Taenaros, Borghini (1989) 288 and Gnoli (1971) 160–164; for Chalcis, Borghini (1989) 212 and Gnoli (1971) 157–159; for Chios, Borghini (1989) 264–265 and Gnoli (1971) 145–146; for Thessaly, Gnoli (1971) 136–138; for Verzirken, Borghini (1989) 166–167 and Gnoli (1971) 203–205; for Teos, Borghini (1989) 133–135 and Fant (1989b) on the quarry; for Iasos, Borghini (1989) 207, 289 and Monna & Pensabene (1977) 108–112; for Docimium, Borghini (1989) 264–265 and Monna & Pensabene (1977) 35–75, and, especially important, Fant (1989a); for Simitthus, Borghini (1989) 214–215 and Röder (1988) on the quarry; for Scyros, Borghini (1989) 192–193, 290–291.
144. For Croceae, see Borghini (1989) 279–281; for Gebel Dokhan, Borghini (1989) 274.
145. For Syene, Borghini (1989) 225–226; for Mons Claudianus, Borghini (1989) 222–223, and Peacock (1988) on the quarry and also Peacock (1994) 363 on the chemical composition of this "granite"; for the Troad, Borghini (1989) 236–237.
146. For a good introduction to this procedure, see Herz & Wenner (1981); also Walker (1984) and Herz (1985).

147. For an overview of quarry studies and transportation, see Ward-Perkins (1992a); also on quarrying Waelkens, De Paepe, & Moens (1988); on transport see Wurch-Kozelj (1988) and Peña (1989). Further see Dodge (1991) 28–32.

148. The tunnelling of Parian marble is described by Pliny, *NH* 36.14. The process of removing large chunks for ease of subsequent working left behind a rock face with a sequence of large scoops out of it; this is described at the Lacedaemonian quarries in ˙ Roman times by Pausanias 3.21.4. See Ward-Perkins (1992a) 16–21 and nn. 7–24 (which are by H. Dodge and B. Ward-Perkins) and figs. 5–11; also Waelkens, De Paepe, & Moens (1988).

149. Waelkens, De Paepe, & Moens (1988) 13.

150. Röder (1971) 303–311, figs. 56–63 for the evidence from Docimium; also Ward-Perkins (1992a) 17 n. 13.

151. Pliny, *NH* 36.70 describes ships carrying obelisks from Egyptian quarries arriving at Rome. Vitruvius 10.2 describes several ways of moving blocks, columns, and other architectural elements on land; the basic methods are well described and illustrated with drawings by Adam (1984) 30–32, by Ling (1985) 18–22 and by Landels (1978) esp. 183–185.

152. Suetonius, *Tib.* 49.2; the translation is that of the Loeb edition: J. C. Rolfe, *Suetonius*, vol. 1 (London and Cambridge, Mass., 1914) 361. I have added the bracketed words [and quarries] to the translation because the actual Latin wording, *ius metallorum*, clearly carries this broad implication (Ward-Perkins (1992a) 24 and nn. 13, 14).

153. On this passage, see Fant (1989a) 7, (1989b) 150, and (1993) 146.

154. I am quoting Ward-Perkins (1992c) 63; see also Ward-Perkins (1992b) 24–26; also Dodge (1988) 69–73.

155. Millar (1977) esp. 185–186.

156. On quarry inscriptions, see Ward-Perkins (1951) 89–104; Dodge (1988) 70; Dodge (1991) 35–36; Fant (1993) 157–158. On the Docimium inscriptions, Fant (1989a) esp. 11–16 and 49–184.

157. Ward-Perkins (1992b) 25 thought the phenomena Flavian; Waelkens, De Paepe, & Moens (1988) 109 agree (adding a nod to Trajan's building program). But Fant (1988b) 151–152 cites evidence from Docimium and Simitthus that permits him to make a strong case for a Hadrianic reorganization; most recently, Fant (1993) 162–163 has made an even better case for assuming there were two such reorganizations; this is not far different from Pensabene's reading of the evidence when there was rather less to go on: Pensabene (1972) 189. On the entire question of Imperial control, see Dodge (1991) 32–34.

158. On stockpiles at Ostia, see Baccini Leotardi (1979) 11–46 and

(1989); also Dodge (1991) 36. On the via Marmorata marble yards and their relationship to Portus, see Fant (1992).

159. See Dodge (1991) 36–38, and Ward-Perkins (1992b) 25 n. 18. On the regular column lengths at Leptis, see Ward-Perkins (1980b) 327 and n. 8. On the problems of 50-foot shafts, and the evidence both for and against their practicality, cf. Ward-Perkins (1992d) 107–110, 114; Peña (1989); Davies, Hemsoll, & Jones (1987).

160. On specialists at Docimium, see Waelkens (1985). On the spread of the so-called marble style, Dodge (1990), esp. 108–109. On import of Phrygian stoneworkers with the stone (into Palestine), Fischer (1988) 162–163.

161. Easily seen in innumerable ancient testimonia, e.g., Pliny, *NH* 24.125, 36.3, 6, 8 44–45 and 51; Seneca, *Ep.* 86.6; *Controv.* 2.1.3.

162. In general on distribution, see Dodge (1988) 73–76. State-owned marble ships and the Ostian *corpus traiectus:* Dodge (1991) 39–40. On Nicomedia, Ward-Perkins (1992c), cf. Dodge (1991) 43. On the shift in trade in white marbles, Walker (1988). On the abandonment of *africano,* Dodge (1991) 42.

163. Corcoran & DeLaine (1994); also, in general on prices of transport of stone, Burford (1960).

Chapter 4: Planning and Layout of Cities and Towns in Roman Italy

1. On the contrast between a predetermined city "plan" and a city street and building pattern that has grown up over time, only partially planned if at all (which he calls an "armature"), see MacDonald (1986) 23–25.

2. Tacitus, *Agricola* 20–21. The translation is that of the Loeb edition: M. Hutton, *Tacitus: Dialogus, Agricola, Germania* (London and Cambridge, Mass., 1914) 206–207.

3. The translation is that of Granger (1931) 1.3.1, pp. 32–35; see Fleury (1990) 121–122. On Vitruvius's particular concept of town planning and its relationship to the world in which he lived, see Hesberg (1989).

4. Granger (1931) 52–53. Fleury (1990) 146–151.

5. Granger (1931) 66–69. Fleury (1990) 188–193.

6. MacDonald (1986) 23–31 on city planning and its relationship to "armatures," and 32–73 on streets, passageways, and stairs, which he called "connective architecture." He rightly emphasizes that these elements in the overall urban design of most Roman foundations have been insufficiently studied, although they are arguably more important to the realities of the city or town than the more apparent buildings set within their web. He deals further with "passage architecture" on

pp. 74–110, concentrating particularly on arches. Cf. the review by Sear (1988) esp. 162–163.

7. On the origins of the amphitheater, see Welch (1994). On Vitruvius's omission of it after 1.7, see Fleury (1990) 190–191.

8. E.g., the early layout scheme of the Piazza d'Armi acropolis at Veii, upon which an orthogonal sanctuary plan was later superimposed, and what little has been learned of the street plan of Acquarossa near Viterbo; Ward-Perkins (1974) 25 and nn. 19, 20. For excellent illustrations and more up-to-date analysis reaching the same basic conclusion, see Gros & Torelli (1988) 36–45. For a more theoretical but essentially similar analysis, see Rykwert (1976) 72–88.

9. Castagnoli (1971) 74–81 is completely convincing on this matter. The passage from Varro is quoted by Solinus 1.17.

10. Castagnoli (1971) 76–77. West: Vitruvius 4.5.1. East: Livy 1.18.6; Dionysius of Halicarnassus, *Ant. Rom.* 2.5.2–3; Plutarch, *Quaest. Rom.* 78; Servius, *ad Aen.* 2.693; Isidorus, *Etym.* 15.4.7. South: Varro, *L. L.* 7.7; Festus 454L; Pliny, *NH* 2.143.

11. Varro, *L. L.* 5.161; Vitruvius 6.3.1. For further information and suggestions, see Crema (1959) 37–42 on the "etrusco-italico" temple plan, and 104–105 on the "atrio tuscanico"; also McKay (1975) 11–29 on the Tuscan atrium plan.

12. Crema (1959) 28–33 on Hippodamus and orthogonal plans in early Italy; Castagnoli (1971) 12–19 on grid patterns, 66–72 on Hippodamus, and 84–93 on Hellenistic cities; Ward-Perkins (1974) 14–17 on "Hippodamean" planning and 18–21 on Hellenistic cities. Owens (1989) provides a brief overview. Further on the implications of orthogonal planning: Rykwert (1976) 31–33, 59–65, who adopts a type of approach that had been sharply, and justly, criticized by Castagnoli (1971) 74–81.

13. See Gros & Torelli (1988) 132–156 for a comprehensive survey of this evidence; also Dilke (1971), Owens (1989) 7–10, and Stambaugh (1988) 243–254. On the influence of south Italian and Sicilian cities, see Ward-Perkins (1974) 22–26; on the earliest Roman towns in Italy, Ward-Perkins (1974) 27–28. On Alba Fucens, see J. Mertens, in Stilwell (1976) 31; also Coarelli & La Regina (1993) 62–98. On Ostia, see Meiggs (1973) 23 and Hermansen (1982) 2–3.

14. Frontinus, *Strat.* 4.1.14; Polybius 4.31.10. This point is emphasized, quite rightly, by Ward-Perkins (1974) 28; also Owens (1989).

15. Reece (1985) 37; see also the several varieties of Roman town plan distinguished by Castagnoli (1971) 96–121.

16. This reading of Pompeii's plan was first proposed by Richardson (1982); Richardson (1988) 36–43 summarizes the arguments more succinctly. It is accepted by Stambaugh (1988) 261. *Contra:* Castagnoli

(1971) 24–35. While Richardson's analysis is appealing and accords well with Vitruvius, it has not won universal acceptance: cf. Zevi (1982), in the same volume as Richardson's original article, who reads the situation differently; Gros & Torelli (1988) 58–60 avoid the question. Laurence (1994) begins to offer what would seem to be an even more radical reinterpretation of the plan of Pompeii (15–19) but then does not pursue or develop the implications (e.g., 20–27).

17. *CIL* 14, Suppl. 1. no. 4338. Ennius, *Ann.* 2, frag. 22 (Vahlen). Livy 1.33.9.

18. Meiggs (1973) 16–23; R. Meiggs, "Ostia," in Stilwell (1976) 658; Hermansen (1982) 1–4. That there might have been an earlier, salt-exporting, settlement on another site near the river is Meiggs's suggestion, one not yet confirmed by archaeological finds.

19. The lack of grid or of other preplanned street pattern in western Ostia from the very earliest times is well emphasized by Hermansen (1982) 4. On the new, probably Sullan, walls, see Meiggs (1973) 34–36.

20. The best overall treatment is Meiggs (1973) 111–148. For a briefer summary, see R. Meiggs, "Ostia," in Stilwell (1976) 658–659, 661. Also Stambaugh (1988) 268–274.

21. Brown (1980) esp. 8–13; Stambaugh (1988) 255–259; see Fentress (1994) on Imperial and later Cosa.

22. Livy 10.45. For the site of the original Samnite town, see Coarelli & La Regina (1993) 226, 228.

23. The common terms *cardo,* to designate the main north-south thoroughfare, and *decumanus* for the east-west avenue of a Roman town, are used conventionally here. Insofar as our evidence goes, these terms seem in fact to have applied only to the streets of military *castra,* not to towns at all: for instance, in describing the laying out of streets, Vitruvius (1.6) does not employ them.

24. On Saepinum: V. Cianfarani, in Stilwell (1976) 781; Anderson (1983b); Coarelli & La Regina (1993) 209–227. On the plan, see Gros & Torelli (1988) 154–155. On Neratius Priscus: SHA *Hadrian* 4.8; R. Syme, "The Jurist Neratius Priscus," *Hermes* 85 (1957) 480–493 = R. Syme, *Roman Papers,* vol. 5 (Oxford, 1988) 478–489.

25. Plutarch, *Romulus* 11. Translation from the Loeb edition: B. Perrin, *Plutarch's Lives,* vol. 1 (London and Cambridge, Mass., 1914) 118–121.

26. Varro, *L. L.* 5.143. Ovid, *Fasti* 4.819–836 provides an account remarkably similar to Plutarch's. On the significance of this rite, and its relationship to the methods of city planning described by Vitruvius, see Rykwert (1976) 44–70.

27. Livy 1.7.3: Romulus's "first act was to fortify the Palatine"; see Tacitus, *Ann.* 12.24; also Richardson (1992) 259.

28. Tacitus, *Ann.* 12.24. See Richardson (1992) 293–294, who works out the route in detail, then points out that Romulus's wall surely would have run inside the line of the *pomerium,* along the top of the Palatine, not at its foot. On the *pomerium* as preserving a set of water boundaries for earliest Rome, see Holland (1961) 55.

29. Livy 1.44.3–5. Translation from the Loeb edition: B. O. Foster, *Livy,* vol. 1 (London and Cambridge, Mass., 1925) 154–157. An excellent commentary is provided by Ogilvie (1965) 179–180.

30. Gros & Torelli (1988) 19–29.

31. See Boatwright (1986) on the problems involved in accepting that Augustus extended the *pomerium;* also Boatwright (1987) 64–66 on the Hadrianic *pomerium.* The extensions under Claudius, Vespasian, and Hadrian are attested by inscribed *cippi* (*CIL* 6.31538, 31539 = *ILS* 248, 311) and so need not be questioned. Caesar's has been much debated but is considered likely by the majority of scholars. For the best survey of the evidence and current thinking on pomerial extensions, see Richardson (1992) 294–296.

32. Livy 5.55.2–5. The translation is from the Loeb edition: B. O. Foster, *Livy,* vol. 3 (London and Cambridge, Mass., 1940) 187, except that I have added two modifying adverbs in the final sentence—"randomly" and "logically"—in an attempt to convey the force of the contrast Livy gives between *sit occupata* and (*sit*) *divisa* there: *formaque urbis sit ocupatae magis quam divisae similis.*

33. See Ogilvie (1965) 750–751 on Livy's passage. For the tradition in other Roman writers: Cicero, *De Div.* 1.30; Tacitus, *Ann.* 15.43; Plutarch, *Camillus,* 32. See discussion by Robinson (1992) 16. For the archaeological evidence of the sack: Blake (1947) 122–124; Coarelli (1983) 129–130.

34. On the magisterial problem: Robinson (1992) 16. On Appius Claudius Caecus's censorship: Frontinus, *Aq.* 5–9; also Stambaugh (1988) 20–22.

35. Cicero, *Contra Rullum: De Lege Agraria* 2.xxxv.95–96. The translation is from the Loeb edition: J. Freese, *Cicero. Pro Quinctio, Pro S. Roscio Amerino, Pro Q. Roscio Comoedo, De Lege Agraria I–III* (London and Cambridge, Mass., 1930) 473.

36. Van Deman (1922); also Duret & Néraudeau (1983) 85–88, and Gros & Torelli (1988) 120–121. See Richardson (1992) 376–377 on the Tabularium; the traditional identification has now been challenged by Purcell (1993), but not the building's architectural significance in its topographical context.

37. This is proposed by Sauron (1987) and accepted by Gros & Torelli (1988) 121–124. Both Duret & Néraudeau (1983) 200–211 and

Stambaugh (1988) 41–42 carefully avoid assigning any urbanistic significance to Pompey's buildings.

38. Cicero, *ad Att.* 13.33a; see similar reactions in 13.20, 13.35.

39. Suetonius, *Jul.* 44. Translation from the Loeb edition: J. C. Rolfe, *Suetonius: The Lives of the Caesars,* vol. I (London and Cambridge, Mass., 1914) 61.

40. For overviews of Caesar's program, see Gros & Torelli (1988) 124–126; Stambaugh (1988) 43–45; Robinson (1992) 17–19.

41. On Cicero and Oppius, see Cicero, *ad Att.* 4.16.8; also Anderson (1984) 39–42.

42. *Lex Julia municipalis: CIL* I². 593 = *ILS* 6085, esp. nos. 20–21, 24–27, 50–51, 68–72. Also see Dudley (1967) 11–12; Robinson (1992) 17–18.

43. Suetonius, *Aug.* 28.3–29.5. For the passages of the *Res Gestae* listed, see the commentary by Brunt & Moore (1967) 53–54, 61–63. The scholarly literature on the individual buildings of Augustus and on his intentions has become enormous; for an overview, see Gros & Torelli (1988) 169–179; Stambaugh (1988) 48–60 is altogether less successful. On the two altars, see Richardson (1992) 157, 287–289 and Anderson (1996) 27–30; on Apollo Palatinus, P. Gros, in Steinby (1993b) 54–57; on Divus Julius, Richardson (1992) 213–214; on Forum Augustum and Mars Ultor temple, Anderson (1984) 65–100 and Bonnefond (1987).

44. Cassius Dio 53.27 on Agrippa's work in the Campus Martius, confirmed by Strabo, *Geog.* 5.3.8; see Roddaz (1984) 252–291. Dudley (1967) 17 points out appositely that Agrippa's reworking of this area "gave Rome a splendid new quarter which may be compared with the New Town of Edinburgh." On the *Horologium,* see Büchner (1982) and Rakob (1987), but note the queries raised by Schütz (1990). On the Mausoleum, see Richardson (1992) 247–249.

45. Suetonius, *Aug.* 29.5. See Richardson (1992) on the individual buildings listed; in addition, on the atrium Libertatis, see Anderson (1984) 21–26, and *contra,* Purcell (1993).

46. Suetonius, *Aug.* 30.1; translation is from the Loeb edition: J. C. Rolfe, *Suetonius: Lives of the Caesars,* 1:169. The division into fourteen regions is affirmed by Pliny, *NH* 3.5.66–67 and Cassius Dio 55.8.

47. On the urban prefecture and the new administrative board and curators: Suetonius, *Aug.* 37, Tacitus, *Ann.* 1.2 and discussions in Brunt & Moore (1967) 14 and Rowell (1962) 113–115; on the fire prevention scheme: Rowell (1962) 115–117. For Agrippa's contribution to the water system: Frontinus, *Aq.* 98–99 and the discussion by Evans (1982); on his reconstruction of the Cloaca Maxima: Cassius Dio

49.43; on his public works in general: Roddaz (1984) 145–156. For an interesting treatment of all of Augustus's changes in city administration and their implications, see Bruun (1991) 140–143.

48. Robinson (1992) 18–19, and Gros & Torelli (1988) 167–169 for general summations; also Roddaz (1984) 145–157 on what Agrippa was involved in. In addition to citations above for individual urbanizing reforms, see Nippel (1984) on police, and Rainbird (1986) on fire protection.

49. For the fire of A.D. 80, see Cassius Dio 66.24; Suetonius, *Titus* 8.3–4. On the Domitianic Campus Martius, see Gros & Torelli (1988) 187–188. On the reworkings under Hadrian, see Boatwright (1987) 33–75, and under Alexander Severus, Coarelli (1987) 432–444. For a general topographical history of the area, see Coarelli (1994) 258–301.

50. On this complex as an example of planned urbanism, see Anderson (1985), Gros & Torelli (1988) 184–186, 198, and Coarelli (1994) 180–197. On the Domus aurea, see Tacitus, *Ann.* 15.42.1 and Suetonius, *Nero* 31; Fabbrini (1983); MacDonald (1982) 20–46; Voisin (1987); and Ball (1994). On the Flavian amphitheater, see Richardson (1992) 7–10 and R. Rea, "Amphitheatrum" in Steinby (1993b) 30–35. On the Meta Sudans, see Richardson (1992) 253; on a possible Neronian predecessor, Panella et al. (1995) 41–42. On the thermae Titi, see Richardson (1992) 396–397; on the thermae Traiani, De Fine Licht (1974) and (1990), also Anderson (1985) esp. 505–509. On the possibility of a Domitianic predecessor to the Arch of Constantine, see Frothingham (1912), Pensabene (1988) 411–412 (*contra:* DeMaria [1988] 294–295) and Steiner & Melucco Vaccaro (1994); *contra:* Panella et al. (1995) esp. 44–46.

51. On these two Fora, see Duret & Néraudeau (1983) 102–114; Anderson (1984) 39–100. The idea that there was an Augustan "blueprint" for the entire sequence of Fora was suggested by Blanckenhagen (1954); it is rejected by Anderson (1984) 73 and by Gros & Torelli (1988) 188–192, and ignored by Stambaugh (1988) 119–122 and Coarelli (1994) 112–127.

52. The one reference to the building as *forum Pacis* occurs in Ammianus Marcellinus (16.10.14); it is also, significantly, omitted from the group that Martial called a *forum triplex* between A.D. 93 and 95 when referring to Domitian's Forum Transitorium and the two earlier fora. See Gros & Torelli (1988) 188–189, Duret & Néraudeau (1983) 114–115, and Anderson (1984) 101–118.

53. On the architectonic achievement of this Forum, and its effect on the templum Pacis, see Anderson (1982); also Duret & Néraudeau (1983) 115–118.

54. On the Domitianic reconstruction of the Forum Julium, see Anderson (1984) 54–62; on Domitianic precedence in the area of Trajan's Forum, Anderson (1984) 148–151. On what Apollodorus's overall plan might have included, see Packer (1994). On the so-called "Terrace of Domitian," between the fora of Augustus and Trajan, see now Tortorici (1993), who argues that this is the remains of a huge Nymphaeum built at the new endpoint of the Aqua Marcia, which had previously served the Capitoline Hill, but had been truncated by Domitian during the excavations of the Quirinal slope (along which it originally ran). The terrace is on a radically different orientation from the Forum of Trajan, so it must be presumed that Trajan and Apollodorus drastically altered, indeed probably completely redesigned, Domitian's original project. Also see L. Lancaster, "The Date of Trajan's Markets," *PBSR* 63 (1995) 25–44.

55. The more-or-less traditional interpretation, recently forcefully reasserted by Packer (1994); also Duret & Néraudeau (1983) 118–121.

56. See L. Richardson, jr., "The Architecture of the Forum of Trajan," *Arch News* 6 (1977): 101–106; Anderson (1984) 152–159; Richardson (1992) esp. 177–178; Claridge (1993).

57. Cf. Blanckenhagen (1954). See Ward-Perkins (1974) 40–42; Anderson (1984) 179–182; Gros & Torelli (1988) 194–196 for assessments of the architectural, symbolic, and urbanistic importance of this sequence of monuments. See also Torelli (1987) esp. 578–582 on the overall urbanistic plan of Domitian's entire building program.

58. Cassius Dio 73.24.1 and Herodian 1.14 are the main sources. Galen, *de comp. med.* 1.1 records the destruction of the libraries of the templum Pacis in the conflagration.

59. Richardson (1992) 350.

60. For a list of Severan building and reconstruction in the city see Benario (1958). On the last Severan emperor's constructions in Rome, see Coarelli (1987).

61. Benario (1958); see further the list (pp. 455–456) and entries on specific buildings in Richardson (1992). A brief but important summary of the urbanistic effect of the Severan program is given by Gros & Torelli (1988) 206–208, and there are also some valuable suggestions in Walker (1990).

62. On the restoration, see SHA *Severus* 23.1 and *CIL* 6.935. For later testimonials of its existence, see SHA *Trig. tyr.* 31.10; Ammianus 16.10.14; Symmachus, *Relat.* 3.7.

63. Anderson (1984) 113–116. See Carettoni et al. (1960) and Rodriguez Almeida (1981) for illustrations and studies of the fragments. That it is Severan is proven beyond doubt by the inclusion on it of the Septizodium, which did not exist prior to that time. On the Forma Urbis in

general see J. C. Anderson, jr., "Post-Mortem Adventures of the Marble Plan of Rome," *Classical Outlook* 59 (1982) 69–73 and Reynolds (1996) 1–24, 45–52.

64. On the location of the Plan and its association with the urban prefect's archive, see Gatti in Carettoni et al. (1960) 1.213–218. On the earlier Vespasianic map and on Agrippa's, see Palmer (1980) 217–218 and nn. 7, 8, 9. Palmer remarks (n. 7, p. 227): "Although the marble plan may have had cadastral relations, its scale is such as to preclude its use for capitation." Agrippa's map is mentioned by the elder Pliny, *NH* 3.17. For further discussion, see Anderson (1984) 116–117; also Reynolds (1996) 53–59.

65. The standard work on the Aurelianic walls remains Richmond (1930). On their use as a customs boundary, see Palmer (1980) esp. 217–220.

66. Tacitus, *Ann.* 15.43.1. The translation is that of Dudley (1967) 21–22.

67. Suetonius, *Nero* 16. Translation from the Loeb edition: J. C. Rolfe, *Suetonius: Lives of the Caesars*, 2:111.

68. Seneca, *Controv.* 2.1.11; Juvenal 3.269–273.

69. *Digest* 43.8, 43.10.1; see Robinson (1992) 36. On the domestic quarters of Rome as shown on the marble plan, see Castagnoli (1976) and Gros & Torelli (1988) 202–206 and figs. 90, 91, and 92.

70. These references are collected and discussed by Robinson (1992) 34–35. They include: Vitruvius 2.8.17 (on wall thickness), and 2.3.2 (on aging bricks); Pliny, *NH* 16.15.36 (on roofing); Strabo, *Geog.* 5.3.7 (on height limits set by Augustus); Suetonius, *Aug.* 89 (on reading from Rutilius). Two further passages that seem to indicate restrictions on heights of buildings are Horace, *Ep.* 1.1.100, and Valerius Maximus 8.1., although the latter does not refer to Rome.

71. Pliny, *Paneg.* 51 (on materials) and the anonymous *Epitome de Caesaribus*, 13.13 (on building heights).

72. Tertullian, *Adversus Val.* 7.1–3.

73. On this entire question, see Balland (1965). Cf. the remarks of Gros & Torelli (1988) 182–183, and of Robinson (1992) 34–37.

74. Varro, *L. L.* 5.146 is the *locus classicus* for this explanation of these names as recalling very early markets, although in both cases the location seems odd—access to the river would hardly aid in the delivery of cattle or vegetables to market—and the spaces cramped. Nonetheless, the ancient tradition is strong and is corroborated by Festus (Paulus *ex Fest.* 27L) for the Boarium. See Wiseman (1987a) 400 and Richardson (1992) 162–163, 164–165 for discussion.

75. The essential study that led to real comprehension of the Circus Flaminius as an urban space was Wiseman (1974); also Wiseman (1976).

76. There were actually two different applications of the term "Subura" to areas of Rome. The first designated the valley between the Oppius and Carinae during the earliest centuries, and fell out of use before the label came to be applied to the bustling inner city area that the major ancient sources designate the "Subura" (especially Martial 1.2, 3; 2.17; 5.22; 6.66; 7.31; 9.37; 10.94; 11.51, 61, 68; 12.3, 18, 21).

77. Gros & Torelli (1988) 61–103; Castagnoli (1978) 19–32; Stambaugh (1988) 1–28.

78. See Richardson (1992) 310–319 (on the various porticus), 143–144 (on the Emporium), 33–35 (Largo Argentina temples), and 50–56 (on the basilicas). Also for the various basilicas, Steinby (1993b) 167–188.

79. Gros & Torelli (1988) 104–126; Castagnoli (1978) 32–34; Stambaugh (1988) 28–66. Also very important is Coarelli (1977).

80. Wiseman (1987a) 403–407.

81. See Giuliani (1982). On the Domus Tiberiana, see Krause (1987). Wiseman (1987a) 407–408 wishes to remove all responsibility for the *Tiberiana* from Tiberius and attribute it to Caligula, but on insufficient grounds since the name *Tiberiana* and the tradition of Tiberius's involvement are attested in the ancient sources. On the Neronian palaces, see Balland (1965) and Ball (1994); on Domitian's Palatine palace, Finsen (1969) and Torelli (1987) esp. 578–582.

82. On the foundation, see Varro, *L. L.* 5.145–147. On the fire of 210 B.C., see Livy 26.27.2, 27.11.16. Plautus, *Curc.* 472 appears to confirm the location on all or at least most of the space later occupied by the templum Pacis. Cicero, *Pro Quinct.* 6.25 calls the entire section of town *macellum*. Further see Anderson (1982) 102–104 and De Ruyt (1983) 250–252. The very existence of the central *macellum* was dismissed by Nabers (1978) 174 and n. 10 on a misreading of the evidence; this is criticized, properly, by De Ruyt (1983) 160–163. On the two streets, see E. Tortorici, "Argiletum" in Steinby (1993b) 127–128, and D. Palombi, "Corneta" in Steinby (1993b) 323.

83. Anderson (1982) 101–105; De Ruyt (1983) 225–252. Also DeRuyt (1983) 163–172 (on the Macellum Liviae) and 172–184 (on the Macellum Magnum).

84. On the disappearance of the Argiletum and Corneta, see Anderson (1982) esp. 105–110. On the Flavian amphitheater complex's extent, see Anderson (1985) esp. 506–509. On the disappearance of private territory in the inner city during the first centuries B.C. and A.D., see Frézouls (1987) esp. 386–392; Stambaugh (1988) 67–85, 89–91 and n. 4 (p. 337); Gros & Torelli (1988) 167–206, esp. 202–206.

85. Packer (1971) 74–79; McKay (1975) 80–89; Castagnoli (1976); Gros & Torelli (1988) 202–206.

86. For an excellent treatment of this side of the suburban expansion of

ancient Rome, see Champlin (1982). Further see Lugli (1923), Quilici (1979) and Purcell (1987a) 30–32; also Purcell (1987b).

87. Cicero, *Phil* 12.x.24: *Hisce ego me viis committam, qui Terminalibus nuper in suburbium, ut eodem die reverterer, ire non sum ausus?*

88. Dionysius of Halicarnassus, *Ant. Rom.* 4.13.3–4. The translation is from the Loeb edition: E. Cary, *The Roman Antiquities of Dionysius of Halicarnassus*, vol. 2 (London and Cambridge, Mass., 1939) 311. See, on this passage, Purcell (1987a) 30, who gives the last two clauses an even more specifically "suburban" translation perfectly in keeping with the original: "It is the fact that town is so interwoven with country which gives the observer some idea of the endless urban sprawl."

89. Martial 4.64.11–17. Note especially lines 12–15:

> *et totam licet aestimare Romam*
> *Albanos quoque Tusculosque colles*
> *et quodcumque iacet sub urbe frigus*
> *Fidenas veteres brevesque Rubras*

90. Anderson (1991) 8–9. Also Quilici (1974). To see this limited view of the *urbs/suburbium* in topographical studies, consider, e.g., Ashby (1927). The baldest example of the misapplication of this image of Rome to the Imperial city and suburbs is M. Rostovtzeff, *A Social and Economic History of the Roman Empire*, 2d ed. (Oxford, 1957) esp. 376. It still persists in historical and topographical writing: e.g., Stambaugh (1988) esp. 89–90, 191–194, who defines Rome from first century B.C. to third century A.D. as the area "enclosed by the third century walls of Aurelian, 1,373 hectares." (p. 337, n. 4).

91. Purcell (1987a) 30–32 and Anderson (1991) 9–11. Champlin (1982) 101–102 tends to underestimate the importance of the smallholdings, but the archaeological record attests their importance: see Quilici (1974) 425–430; also such recent studies as Arthur (1991) esp. 55–88, and more generally much of the testimony collected in Barker & Lloyd (1991), esp. 10–17 (by Vallat) and 233–240 (by Lloyd). On the limited geographical extent of the *insula* in Rome, see Packer (1967) 80–83 and Quilici (1974) 420.

92. Anderson (1991) 9; also Purcell (1987b). Literary testimonia of *rus in urbe* in the first century A.D. include Suetonius, *Nero* 31; Tacitus, *Ann.* 15.42; Martial, *De Spect.* 1.2.7–8. Disappearance of space in the city: Stambaugh (1988) 39–45, also 90: "about half the city's space was occupied by public buildings."

93. On Trajan's ordinance, see Pliny, *Ep.* 6.19 (cited by Bloch [1947] 338); also Sirago (1958) 81–85, and Champlin (1982) 103. For the urban/suburban continuum and how it changed in the later Empire, see Coarelli (1986).

Chapter 5: Public Architecture and Shared Space

1. In including religious architecture together with all other forms of public building, I am following MacDonald (1986) 111–142. For some pertinent comments on the problems in lumping together administrative and recreational, rather than regarding them as separate categories (as here), see Sear (1992) 292–293.

2. The finest modern treatments of the history and typology of Roman public architecture are, first, Crema (1959), and then Boëthius (1978) and Ward-Perkins (1981), which were originally issued as a single volume in 1970. Also commendable on a more introductory level is Sear (1982; rev. ed. 1989). While many others have appeared, these seem to me the most satisfactory.

3. MacDonald (1986) 5–110 is the essential discussion of these elements, which added together create what he labels the "armature" of the Roman city or town. I prefer to avoid the term "armature" since I find it misleading, but MacDonald's concept and description are basic and essential to considering Roman spaces and their architecture.

4. This point was raised by Coarelli (1983b) esp. 200–206, discussed by Wiseman (1987a) esp. 396–399, and taken further again by Wallace-Hadrill (1988) 58–68 and (1994) esp. 17–23.

5. Stambaugh (1978) 579–580.

6. Ling (1990) considers the problems faced by the stranger attempting to find his way around Pompeii; also see Stambaugh (1978) 587–588.

7. For booksellers, see Martial 1.2.5–8, 1.3.1–2, 1.117.9–12; also Anderson (1984) 106. For wine, see SHA *Aurelianus* 48.4; also Purcell (1985) 14–15. For further examples, see Stambaugh (1978) 585–586.

8. Vitruvius 4.5.2. The translation is from Granger (1931) 230–233.

9. For civic business and offices, see Stambaugh (1978) 580–583; on the so-called *templa rostrata* and their uses, see Ulrich (1994) esp. 81–155. For art works and libraries, see Stambaugh (1978) 586–587.

10. See Richardson (1978c) on the entire Concordia tradition; on Camillus's vow, see Momigliano (1942); on the Augustan temple to Concordia, see Kellum (1990); on the vow to *Concordia Nova*, see Weinstock (1971) 260–266.

11. Stambaugh (1978) 567 and n. 88, 584 and n. 226, a dedication recorded in Festus 242M. For a number of further examples of this sort of political dedication in Rome during the fourth to second century B.C., see Richardson (1991).

12. Anderson (1984) 53–54 (on Venus Genetrix), 65–73 (on Mars Ultor), 101 (on Peace), 132–133 (on Minerva), 158–159 (on Deified Trajan). Further on Venus Genetrix, see Ulrich (1993); on Mars Ultor, see Zanker (1988) 193–201; on Deified Trajan, see Boatwright (1987) 74–

94, Claridge (1993) and—*contra*—Packer (1994) and (1995) 349.

13. For first building, see Livy 1.38.7, 1.55.1–56.1, 2.8.6–8. For the Sullan rebuilding, see Plutarch, *Sulla* 27 and Tacitus, *Hist.* 3.72. For the Domitianic rebuilding, see Plutarch, *Poplic.* 15.3 and Suetonius, *Dom.* 5. Further see P.-M. Martin (1983).

14. Vitruvius 5.1.1–2. Translation from Granger (1931) 254–257. The archaeological evidence from Italy confirms Vitruvius on the shape of the basic Roman type of forum; see Russell (1968). On the *spectacula* and *maeniana* as determinants of forum planning, see Welch (1994) 69–78.

15. Vitruvius 5.9.1–9. The placement of this passage at the end of his long discussion of theaters has perhaps caused less attention to be paid to it than it deserves. That Vitruvius considers the *porticus* an essential architectural form in contexts far beyond the theater is manifest.

16. See Lugli (1946) pl. 4; also Richardson (1978b) 359–362 and (1992) 42, 81.

17. On the arcades of the basilicas, see Coarelli (1985) 212 (fig. 35) for the Aemilia, and 9–10 (fig. 1) for the Julia. It is likely that the earlier form of the Basilica Aemilia did have a colonnaded front: Coarelli (1985) 203–209. For the decorative arrangements of both façades in the Imperial period, see Nash (1968) 1:186–187, 278.

18. Vitruvius 5.1.4–10 (basilicas), 5.2 (treasury, prison, senate house), 5.3–5.8 (theaters), 5.9 (colonnades and porticoes), 5.10 (baths), 5.11 (exercise grounds), 5.12 (harbors).

19. Vitruvius 5.4. Translation from Granger (1931) 257.

20. See Robertson (1969) 268; also Crema (1959) 62–66, who derives the word "basilica" from the Greek στοὰ Βασιλεὺς.

21. Livy 39.44.7; *De viris illustribus* 47; Plutarch, *Cato* 19.2. On its destruction: Asconius, *Cic. in Mil.* 29 (Colson, p. 138). For discussion see Coarelli (1985) 59–63; Richardson (1992) 56.

22. Richardson (1988) 97.

23. On the architecture of this building generally, and particularly on the related questions of whether or not it had a second storey and its roofing system (if any) over the nave, see Robertson (1969) 268–269 and Richardson (1988) 96–99.

24. Richardson (1988) 97.

25. By far the most important source on this building is Packer (1996), which was not available to me at the time of writing; see Packer's summary in Steinby (1995) 352–353. See also Crema (1959) 370; Blake & Bishop (1973) esp. 15; Anderson (1984) 144–145; Richardson (1992) 176.

26. Anderson (1984) 160–167; Packer (1995) 349.

27. See Crema (1959) 578, Robertson (1969) 270–271, and Ward-

Perkins (1981) 426–428 and 442–445 on the continuity of the basilica and examples from late antiquity.

28. Richardson (1978b), (1992) 102–104. The main publication of the Diocletianic building is Bartoli (1963). Also important are Nash (1968) 1:301–303 and Morselli & Tortorici (1989) 1–263.

29. Vitruvius 5.2.1–2. Translation from Granger (1931) 263.

30. See Coarelli (1983) 119–160 and (1985) 11–27.

31. Pliny, *NH* 7.212.

32. See Coarelli (1983) 161–198 on the *Volcanal* and the *lapis niger*; (1985) 28–38 on the *Puteal* and the fig tree, and 39–52 on the *columna Maenia*.

33. Coarelli (1985) 22–27 and 53–58.

34. Hanson (1959) esp. 37–39; also Richardson (1957) on the examples at Cosa and Paestum, as well as that at Rome.

35. On the *aerarium*, see Macrobius, *Sat.* 1.8.3; Paulus *ex Fest.* 2L; Appian, *BellCiv* 1.31; Asconius, *Cic. in Mil.* 36 (Colson, p. 140). For the single entranceway, see Plutarch, *Ti. Gracchus* 10.6. Further see Lugli (1946) 149–151; Richardson (1980) 51–62 and (1992) 343–344. On the treasury at Pompeii, see Richardson (1988) 140 and (1992) 344.

36. Sallust, *Cat.* 55.2–5. The translation is from J. C. Rolfe's Loeb edition: *Sallust* (London and Cambridge, Mass., 1930) 115.

37. Frank (1924) 39–47; Lugli (1946) 107–111; Nash (1968) 1:206–208; Coarelli (1985) 64–76; Richardson (1992) 71.

38. Basilica Porcia: Platner & Ashby (1929) 82; Coarelli (1985) 59–64; Richardson (1992) 56. On the basilica at Pompeii and its uses, see Richardson (1988) 97.

39. Nash (1976); Anderson (1984) 51–54 and 62–63.

40. On the location of the city prefecture in the templum Pacis after A.D. 192, see Anderson (1984) esp. 116–117, accepted by Richardson (1992) 287. On the *praefectura urbana* (offices on the Oppius), see Nash (1976), followed by Richardson (1992) 321.

41. Livy 43.16.11–13. The translation is from A. C. Schlesinger's Loeb edition: *Livy XIII, Books xliii–xlv* (London and Cambridge, Mass., 1968) 59.

42. Anderson (1984) 21–26; Richardson (1992) 41; Packer (1995) 349. On the fragment of the marble plan, see Carettoni et al. (1960) vol. 2, pl. 28 and Rodriguez Almeida (1981) vol. 2, pl. 21.

43. Pliny, *NH* 36.33; Ovid, *Ars amat.* 1.82 and *Rem. amat.* 660. Also Cicero, *ad Att.* 4.16.14. The location on the clivus Argentarius is urged by Anderson (1984) 21–26 (see also Ulrich [1986], and Richardson [1992] 14 and 41), but a location on the Capitoline Hill and an identification of the atrium Libertatis with the structure traditionally identified as the Tabularium has been asserted by Purcell (1993).

44. The inscriptions are *CIL* I². 736, 737 = 6.1313, 1314 = *ILS* 35, 35a (Catulus) and *CIL* 6.916 = 31201 (Claudius); for the L. Cornelius inscription, see Molisani (1971), and chapter 1 and fig. 1.1, above. See Lugli (1946) 42–46; Nash (1968) 2:402–408; Richardson (1992) , 376–377 for the traditional identification. *Contra:* Purcell (1993). It is difficult to see how this complex could possibly have been called an "atrium" of any kind, since it has none of the characteristics otherwise associated with *atria* by Vitruvius or in the archaeological record. Despite the ingenuity of Purcell's argument, the traditional identification remains the most convincing.

45. On libraries outside Rome, see Richardson (1977), and (1988) 273–275. For libraries in Rome, see Richardson (1992) 58–59 and Steinby (1993b) 196–197.

46. Anderson (1984) 172–177.

47. Livy 33.27.4. See Kleiner (1985) 14–15.

48. Livy 37.3.7. The translation is from E. T. Sage's Loeb edition, *Livy X: Books xxxv–xxxvii* (London and Cambridge, Mass., 1965) 299. Also Kleiner (1985) 15–16.

49. On Republican arches, see Kleiner (1985) 16–19; on Augustan arches, Kleiner (1985) 20–34; also Richardson (1992) 22.

50. Nash (1968) 1:74–78 and 102–103. See Koeppel (1983) and Kleiner (1985) 59–62.

51. Kleiner (1985) 69–93.

52. Nash (1968) 1:133–135.

53. On Domitian's many arches, see Suetonius, *Dom.* 13 and Cassius Dio 68.1.1. On the Triumphalis, Martial 8.65. For the Palatine arch, see Richardson (1992) 25.

54. For each of these later examples, see the entries in Richardson (1992) 23–30.

55. See MacDonald (1986) 5–110, esp. 5–31, on the function of arches within the context of Roman town street patterns. On all the provincial and Italian arches listed, see Kähler (1939); on the arches of Narbonese Gaul, see Kleiner (1985) 40–50; Anderson (1987).

56. Richardson (1992) 270–271 with bibliography.

57. Tortorici (1993).

58. MacDonald (1986) 111–112; Yegül (1992) 30–47, esp. 43.

59. MacDonald (1986) 115–116.

60. Cicero, *ad Fam.* 14.20; Pliny, *Ep.* 2.17.26; Apuleius, *Met.* 1.23.

61. Yegül (1992) 48–55 with examples, notably the Greek baths at Gela in Sicily.

62. Vitruvius 5.11.1.

63. Yegül (1992) 57–66; Nielsen (1990) 1:25–34.

64. Meiggs (1973) 411–413; Pavolini (1983) 105–109; Nielsen (1990) vol. 2: no. C 27 and fig. 69; Yegül (1992) 68 and fig. 73.

65. Martial 6.42, lines 1–3, 8–24. The translation is from W. C. A. Ker's Loeb edition: *Martial, Epigrams* 1 (London and Cambridge, Mass., 1968) 382–385.

66. E.g., the list in Richardson (1992) 48–50, and on the terms *thermae* and *balneum*, 385–386.

67. Cassius Dio 53.27.1 and 54.29.4. On the Aqua Virgo, see Frontinus, *Aq.* 1.10. On collections and decoration, see Pliny, *NH* 34.62, 35.26, 36.189. In general, Richardson (1992) 386–387.

68. See the lists in Platner & Ashby (1929) 518–536, and in Richardson (1992) 386–398.

69. On the Baths of Titus, see Lugli (1946) 353–355; Nash (1968) 2:469–471; Anderson (1985) 499.

70. The most important architectural and archaeological studies of Trajan's Baths are De Fine Licht (1974) and (1990). Further see Nielsen (1990) 1:49–51; Yegül (1992) 142–146.

71. Yegül (1992) 43–46 and 172–180.

72. Seneca, *Ep. Mor.* 56. The translation is from R. M. Gummere's Loeb edition: *Seneca IV: Epistulae Morales I, Books i–lxv* (London and Cambridge, Mass., 1979) 372–375.

73. Yegül (1992) esp. 32–46.

74. See Anderson (1985) 503–509. *Contra:* Yegül (1992) 142–144, n. 41 (pp. 442–443), but cf. the comments of DeLaine (1988) esp. 19.

75. On women in the baths, see Jerome, *Chron.* 146. Also see Yegül (1992) 172–180.

76. Dionysius of Halicarnassus, *Ant. Rom.* 3.68. The translation is from E. Cary's Loeb edition: *Dionysius of Halicarnassus, Roman Antiquities II: Books 3 and 4* (London and Cambridge, Mass., 1939) 240–243.

77. Ovid, *Ars amat.* 1.135–142.

78. On circuses in general, see Humphrey (1986). On the Circus Maximus, ibid., pp. 56–244; on the Circus Vaticanus, ibid., 545–552. See Crema (1959) 99–100 on derivations of the circus form.

79. Nash (1968) 2:387–390; Richardson (1992) 82, 366–367.

80. Livy, *Epit.* 16; Valerius Maximus 2.4.7.

81. Welch (1994) asserts this new interpretation of the *ludi* in the Roman Forum and of the architectural origins of the Roman amphitheater with conviction. For the more traditional view of a Campanian origin for the building type, see Crema (1959) 95–96; also Richardson (1992) 6.

82. On the amphitheater at Pompeii, see Crema (1959) 98 and Richardson (1988) 134–138; at Alba Fucens, Coarelli & La Regina (1993) 92.

83. On the early amphitheaters in Rome, see Richardson (1992) 6; also Palombi (pp. 35, 36) and Viscogliosi (pp. 36–37) in Steinby (1993b).

84. See R. Rea, "Amphitheatrum," in Steinby (1993b) 30–35; Richardson (1992) 7–10.
85. See Coarelli (1974) 166–174; Anderson (1985). On the spectacles of the amphitheaters and their production, as well as their social siginificance, see Girod (1983).
86. One of the few examples of a theater that seems to have had a regular function in addition to shows and spectacles may be provided by the theater at Saepinum. There, the back of the *cavea* intersected the city wall at one point, and the wall was pierced for a gateway that allowed access to the theater's *scaena* and *orchestra* from outside the town. It is generally thought this was intended for bringing in livestock and other items for country fairs held in the theater; cf. V. Cianfarani, "Saepinum," in Stilwell (1976) 781; Anderson (1983b) 4–6; Coarelli & La Regina (1993) 225–226.
87. For instance, *dolia* used for this purpose may still be seen in the seating of the Circus of Maxentius on the via Appia.
88. Of particular importance on this subject are Frézouls (1982), Small (1983), Isler (1989), Sear (1990), Tosi (1994), and Gros (1994c).
89. Lauter (1976) esp. 415, followed by Sear (1990) 249–250.
90. Richardson (1988) 77, cf. Sear (1990) 249.
91. See Sear (1990) 250. On the theater at Tusculum, see Ashby (1910) esp. 353. For the early first century B.C. reworking of the large theater at Pompeii, see Richardson (1988) 80.
92. Livy, *Epit.* 48; Tacitus, *Ann.* 14.20; Valerius Maximus 2.4.1–2.
93. The best extant parallel to this in Roman architecture is the Roman theater at Orange (ancient Arausio) in Provence. Tosi (1994) 180–183 asserts that Vitruvius was drawing on the architecture of Pompey's theater in laying out the details of his "Roman" theater building and demonstrates quite convincingly that what we know of Pompey's complex is closer than the theaters of Marcellus or Statilius Taurus to Vitruvius's prescription. But she fails to account for the likelihood that Vitruvius had seen theaters outside Rome in the course of his travels while serving in Julius Caesar's army and could have had access to written treatises on stone theaters in Italy or the Roman West that antedated the late specimens in Rome.
94. See Sauron (1987) on the significance of Pompey's theater in its urban setting, a theoretical suggestion not widely accepted; cf. Rodriguez Almeida (1981) 148–150 and pl. 32; Richardson (1992) 383–385. On the discovery and appearance of the theater itself, see Coarelli (1972). The nature and appearance of the Venus shrine atop the *cavea* remains a matter of debate and dispute; cf. Hill (1944); Hanson (1959) 43–58; Richardson (1987); Stambaugh (1988) 41–42 and n. 10 (p. 330).

95. Gros (1987) esp. 342–343 makes a strong case for the incorporation of these three theaters into a "symbolic" piece of urbanism, integrated into the Augustan city. See Frézouls (1981) on the political implications of Pompey's construction.

96. Strabo, *Geog.* 5.3.8 (C 236). The translation is from H. L. Jones's Loeb edition: *The Geography of Strabo* 2 (London and Cambridge, Mass., 1923): 407. N.B., the comments of Gros (1987) 343 on this passage.

97. On the *theatrum tectum* at Pompeii, see Richardson (1988) 131–134. On the Domitianic *odeum* in Rome, see Platner & Ashby (1929) 371; Crema (1959) 302; Richardson (1992) 276.

Chapter 6: Quotidian Architecture and Individual Space

1. See the attempt at a survey of such material in the Roman Campagna by Quilici Gigli (1994), which demonstrates both the importance of the subject and the frustrating lack of precise information in the area around Rome and Latium and, indeed, in most of Italy. The well-established pattern of excavated villas of the Roman period in the European provinces, especially in France, Germany, and Britain, has yielded sufficient data to allow theories concerning the social structures implied by their layout and architecture to be formulated, but these theories are much debated and not yet well synthesized; see, e.g., Smith (1978) and (1987)—but *contra*: Webster & Smith (1987)—or Clarke (1990).

2. On *fauces*, see Richardson (1988) 387–388. For some interesting speculations on the social meaning of the *fauces* type of entrance to a Roman house, see Wallace-Hadrill (1994) 118.

3. Vitruvius 6.1–2.

4. Richardson (1988) 386–387.

5. Richardson (1988) 111–112 (Epidio Rufo), 118 (Fontana Grande), 160 (Menandro), 310 (Dioscuri).

6. Richardson (1988) 385 (Ceii), 386 (Grata Metallica), 387 (Nozze).

7. Vitruvius 6.2; Richardson (1988) 295 (Giulia Felice).

8. Richardson (1988) 118–119 (Polybio), 384 (two numbered houses). The excavator of the Casa del Chirurgio, Amedeo Maiuri, asserted it was testudinate and lacked a *compluvium*, but this is often questioned, e.g., by Richardson (1988) 370, n. 3.

9. Vitruvius 6.3–7. Richardson (1988) 389–398. For the Casa di Sallustio, see Laidlaw & Packer (1971), also Stambaugh (1988) 163–164; Casa del Fauno, McKay (1975) 43–44.

10. Vitruvius 6.3.8–11. An example of the Corinthian *oecus* is that of the Casa del Labirinto at Pompeii (Richardson [1988] 165–166); of the tetrastyle *oecus*, the Casa delle Nozze d'Argento (Richardson [1988]

156); of the Egyptian *oecus* the magnificent example that replaced the main *triclinium* in the Casa dell'Atrio a mosaico at Herculaneum (McKay [1975] 53–54); and of the Cyzicene perhaps the rectangular hall that opened off the gardens in the *praedium* of Julia Felix at Pompeii (McKay [1975] 53).

11. See with texts of the graffiti, McKay [1975] 82.

12. In this topic, as in others, I am much indebted to the work of A. Wallace-Hadrill, esp. (1994) 65–90 (his chapter "Houses and Urban Texture"), whose extraordinarily perceptive analyses I am in large part following. Also essential for looking at the less than wealthy housing of Pompeii is Packer (1975).

13. I have chosen the *insula* of the Menander (I.x) because it enjoys one of the most comprehensive and reliable excavation reports of any sector of the city (O. Elia, "Relazione sullo scavo dell'Insula X della Regio I[i]," *NSA* 1934, 264–344). There is also a good descriptive survey in La Rocca & DeVos (1976) 172–188. The work of a British team of archaeologists, led by R. Ling, has further clarified our knowledge of the entire *insula* (see Ling [1983], with final report in preparation), as has the survey by Wallace-Hadrill (1994) 193–194. We are rarely so well informed. On Pompeiian city blocks in general, and especially Regio 7, see Laurence (1994) 104–121.

14. Wallace-Hadrill (1994) 56–57.

15. Wallace-Hadrill (1994) 39, 43–44.

16. By Moeller (1976) 39. Jongman (1988) 163 casts doubt on this; Wallace-Hadrill (1994) 193 does not enter the fray. On the tool chest in the Casa del Fabbro, see Wallace-Hadrill (1994) 136.

17. Strocka (1991).

18. Maiuri (1960) 188 for a good example. The ranked classification was originally applied to Herculaeum by Maiuri (1958) *passim*, esp. 248. The presumptions have continued to creep into more modern analyses of the social structure revealed in Roman urban contexts: e.g., Raper (1977) esp. 192–193, and Raper (1979). This is discussed in detail by Wallace-Hadrill (1991b) 250–264 and (1994) 118–131.

19. See Wallace-Hadrill (1994) 141, quoting the Neapolitan novelist Luciano De Crescenzo: "In Naples, the working class lived in the basements, the nobles on the so-called *primo piano nobile* and the bourgeoisie on the upper floors. This social stratification of a vertical type has obviously favoured cultural exchanges between the classes."

20. Vitruvius 6.5. The translation is Granger (1934) 36–39.

21. See Wallace-Hadrill (1994) 38–63 "The articulation of the house," esp. 39, 40 (Casa del Menandro); 39, 43 (Casa degli Amanti); 56 (Casa del Fabbro).

22. Wallace-Hadrill (1994) 40.

23. Vitruvius 6.3.6.
24. See Wallace-Hadrill (1994) 44–51; also his chapter "Luxury and Status," 143–174.
25. See I. Jacopi, "Domus: Augustus (Palatium)," in Steinby (1995) 46–48.
26. Suetonius, *Vit.* 15.3; Tacitus, *Hist.* 1.27; Plutarch, *Galb.,* 24.3. See Giuliani (1982) 241–254; Krause (1987) and "Domus Tiberiana," in Steinby (1995) 197–199; Richardson (1992) 136–137.
27. See M. de Vos, "Domus Transitoria," in Steinby (1995) 199–202; Richardson (1992) 138–139.
28. Tacitus, *Ann.* 15.42.1; Suetonius, *Nero* 31. Major discussions of the remains and the architecture include: Boëthius (1960) 94–128; Nash (1968) 1:339–348; MacDonald (1982) 20–46; Fabbrini (1983) and "Domus Aurea," in Steinby (1995) 56–63; Hemsoll (1990); Richardson (1992) 119–121; and Ball (1994). Warden (1981) raises some important doubts as to whether the remains on the Oppius should be connected with Nero's Domus Aurea at all; while the analysis has won few adherents, the questions deserve further attention.
29. Especially important to an understanding of the architecture of this palace is MacDonald (1982) 52–69. Also see Crema (1959) 316–319; Finsen (1969); Giuliani (1982) 246–254; Richardson (1992) 114–117; and L. Sasso D'Elia, "Domus Augustana," in Steinby (1995) 40–45.
30. Statius, *Silvae* 4.2. The translation is from J. H. Mozley's Loeb edition, *Statius I* (London and Cambridge, Mass., 1982) 212–215.
31. Packer (1971) 57–58 and 117, plan 64.
32. First published in Maiuri (1958) 280–302. See the descriptions and discussion in Packer (1971) 55–56 and 116, plans 60, 61; also Stambaugh (1988) 174–175 and McKay (1975) 82–83.
33. Cf. Castagnoli (1976), esp. 45–47. The ancient sources include *CIL* 4.138, which refers to the insula Arriana Polliana at Pompeii clearly meaning the entire city block; *CIL* 6.29791, which describes a multi-unit apartment building with six apartments and eleven shops for rent; the legal citations *Digest* 33.7.7 (which refers to an *insula* in which an apartment—*cenaculum*—was located), 17.2.52.10 (portions of an *insula*), and 39.1.3.2 (common space in an *insula*); the best-known reference of all is Festus 98–99L, which says "They are properly called *insulae* that are not joined by party walls, and are encircled by a passageway (sidewalk? street?) either public or private" (the translation is mine). The texts of the Regionary Catalogues are available in Valentini & Zucchetti (1940–53) 1:63–251. On the impossibility of resolving the evidence of the Regionaries on *insulae* with the topography of the Constantinian city, see Packer (1967) and Hermansen (1978).
34. Packer (1971) 79 suggests that the term covered "any type of multiple

dwelling"; Castagnoli (1976) 47–49 goes even further, suggesting it can refer to any unit of habitation whatsoever. This last must be incorrect; the Regionary Catalogues list *domus,* seeming to indicate the houses of the wealthy senatorial families of the period, separately. Probably Packer is correct in regarding it as a loose blanket term for multiple dwellings as employed in our ancient sources.

35. Vituvius 2.8.17. The translation is that of Granger (1931) 127. Note that Vitruvius is distinguishing between the strength of walls of sun-dried brick (*lateres*), which he feels cannot support a second storey at a width of a foot and a half, and baked brick (*testacea*) which, with strong cores of *opus caementicium,* can. The passage about these walls reads in Latin, with important terms highlighted: Itaque pilis lapideis structuris *testaceis,* parietibus *caementiciis* altitudines exstructae contignationibus crebris coaxtae *cenaculorum* ad summas utilitates perficiunt despectationes.

36. The first typology is that of Boëthius (1960) 159–161; the second that of Packer (1971) 6–15. Both have strengths and limitations.

37. This description is adapted from Packer (1971) 127–134 as modified by Stambaugh (1988) 175 and further modified by me. Numbers refer to Packer's plans 2 (ground floor) and 3 (second floor), p. 94 (fig. 6.3 here).

38. For detailed analysis of the design of the Garden Apartments, see Watts and Donald (1987). More generally, see Meiggs (1973) 139–140, 242; Pavolini (1983) 156–157.

39. Hermansen (1970) and (1982) 17–43 is essential for the terminology of apartment rooms and for the *medianum* in particular. Ulpian's remarks paraphrased here occur at *Digest* 9.3.1.10–9.3.5.2. On the vocabulary of these passages, see Frier (1980) esp. 3–20.

40. See especially Frier (1980); also Casey (1985) on the legal testimonia for all these subjects.

41. See on the Ara Coeli complex, Nash (1968) 1:506–507, and Packer (1971) 75; on the SS. Giovanni e Paolo example, Packer (1971) 75; the Porta S. Lorenzo *insula:* Packer (1971) 75; on the Galleria Colonna *insula:* Packer (1971) 75–76, 121 (plan 73), and Gros & Torelli (1988) 201–202; on the via Giulio Romano *insula:* Packer (1968); on the others: McKay (1975) 88–89.

42. See Gros & Torelli (1988) 202–206, figs. 90, 91, 92. For detailed consideration of the individual fragments, see Rodriguez Almeida (1981) 78–92, Tav. IX, no. 11a–d (clivus Suburanus), 144, Tav. XXIX, no. 37A (Janiculum), 86–87, Tav. X, no. 11e–i (vicus Patricius). This information had been summarized previously by Packer (1971) 76–77 but without the advantage of numerous fragments published subsequently.

43. Burning and collapse: Seneca, *De Benef.* 4.6.2; 6.15.7; *De Ira* 3.35.5; noise: Martial 12.27; high rents: Martial 3.30; bad neighbors: Martial 1.117; 4.38; traffic: Martial 5.22; high stairs: Martial 7.20; cf. Castagnoli (1950). Yavetz (1958), who deals primarily with the Republic, comes to the conclusion that there had been little change over the centuries, as does Packer (1971) 74–78.

44. Juvenal 3.190–202, 223–225, 232–248, 268–274. The translation is that of the Loeb edition: G. G. Ramsay, *Juvenal and Persius* (London and Cambridge, Mass., 1918) 46–53.

45. For the best overall description of the remains at Sette Bassi: Ashby (1907) 97–112, and (1927) 156–159. See Colini (1958) on the topography and Bloch (1958) on the dating of the remains.

46. Widrig (1986) 141–157, and (1987) 227–254.

47. The remains of many such farms and smallholdings are described by Ashby (1907) and (1910). See examples from recent excavations provided by Arthur (1991) and Quilici Gigli (1994). On social structure implied by villa design: Smith (1978) and (1987)—strongly opposed by Webster & Smith (1987)—and Clarke (1990). On social stratification between town and country, see Patterson (1991).

48. Cicero, *De Leg.* 2.23.58 and 2.24.61.

49. See Robinson (1992) 124–127, and Purcell (1987a).

50. Meiggs (1973) 455–456.

51. Meiggs (1973) 457. On the tomb of Cartilius Poplicola, see Panciera (1966).

52. For a good description of these *columbaria*, see Pavolini (1983) 261–270.

53. On the tomb of G. Ennius Marsus, see Anderson (1983b), Coarelli & La Regina (1993) 224–225.

54. See the list and details given in Richardson (1992) 351–361.

55. See Anderson (1984) 154–159 and Claridge (1993).

56. On the Imperial mausolea, see Richardson (1992) 247–249 (Augustus) and 249–251 (Hadrian).

57. Tomb of the Scipios: Nash (1968) vol. 2: 352–256. In general, on tombs in their cemetery contexts: Purcell (1987a).

58. See the pioneering article by N. Purcell (1994). There have been valuable earlier studies on particular aspects of certain kinds of *tabernae* (e.g., Hermansen [1974] and [1982] 125–205; Packer [1978]), on certain types of quotidian spaces, especially in Rome (e.g., De Ruyt [1983] on *macella*; MacMullen [1970] and Wiseman [1974] on open markets, now supplemented by Frayn [1993] and Ligt [1993]; Andreau, Etienne, and Morel [all 1987] on commercial spaces in ancient Rome), and on specific types of evidence for the *tabernae* (e.g., Staccioli [1959]).

59. On Capua, see Asconius, *in Pis.* 10c. *Tabernae* in time of Tarquinius Priscus, Livy 1.35.10 and Dionysius of Halicarnassus, *Ant. Rom.* 3.67.4. *Tabernae Veteres,* Plautus, *Curc.* 480; Livy 44.16.10; Cicero, *Acad.* 2.70. *Tabernae Novae,* Livy 3.48.5 and 40.51.5; Varro, *L. L.* 6.59; Cicero, *De Orat.* 2.266. *Tabernae* in Forum Boarium, Livy 35.40. See Morel (1987) 133–137 and Purcell (1994) 660–661 for surveys of the early development and distribution of the *taberna;* see Wallace-Hadrill (1991b) 262–264 and Richardson (1992) 375 on the various groups of *tabernae* in and near the Forum.

60. On shops in the Markets of Trajan, see Ungaro & Messa (1989) esp. 17–27; on shops on the marble plan: Staccioli (1959). On shops at Ostia: Girri (1956). On shops at Pompeii and Herculaneum: Wallace-Hadrill (1991b) esp. 260–262; cf., on Pompeii, Laurence (1994) 51–69, who mistakenly asserts that *tabernae* did not tend to occur on the main thoroughfares but only on the less important streets of Pompeii, when exactly the opposite was in fact the case. He is correct in asserting that certain types of businesses, especially the relatively noisy workshops such as *officinae lanifricariae* and *officinae tinctoriae* tend to be excluded from main streets, but this cannot be extended to the *taberna* as an architectural unit in Pompeii.

61. Purcell (1994) 661–662 suggests the apposite example of Cicero, *Dom.* 89–90.

62. See, for instance, Boëthius (1960) chaps. 2 and 4.

63. Livy 6.25.8–11. The translation is from the Loeb edition: B. O. Foster, *Livy,* vol. 3 (London and Cambridge, Mass., 1940) 284–287.

64. Cicero, *ad Att.* 14.9.1.

65. On the thermopolium in via di Diana, see Meiggs (1973) 428–429; Hermansen (1982) 130–132; Pavolini (1983) 83. On the bakery in via dei Molini, see Meiggs (1973) 274; Pavolini (1983) 77–79. On the fullery of Stephanus, see La Rocca & DeVos (1976) 194–197; on the *stabulum* of Hermes, see Packer (1978) 6–9.

66. Laidlaw & Packer (1971); also La Rocca & DeVos (1976) 326–327 and Stambaugh (1988) 162–164, 171.

67. Plautus, *Curc.* 466–482. The translation is that of Dudley (1967) 75–76.

68. On fruit and vegetables, see 7.31.9–12, 10.94.5–6; books, 1.2.7–8, 1.3.1–2,1.117.9–12; prostitutes, 2.17. See Castagnoli (1950) and Anderson (1984) 120–121. As late as the second half of the first century B.C. there were apparently individual houses in the area of the lower Argiletum (Cicero, *ad Att.* 1.14.7, 12.32.2) but these are never mentioned in subsequent sources and had very likely been absorbed in the expansion of the Fora of Caesar and Augustus.

69. I follow the brilliant analysis by Wiseman (1974), reinforced in (1976).

See also MacMullen (1970), Frayn (1993), and Ligt (1993) on the nature and importance of market days in Italy and throughout the Roman world.

70. Morel (1987) 129–131.
71. Morel (1987) 132–133. Also Etienne (1987) esp. 236–238. See now the essential study of the via Marmorata marble depot by Fant (1992).
72. Morel (1987) 141; on the locations of the various streets see Richardson (1992) 375.
73. See the list given by Morel (1987) 143.
74. This conclusion was first drawn by Boëthius (1960) esp. 129–185, who was followed by Packer (1971), MacDonald (1986), and Purcell (1994) as well as by me. The insight is of tremendous importance to our understanding of Roman society as well as of Roman quotidian architecture.
75. Cicero, *In Pis.* 67. The translation is mine; the Latin reads: *pistor domi nullus, nullus cella; panis et vinum a propola atque de cupa.* See Purcell (1994) 66.

Bibliography

The abbreviations used in this bibliography are those of *L'Année Philologique*.

Adam (1984). J.-P. Adam. *La construction romaine*. Paris, 1984.

Adam (1994). J.-P. Adam. *Roman Building: Materials and Techniques*. English translation by Anthony Mathews of Adam (1984). Bloomington & Indianapolis, 1994.

Alzinger (1989). W. Alzinger. "Vitruvs Basilika und der archäologische Befund." In Geertman & DeJong (1989) 212–216.

Amalfitano, Camodeca, & Medri (1990). P. Amalfitano, G. Camodeca, and M. Medri, eds. *I Campi Flegrei: un itinerario archeologico*. Venice, 1990.

Anderson (1982). J. C. Anderson, jr. "Domitian, the Argiletum, and the Temple of Peace." *AJA* 86 (1982) 101–110.

Anderson (1983a). J. C. Anderson, jr. "A Topographical Tradition in Fourth Century Chronicles: Domitian's Building Program." *Historia* 32 (1983) 93–105.

Anderson (1983b). J. C. Anderson, jr. "Saepinum: A Samnite and Roman Town in the Abruzzi." *AugAge* 2 (1982–1983) 1–8.

Anderson (1984). J. C. Anderson, jr. *Historical Topography of the Imperial Fora*. Collection Latomus, vol. 182. Brussels, 1984.

Anderson (1985). J. C. Anderson, jr. "The Date of the *Thermae Traiani* and the Topography of the *Oppius Mons*," *AJA* 89 (1985) 499–509.

Anderson (1987). J. C. Anderson, jr. "The Date of the Arch at Orange." *BJ* 187 (1987) 159–192.

Bibliography

Anderson (1991). J. C. Anderson, jr. *Roman Brick Stamps: The Thomas Ashby Collection in the American Academy in Rome*. Archaeological Monographs of the British School at Rome, vol. 3. London, 1991.

Anderson (1996). J. C. Anderson, jr. "The Ara Pacis Augustae: Legends, Facts, and Flights of Fancy." In M. Boatwright and H. Evans, eds., *Shapes of City Life in Rome and Pompeii* (New Rochelle, N.Y., 1996) 27–51.

André (1985). J.-M. André. "Le prologue scientifique et la rhétorique. Les préfaces de Vitruve." *BAGB* 44 (1985) 375–384.

André (1988). J.-M. André. "La rhétorique dans les préfaces de Vitruve. Le statut culturel de la science." *Filologia e Forme litterarie. Studi offerti a F. della Corte* 3 (Urbino, 1988) 265–289.

Andreau (1987). J. Andreau. "L'espace de la vie financière à Rome." In Pietri (1987) 157–174.

Arthur (1991). P. Arthur. *Romans in Northern Campania: Settlement and Land-use around the Massico and the Garigliano Basin*. Archaeological Monographs of the British School at Rome, vol. 1. London, 1991.

Asgari (1988). N. Asgari. "The Stages of Workmanship of the Corinthian Capital in Proconnesus and Its Export Form." In Herz & Waelkens (1988) 115–125.

Ashby (1907). T. Ashby. "The Classical Topography of the Roman Campagna. Part III, sect. 1." *PBSR* 4 (1907) 1–159.

Ashby (1910). T. Ashby. "The Classical Topography of the Roman Campagna. Part III, sect. 2." *PBSR* 5 (1910) 213–432.

Ashby (1927). T. Ashby. *The Roman Campagna in Classical Times*. London, 1927; reprint: London, 1970.

Ashby (1935). T. Ashby. *The Aqueducts of Ancient Rome*. Oxford, 1935.

Astin (1990). A. E. Astin. "The Role of Censors in Roman Economic Life." *Latomus* 49 (1990) 20–36.

Aubert (1993). J.-J. Aubert. "Workshop Managers." In Harris (1993a) 171–182.

Aubert (1994). J.-J. Aubert. *Business Managers in Ancient Rome: A Social and Economic Study of Institores, 200 B.C.–A.D. 250*. Columbia Studies in the Classical Tradition, vol. 21. Leiden, New York, Cologne, 1994.

Baccini Leotardi (1979). P. Baccini Leotardi. *Marmi di cava rinvenuti ad Ostia e considerazioni sul commercio dei marmi in età romana*. Scavi di Ostia, vol. 10. Rome, 1979.

Baccini Leotardi (1989). P. Baccini Leotardi. *Nuove testimonianze sul commercio dei marmi in età imperiale*. Rome, 1989.

Badian (1972). E. Badian. *Publicans and Sinners: Private Enterprise in the Service of the Roman Republic*. Oxford, 1972.

Baldwin (1989). B. Baldwin. "The Non-architectural Side of Vitruvius." *Prudentia* 21.2 (1989) 4–12.

Baldwin (1990). B. Baldwin. "The Date, Identity, and Career of Vitruvius." *Latomus* 94 (1990) 425–434.

Ball (1994). L. F. Ball. "A Reappraisal of Nero's Domus Aurea." In J. Humphrey, ed., *Rome Papers.* Journal of Roman Archaeology Supplementary Series, no. 11 (Ann Arbor, 1994) 183–254.

Balland (1965). M. A. Balland. "*Nova Urbs* et 'Neapolis.'" Remarques sur les projets urbanistiques de Néron." *MEFRA* 77 (1965) 349–393.

Barker & Lloyd (1991). G. Barker and J. Lloyd, eds. *Roman Landscapes. Archaeological Survey in the Mediterranean Region.* Archaeological Monographs of the British School at Rome, vol. 2. London, 1991.

Bartoli (1963). A. Bartoli. *Curia Senatus.* Rome, 1963.

Barton (1989a). I. M. Barton, ed. *Roman Public Buildings.* Exeter Studies in History no. 20. Exeter, 1989.

Barton (1989b). I. M. Barton. "Religious buildings." In Barton (1989a) 67–96.

Bauer (1983). H. Bauer. "Porticus Absidata." *MDAI(R)* 90 (1983) 130–139.

Benario (1958). H. W. Benario. "Rome of the Severi." *Latomus* 17 (1958) 712–722.

Benndorf (1902). O. Benndorf. "Antike Baumodelle." *JÖAI* 5 (1902) 175–195.

Bianchi-Bandinelli (1950). R. Bianchi-Bandinelli. *Storicità dell'arte classica.* 2d ed. Florence, 1950.

Bianchi-Bandinelli (1958). R. Bianchi-Bandinelli. "Apollodoro di Damasco." In R. Bianchi-Bandinelli, ed., *Enciclopedia dell'arte antica classica e orientale,* 1 (Rome, 1958) 477–480.

Bianchi-Bandinelli (1969). R. Bianchi-Bandinelli. *Rome: le centre du pouvoir.* Paris, 1969.

Birley (1981). A. J. Birley. *The Fasti of Roman Britain.* Oxford, 1981.

Blake (1947). M. A. Blake. *Ancient Roman Construction in Italy from Prehistoric Times to Augustus.* Washington, D.C., 1947.

Blake (1959). M. A. Blake. *Ancient Roman Construction in Italy from Tiberius through the Flavians.* Washington, D.C., 1959.

Blake & Bishop (1973). M. A. Blake and D. T. Bishop. *Roman Construction in Italy from Nerva through the Antonines.* Philadelphia, 1973.

Blanckenhagen (1954). H. P. von Blanckenhagen. "The Imperial Fora." *JSAH* 13.4 (1954) 21–27.

Bloch (1944). H. Bloch. "The Aqua Traiana." *AJA* 48 (1944) 337–341.

Bloch (1947). H. Bloch. *I bolli laterizi e la storia edilizia romana.* Rome, 1947. Reprinted, with indices, from *BCAR* 64 (1936) 141–225; 65 (1937) 83–187; 66 (1938) 61–221. 2d reprinting: Rome, 1968.

Bloch (1958). H. Bloch. "Sette Bassi Revisited." *HSCP* 63 (1958) 401–414.

Boatwright (1986). M. T. Boatwright. "The Pomerial Extension of Augustus." *Historia* 35 (1986) 13–27.

Boatwright (1987). M. T. Boatwright. *Hadrian and the City of Rome.* Princeton, 1987.

Bodel (1983). J. P. Bodel. *Roman Brick Stamps in the Kelsey Museum.* University of Michigan, Kelsey Museum of Archaeology Studies, vol. 6. Ann Arbor, 1983.

Boëthius (1930). A. Boëthius. "Till frågan om Pantheons byggnadshistoria." *Eranos* 28 (1930) 201–203.

Boëthius (1932). A. Boëthius. "The Neronian *Nova Urbs,*" *ORom* 2 (1932) 84–97

Boëthius (1934). A. Boëthius. "Remarks on the Development of Domestic Architecture in Rome." *AJA* 24 (1934) 158–170.

Boëthius (1939). A. Boëthius. "Vitruvius and the Roman Architecture of His Age." In K. Hanell, E. Knudtzon, and N. Valmin, eds., *ΔΡΑΓΜΑ. Festschrift für M. P. Nilsson.* Acta Instituti Romani Regni Sueciae, ser. altera 1 (Lund, 1939) 114–143.

Boëthius (1945). A. Boëthius. "Maeniana: A Study of the Forum Romanum of the Fourth Century B.C.." *Eranos* 43 (1945) 89–110.

Boëthius (1960). A. Boëthius. *The Golden House of Nero.* Ann Arbor, 1960.

Boëthius (1978). A. Boëthius. *Etruscan and Early Roman Architecture.* 2d ed., rev. by R. Ling and T. Rasmussen. Harmondsworth & New York, 1978.

Bommelaer (1989). J.-Fr. Bommelaer. "Sur les rapports de Vitruve avec la science de son temps: questions de topographie et de géographie." In Geertman & DeJong (1989) 22–30.

Bonnefond (1987). M. Bonnefond. "Transferts de fonctions et mutation idéologique: le Capitole et le Forum d'Auguste." In Pietri (1987) 251–278.

Boren (1957–58). H. C. Boren. "The Urban Side of the Gracchan Economic Crisis." *AHR* 63 (1957–58) 890–902.

Borghini (1989). G. Borghini, ed. *Marmi antichi.* Ministero per i Beni Culturali ed Ambientali-Istituto Centrale per il Catalogo e la Documentazione. Rome, 1989.

Boyd (1953). M. J. Boyd. "The Porticus of Metellus and Octavia and Their Two Temples." *PBSR* 21 (1953) 152–159.

Briggs (1927). M. S. Briggs. *The Architect in History.* Oxford, 1927.

Brodribb (1979). G. Brodribb. "Markings on Tile and Brick." In McWhirr (1979) 211–221.

Brodribb (1987). G. Brodribb. *Roman Brick and Tile.* Gloucester, 1987.

Brothers (1989). A. J. Brothers. "Buildings for Entertainment." In Barton (1989a) 97–125.

Broughton (1952). T. R. S. Broughton. *The Magistrates of the Roman Republic.* 2 vols. New York, 1952.

Brown (1961). F. E. Brown. *Roman Architecture.* London & New York, 1961.

Brown (1963). F. E. Brown. "Vitruvius and the Liberal Art of Architecture." *Bucknell Review* 11.4 (1963) 99–107.

Brown (1980). F. E. Brown. *Cosa: The Making of a Roman Town.* Ann Arbor, 1980.

Brunt (1971). P. A. Brunt. *Italian Manpower.* Oxford, 1971.

Brunt (1974). P. A. Brunt. "The Roman Mob." In M. I. Finley, ed., *Studies in Ancient Society* (London & Boston, 1974) 74–102.

Brunt (1980). P. A. Brunt. "Free Labour and Public Works at Rome." *JRS* 70 (1980) 81–100.

Brunt (1990). P. A. Brunt. "Publicans in the Principate." In P. A. Brunt, *Roman Imperial Themes* (Oxford, 1990) 354–432.

Brunt & Moore (1967). P. A. Brunt and J. M. Moore, eds. *Res Gestae Divi Augusti.* Oxford, 1967.

Bruun (1991). Chr. Bruun. *The Water Supply of Ancient Rome: A Study of Roman Imperial Administration.* Societas Scientiarum Fennica: Commentationes Humanarum Litterarum, vol. 93. Helsinki, 1991.

Büchner (1982). E. Büchner. *Die Sonnenuhr des Augustus.* Mainz, 1982.

Buora (1985). M. Buora. "Sul commercio dei laterizi tra Aquileia e la Dalmazia." *AAAd* 26 (1985) 209–226.

Burford (1960). A. Burford. "Heavy Transport in Classical Antiquity." *Economic History Review* 13.1 (1960) 1–18.

Burford (1963). A. Burford. "The Builders of the Parthenon." In G. T. W. Hooker, ed., *Parthenos and Parthenon.* Greece and Rome, Suppl. to vol. 10 (Oxford, 1963) 23–35.

Burford (1972). A. Burford. *Craftsmen in Greek and Roman Society.* London, 1972.

Burkert (1992). W. Burkert. "Perikles von Mylasa, Architekt des Tempels der Venus und Roma." In H. Froning, T. Hölscher, & H. Mielsch, eds., *Kotinos. Festschrift für Erika Simon* (Mainz, 1992) 415–417.

Calabi Limentani (1958). E. Calabi Limentani. "Architetto." In R. Bianchi-Bandinelli, R., ed., *Enciclopedia dell'arte antica classica e orientale.* 1 (Rome, 1958) 572–578

Callebat (1973). L. Callebat, ed. *Vitruve, De l'architecture, Livre VIII.* Paris, 1973.

Callebat (1982). L. Callebat. "La prose du 'De Architectura' de Vitruve." *ANRW* 2.30.1 (Berlin, 1982) 696–722.

Callebat (1989). L. Callebat. "Organisation et structures du *De Architectura* de Vitruve." In Geertman & DeJong (1989) 34–38.

Callebat (1994). L. Callebat. "Rhétorique et architecture dans le *De Architectura* de Vitruve." In Gros (1994a) 31–46.

Bibliography

Callebat & Fleury (1986). L. Callebat & P. Fleury, eds. *Vitruve, De l'architecture, Livre X*. Paris, 1986.

Campbell (1938). W. A. Campbell. "The 4th and 5th Seasons of Excavations at Antioch-on-the-Orontes: 1935–1936." *AJA* 42 (1938) 205–217.

Carettoni et al. (1960). G. Carettoni, G. Gatti, L. Cozza, and A. Colini. *Forma Urbis Romae. La Pianta Marmorea di Roma antica*. 2 vols. Rome, 1960.

Carpenter (1970). R. Carpenter. *The Architects of the Parthenon*. Hardmondsworth & Baltimore, 1970.

Carter (1989). J. M. Carter. "Civic and Other Buildings." In Barton (1989a) 31–65.

Casey (1985). J. Casey. "The Roman Housing Market." In Grew & Hobley (1985) 43–48.

Casson (1978). L. Casson. "Unemployment, the Building Trade, and Suetonius, *Vesp.* 18." *BASP* 15 (1978) 43–51.

Castagnoli (1941). F. Castagnoli. "Gli edifici rappresentati in un rilievo del sepolcro degli Haterii." *BCAR* 69 (1941) 59–69.

Castagnoli (1950). F. Castagnoli. "Roma nei versi di Marziale." *Athenaeum* 28 (1950) 67–78.

Castagnoli (1971). F. Castagnoli. *Orthogonal Town Planning in Antiquity*. Cambridge, Mass., 1971.

Castagnoli (1976). F. Castagnoli. "L'insula nei cataloghi regionari di Roma." *RFIC* 104 (1976) 45–52.

Castagnoli (1978). F. Castagnoli. *Roma antica: profilo urbanistico*. Guide allo studio della civiltà romana, vol. 1.3. Rome, 1978.

Castagnoli (1980). F. Castagnoli. *Topografia e urbanistica di Roma antica*. 3d ed. Turin, 1980.

Champlin (1982). E. Champlin. "The *suburbium* of Rome." *AJAH* 7 (1982) 97–117.

Champlin (1983). E. Champlin. "Figlinae Marcianae." *Athenaeum* 61 (1983) 257–264.

Chevallier (1974). R. Chevallier. "Vitruve et l'Italie." In *Litterature greco-romaine et géographie historique. Mélanges offerts à Roger Dion. Collection Caesarodunum*, 9 bis (Paris, 1974) 161–166.

Chevallier (1983). R. Chevallier, ed. *Présence de l'architecture et de l'urbanisme romains. Homage à Paul Defournet. Collection Caesarodunum*, 18 bis (Paris, 1983).

Claridge (1988). A. Claridge. "Roman Statuary and the Supply of Statuary Marble." In Fant (1988a) 139–152.

Claridge (1993). A. Claridge. "Hadrian's Column of Trajan." *JRA* 6 (1993) 5–22.

Clarke (1963). M. L. Clarke. "The Architects of Greece and Rome." *Architectural History* 6 (1963) 14–30.

Clarke (1990). S. Clarke. "The Social Significance of Villa Architecture in Celtic North West Europe." *Oxford Journal of Archaeology* 9 (1990) 337–353.

Clarke (1991). J. R. Clarke. *The Houses of Roman Italy, 100 B.C.-A.D. 250: Ritual, Space, and Decoration.* Berkeley & Los Angeles, 1991.

Coarelli (1968). F. Coarelli. "L'ara di Domizio Enobarbo e la cultura artistica in Roma nel II secolo A. C." *DArch* 2 (1968) 302–368.

Coarelli (1972). F. Coarelli. "Il complesso pompeiano del Campo Marzio e la sua decorazione scultorea." *RPAA* 44 (1972) 99–121.

Coarelli (1974). F. Coarelli. *Guida archeologica di Roma.* Verona, 1974.

Coarelli (1977). F. Coarelli. "Public Building in Rome between the Second Punic War and Sulla." *PBSR* 45 (1977) 1–23.

Coarelli (1979). F. Coarelli. "La riscoperta del sepolcro degli Haterii." In Kopcke & Moore (1979) 255–270.

Coarelli (1983a). F. Coarelli. *Il Foro Romano. Periodo arcaico.* Rome, 1983.

Coarelli (1983b). F. Coarelli. "Architettura sacra e architettura privata nella tarda Repubblica." In Gros (1983a) 191–217.

Coarelli (1985). F. Coarelli, *Il Foro Romano. Periodo repubblicano e augusteo.* Rome, 1985.

Coarelli (1986). F. Coarelli. "L'Urbs e il suburbio." In A. Giardina, ed., *Roma politica economia paesaggio urbano.* Società romana e impero tardoantico, vol. 2 (Bari, 1986) 1–58.

Coarelli (1987). F. Coarelli. "La situazione edilizia di Roma sotto Severo Alessandro." In Pietri (1987) 429–456.

Coarelli (1989). F. Coarelli. "La casa dell'aristocrazia romana secondo Vitruvio." In Geertman & DeJong (1989) 178–187.

Coarelli (1994). F. Coarelli. *Guide Archeologiche Mondadori: Roma.* 2d ed., rev., with the collaboration of Luisanna Usai, of Coarelli (1974). Milan, 1994.

Coarelli & La Regina (1993). F. Coarelli and A. La Regina. *Guide Archeologiche Laterza 9: Abruzzo, Molise.* 2d ed. Bari, 1993.

Colini (1938). A. M. Colini. "Piazza Nicosia." *BCAR* 46 (1938) 272–273.

Colini (1958). A. M. Colini. "La villa di Sette Bassi." *Capitolium* 33 (1958) 14–17.

Colson (1980). F. H. Colson, ed. *Cicero, Pro Milone, with Asconius' Commentary Appended.* New ed. (Bristol, 1980).

Corcoran & DeLaine (1994). S. Corcoran and J. DeLaine. "The Unit Measurement of Marble in Diocletian's Prices Edict." *JRA* 7 (1994) 263–273.

Coulton (1977). J. J. Coulton. *Greek Architects at Work.* London, 1977.

Coulton (1983). J. J. Coulton. "Greek Architects and the Transmission of Design." In Gros (1983a) 453–468.

Crema (1959). L. Crema. *L'architettura romana.* Enciclopedia classica 3.12.1. Turin, 1959.

Curchin (1986). L. A. Curchin. "Non-slave Labour in Roman Spain." *Gérion* 4 (1986) 177–187.

D'Arms (1980). J. H. D'Arms. "Republican Senators' Involvement in Commerce in the Late Republic: Some Ciceronian Evidence." *MAAR* 36 (1980) 77–90.

D'Arms (1981). J. H. D'Arms. *Commerce and Social Standing in Ancient Rome.* Cambridge, Mass., 1981.

Davies, Hemsoll, & Jones (1987). P. Davies, D. Hemsoll, and M. Wilson Jones. "The Pantheon: Triumph of Rome or Triumph of Compromise?" *Art History* 10 (1987) 133–153.

De Fine Licht (1974). K. De Fine Licht. *Untersuchungen an den Trajansthermen zu Rom.* ARID, Suppl. 7. Copenhagen, 1974.

De Fine Licht (1990). K. De Fine Licht. *Sette Sale. Untersuchungen an den Trajansthermen zu Rom 2.* ARID, Suppl. 20. Rome, 1990.

DeLaine (1988). J. DeLaine. "Recent Research on Roman Baths." *JRA* 1 (1988) 11–32.

DeLaine (1993). J. DeLaine. "Roman Baths and Bathing." *JRA* 6 (1993) 348–358.

Deli (1992). A. Deli. "La Basilica di Vitruvio." In F. Milesi, ed., *Fano Romana* (Fano, 1992) 209–220.

DeMaria (1988). S. DeMaria. *Gli archi onorari di Roma e dell'Italia romana.* Bibliotheca Archaeologica, vol. 7. Rome, 1988.

De Ruggiero (1895). E. De Ruggiero. *Dizionario epigrafico di antichità romana,* vol. 1. Rome 1895.

De Ruyt (1983). C. De Ruyt. *Macellum. Marché alimentaire des Romains.* Publications d'histoire d'art et d'archéologie de l'Université Catholique de Louvain, vol. 35. Louvain, 1983.

Dilke (1971). O. A. W. Dilke. *The Roman Land Surveyors: An Introduction to the Agrimensores.* Newton Abbot, 1971.

Dinsmoor (1950). W. B. Dinsmoor. *The Architecture of Ancient Greece.* 3d ed., rev. London, 1950.

Dobson (1965). B. Dobson. "The Praefectus Fabrum in the Early Principate." In M. Jarrett & B. Dobson, eds., *Britain and Rome: Essays Presented to Eric Birley* (Kendal, 1965) 61–84.

Dodge (1988). H. Dodge. "Decorative Stones for Architecture in the Roman Empire." *Oxford Journal of Archaeology* 7.1 (1988) 65–80.

Dodge (1990). H. Dodge. "The Architectural Impact of Rome in the East." In Henig (1990) 108–120.

Dodge (1991). H. Dodge. "Ancient Marble Studies: Recent Research." *JRA* 4 (1991) 28–50.

Dodge & Ward-Perkins (1992). H. Dodge and B. Ward-Perkins, eds. *Marble in Antiquity: Collected Papers of J. B. Ward-Perkins.* Archaeological Monographs of the British School at Rome, vol. 6. London, 1992.

Dolci (1980). E. Dolci. *Carrara: cave antiche.* Carrara, 1980.

Dolci (1988). E. Dolci. "Marmora Lunensia: Quarrying Technology and Archaeological Use." In Herz & Waelkens (1988) 77–84.

Dolci (1989). E. Dolci, ed. *Il marmo nella civiltà romana. La produzione e il commercio.* Carrara, 1989.

Donderer (1996). M. Donderer. *Die Architekten der späten römischen Republik und der Kaiserzeit. Epigraphische Zeugnisse.* Erlanger Forschungen Reihe A, Geisteswissenschaften Band 69. Erlangen, 1996.

Downey (1961). G. Downey. *A History of Antioch in Syria.* Princeton, 1961.

Drerup (1959). H. Drerup. "Bildraum und Realraum in der römischen Architektur." *MDAI(R)* 66 (1959) 147–174.

Dudley (1967). D. R. Dudley. *Urbs Roma. A Source Book of Classical Texts on the City and Its Monuments.* Aberdeen, 1967.

Duncan-Jones (1965). R. Duncan-Jones. "Land Costs at Rome." *PBSR* 33 (1965) 177–188.

Duncan-Jones (1985). R. Duncan-Jones. "Who Paid for Public Buildings in Roman Cities?" In Grew & Hobley (1985) 28–33.

Duret & Néraudeau (1983). L. Duret and J.-P. Néraudeau. *Urbanisme et métamorphoses de la Rome antique.* Paris, 1983.

Etienne (1987). R. Etienne. "*Extra portam trigeminam:* espace politique et espace économique à l'*Emporium* de Rome." In Pietri (1987) 235–249.

Ettlinger (1977). L. D. Ettlinger. "The Emergence of the Italian Architect." In S. Kostof, ed., *The Architect: Chapters in the History of the Profession* (Oxford, 1977) 96–123.

Evans (1982). H. B. Evans. "Agrippa's Water Plan." *AJA* 86 (1982) 101–111.

Evans (1983). H. B. Evans. "Nero's *Arcus Caelimontani,*" *AJA* 87 (1983) 392–399.

Evans (1994). H. B. Evans. *Water Distribution in Ancient Rome: The Evidence of Frontinus.* Ann Arbor, 1994.

Fabbrini (1983). L. Fabbrini. "Domus Aurea: una nuova lettura planimetrica del palazzo sul colle Oppio." *ARID,* Suppl. X (1983) 169–186.

Fant (1985). J. C. Fant. "Four Unfinished Sarcophagus Lids at Docimium and the Roman Imperial Quarry System in Phrygia." *AJA* 89 (1985) 655–662.

Fant (1988a). J. C. Fant, ed. *Ancient Marble Quarrying and Trade.* British Archaeological Reports, S453. Oxford, 1988.

Fant (1988b). J. C. Fant. "The Roman Emperors in the Marble Business:

Capitalists, Middlemen or Philanthropists?" In Herz & Waelkens (1988) 147–158.

Fant (1989a). J. C. Fant. *Cavum Antrum Phygiae. The Organization and Operations of the Roman Imperial Marble Quarries in Phrygia.* British Archaeological Reports, S482. Oxford, 1989.

Fant (1989b). J. C. Fant. "Poikiloi Lithoi: The Anomalous Economics of the Roman Imperial Marble Quarry at Teos." In S. Walker and A. Cameron, eds., *The Greek Renaissance in the Roman Empire.* Bulletin of the Institute of Classical Studies, University of London, Supplement 55 (London, 1989) 206–218.

Fant (1992). J. C. Fant. "The Imperial Marble Yard at Portus." In Waelkens, Herz, & Moens (1992) 115–120.

Fant (1993). J. C. Fant. "Ideology, Gift, and Trade: A Distribution Model for the Roman Imperial Marbles." In Harris (1993) 145–170.

Fensterbusch (1964). C. Fensterbusch, ed. *Vitruv. Zehn Bücher über Architektur.* Darmstadt, 1964.

Fentress (1994). E. Fentress. "Cosa in the Empire: The Unmaking of a Roman Town." *JRA* 7 (1994) 208–222.

Ferri (1953). S. Ferri. "Note archeologiche al testo di Vitruvio." *PP* 30 (1953) 214–224.

Ferri (1960). S. Ferri. *Vitruvio. Architettura dai libri I–VII.* Rome, 1960.

Finley (1973). M. I. Finley. *The Ancient Economy.* Berkeley & Los Angeles, 1973.

Finsen (1969). H. Finsen. *La résidence de Domitien sur le Palatin.* ARID, Suppl. 5. Copenhagen, 1969.

Fischer (1988). M. Fischer. "Marble Imports and Local Stone in the Architectural Decoration of Roman Palestine." In Herz & Waelkens (1988) 161–170.

Fitch & Goldman (1994). C. R. Fitch and N. W. Goldman. *Cosa: The Lamps.* Memoirs of the American Academy in Rome, vol. 39. Ann Arbor, 1994.

Fleury (1990). P. Fleury, ed. *Vitruve, De l'architecture, Livre I.* Paris, 1990.

Fleury (1993). P. Fleury. *La mécanique de Vitruve.* Caen, 1993.

Fleury (1994). P. Fleury. "Le *De Architectura* et les traités de mécanique ancienne." In Gros (1994a) 187–212.

Frank (1924). T. Frank. *Roman Buildings of the Republic.* PAAR, vol. 3. Rome, 1924.

Frank (1933). T. Frank. *An Economic Survey of Ancient Rome,* vol. 1. Baltimore, 1933.

Frayn (1993). J. Frayn. *Markets and Fairs in Roman Italy: Their Social and Economic Importance from the Second Century B.C. to the Third Century A.D.* Oxford, 1993.

Frézouls (1981). E. Frézouls. "La construction du *Theatrum Lapideum* et son contexte politique." *Actes du colloque de Strasbourg, 5–7 novembre*

1981, Théâtre et spectacles dan l'antiquité (Strasbourg, 1981) 193–214.

Frézouls (1982). E. Frézouls. "Aspects de l'histoire architecturale du théâtre romain." *ANRW* 2.12.1 (1982) 343–441.

Frézouls (1987). E. Frézouls. "Rome ville ouverte. Réflexions sur les problèmes de l'expansion urbaine d'Auguste à Aurélien." In Pietri (1987) 347–372.

Frier (1977). B. W. Frier. "The Rental Market in Early Imperial Rome." *JRS* 67 (1977) 27–37.

Frier (1978). B. W. Frier. "Cicero's Management of His Urban Properties." *CJ* 74 (1978) 1–6.

Frier (1980). B. W. Frier. *Landlord and Tenant in Imperial Rome*. Princeton, 1980.

Frothingham (1912). A. L. Frothingham. "Who Built the Arch of Constantine?" *AJA* 16 (1912) 368–386.

Garnsey (1976). P. Garnsey. "Urban Property Investment." In M. I. Finley, ed., *Studies in Roman Property* (Cambridge, 1976) 123–132.

Garnsey (1980a). P. Garnsey, ed. *Non-Slave Labour in the Greco-Roman World*. Cambridge Philological Society, Suppl. 6. Cambridge, 1980.

Garnsey (1980b). P. Garnsey. "Non-slave Labour in the Roman world." In Garnsey (1980a) 34–47.

Garnsey (1981). P. Garnsey. "Independent Freedmen and the Economy of Roman Italy under the Principate." *Klio* 63 (1981) 359–372.

Geertman & DeJong (1989). H. Geertman and J. J. DeJong, eds. *Munus non ingratum. Proceedings of the International Symposium on Vitruvius' De Architectura and the Hellenistic and Republican Architecture (Leiden 20–23 January, 1987)*. BABESCH: Bulletin Antike Beschaving (Annual Papers on Classical Archaeology), Supplement 2. Leiden, 1989.

Geertman (1994). H. Geertman. "Teoria e attualità della progettistica architettonica di Vitruvio." In Gros (1994a) 7–30.

Girod (1983). R. Girod. "Amphithéâtre et 'show Business'." In Chevallier (1983) 41–44.

Girri (1956). G. Girri. *La taberna nel quadro urbanistico e sociale di Ostia*. Milan, 1956.

Giuliani (1982). C. F. Giuliani. "Note sull'architettura delle residenze imperiali dal I al II secolo d. Cr." *ANRW* 2.12.1 (1982) 233–258.

Gjerstad (1953–73). E. Gjerstad. *Early Rome*. 6 vols. Lund, 1953–1973.

Gnoli (1971). R. Gnoli. *Marmora romana*. Rome, 1971.

Goguey (1978). D. Goguey. "La formation de l'architecte: culture et technique." In *Recherches sur 'les artes' à Rome* (troisieme cycle, Dijon, octobre 1978), Publications de l'Université de Dijon 68 (Paris, 1978) 100–115.

Goujard (1975). R. Goujard, ed. *Caton: De L'Agriculture*. Paris, 1975.

Granger (1931). F. Granger, ed. *Vitruvius: On Architecture, Books 1–5*, vol. 1. London & New York, 1931.

Granger (1934). F. Granger, ed. *Vitruvius: On Architecture, Books 6–10*, vol. 2. London & New York, 1934.

Grew & Hobley (1985). F. Grew and B. Hobley, eds. *Roman Urban Topography in Britain and the Western Empire*. The Council for British Archaeology, Research Report no. 59. London, 1985.

Grimal (1961). P. Grimal, ed. *Frontin, Les Aqueducs de la ville de Rome.* 2d ed. Paris, 1961.

Gros (1967). P. Gros. "Trois temples de la Fortune." *MEFRA* 79 (1967) 503–566.

Gros (1973). P. Gros. "Hermodoros et Vitruve." *MEFRA* 85 (1973) 136–161.

Gros (1975). P. Gros. "Structures et limites de la compilation vitruvienne dans les livres III et IV." *Latomus* 34 (1975) 986–1009.

Gros (1976a). P. Gros. "Les premières générations d'architectes hellénistiques à Rome." In R. Bloch, ed., *L'Italie préromaine et la Rome républicaine I. Mélanges offerts à Jacques Heurgon*. Collection de l'école française de Rome, vol. 27 (Rome, 1976) 387–409.

Gros (1976b). P. Gros. *Aurea templa. Recherches sur l'architecture religieuse de Rome à l'époque d'Auguste*. Bibliothèque des écoles françaises d'Athènes et de Rome, vol. 231. Rome, 1976.

Gros (1978a). P. Gros. "Le dossier vitruvien d'Hermogénès." *MEFRA* 90, 2 (1978) 687–703.

Gros (1978b). P. Gros. "Vie et mort de l'art hellénistique selon Vitruve et Pline." *REL* 56 (1978) 289–313.

Gros (1978c). P. Gros. *Architecture et société à Rome et en Italie centro-méridionale aux derniers siècles de la République*. Collection Latomus, vol. 156. Brussels, 1978.

Gros (1982). P. Gros. "Vitruve: l'architecture et sa theorie, à la lumière des études recentes." *ANRW* 2.30.1 (1982) 659–695.

Gros (1983a). P. Gros, ed. *Architecture et société, de l'archaisme grec à la fin de la République romaine*. Actes du colloque international organisé par le Centre de la recherche scientifique de l'école française de Rome (Rome 2–4 decembre 1980). Collection de l'école française de Rome, vol. 66 (= *MEFRA* Suppl. 66). Paris & Rome, 1983.

Gros (1983b). P. Gros. "Statut social et rôle culturel des architectes (période hellénistique et augustéene)." In Gros (1983a) 425–452.

Gros (1987). P. Gros. "La fonction symbolique des édifices théâtraux dans le paysage urbain de la Rome augustéene." In Pietri (1987) 319–346.

Gros (1989). P. Gros. "L'*auctoritas* chez Vitruve: contribution a l'étude de la semantique des ordres dans le *De Architectura*." In Geertman & DeJong (1989) 126–133.

Gros (1990). P. Gros, ed. *Vitruve, De l'architecture, Livre III.* Paris, 1990.

Gros (1992). P. Gros, ed. *Vitruve, De l'architecture, Livre IV.* Paris, 1992.

Gros (1994a). P. Gros, ed. *Le Projet de Vitruve. Objet, destinaires et réception du De Architectura.* Collection de l'école française de Rome, vol. 192. Rome, 1994.

Gros (1994b). P. Gros. "*Munus non ingratum.* Le traité vitruvien et la notion de service." In Gros (1994a) 75–90.

Gros (1994c). P. Gros. "La schéma du théâtre latin et sa signification dans la système normatif du *De Architectura.*" *RA,* 1994, 57–80.

Gros & Torelli (1988). P. Gros and M. Torelli. *Storia dell'urbanistica. Il mondo romano.* Bari, 1988.

Gullini (1983). G. Gullini. "Terrazza, edificio, uso dello spazio. Note su archittetura e società nel periodo medio e tardo repubblicano." In Gros (1983a) 119–189.

Hannestad (1986). N. Hannestad. *Roman Art and Imperial Policy.* Jutland Archaeological Society Publications no. xix. Aarhus, Denmark, 1986.

Hanson (1959). J. A. Hanson. *Roman Theater-temples.* Princeton Monographs in Art and Archaeology, vol. 33. Princeton, 1959.

Hardy (1912). E. G. Hardy. *Roman Laws and Charters.* Oxford, 1912.

Harris (1980). W. V. Harris. "Roman Terracotta Lamps: The Organization of an Industry." *JRS* 70 (1980) 126–145.

Harris (1993a). W. V. Harris, ed. *The Inscribed Economy: Production and Distribution in the Roman Empire in the Light of 'Instrumentum Domesticum.'* Journal of Roman Archaeology Supplementary series, no. 6. Ann Arbor, 1993.

Harris (1993b). W. V. Harris. "Production, Distribution, and *Instrumentum Domesticum,*" in Harris (1993a) 186–189.

Haselberger (1989). L. Haselberger. "Die Zeichnungen in Vitruvs *De Architectura.* Zur Illustration antiker Schriften über das Konstruktionswesen." In Geertman & DeJong (1989) 69–70.

Haselberger (1994). L. Haselberger. "Ein Giebelriß der Vorhalle des Pantheon. Die Werkriße vor dem Augustusmausoleum." *MDAI(R)* 101 (1994) 279–308.

Haselberger (1995). L. Haselberger. "Deciphering a Roman Blueprint." *Scientific American,* June 1995, 84–89.

Heilmeyer (1975). W.-D. Heilmeyer. "Apollodoros von Damaskos, der Architekt des Pantheon." *JDAI* 90 (1975) 316–347.

Helen (1975). T. Helen. *Organization of Roman Brick Production in the First and Second Centuries AD: An Interpretation of Roman Brick Stamps.* Helsinki, 1975.

Hemsoll (1990). D. Hemsoll. "The Architecture of Nero's Golden House." In Henig (1990) 10–38.

Henig (1990). M. Henig, ed. *Architecture and Architectural Sculpture in the Roman Empire.* Oxford, 1990.

Hermansen (1970). G. Hermansen. "The *Medianum* and the Roman Apartment." *Phoenix* 24 (1970) 342–347.

Hermansen (1974). H. Hermansen. "The Roman Inns and the Law: The Inns of Ostia." In J. A. S. Evans, ed., *Polis and Imperium: Studies in Honour of E. T. Salmon* (Toronto, 1974) 167–181.

Hermansen (1978). G. Hermansen. "The Population of Imperial Rome: The Regionaries." *Historia* 27 (1978) 129–168.

Hermansen (1982). G. Hermansen. *Ostia: Aspects of Roman City Life.* Edmonton, 1982.

Herz (1955). N. Herz. "Petrofabric Analysis and Classical Archaeology." *American Journal of Science* 200.3 (1955) 299–305.

Herz (1985). N. Herz. "Isotopic Analysis of Marble." In G. Rapp Jr. and J. A. Gifford, eds., *Archaeological Geology* (New Haven, 1985) 331–351.

Herz (1988). N. Herz. "Geology of Greece and Turkey: Potential Marble Source Regions." In Herz & Waelkens (1988) 7–10.

Herz & Waelkens (1988). N. Herz and M. Waelkens, eds. *Classical Marble: Geochemistry, Technology, Trade.* Nato ASI Series, vol. 153. Dordrecht, London, & Boston, 1988.

Herz & Wenner (1981). N. Herz and D. Wenner. "Tracing the Origins of Marble." *Archaeology* 34.5 (1981) 14–21.

Hesberg (1989). H. von Hesberg. "Vitruv und die Stadtplanung in spätrepublikanischer und augusteischer Zeit." In Geertman & DeJong (1989) 134–140.

Hill (1944). D. K. Hill. "The Temple above Pompey's Theater." *CJ* 39 (1944) 360–365.

Hodge (1981). A. T. Hodge. "Vitruvius, Lead Pipes, and Lead Poisoning." *AJA* 85 (1981) 486–491.

Hodge (1984). A. T. Hodge. "How Did Frontinus Measure the Quinaria?" *AJA* 88 (1984) 205–216.

Hodge (1992). A. T. Hodge. *Roman Aqueducts and Water Supply.* London, 1992.

Hoepfner & Schwander (1990). W. Hoepfner and E.-L. Schwandner, eds. *Hermogenes und die Hochhellenistische Architektur.* International Congress of Classical Archaeology no. 13. Mainz am Rhein, 1990.

Hoepfner (1990). W. Hoepfner. "Bauten und Bedeutung des Hermogenes." In Hoepfner & Schwander (1990) 1–34.

Holland (1961). L. A. Holland. *Janus and the Bridge.* PAAR, vol. 21. Rome, 1961

Holloway (1966). R. R. Holloway. "The Tomb of Augustus and the Princes of Troy." *AJA* 70 (1966) 171–173.

Horsfall (1988). N. Horsfall. "Patronage of Art in the Roman World." *Prudentia* 20 (1988) 9–28.

Humphrey (1986). J. H. Humphrey. *Roman Circuses: Arenas for Chariot Racing.* London, 1986.

Huxley (1959). G. L. Huxley. *Anthemius of Tralles: A Study in Later Greek Geometry.* Cambridge, Mass., 1959.

Isler (1989). H. P. Isler. "Vitruvs Regeln und die erhaltenen Theaterbauten." In Geertman & DeJong (1989) 141–153

Janvier (1969). Y. Janvier. *La législation du bas-Empire romain sur les édifices publics.* Aix-en-Provence, 1969.

Jeppesen (1958). K. Jeppesen. *Paradeigmata.* Jutland Archaeological Society Publications vol. 4. Aarhus, Denmark, 1958.

Jeppesen (1989). K. Jeppesen. "Vitruvius in Africa." In Geertman & DeJong (1989) 31–33.

Jones (1992). B. W. Jones. *The Emperor Domitian.* London & New York, 1992.

Jongman (1988). W. Jongman. *The Economy and Society of Pompeii.* Amsterdam, 1988.

Jouffroy (1986). H. Jouffroy. *La construction publique en Italie et dans l'Afrique romaine.* Strasbourg, 1986.

Kähler (1939). H. Kähler. "Triumphbogen." *RE* VII A (Stuttgart, 1948) cols. 373–493, figs. 1–24.

Kellum (1990). B. A. Kellum. "The City Adorned: Programmatic Display at the *Aedes Concordiae Augustae.*" In K. Raaflaub and M. Toher, eds., *Between Republic and Empire* (Berkeley & Los Angeles, 1990) 276–307.

Kienast (1980). D. Kienast. "Zur Baupolitik Hadrians in Rom." *Chiron* 10 (1980) 391–412.

Kleiner (1985). F. S. Kleiner. *The Arch of Nero in Rome.* Archaeologia, vol. 54. Rome, 1985.

Kleiner (1992). D. E. E. Kleiner. *Roman Sculpture.* New Haven, 1992.

Knell & Wesenberg (1984). H. Knell and B. Wesenberg, eds. *Vitruv-Kolloquium des Deutschen Archaeologen-Verbandes, durchgefuhrt an der Technischen Hochschule Darmstadt, 17–18 Juni 1982 (THD Schriftenr. Wissensch. und Technik 22).* Darmstadt, 1984.

Koeppel (1980). G. M. Koeppel. "Fragments from a Domitianic Monument in Ann Arbor and Rome." *Bulletin of the Museums of Art and Archaeology, the University of Michigan* 3 (1980) 14–29.

Koeppel (1983). G. M. Koeppel. "Two Reliefs from the Arch of Claudius in Rome." *MDAI(R)* 90 (1983) 103–109.

Kopcke & Moore (1979). G. Kopcke and M. B. Moore, eds. *Studies in Classical Art and Archaeology: A Tribute to Peter Heinrich von Blanckenhagen.* Locust Valley, New York, 1979.

Krause (1987). C. Krause. "La Domus Tiberiana e il suo contesto urbano." In Pietri (1987) 781–798.

Kreeb (1990). M. Kreeb. "Hermogenes: Quellen- und Datierungsprobleme." In Hoepfner & Schwandner (1990) 103–114.

Laidlaw & Packer (1971). A. Laidlaw and J. Packer. "Excavations in the House of Sallust in Pompeii." *AJA* 75 (1971) 206–207.

Lamprecht (1984). H. O. Lamprecht. *Opus Caementicium: Bautechnik der Römer.* Düsseldorf, 1984.

Landels (1978). J. G. Landels. *Engineering in the Ancient World.* Berkeley & Los Angeles, 1978.

Langdon (1988). M. K. Langdon. "Hymettiana II: an Ancient Quarry on Mt. Hymettos." *AJA* 92 (1988) 75–83.

La Rocca & DeVos (1976). E. La Rocca and M. and A. DeVos. *Guida archeologica di Pompeii.* Verona, 1976.

Laserre (1967). F. Laserre, ed. *Strabon, Géographie, Livres 5 et 6.* Paris, 1967.

Laurence (1994). R. Laurence. *Roman Pompeii: Space and Society.* London & New York, 1994.

Lauter (1971). H. Lauter. "Heiligtum oder Markt?" *AA,* 1971, 55–62.

Lauter (1976). H. Lauter. "Die hellenistischen Theater der Samniten und Latiner in ihrer Beziehung zur Theaterarchitektur der Griechen." In P. Zanker, ed., *Hellenismus in Mittelitalien* 2 (Göttingen, 1976) 413–430.

Lauter (1986). H. Lauter. *Die Architektur des Hellenismus.* Darmstadt, 1986.

Lawrence (1983). A. W. Lawrence. *Greek Architecture.* Rev., with additions, by R. A. Tomlinson. London, 1983.

Leon (1971). C. Leon. *Die Bauornamentik des Trajansforums.* Vienna, Cologne, and Graz, 1971.

Ligt (1993). L. de Ligt. *Fairs and Markets in the Roman Empire: Economic and Social Aspects of Periodic Trade in a Pre-industrial Society.* Dutch Monographs on Ancient History and Archaeology, vol. 11. Amsterdam, 1993.

Ling (1983). R. Ling. "The Insula of the Menander at Pompeii: Interim Report." *AntJ* 63 (1983) 34–57.

Ling (1985). R. Ling. "The Mechanics of the Building Trade." In Grew & Hobley (1985) 14–27.

Ling (1990). R. Ling. "A Stranger in Town: Finding the Way in an Ancient City." *G&R* 37 (1990) 204–214.

Ling (1991). R. Ling. "The Architecture of Pompeii." *JRA* 4 (1991) 248–256.

Loane (1938). H. J. Loane. *Industry and Commerce in the City of Rome.* Baltimore, 1938.

Lugli (1923). G. Lugli. "Il suburbio di Roma." *BCAR* 51 (1923) 3–52.

Lugli (1938). G. Lugli. "Nuove forme dell'architettura romana nell'età dei Flavi." *Atti del Convegno Nazionale di Storia dell'Architettura* 3 (1938) 95–102.

Lugli (1946). G. Lugli. *Roma antica: il centro monumentale*. Rome, 1946.

Lugli (1957). G. Lugli. *La tecnica edilizia romana con particolare riguardo a Roma e Lazio*. 2 vols. Rome, 1957.

Lugli (1960). G. Lugli, ed. *Fontes ad topographiam veteris urbis Romae pertinentes, VIII.I: Regio X (Mons Palatinus)*. Rome, 1960.

Lundström (1912). V. Lundström. "Bidrag till Roms topografi I: Pantheon-biblioteket." *Eranos* 10 (1912) 64–72.

MacDonald (1977). W. L. MacDonald. "Roman Architects." In S. Kostof, ed., *The Architect: Chapters in the History of the Profession* (Oxford, 1977) 28–58.

MacDonald (1982). W. L. MacDonald. *The Architecture of the Roman Empire*, vol. 1: *An Introductory Study*. 2d ed., rev. New Haven, 1982.

MacDonald (1986). W. L. MacDonald. *The Architecture of the Roman Empire*, vol. 2: *An Urban Appraisal*. New Haven, 1986.

MacMullen (1959). R. MacMullen. "Roman Imperial Buildings in the Provinces." *HSCPh* 64 (1959) 207–235.

MacMullen (1970). R. MacMullen. "Markets Days in the Roman Empire." *Phoenix* 24 (1970) 333–341.

Maiuri (1958). A. Maiuri. *Ercolano. I nuovi scavi (1927–1958)*. 2 vols. Rome, 1958.

Maiuri (1960). A. Maiuri. *Pompeii*. Novara, 1960.

Malissard (1983). A. Malissard. "Incendium et ruinae. A propos des villas et monuments dan les *Histoires* et les *Annales* de Tacite." In Chevallier (1983) 45–56.

Marchetti-Longi (1936). G. Marchetti-Longi. "'Theatrum Lapideum,' 'Curia Pompeia' e 'Trullum Dominae Maraldae' (Topografia antica e medioevale di Roma)." *RPAA* 12 (1936) 233–319.

McCredie (1979). J. R. McCredie. "The Architects of the Parthenon." In Kopcke & Moore (1979) 69–74.

McKay (1975). A. G. McKay. *Houses, Villas, and Palaces in the Roman World*. London, 1975.

McKay (1978). A. G. McKay. *Vitruvius: Architect and Engineer*. New York & London, 1978.

McWhirr (1979). A. McWhirr, ed. *Roman Brick and Tile: Studies in Manufacture, Distribution and Use in the Western Empire*. Oxford, 1979.

Mansuelli (1982a). G. Mansuelli. "La città romana nei primi secoli dell'impero." *ANRW* 2.12.1 (1982) 145–178.

Mansuelli (1982b). G. Mansuelli. "Forme e significati dell'architettura in Roma nell'età del principato, *ANRW* 2.12.1 (1982) 212–232.

Martin (1983). P.-M. Martin. "Architecture et politique: le temple de Jupiter Capitolin." In Chevallier (1983) 9–30.

Martin (1982). S. D. Martin. "Building Contracts in Classical Roman Law." Ph.D. diss., University of Michigan, Ann Arbor, 1982.

Martin (1989). S. D. Martin. *The Roman Jurists and the Organization of* *Private Building in the Late Republic and Early Empire.* Collection Latomus, vol. 204. Brussels, 1989.

Meiggs (1973). R. Meiggs. *Roman Ostia.* 2d ed. Oxford, 1973.

Meiggs (1980). R. Meiggs. "Sea-Borne Timber Supplies to Rome." *MAAR* 36 (1980) 185–196.

Meiggs (1982). R. Meiggs. *Trees and Timber in the Ancient Mediterranean World.* Oxford, 1982.

Merrill (1904). W. A. Merrill. "Notes on the Influence of Lucretius on Vitruvius." *TAPhA* 35 (1904) 16–21.

Mertens (1983). J. Mertens. "Alba Fucens, une cité antique dans un village moderne." In Chevallier (1983) 407–418.

Millar (1977). F. Millar. *The Emperor in the Roman World.* London, 1977.

Millar (1983). F. Millar. "Empire and City, Augustus to Julian: Obligations, Excuses, and Status." *JRS* 73 (1983) 76–96.

Moeller (1976). W. O. Moeller. *The Wool Trade of Ancient Pompeii.* Leiden, 1976.

Molisani (1971). G. Molisani. "Lucius Cornelius Quinti Catuli Architectus." *RAL* 26 (1971) 1–10.

Momigliano (1942). A. Momigliano. "Camillus and Concord." *CQ* 36 (1942) 111–120.

Monna & Pensabene (1977). D. Monna and P. Pensabene. *Marmi dell'Asia Minore.* Rome, 1977.

More (1969). J. More. "The Fabri Tignarii of Rome." Ph.D. diss., Harvard University, Cambridge, Mass., 1969.

Morel (1987). J.-P. Morel. "La topographie de l'artisanat et du commerce dans la Rome antique." In Pietri (1987) 127–155.

Morel (1989). J.-P. Morel. "The Transformation of Italy, 300–130 B.C.: The Evidence of Archaeology." In *CAH*, 2d ed., vol. 8 (Cambridge, 1989) 477–516.

Morgan (1971). M. G. Morgan. "The Portico of Metellus: A Reconsideration." *Hermes* 99 (1971) 480–505.

Morselli & Tortorici (1989). C. Morselli and E. Tortorici. *Curia, Forum Iulium, Forum Transitorium.* Rome, 1989.

Nabers (1978). N. Nabers. "The Architectural Variations of the Macellum." *ORom* 9.20 (1978) 173–175.

Nash (1968). E. Nash. *A Pictorial Dictionary of Ancient Rome.* 2 vols. 2d ed. London & New York, 1968.

Nash (1976). E. Nash. "Secretarium Senatus." In L. Bonfante and H. von Heintze, eds., *In Memoriam Otto J. Brendel* (Mainz, 1976) 191–204

Nielsen (1990). I. Nielsen. *Thermae et Balnea: The Architecture and Cultural History of Roman Public Baths.* 2 vols. Aarhus, Denmark, 1990.

Nippel (1984). W. Nippel. "Policing Rome." *JRS* 74 (1984) 20–29.

Nordh (1949). A. Nordh. *Libellus de regionibus urbis Romae*. Lund, 1949.

Novara (1983). A. Novara. "Les raisons d'écrire de Vitruve ou la revanche de l'architecte." *BAGB* 42 (1983) 284–308.

Novara (1994). A. Novara. "Faire oeuvre utile: la mésure de l'ambition chez Vitruve." In Gros (1994a) 47–61.

Ogilvie (1965). R. Ogilvie. *A Commentary on Livy, Books 1–5*. Oxford, 1965.

Ohr (1975). K. Ohr."Die form der Basilika bei Vitruv." *BJ* 175 (1975) 113–128.

Olcese (1993). G. Olcese. "Archeologia e archeometria dei laterizi bollati urbani: primi risultati e prospettive di ricerca." In Harris (1993a) 121–128.

Onians (1990). J. Onians. "Quinitilian and the Idea of Roman Art." In Henig (1990) 1–9.

Owens (1989). E. J. Owens. "Roman town planning." In Barton (1989a) 7–30.

Packer (1967). J. E. Packer. "Housing and Population in Imperial Ostia and Rome." *JRS* 57 (1967) 80–95.

Packer (1968a). J. E. Packer. "La casa di Via Giulio Romano." *BCAR* 81 (1968) 127–148.

Packer (1968b). J. E. Packer. "Structure and Design in Ancient Ostia." *Technology and Culture* 9 (1968) 357–388.

Packer (1969). J. E. Packer. "Roman Imperial Building, 31 B.C.–A.D. 138." In C. Roebuck, ed., *The Muses at Work* (Cambridge, Mass., & London, 1969) 36–59.

Packer (1971). J. E. Packer. *The Insulae of Imperial Ostia*. MAAR, vol. 31 (Rome, 1971).

Packer (1975). J. E. Packer. "Middle and lower class housing in Pompeii and Herculaneum." In B. Andreae and H. Kyrieleis, eds., *Neue Forschungen in Pompeji* (Recklinghausen, 1975) 133–146.

Packer (1978). J. E. Packer. "Inns at Pompeii." *Cronache Pompeiane* 4 (1978) 5–53.

Packer (1988). J. E. Packer. "Imperial Construction: Rome and Central Italy." In M. Grant & E. Kitzinger, eds., *Civilization of the Ancient Mediterranean*, 1 (New York, 1988) 299–311.

Packer (1994). J. E. Packer. "Trajan's Forum Again: The Column and the Temple of Trajan in the Master Plan Attributed to Apollodorus(?)." *JRA* 7 (1994) 163–182.

Packer (1995). J. E. Packer. "Forum Traiani." In Steinby (1995) 348–356.

Packer (1996). J. E. Packer. *The Forum of Trajan in Rome: A Study of the Monuments*. Berkeley & Los Angeles, 1996.

Palmer (1980). R. E. A. Palmer. "Customs on market goods imported into the city of Rome." *MAAR* 36 (1980) 217–233.

Palmer (1983). R. E. A. Palmer. "On the Track of the Ignoble." *Athenaeum* 61 (1983) 343–361.

Panciera (1966). S. Panciera. "Il sepolcro ostiense di C. Cartilius Poplicola e una scheda epigrafica di G. Marini," *ArchClass* 18 (1966) 50–64.

Panella et al. (1995). C. Panella, P. Pensabene, M. Milella, and M. Wilson Jones. "Scavo nell'area della Meta Sudans e ricerche sull'Arco di Costantino." *Archeologia Laziale* 12 (1995) 41–61.

Paribeni (1943). R. E. Paribeni. "Apollodorus di Damasco." *RAL*, ser. 7, 4 (1943) 124–140.

Patterson (1991). J. Patterson. "Settlement, City, and Elite in Samnium and Lycia." In Rich & Wallace-Hadrill (1991) 147–168.

Pavolini (1983). C. Pavolini. *Guide Archeologiche Laterza, 8: Ostia.* Bari, 1983.

Peacock (1988). D. P. S. Peacock. "The Roman Quarries of Mons Claudianus Egypt: An Interim Report." In Herz & Waelkens (1988) 97–101.

Peacock (1994). D. P. S. Peacock. "Roman Stones." *JRA* 7 (1994) 361–363.

Pearse (1974). J. L. D. Pearse. "The Organization of Roman Building during the Late Republic and Early Empire." Ph.D. diss., Cambridge University, Cambridge, 1974.

Pedotti (1969). B. Pedotti. *L'architettura e la figura dell'architetto secondo Vitruvio.* Florence, 1969.

Pellati (1949). F. Pellati. "La basilica di Fano et la formazione del trattato di Vitruvio." *RPAA* 33–34 (1947–49) 153–174.

Peña (1989). J. T. Peña. "*P. Giss. 69*: Evidence for the Supplying of Stone Transport Operations in Roman Egypt and the Production of Fifty Foot Monolithic Column Shafts." *JRA* 2 (1989) 126–132.

Pensabene (1972). P. Pensabene. "Considerazione sul trasporto di manufatti marmorei in eta imperiale a Roma e in altri centri occidentali." *DArch* 6 (1972) 317–362.

Pensabene (1982a). P. Pensabene. "Il Marmo nell'Impero Romano." *BMAH* 53.2 (1982) 21–32.

Pensabene (1982b). P. Pensabene. "Osservazioni sulla diffusione dei marmi e il loro prezzo nella Roma Imperiale." *BMAH* 53.2 (1982) 57–70.

Pensabene (1985). P. Pensabene, ed. *Marmi antichi. Problemi d'impiegi, di restauro e d'identificazione.* Studi Miscellanei, vol. 26, 1981–1983 (Rome, 1985).

Pensabene (1988). P. Pensabene. "The Arch of Constantine: Marble Samples." In Herz & Waelkens (1988) 411–418.

Pensabene (1989). P. Pensabene. "Amministrazione dei marmi e sistema distributivo nel mondo romano." In Borghini (1989) 43–54.

Perring (1991). D. Perring. "Spatial Organisation and Social Change in Roman Towns." In Rich & Wallace-Hadrill (1991) 273–293.

Phillips (1973). E. J. Phillips. "The Roman Law on the Demolition of Buildings." *Latomus* 32 (1973) 86–95.

Picard (1983). G. C. Picard. "Les centres civiques ruraux dans l'Italie et la Gaule romaine." In Gros (1983a) 415–423.

Pietri (1987). C. Pietri, ed. *L'Urbs: Espace Urbain et Histoire.* Collection de l'école française de Rome, Suppl. 98. Rome, 1987.

Pisani Sartorio & Steinby (1989). G. Pisani Sartorio and E. M. Steinby. "Costruire l'Impero: Materiali tecniche e arti edilizie dei Romani." *Archeo* 56 (Ottobre 1989) 53–97.

Platner & Ashby (1929). S. Platner and T. Ashby. *A Topographical Dictionary of Ancient Rome.* Oxford, 1929. Reprint: Rome, 1965.

Plommer (1973). H. Plommer. *Vitruvius and Later Roman Building Manuals.* Cambridge, 1973.

Promis (1873). C. Promis. "Gli architetti e l'architettura presso i romani." *MAT* 27 (1873) 1–187

Purcell (1983). N. Purcell. "The *Apparitores:* A Study in Social Mobility." *PBSR* 51 (1983) 125–173.

Purcell (1985). N. Purcell, "Wine and Wealth in Ancient Italy." *JRS* 75 (1985) 1–19.

Purcell (1987a). N. Purcell. "Tomb and Suburb." In H. von Hesberg and P. Zanker, eds., *Römische Gräberstraßen* (Munich, 1987) 25–41.

Purcell (1987b). N. Purcell. "Town in Country and Country in Town." In E. G. MacDougall, ed., *Ancient Roman Villa Gardens.* Dumbarton Oaks Colloquium on the History of Landscape Architecture, vol. 10 (Washington, D.C., 1987) 187–203.

Purcell (1993). N. Purcell. "Atrium Libertatis." *PBSR* 61 (1993) 125–155.

Purcell (1994). N. Purcell. "The City of Rome and the *Plebs Urbana* in the Late Republic." In *CAH,* 2d ed., vol. 9 (Cambridge, 1994) 644–688.

Purcell (1995a). N. Purcell. "Forum Romanum (the Republican Period)." In Steinby (1995) 325–336.

Purcell (1995b). N. Purcell. "Forum Romanum (the Imperial Period)." In Steinby (1995) 336–342.

Quilici (1974). L. Quilici. "La campagna romana come surburbio di Roma antica." *PP* 29 (1974) 410–438.

Quilici (1979). L. Quilici. "La villa nel suburbio romano: problemi di studio e di inquadrimento storico-topografico." *ArchClass* 31 (1979) 309–317.

Quilici Gigli (1994). S. Quilici Gigli. "The Changing Landscape of the Roman Campagna. Lo sfruttamento del territorio in età imperiale." In J. Carlsen, P. Orsted, and J. E. Skydsgaard, eds., *Landuse in the Roman Empire.* ARID, Suppl. 22 (Rome, 1994) 135–144.

Rainbird (1986). J. Rainbird. "The Fire Stations of Imperial Rome." *PBSR* 54 (1986) 147–169.

Rakob (1976). F. Rakob. "Hellenismus in Mittelitalien: Bautypen und Bautechnik." In P. Zanker, ed., *Hellenismus in Mittelitalien*, 2 (Göttingen, 1976) 366–386.

Rakob (1984). R. Rakob. "Metrologie und plan-figuren einer Kaiserlichen Bauhütte." In *Bauplanung und Bautheorie der Antike.* Deutsches Archäologisches Institut, Diskussionen zur archäologischen Bauforschung, vol. 4 (Berlin, 1984) 220–237.

Rakob (1987). F. Rakob. "Die Urbanisierung des nördliche Marsfeldes. Neue Forschungen im areal des Horologium Augsusti." In Pietri (1987) 687–712.

Raper (1977). R. A. Raper. "The Analysis of the Urban Structure at Pompeii: A Sociological Examination of Land Use." In D. L. Clarke, ed., *Spatial Archaeology* (Cambridge, 1977) 189–221.

Raper (1979). R. A. Raper. "Pompeii: planning and social implications." In B. C. Burnham and J. Kingsbury, eds., *Space, Hierarchy, and Society: Interdisciplinary Studies in Social Area Analysis*. B.A.R. International Series, vol. 59 (Oxford, 1979) 137–148.

Rawson (1975). E. Rawson. "Architecture and Sculpture: The Activities of the Cossuttii." *PBSR* 43 (1975) 36–47.

Rawson (1976). E. Rawson. "The Ciceronian Aristocracy and Its Properties." In M. I. Finley, ed., *Studies in Roman Property.* (Cambridge, 1976) 85–102.

Rawson (1985). E. Rawson. *Intellectual Life in the Late Roman Republic.* London, 1985.

Reece (1985). R. Reece. "Roman Towns and Their Plans." In Grew & Hobley (1985) 37–40.

Reynolds (1996). D. W. Reynolds. "*Forma Urbis Romae:* The Severan Marble Plan and the Urban Form of Ancient Rome." Ph.D. diss., University of Michigan, 1996.

Rich & Wallace-Hadrill (1991). J. Rich and A. Wallace-Hadrill, eds. *City and Country in the Ancient World.* London & New York, 1991.

Richardson (1957). L. Richardson, jr. "Comitium and Curia: Cosa and Rome." *Archaeology* 10 (1957) 49–55.

Richardson (1976). L. Richardson, jr. "The Evolution of the Porticus Octaviae." *AJA* 80 (1976) 57–64.

Richardson (1977a). L. Richardson, jr. "Hercules Musarum and the Porticus Philippi in Rome." *AJA* 81 (1977) 355–361.

Richardson (1977b). L. Richardson, jr. "The Libraries of Pompeii." *Archaeology* 30 (1977) 394–402.

Richardson (1978a). L. Richardson, jr. "*Honos et Virtus* and the Sacra Via." *AJA* 82 (1978) 240–246.

Richardson (1978b). L. Richardson, jr. "Curia Julia and Janus Geminus." *MDAI(R)* 85 (1978) 359–369.

Richardson (1978c). L. Richardson, jr. "Concordia and Concordia Augusta: Rome and Pompeii." *PP* 33 (1978) 265–272.

Richardson (1979). L. Richardson, jr. "Basilica Fulvia, Modo Aemilia." In Kopcke & Moore (1979) 209–216.

Richardson (1982). L. Richardson, jr. "The City-Plan of Pompeii." In A. de Franciscis, ed., *La regione sotterata dal Vesuvio. Studi e prospettive* (Naples, 1982) 341–351.

Richardson (1987). L. Richardson, jr. "A Note on the Architecture of the *Theatrum Pompeii* in Rome." *AJA* 91 (1987) 123–126.

Richardson (1988). L. Richardson, jr. *Pompeii: An Architectural History.* Baltimore & London, 1988.

Richardson (1991). L. Richardson, jr. "Urban Development in Ancient Rome and the Impact of Empire." In A. Molho, K. Raaflaub, and J. Emlen, eds., *City States in Classical Antiquity and Medieval Italy: Athens and Rome, Florence and Venice.* (Stuttgart, 1991) 381–402.

Richardson (1992). L. Richardson, jr. *A New Topographical Dictionary of Ancient Rome.* Baltimore & London, 1992.

Richmond (1930). I. A. Richmond. *The City Wall of Imperial Rome.* Oxford, 1930.

Richmond (1961). I. A. Richmond. "Roman timber building." In W. E. M. Jope, ed., *Studies in Building History* (London, 1961) 15–26.

Ridley (1989). R. T. Ridley. "The Fate of an Architect: Apollodoros of Damascus." *Athenaeum* 67 (1989) 551–565.

Robinson (1992). O. F. Robinson. *Ancient Rome: City Planning and Administration.* London & New York, 1992.

Roddaz (1984). J.-M. Roddaz. *Marcus Agrippa.* Bibliothèque des écoles françaises d'Athènes et de Rome, vol. 253. Rome, 1984.

Roddaz & Fabre (1982). J.-M. Roddaz and G. Fabre. "Recherches sur la *familia* de M. Agrippa." *Athenaeum* 60 (1982) 84–112.

Röder (1971). J. Röder. "Marmor Phryium. Die antiken Marmorbrüche von Iscehisar in Westanatolien." *JDAI* 86 (1971) 253–312.

Röder (1988). G. Röder. "Numidian Marble and Some of Its Specialities." In Herz & Waelkens (1988) 91–96.

Rodriguez Almeida (1981). E. Rodriguez Almeida. *Forma urbis marmorea: aggiornamento generale 1980.* 2 vols. Rome, 1981.

Rodriguez Almeida (1994). E. Rodriguez Almeida. "Marziale in Marmo." *MEFRA* 106 (1994) 197–217.

Romano (1985). E. Romano. "Per la cronologia di Vitruvio." *QCTC* 2–3 (1984–85) 45–52.

Rowell (1962). H. T. Rowell. *Rome in the Augustan Age.* Norman (OK), 1962.

Ruffel & Soubirain (1962). M. Ruffel and J. Soubirain. "Vitruve ou Mamurra?" *Pallas* 11 (1962) 123–179.

Russell (1968). J. Russell. "The Origin and Development of Republican Forums." *Phoenix* 22 (1968) 304–317.

Rykwert (1976). J. Rykwert. *The Idea of a Town: The Anthropology of Urban Form in Rome, Italy, and the Ancient World*. London, 1976.

Saliou (1994). C. Saliou. *Les lois des bâtiments: Voisinage et habitat urbain dans l'empire romain. Recherches sur les rapports entre le droit et la construction privée du siècle d'Auguste au siècle de Justinien*. Institut français d'archéologie du Proche-Orient, Bibliothèque archéologique et historique, vol. 116. Beirut, 1994.

Sallmann (1984). K. Sallmann. "Bildungsvorgaben des Fachschriftstellers: Bemerkungen zur Pädagogik Vitruvs." In Knell & Wesenberg (1984) 11–26.

Sauron (1987). G. Sauron. "Le complexe pompéien du Champ du Mars: nouveauté urbanistique à finalité idéologique." In Pietri (1987) 457–473.

Scheid (1987). J. Scheid. "Les sanctuaires de confins dans la Rome antique. Réalité et permanence d'une représentation idéale de l'espace romain." In Pietri (1987) 583–595.

Schrijvers (1989a). P. H. Schrijvers. "Vitruve et la vie intellectuelle de son temps." In Geertman & DeJong (1989) 13–21.

Schrijvers (1989b). P. H. Schrijvers. "Vitruve I.1.1: explication de texte." In Geertman & DeJong (1989) 49–54.

Schütz (1990). M. Schütz. "Zur Sonnenuhr des Augustus auf dem Marsfeld." *Gymnasium* 97 (1990) 432–457.

Schwandner (1990). E.-L. Schwandner. "Beobachtungen zur hellenistischen Tempelarchitektur von Pergamon." In Hoepfner & Schwandner (1990) 85–102.

Sear (1982). F. B. Sear. *Roman Architecture*. London, 1982.

Sear (1988). F. B. Sear. "MacDonald's *Architecture II*." *JRA* 1 (1988) 162–165.

Sear (1989). F. B. Sear. *Roman Architecture*. 2d ed., rev., of Sear (1982). London, 1989.

Sear (1990). F. B. Sear. "Vitruvius and Roman Theater Design." *AJA* 94 (1990) 249–258.

Sear (1992). F. B. Sear. "Introducing Roman Public Buildings." *JRA* 5 (1992) 291–293.

Setälä (1977). P. Setälä. *Private Domini in Roman Brick Stamps of the Empire*. Helsinki, 1977.

Shackleton-Bailey (1965–70). D. K. Shackleton-Bailey, ed. *Cicero's Letter's to Atticus*. 7 vols. Cambridge, 1965–1970.

Shackleton-Bailey (1980). D. K. Shackleton-Bailey, ed. *Cicero: Epistulae ad Quintum Fratrem et M. Brutum*. Cambridge, 1980.

Shipley (1931). F. W. Shipley. "Chronology of Building Operations in Rome from the Death of Caesar to the Death of Augustus." *MAAR* 9 (1931) 7–60.

Sirago (1958). V. A. Sirago. *L'Italia agraria sotto Traiano.* Louvain, 1958.

Skydsgaard (1980). J. E. Skydsgaard. "Non-Slave Labour in Rural Italy during the Late Republic." In Garnsey (1980a) 65–72.

Skydsgaard (1983). J. E. Skydsgaard. "Public Building and Society in Ancient Rome." *ARID,* Suppl. X (1983) 223–228.

Small (1983). D. B. Small. "Studies in Roman Theater Design." *AJA* 87 (1983) 55–68.

Smith (1978). J. T. Smith. "Villas as the Key to Social Structure." In M. Todd, ed., *Studies in the Romano-British Villa* (Leicester, 1978) 149–185.

Smith (1987). J. T. Smith. "The Social Structure of a Roman Villa." *Oxford Journal of Archaeology* 6 (1987) 213–255.

Soubirain (1969). J. Soubirain, ed. *Vitruve: De l'architecture, Livre IX.* Paris, 1969.

Staccioli (1959). R. A. Staccioli. "Le *tabernae* a Roma attraverso la Forma Urbis." *RAL* 8.14 (1959) 56–66.

Stambaugh (1978). J. E. Stambaugh. "The Functions of Roman Temples." *ANRW* 2.16.1 (1978) 554–608.

Stambaugh (1988). J. E. Stambaugh. *The Ancient Roman City.* Baltimore & London, 1988.

Stampolides (1990). N. C. Stampolides. "Hermogenes, sein Werk und seine Schüle vom Ende des 3. bis zum Ende des 1 Jhs. v. Chr." In Hoepfner & Schwander (1990) 115–122.

Steinby (1976). E. M. Steinby. *La cronologia delle figlinae doliari urbane dalla fine della età repubblicana fino all'inizio del III secolo.* Rome, 1976. Updated to 1977 in *BCAR* 84 (1974–75) 7–132.

Steinby (1978). E. M. Steinby. "Ziegelstempel von Rom und Umgebung." *RE* Supplbd. XV (Stuttgart, 1978) cols. 1489–1531.

Steinby (1979). E. M. Steinby. "La produzione laterizia." In F. Zevi, ed., *Pompei 79* (Naples, 1979) 265–271.

Steinby (1981). E. M. Steinby. "La diffusione dell'opus doliare urbano." In A. Giardina and A. Schiavone, eds., *Merci, mercati e scambi nel Mediterraneo.* Società romana e produzione schiavistica, vol. 2 (Bari, 1981) 238–245.

Steinby (1982). E. M. Steinby. "I senatori e l'industria laterizia urbana." *Tituli* 4 (1982) 227–237.

Steinby (1983). E. M. Steinby. "L'edilizia come industria publica e privata." *ARID,* Suppl. X (1983) 219–222.

Steinby (1986). E. M. Steinby. "L'industria laterizia di Roma nel tardo impero." In A. Giardina, ed., *Roma: Politica Economia Paesaggio urbano.* Società romana e impero tardo antico, vol. 2. (Bari, 1986) 99–164.

Steinby (1993a). E. M. Steinby. "L'organizzazione produttiva dei laterizi: un modello interpretativo per l'*instrumentum* in genere." In Harris (1993) 139–144.

Steinby (1993b). E. M. Steinby, ed. *Lexicon Topographicum Urbis Romae,* vol. 1 (A-C). Rome, 1993.

Steinby (1995). E. M. Steinby, ed. *Lexicon Topographicum Urbis Romae,* vol. 2 (D-H). Rome, 1995.

Steiner & Melucco Vaccaro (1994). A. Steiner and A. Melucco Vaccaro. "Chi costruì l'arco di Costantino?" *Archeo* 9.5 (1994) 38–45.

Stilwell (1976). R. Stilwell, ed. *Princeton Encyclopedia of Classical Sites.* Princeton, 1976.

Strocka (1991). V. Strocka. *Casa del Labirinto.* Häuser in Pompeji, vol. 4. Munich, 1991.

Strong (1968). D. E. Strong. "The Administration of Public Building in Rome during the Late Republic and Early Empire." *BICS* 15 (1968) 97–109.

Stucchi (1989). S. Stucchi. "*Tantis Viribus.* L'area della colonna nella concezione generale del Foro di Traiano." *ArchClass* 49 (1989) 237–292.

Suolahti (1963). J. Suolahti. *The Roman Censors.* Helsinki, 1963.

Thielscher (1961). P. Thielscher. "Vitruvius Mamurra." In *RE* IX A 1 (Stuttgart, 1961) cols. 419–489.

Thompson (1987). H. A. Thompson. "The Impact of Roman Architects and Architecture on Athens, 170 B.C.–A.D. 170." In S. Macready and F. H. Thompson, eds., *Roman Architecture in the Greek World.* Society of Antiquaries Occasional Papers (n.s.), vol. 10 (London, 1987) 1–17.

Thornton (1986). M. K. Thornton. "Julio-Claudian Building Programs: Eat, Drink and Be Merry." *Historia* 35 (1986) 28–44.

Thornton & Thornton (1989). M. K. Thornton and J. L. Thornton. *Julio-Claudian Building Programs: A Quantitative Study in Political Management.* Wauconda, Ill., 1989.

Tomber (1987). R. Tomber. "Evidence for Long-distance Commerce: Imported Bricks and Tiles at Carthage." *RCRF* 25/26 (1987) 161–174.

Tomlinson (1989). R. Tomlinson. "Vitruvius and Hermogenes." In Geertman & DeJong (1989) 71–75.

Torelli (1980). M. Torelli. "Industria estrattiva, lavoro artigianale, interessi economici: qualche appunto." *MAAR* 36 (1980) 313–324.

Torelli (1987). M. Torelli. "Culto imperiale e spazi urbani in età Flavia." In Pietri (1987) 563–582.

Torrence (1994). E. M. Torrence. "Vitruvius and the Profession of 'Architectus': 'Fabrica aut Ratiocinatio'?" M.A. thesis, University of Georgia, Athens, 1994.

Tortorici (1993). E. Tortorici. "'La terrazza domitianea', l'*aqua Marcia* ed il taglio della sella tra Campidoglio e Quirinale." *BCAR* 95.2 (1993) 7–24.

Tosi (1994). G. Tosi. "Il significato dei disegni planimetrici vitruviani relativi al teatro antico." In Gros (1994a) 171–185.

Toynbee (1951). J. M. C. Toynbee. *Some Notes on Artists in the Roman World.* Collection Latomus, vol. 6. Brussels, 1951.

Treggiari (1969). S. M. Treggiari. *Roman Freedmen during the Late Republic.* Oxford, 1969.

Treggiari (1980). S. M. Treggiari. "Urban Labour in Rome: *Mercennarii* and *Tabernarii,*" in Garnsey (1980a) 48–64.

Ulrich (1986). R. Ulrich. "The Fountain of the Appiades." *MDAI(R)* 93 (1986) 405–423.

Ulrich (1993). R. Ulrich. "Julius Caesar and the Creation of the Forum Julium." *AJA* 97 (1993) 49–70.

Ulrich (1994). R. Ulrich. *The Roman Orator and the Sacred Stage: The Roman Templum Rostratum.* Collection Latomus, vol. 222. Brussels, 1994.

Ulrich (1996). R. Ulrich. "*Contignatio,* Vitruvius, and the Campanian Builder." *AJA* 100 (1996) 137–152.

Ungaro & Messa (1989). L. Ungaro and L. Messa. *I Mercati Traianei e la Vita Commerciale nella Roma Antica.* Comune di Roma Assessorato alla Cultura, Centro di Coordinamento didattico, vol. 3. Rome, 1989.

Valentini & Zucchetti (1940–53). R. Valentini and G. Zucchetti. *Codice topografico della città di Roma.* 4 vols. Rome, 1940–1953.

Van Deman (1912). E. B. Van Deman. "Methods of Determining the Date of Roman Concrete Monuments." *AJA* 16 (1912) 230–251.

Van Deman (1922). E. B. Van Deman. "The Sullan Forum." *JRS* 12 (1922) 1–31.

Waelkens (1985). M. Waelkens. "From a Phrygian Quarry: The Provenance of the Statues of the Dacian Prisoners in Trajan's Forum at Rome." *AJA* 89 (1985) 641–653.

Waelkens, De Paepe, & Moens (1988). M. Waelkens, H. De Paepe, and L. Moens. "Quarries and the Marble Trade in Antiquity." In Herz & Waelkens (1988) 11–28.

Waelkens, Herz, & Moens (1992). M. Waelkens, N. Herz, and L. Moens, eds. *Ancient Stones: Quarrying, Trade and Provenance.* Acta Archaeologica Lovaniensia. Monographie, Katholieke Universiteit Leuven, vol. 4. Louvain, 1992.

Walker (1984). S. Walker. "Marble Origins by Isotopic Analysis." *World Archaeology* 16 (1984) 204–221.

Walker (1988). S. Walker. "From West to East: Evidence for a Shift in the Balance of Trade in White Marbles." In Herz & Waelkens (1988) 187–196.

Walker (1990). S. Walker. "*Dignam Congruentque Splendori Patriae:* Aspects of Urban Renewal under the Severi." In Henig (1990) 138–142.

Wallace-Hadrill (1988). A. Wallace-Hadrill. "The Social Structure of the Roman House." *PBSR* 56 (1988) 43–97.

Wallace-Hadrill (1990a). A. Wallace-Hadrill. "The Social Spread of Roman Luxury: Sampling Pompeii and Herculaneum." *PBSR* 58 (1990) 145–192.

Wallace-Hadrill (1990b). A. Wallace-Hadrill. "Roman Arches and Greek Honours: The Language of Power at Rome." *PCPhS* 36 (1990) 143–181.

Wallace-Hadrill (1991a). A. Wallace-Hadrill. "Houses and Households: Sampling Pompeii and Herculaneum." In B. Rawson, ed., *Marriage, Divorce, and Children in Ancient Rome* (Canberra & Oxford, 1991) 191–227.

Wallace-Hadrill (1991b). A. Wallace-Hadrill. "Elites and Trade in the Roman Town." In Rich & Wallace-Hadrill (1991) 241–272.

Wallace-Hadrill (1994). A. Wallace-Hadrill. *Houses and Society at Pompeii and Herculaneum.* Princeton, 1994.

Walton (1924). A. Walton. "The Date of the Arch of Constantine." *MAAR* 4 (1924) 169–180.

Ward-Perkins (1951). J. B. Ward-Perkins. "Tripolitania and the Marble Trade." *JRS* 41 (1951) 89–104.

Ward-Perkins (1971). J. B. Ward-Perkins. "Quarrying in Antiquity: Technology, Tradition, and Social Change." *PBA* 57 (1971) 137–158.

Ward-Perkins (1974). J. B. Ward-Perkins. *Cities of Ancient Greece and Italy: Planning in Classical Antiquity.* New York & London, 1974.

Ward-Perkins (1980). J. B. Ward-Perkins. "The Marble Trade and Its Organization: Evidence from Nicomedia." *MAAR* 36 (1980) 325–338.

Ward-Perkins (1981). J. B. Ward-Perkins. *Roman Imperial Architecture.* Harmondsworth & New York, 1981.

Ward-Perkins (1992a). J. B. Ward-Perkins. "Materials, Quarries, and Transportation." In Dodge & Ward-Perkins (1992) 13–22. Rev., with notes, by H. Dodge & B. Ward-Perkins.

Ward-Perkins (1992b). J. B. Ward-Perkins. "The Roman System in Operation." In Dodge & Ward-Perkins (1992) 23–30. Rev., with notes, by H. Dodge & B. Ward-Perkins.

Ward-Perkins (1992c). J. B. Ward-Perkins. "Nicomedia and the Marble Trade." In Dodge & Ward-Perkins (1992) 61–106. Rev., with additional notes, by H. Dodge & B. Ward-Perkins.

Ward-Perkins (1992d). J. B. Ward-Perkins. "Columna Divi Antonini." In Dodge & Ward Perkins (1992) 107–114. Rev., with additional notes, by H. Dodge & B. Ward-Perkins.

Warden (1981). P. G. Warden. "The Domus Aurea Reconsidered." *JSAH* 40 (1981) 271–278.

Wataghin Cantano (1966). G. Wataghin Cantano. *La Domus Augustana. Personalità e problemi dell'architettura Flavia.* Università di Torino, Facoltà di lettere e filosofia, archeologia e storia dell'arte, vol. 10. Turin, 1966.

Waters (1969). K. A. Waters. "Traianus Domitiani Continuator." *AJPh* 96 (1969) 385–405.

Watson (1965). A. Watson. *The Law of Obligations in the Later Roman Republic.* Oxford, 1965.

Watts & Donald (1987). C. M. Watts and J. Donald. "Geometrical Ordering of the Garden Houses at Ostia." *JSAH* 46 (1987) 265–276.

Weaver (1972). P. R. C. Weaver. *Familia Caesaris: A Social Study of the Emperors' Freedmen and Slaves.* Cambridge, 1972.

Webster & Smith (1987). G. Webster and L. Smith. "Reply to J. T. Smith." *Oxford Journal of Archaeology* 6 (1987) 69–89.

Weinstock (1971). S. Weinstock. *Divus Julius.* Oxford, 1971.

Welch (1994). K. E. Welch. "The Roman Arena in Late Republican Italy: A New Interpretation." *JRA* 7 (1994) 59–79.

Whittaker (1980). C. R. Whittaker. "Rural Labour in Three Roman Provinces." In Garnsey (1980a) 73–99.

Widrig (1986). W. Widrig. "Excavations on the Ancient Via Gabina: Second Preliminary Report." *NSA* ser. 8, vol. 37 (1983 [published 1986]) 131–166.

Widrig (1987). W. Widrig. "Land Use at the Via Gabina Villas." In E. H. MacDougall, ed., *Ancient Roman Villa Gardens.* Dumbarton Oaks Colloquium on the History of Landscape Architecture, vol. 10 (Washington, D.C., 1987) 225–260.

Wiegand (1894). Th. Wiegand. "Die puteolanische Bauinschrift." *Jahrbüch für Klassische Philologie,* Suppl. XX (1894) 660–778.

Wilkes (1979). J. J. Wilkes. "Importation and Manufacture of Stamped Bricks and Tiles in the Roman Province of Dalmatia." In McWhirr (1979) 65–72.

Winter (1974). R. Winter. *The Forest and Man.* New York, 1974.

Wiseman (1974). T. P. Wiseman. "The Circus Flaminius." *PBSR* 42 (1974) 3–26.

Wiseman (1976). T. P. Wiseman. "Two Questions on the Circus Flaminius." *PBSR* 44 (1976) 44–47.

Wiseman (1979). T. P. Wiseman. "Tile-stamps and Roman Nomenclature." In McWhirr (1979) 221–230.

Wiseman (1985). T. P. Wiseman. *Catullus and His World.* Cambridge (U.K.), 1985.

Wiseman (1987a). T. P. Wiseman. "*Conspicui postes tectaque digna Deo:* The Public Image of Aristocratic and Imperial Houses in the Late Republic and Early Empire." In Pietri (1987) 393–413.

Wiseman (1987b). T. P. Wiseman. "Reading the City: History, Poetry, and the Topography of Rome." *J.A.C.T. Review,* ser. 2, no. 1 (1987) 3–6.

Bibliography

Wiseman (1987c). T. P. Wiseman. *Roman Studies Literary and Historical.* Collected Classical Papers, vol. 1. Liverpool, 1987.

Wurch-Kozelj (1988). M. Wurch-Kozelj. "Methods of Transporting Blocks in Antiquity." In Herz & Waelkens (1988) 55–64.

Wycherley (1964). R. E. Wycherley. "The Olympieion at Athens." *GRBS* 5 (1964) 161–179.

Yavetz (1958). Z. Yavetz. "The Living Conditions of the Urban Plebs in Republican Rome. " *Latomus* 17 (1958) 500–517.

Yegül (1992). F. Yegül. *Baths and Bathing in Classical Antiquity.* Cambridge, Mass., 1992.

Zanker (1988). P. Zanker. *The Power of Images in the Age of Augustus.* Ann Arbor, 1988.

Zevi (1982). F. Zevi. "Urbanistica di Pompeii." In A. de Franciscis, ed. *La regione sotterata dal Vesuvio. Studi e prospettive* (Naples, 1982) 353–365.

Zimmer (1984). G. Zimmer. "Zollstöcke römischer Architekten." In *Bauplanung und Bautheorie der Antike.* Deutsches Archäologisches Institut, Diskussionen zur archäologischen Bauforschung, vol. 4 (Berlin, 1984) 265–276.

Index

ANCIENT SOCIETY AND HISTORY

The series Ancient Society and History offers books, relatively brief
in compass, on selected topics in the history of ancient Greece and
Rome, broadly conceived, with a special emphasis on comparative
and other nontraditional approaches and methods. The series,
which includes both works of synthesis and works of original scholarship, is aimed at the widest possible range of specialists and
nonspecialist readers.